KURSK

KURSK

THE GREATEST BATTLE
EASTERN FRONT 1943

LLOYD CLARK

headline
review

First published in 2011 by HEADLINE REVIEW
An imprint of HEADLINE PUBLISHING GROUP

Cataloguing in Publication Data is available from the British Library

ISBN 978 0 7553 3638 8

Typeset in Garamond by Palimpsest Book Production Limited,
Falkirk, Stirlingshire

Printed and bound in Great Britain by Clays Ltd, St Ives plc

Headline's policy is to use papers that are natural, renewable and
recyclable products and made from wood grown in sustainable forests.
The logging and manufacturing processes are expected to conform
to the environmental regulations of the country of origin.

HEADLINE PUBLISHING GROUP
An Hachette UK Company
338 Euston Road
London NW1 3BH

www.headline.co.uk
www.hachette.co.uk

Contents

Acknowledgements   ix
Maps   xiii

Introduction   xv
Dramatis Personae   xxi
Prologue   xxiii

1   The Origins of Annihilation I
    Germany and the Germans 1918–41   1

2   The Origins of Annihilation II
    The Soviet Union and the Soviets 1918–41   35

3   Invasion
    Barbarossa: December 1940–September 1941   67

4   Heading South
    Moscow to Stalingrad: October 1941–early February 1943   117

5   Uneasy Calm
    Zitadelle Preliminaries: February–July 1943   165

6 Breaking In
  Zitadelle Launched: 5 July   219

7 Breaking Through
  Zitadelle: 6–8 July   261

8 Anticipation
  Zitadelle: 9–11 July   309

9 Finale
  Zitadelle: 12 July and After   341

Conclusion   383
Epilogue   390
Notes   393
Bibliography   435
Order of Battle   448
Rank Equivalents   457
Index   459

For the boys: Charles (Nobby), John C., Brent, Freddie, Henry, Len, Steve, John H. and Nicholas. Outnumbered but awesome. For two more girls: Tilda and Orla. Even more formidable.

Acknowledgements

This book has been, without doubt, the most demanding that I have written. Pulling together the research has proved a massive effort under some trying conditions and I was extremely fortunate to have been helped in my task by some outstanding people. No matter where I travelled in the world, more often than not I came across folk who did their utmost to help me. I feel particularly honoured and privileged to have spent so much time with veterans of the Battle of Kursk. In common with my previous experience with veterans, they were unfailingly courteous, helpful and made me promise that I would do justice to their experiences. I hope that they find this book worthy. All errors and omissions that you may find in this book however, are mine and mine alone.

I should like to thank the staff at the following archives, libraries, museums and other institutions for the help they have given to me over the three years that this book was in preparation: the National Archives, London; the Imperial War Museum, London; the Liddell Hart Centre for Military Archives, King's College London; the Royal

Historical Society, London; the Institute for Historical Research, University of London; the School of Slavonic and East European Studies, University College London; the University of London Library; the Central Library, the Royal Military Academy Sandhurst; the Prince Consort's Library, Aldershot; the British Museum, London; the Tank Museum, Bovington, Dorset; Das Bundesarchiv, Freiburg and Koblenz; the National Archives, Maryland and Washington D.C.; the Library of Congress, Washington D.C., and the Central Archive of the Russian Ministry of Defence, Podolsk.

I am grateful for having been granted permission to quote from the following books: *Panzer Operations* by Erhard Raus, published by Frontline Books; *Red Road from Stalingrad* by Mansur Abdulin, published by Pen and Sword Books; *In Deadly Combat – A German Soldier's Memoir of the Eastern Front* by Gottlob Herbert Bidermann, published by the University Press of Kansas © 2000; *800 Days on the Eastern Front: A Russian Soldier Remembers World War II* by Nikolai Litvin, published by the University Press of Kansas © 2007, and *Panzer Leader* by Heinz Guderian published by Penguin Books Limited in the UK and to Elisabeth Gräfin Schulenburg for the US permissions. While I have endeavoured to trace the copyright-holders of all material from which I have quoted, I have failed to trace some while others have not responded to my emails, letters and telephone calls. I would, however, be pleased to rectify any omission in future editions should copyright-holders contact me.

My thanks are also due to: the Ministry of Defence; the Commandant of the Royal Military Academy Sandhurst; Andrew Orgill's superb team in the Royal Military Academy's Central Library, and to Sean McKnight and Dr Duncan Anderson for granting me a term's sabbatical to finish this book. I am also indebted to my colleagues in the Department of War Studies for picking up my responsibilities so willingly during my absence. I should like to extend my gratitude to General Sir Richard Dannatt, Major General Anthony

Deane-Drummond, Lieutenant Colonel Roger Morton and Major Tony Borgnis for their time and inspiration. I am indebted to my military students at Sandhurst and on the Army's Military Analysis Course, and to my post-graduate civilian students at the University of Buckingham for their constructive criticism. Professors John Adamson, Saul David and Gary Sheffield along with Ro Horrocks and her battlefield tourists – too many to mention, but you know who you are – need to be thanked for their comments and encouragement.

I am deeply grateful for the unstinting humour, diligence and determination of the small team who assisted me with the research for this book: Debbie Fields, Leo Berger, David Rogers and Alex Kuzin – we got there in the end! I am also appreciative of Graeme Reid-Davis's help with some translations and pronunciations, Ian Breen's tolerance whilst driving me across foreign fields and Mark Waterhouse's map-reading skills. I am beholden to Charlie Viney, my exceptional agent, for his unfailing enthusiasm and support. I have also been extremely fortunate working with two professional, and patient, editorial teams at my publishers in the UK and US and my thanks are due to Martin Fletcher and Emily Griffin at Headline, and Jofie Ferrari-Adler, Jamison Stoltz and Morgan Entrekin at Grove Atlantic. My gratitude is further extended to Marion Paull for her truly excellent copyedit, Lorraine Jerram for her proofreading, and Alan Collinson at Geo-Innovations for the maps.

My deepest thanks, however, are due to the people who kept me sane over the days, weeks, months and years, ensuring that my feet remained firmly planted on the ground, enthused me in dark moments and put up with my frequent trips away from home. Catriona, Freddie, Charlotte and Henry, you are the best family a man could ever want.

Lloyd Clark
Wigginton Bottom and Camberley, November 2010

Maps

1: Operation Barbarossa, 1941   xxii
2: The Soviet Counterblows, 1941–3   xxviii
3: The Eve of Battle, 4 July 1943   34
4: Voronezh Front, 4–8 July 1943   66
5: Central Front, 4–10 July 1943   116
6: Voronezh Front, 9–11 July 1943   164
7: Voronezh Front, 12–15 July 1943   218
8: Prokhorovka, 10–11 July 1943   260
9: Prokhorovka, 11–13 July 1943   308
10: Soviet Advances, August–December 1943   340

Introduction

The Battle of Kursk was the greatest land battle the world has ever seen on a fighting front that epitomized 'total war'. Here was a barbaric campaign of passion and intensity, which was deeply rooted in ideology and centred on annihilation. It was a confrontation characterized by hideous excess and outrageous atrocities, involving the two largest national armies ever amassed, and fought over four years in operations stretching from the Arctic Circle to the Black Sea. It concluded with Germany having incurred nearly three million military dead and the Soviet Union a staggering 10 million. The Soviet losses alone equated to the total number of dead from all belligerent nations on all fronts during the Great War. Every week Stalin's armed forces accumulated a football stadium's worth of dead, and every three months mourned as many lives as the United States did in the entire war. Seventeen million civilians also perished as a direct result of the fighting between 22 June 1941 and 8 May 1945, in a conflict that set new standards in depravity and inhumanity. It was a war that proved to be another national trauma in a turbulent century for the Soviet Union's ill-fated population, one that placed the enemy on the outskirts of their capital city and demanded seemingly endless sacrifice before it was over.

Although the Russo-German war changed the world forever, its significance is not well represented in the national consciousnesses of the United Kingdom, Commonwealth countries and the United States. The general public of these nations does not seem to identify with the scale and importance of the fighting in Russia when compared with the more modestly influential northwest European campaign. While the Normandy landings during the summer of 1944 did mark a major turning point in the war in Europe, we should remember that by the end of that year, 91 Allied divisions in northwest Europe faced 65 German divisions across a 250 mile front, while at the same time in the East, 560 Soviet divisions fought 235 German divisions across 2000 miles.

The lack of appreciation for the Eastern Front in the West, although regrettable, is, however, understandable. For those nations not involved in that particular fight, the historical vista that it presents is unlikely to be one with which their populations are particularly well acquainted. People are naturally influenced by their own nation's campaigns and battles – 'our history, our heritage, our war dead' – but in so doing are in danger of overemphasizing the importance of that fighting on events and outcomes. To the people of the United Kingdom, for example, the confrontation between the Soviet Union and Germany not only lacks the immediacy of the liberation of France, but also an obvious relevance to their everyday lives. Here is a campaign fought by soldiers speaking in foreign tongues led by vile autocrats on battlefields many hundreds of miles away. What is more, there have been very few cultural reference points connected with that conflict for the population to soak up and share. Books about the Eastern Front – although not totally absent from the shelves of bookshops and libraries – have been severely under-represented in the history sections, the media has not shown any great appetite for the subject and, although some programmes about the war in Russia are to be found tucked away on 'specialist' television channels, very few mainstream films have been set in the East. Over the decades since the end of the Second World War, therefore, people living in the countries of the old Western Alliance have not been particularly likely to happen upon material – academic or otherwise – to raise their awareness of the Russo-German war.

In the last 20 years there has been a slow but gradual improvement in this situation. The lowering of the Iron Curtain heralded a haphazard erosion of the restrictions placed on the free flow of information and ideas that had previously so stifled a wider understanding of the Eastern Front. Now, nearly a generation since the fall of the Berlin Wall, the world is gaining a fuller, more accurate, better balanced and more vibrant picture of the fighting there than ever before. The nations of the former Soviet Union have a new outlook, which is reflected in a diminution of state bureaucracy, the opening of archives and closer links with foreign academic institutions. A new spirit of cooperation has been born. Nurtured by the email boom and given strength by low-priced air travel, circumstances have developed that are far more conducive to the undertaking of a fundamental reassessment of the Russo-German conflict than had previously been the case. It has been a slow and sometimes painful process, but its success should be measured not merely by the weight of the academic papers produced under the new conditions, but also by new initiatives, such as British, American and French units joining 10,500 Russian troops marching across Red Square to mark the 65th anniversary of the end of the war.

For students of the Eastern Front, the improvement in access to state documents, veterans of the conflict and the old battlefields has been thrilling and has encouraged a new generation of writers to take up the challenge of interpreting the campaign. The subject has been vitalized by a plethora of ground-breaking studies by academics such as David Glantz, and popularized by bestsellers from the pen of Antony Beevor. Thus, slowly, the West's historical landscape has begun to broaden to incorporate the fighting in the East, which has persuaded historians not only to explore that campaign in greater breadth and depth, but also to re-evaluate the course, outcome and consequences of the Second World War. *Kursk* was partly prompted by the new energy that currently surrounds the study of the Russo-German war, but was also born of my frustration at being unable to find a text that placed the battle in its proper context and with the requisite detail. There are plenty of books that make sweeping generalizations about the fighting in the Kursk salient, and many that provide such mind-numbing technical information about formations and equipment as to render it impossible to deduce what happened, but precious few that provide a satisfying overview. It is peculiar that such a massive confrontation (which eventually occupied four million men, 69,000 guns and mortars, 13,000 tanks and self-propelled guns and almost 12,000 aircraft) should remain so relatively obscure. Even more so when one considers the exceptional influence that the battle had on subsequent events. In the words of historian John Hughes-Wilson, that Kursk is 'one of the most decisive battles of the world is no exaggeration . . . [it had] *epic* significance.'

This volume, therefore, seeks to provide the overview that places the Battle of Kursk in the context required to do justice to its pivotal position in the course of the fighting on the Eastern Front. To do this, *Kursk* does not just take a snapshot of the campaign in July 1943 and provide highlights of the previous year's combat, but subjects Germany and the Soviet Union to a political, economical, military and social examination from the last days of the Great War onwards. By charting the rise of Hitler and Stalin into determined, aggressive and ruthless dictators able to bend the equally vulnerable Germany and Soviet Union to their wills, we will be able to achieve some under-standing of both the political motivations and the ideological fervour behind their ambitions. Through an examination of how these auto-crats sought to achieve their goals, it will also be possible to assess how well prepared their nations were for the tasks that their leaders handed to them. The chances of success depended greatly on the belligerents' mental and physical preparedness for the trials ahead along with the critical relationships between state, economy, armed forces and people. Such factors also helped to shape and determine the fighting methods that the combatants deployed. In blitzkrieg the Wehrmacht had a totemic operational technique, but by 1943 the improving Soviets had not only identified ways of countering it, but were also on the verge of re-establishing their own manoeuvre-warfare credentials. Critical to both was the ability to sustain the campaign and operations over protracted periods. This was not just a case of securing the vital raw resources and manufacturing facilities to turn iron into tanks and oil into fuel, but ensuring that necessities got to where they were needed in time to make a difference. Such issues constantly challenged the leading political and military figures of the day and had a seismic influence on strategy, but also had a direct impact on the hapless soldier at the sharp end trying to carry out his duty. As a result, although *Kursk* maintains the necessary focus on the decision makers, it has the fighting man at its heart. It should be remembered that those who fought to secure a brighter, safer future for their children in the Great War were the fathers who watched their sons march off to fight in an even more devastating conflict. By endeavouring to unravel the tangled skein of issues that surround the Battle of Kursk, it is hoped that we might take a step closer to understanding the reasons why another doomed generation were dragged from their families and sent to fight in hell.

Dramatis Personae

SOVIET UNION

Marshal Georgi Zhukov – Deputy Supreme Commander

General Konstantin Rokossovsky – Commander Central Front

General Nikolai Vatutin – Commander Voronezh Front

General Ivan Konev – Commander Steppe Front

GERMANY

Field Marshal Wilhelm Keitel – Chief of Armed Forces High Command (OKW)

Colonel-General Kurt Zeitzler – Chief of Army High Command (OKH)

Colonel-General Heinz Guderian – Inspector General of Panzer Troops

Field Marshal Günther von Kluge – Commander Army Group Centre

Colonel-General Walter Model – Commander Ninth Army

Field Marshal Erich von Manstein – Commander Army Group South

Colonel-General Hermann Hoth – Commander Fourth Panzer Army

Colonel-General Werner Kempf – Commander Army Detachment Kempf

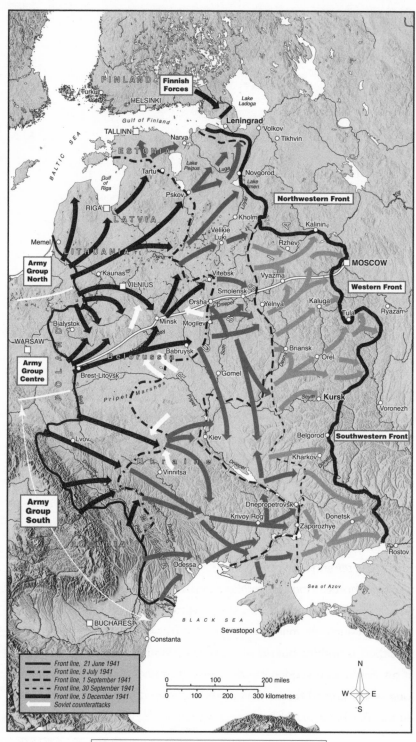

Map 1: Operation Barbarossa, 1941

Prologue

I walk in the dusty tracks of the Wehrmacht's most powerful division under a scorching sun. The flat landscape is pregnant with ripe crops wavering gently in a tender breeze. There are no hedgerows, buildings or people. An unseen road springs from the village of Butovo, but I hear no traffic. There is an intense silence, which helps me to imagine the battle fought here in July 1943. This place is remote. Kursk is 65 miles to the north and Belgorod 30 miles to the southeast. This open steppe land is unlike anything in England and like nothing I have seen elsewhere in Europe. It reminds me most of the American mid-west and feels a long way from home. I look at the sketch map that has been provided for me to help pick out the landmarks. The village of Cherkasskoe lies shimmering a couple of miles to my left, a shallow ditch to my right, otherwise there is nothing but massive fields. I continue northwards and arrive at my destination suddenly – the western-most tentacle of a three-mile long *balka*. The 50 feet wide and 20 feet deep dried river bed was used during the battle to house a headquarters, field kitchen and a small medical aid station. It was a chasm that offered just a little safety as the landscape erupted around it.

I negotiate the *balka*'s grassy bank and drop down into the cool air at the bottom. I can hear voices and walk towards them to find Mykhailo Petrik and his son, Anton, enjoying a joke. Mykhailo was an infantryman during the Battle of Kursk and had been stationed in a dug-out not far from here during the opening days of the German offensive. We had met for the first time a week before and he had mentioned that he was keen to show his son the old battlefield and invited me to join them. We shook hands. Mykhailo's were rough from years spent working as a mechanic near Smolensk; his son's were soft after years spent working as a doctor in London and Moscow. 'This is where I came to pick up the food for the section the night before the attack,' Mykhailo explains. 'It was full of people, full of activity but there was tension in the air. We knew that the Germans would strike soon. It was an anxious time.'

Anton produces a collapsible chair and, declining with a dismissive wave my offer to steady him, Mykhailo slumps into it. He tells us about joining up in Kiev – 'a crush of people and a forlorn party official taking names'; his training – 'they tried to starve us to death'; and his eventual deployment at the front during the battle for Moscow in December 1941 – 'a nightmare spread over weeks'. His memory is good but details are lacking, until he comes to describe his DP light machine gun. 'It fired a 7.62mm round from a pan magazine perched on top. It was light enough to fire from the hip, but for accuracy we used its bi-pod. It was a good weapon, but of an old design and was prone to overheating. We fired it in short bursts, but had to be careful not to cook it.' Mykhailo proceeds to run through the parts of the weapon in loving detail and dismantles an imaginary DP on his lap, and then reassembles it while mumbling to himself. He completes his task with a smile, delighted that he can still remember the process. Anton and I applaud and he makes a little seated bow.

We leave the *balka* for the position that Mykhailo's platoon occupied on the morning of 5 July. We walk in bursts of a couple of hundred yards to allow our guide to catch his breath. 'The landscape has changed over the years,' he says as Anton places a baseball cap on his father's balding head, 'but nothing that blocks the memory. It is all still recognizable.' I ask him how many times he had been back to the battlefield since the end of the war. 'Just once,' he replies. 'I returned in the 1970s with an old comrade who lived in Belgorod and was making a study of the battle. I do not think that he ever finished it. He died many years ago, but the maps that I copied for you are the ones that we drew during that visit. We spent a day wandering around, making sense of the ground and using some information that we collected and some we had been given by others.' 'But are you sure of your bearings now, all these years later?' I ask. 'Oh, yes,' Mykhailo shoots back, 'I spent yesterday out here hunting around.' I look at Anton who is shaking his head with incredulity and adds with a smile, 'This is an eighty-six-year-old man who disregards the advice of his physician son and likes to wander off in the middle of nowhere.'

We arrive at the edge of a field around half a mile from the *balka*, towards Cherkasskoe. 'Our section was dug in here,' Mykhailo announces with authority. 'The Germans came towards us from that direction.' I had been so engaged in conversation that I had failed to relate the ground to the battle as we walked. I turn and am astounded by the scene that greets me – a broad front of wide-open fields under a huge sky. I immediately imagine a wall of steel and field grey advancing towards us. I turn to Mykhailo and he opens wide his bright blue eyes and nods his head slowly as if to say, 'Frightening, eh?' He gives Anton and me a moment to absorb the scene and then fills in the detail. 'We were targeted by dive bombers, artillery and tanks. There was an awful crescendo. But then it stopped, as the infantry rushed forward, and was replaced by the drilling sound of German machine guns and the explosion of mortars. That was when I was hit.' His hand moves up to his neck and for the first time I see an old scar. 'It was the last time that I saw my comrades,' he says. 'They were blown away by the enemy.' He pauses and stares into the distance. 'Blown away by the Nazis.' The crops rustle and there is a short silence before Mykhailo declares, 'It's time to move on.'

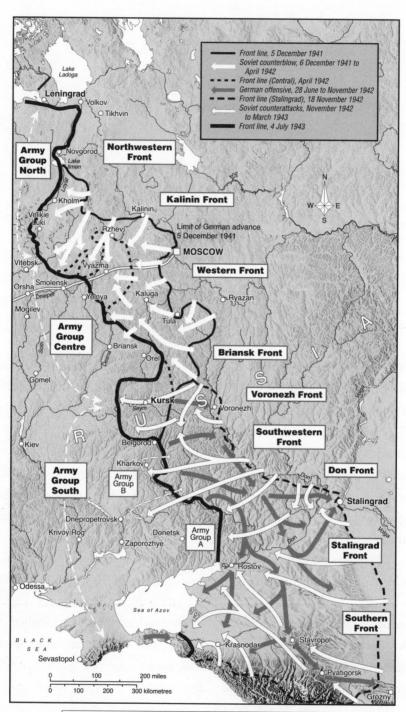

Map 2: The Soviet Counterblows, 1941–3

The following legend and labels appear on the map:

Front line, 5 December 1941
Soviet counterblow, 6 December 1941 to April 1942
Front line (Central), April 1942
German offensive, 28 June to November 1942
Front line (Stalingrad), 18 November 1942
Soviet counterattacks, November 1942 to March 1943
Front line, 4 July 1943

Lake Ladoga
Leningrad
Volkov
Tikhvin
Army Group North
Novgorod
Lake Ilmen
Kholm
Northwestern Front
Velikie Luki
Kalinin
Kalinin Front
Rzhev
Limit of German advance 5 December 1941
MOSCOW
Vitebsk
Vyazma
Western Front
Orsha
Smolensk
Dnieper
Mogilev
Kaluga
Ryazan
Army Group Centre
Briansk
Tula
Yelnya
Gomel
Orel
Brian sk Front
Voronezh Front
Kursk
Seym
Voronezh
Kiev
Belgorod
Southwestern Front
Army Group South
Kharkov
Army Group B
Don Front
Stalingrad
Dnepropetrovsk
Krivoy Rog
Donetsk
Army Group A
Don
Voiga
Stalingrad Front
Zaporozhye
Rostov
Odessa
Sea of Azov
BLACK SEA
Krasnodar
Stavropol
Southern Front
Sevastopol
Pyatigorsk
Grozny

0   100   200 miles
0   100   200   300 kilometres

CHAPTER 1

The Origins of Annihilation I

(Germany and the Germans 1918–41)

The day dawned stormy and was to become shocking. On the morning of 12 July 1943 the Germans thrust towards the village of Prokhorovka some 50 miles southeast of Kursk. Acutely aware that his Tiger company would take the initial shock of any enemy counter-attack, 29-year-old SS-Untersturmführer Michael Wittmann's senses were heightened to any movement before him. His commanders stood in their open turrets scanning the featureless steppe through their field glasses, but it was Wittmann who alerted them to the dust cloud thrown up by the approaching enemy armour.

There was no panic – well-rehearsed drills led to a smooth reaction. Crisp orders were issued and immediately followed by experienced crew who understood that vacillation and panic led to confusion and death. The Tigers advanced, their engines whining as they climbed a low rise before juddering to a halt. The 100 tank Soviet wave sped towards them in an attempt to get close enough for their guns to penetrate the panzers' armour before the powerful German 88mm guns had an opportunity to pick them off. The Tiger gunners peered down their optical sights at the olive-green armour a mile away, but even as their cross hairs settled on a target, the T-34s dipped into a gentle fold in the ground like an armada sailing on a rolling sea. A tense minute passed before the enemy rose again and now they were just half a mile away. Anticipating the breaking wave, the Tiger commanders gave the order to fire. The 63 ton beasts jerked as their high-velocity guns blasted off their armour-piercing rounds.

The T-34s were devastated. An intense white explosion stopped one dead, another slew to the right before coming to a blazing stop while a third was ripped apart and disembowelled with appalling ease. The German intercoms were alive with impassioned voices as commanders sought to break up the enemy formation and the five-man crews fought for their lives. The T-34s plunged on as the Tigers found new fire positions and unleashed more destruction. Wittmann's skilful gunner, Helmut Gräser, took rapid aim and loosed off. The round buried itself into a victim and dislodged the turret. The Tiger was re-positioned, the gun erupted, another hit.

The Soviets closed to within a couple of hundred feet and returned fire on the move. Wittmann's Tiger was hit twice – the tank, ringing like a bell, was saved by two inches of steel – and four from his company were disabled. The field was littered with burning wrecks sending plumes of black smoke into the steel grey sky. The officer of one T-34 lay dead, slumped across his hatch as flames licked around the turret and his crew screamed from within. The acrid air hung heavy over the charred corpses and the broken bodies of the wounded.

The clash of arms at Prokhorovka was the greatest tank battle of the Second World War and was indicative of a new 'totality' to the fighting on the Eastern Front by 1943. The fathers of those who fought that summer in the Kursk salient had participated in the previous shattering conflict, which had been meant to safeguard the future of the next generation. Yet from the ruin of the Great War two new edifices to war arose. Their tyrannical architects – Adolf Hitler and Joseph Stalin – were guided by fervent ideologies and driven by unbridled ambition and a quest for supreme power.

The very idea of fighting another war was abhorrent to most Germans in 1918 for the nation was on its knees, the people starving, the armed forces broken, the economy crushed and politics in crisis. The decline from a strong, confrontational war-maker to feeble, tentative peace-maker was so abrupt that it destabilized the nation and left its population reeling. Although the *dénouement* was overseen by the military dictatorship of Generals Paul von Hindenburg and Erich Ludendorff, as the Allies advanced irrepressibly towards Germany during the autumn of 1918, the population's angst focused more and more on Kaiser Wilhelm II. The increasingly peripheral head of state was a reform-shy, anti-democratic figure. He had led Germany into the war but by the end of October 1918 was effectively confronted with a notice of eviction. It was served by a series of mutinies, which initially centred on the ports of Wilhelmshaven and Kiel, where rumours had spread that the fleet was to be sent into a final battle against the Royal Navy. The uprisings encouraged Communists, such as Richard Krebs, who later wrote in his autobiography, *Out of the Night*:

> Then came stirring news. Mutiny in the Kaiser's Fleet ... I saw women [in Kiel] who laughed and wept because they had their men in the Fleet. From windows and doors in the front of the food stores sounded the anxious voices: 'Will the Fleet sail out? ... No, the Fleet must not sail! It's murder! Finish the war!' Youngsters in the street yelled, 'Hurrah.'

As mutinies rolled across Germany, soldiers' and workers' councils seized power in numerous cities to the cry of 'peace and democracy'. The abdication of the Kaiser on 9 November and the announcement of an armistice two days later successfully diluted the venomous radicalism that the status quo so feared, but there was too much momentum to thwart some change. The result was a very orderly and restrained revolution, which led to the establishment of the Weimar Republic and moderate coalition governments clutching at little more than hopeful democratic intentions with which to undertake the rebuilding of Germany. Unimpressed and frustrated, Communists and Nationalists fought each other on city streets. In January 1919, Berliner Hilda Brandt wrote to an English friend:

> Most of us just want peace. To take up the wretched strands of our lives and move on. To have fighting on our doorstep – so much uncertainty – is too much to bear. I have lost Gerd [husband] and Friedrich [son] and for what? It is as though the barbarity of the fighting front has seeped into our souls without us knowing . . . We are hurting, still grieving and feel helpless. We yearn for leadership and stability, not thugs and more conflict.

Yet there was one thing about which the political extremists agreed: the 'vacuous' Weimar Republic committed an act of treachery when it signed the Treaty of Versailles in June 1919.

The treaty – which was designed by the victorious Allies – formally brought the Great War to an end and significantly shaped Europe's future. It punished Germany by emasculating the country's military forces – disbanding the general staff, abolishing conscription, the airforce and panzer force, and limiting the army to 100,000 men and the navy to 15,000 personnel with just six battleships. Any military threat to the West was further undermined by the demilitarization of the Rhineland, while humiliation was heaped on the vanquished, not to mention economic purdah, by the loss of 13 per cent of German terri-tory, 12 per cent of its population and all its colonial possessions. Yet even though these provisions were far-reaching and intended to hurt, no aspect of the treaty attracted more contempt in Germany than

Article 231, which asserted German culpability for starting the war and was used as a lever to extract war-damage reparations amounting to 136,000 million gold marks. It was scant compensation to be told by the Allies that the treaty was a 'restrained compromise', which the outraged German press called a 'diktat'. Reflecting the national mood, *Deutsche Zeitung* reported on 28 June 1919:

> Today in the Hall of Mirrors in Versailles, the disgraceful Treaty is being signed. Do not forget it! The German people will, with unstinting labour, work to regain the place among the nations to which it is justly entitled. Then will come vengeance for the shame of 1919.

The Germans were not the only ones who believed that the Treaty of Versailles was fatally flawed and would lead to future conflict. The French press, for example, thought the settlement too lenient. Field Marshal Ferdinand Foch opined: 'This is not peace. It is an armistice for twenty years.' British economist John Maynard Keynes agreed, not because the treaty was too lame but because the reparations were too great for Germany to bear. He argued: 'The treaty, by overstepping the limits of the possible, had in practice settled nothing.'

Although the fledgling republic was checkmated and had little option but to agree to abide by the treaty's provisions, right-wing politicians, Nationalists and some ex-military leaders lambasted the new regime for their complicity in signing the document, criticized the left for disrupting an 'undefeated army' with their 'selfish uprisings' and the 'greedy Jews' for engaging 'in profiteering, careless of whether Germany won the war or not'. These 'November criminals' who had 'stabbed Germany in the back' would, the disillusioned suggested, be made to pay for their disloyalty and subversion. Such an argument was central to the developing ideology of Adolf Hitler and the Nazi Party during the 1920s.

Although Hitler later wrote that he became politicized while a 'coffee-house dreamer' during his five years in cosmopolitan Vienna before the Great War, his political awareness really developed while he was serving in the German army on the Western Front. During his time as a junior soldier, his drifter's life found a purpose and he became attracted to extreme nationalism. Drawing on his experience of dislocation, struggle and loneliness in the capital of the fading Austro-Hungarian Empire, Hitler bored his comrades with mini-lectures about the benefits of territorial expansion after the unification of German-speaking peoples. He also harangued Communists, Jews and sectors of the home front whom he believed to be undermining the nation's ability to win the war. Hitler immediately knew where to point the finger of blame, therefore, when the war was lost. Receiving the news in hospital while recovering from wounds received in a gas attack, he later wrote:

> Everything went black before my eyes; I tottered and groped my way back to the dormitory, threw myself on my bunk, and dug my burning head into my blanket and pillow . . . And so it had all been in vain. In vain all the sacrifices and privations . . . Miserable and degenerate criminals! . . . There followed terrible days and even worse nights – I knew that all was lost . . . In these nights hatred grew in me, hatred for those responsible for this deed . . . I, for my part, decided to go into politics.

Hitler remained in the army after the war and was posted to Munich, a hot-bed of right-wing extremism. He became active in what was soon to become the Nationalsozialistische Deutsche Arbeiterpartei (NSDAP) or Nazi Party. Attracted to the organization's devotion to Germany and aspirational leanings towards imperialistic nationalism, which were intertwined with anti-Semitism, by the time Hitler left the army in April 1920 he had become the meagrely supported party's leading orator. His poorly prepared but passionately delivered diatribes pandered to the workers with vague suggestions of socialist ideas (which were later dropped) and became increasingly well received by audiences that grew steadily from dozens to thousands. Hitler connected particularly well with former soldiers and one of them, fellow Nazi Gregor Strasser, later wrote:

> [W]e became nationalists on the battlefield . . . we could not help coming home with the brutal intention of gathering the whole nation around us and teaching them that the greatness of a nation depends on the willingness of the individual to stand up for the nation.

By the summer of 1921, Hitler was chairman of the party with unlimited powers and supreme self-confidence. He worked increasingly hard to give the impression that he lived to represent the common man, but as his private secretary during the Second World War was to later write, Hitler was 'a man whose honourable façade hid a criminal lust for power'. This aspect of his personality, when coupled with an impatience for national recognition, led to Hitler undertaking a classic (if somewhat desperate) political stunt. In late 1923, as Germany was gripped by hyperinflation and unable to fulfil its Versailles reparations commitments, he decided to seize power in Munich. On 8 November, Hitler, assisted by the Nazis' thuggish, brown-shirted private army, known as the *Stormabteilungen* (SA), hijacked a political meeting in a Munich beer hall and, firing a pistol above his head, announced, 'The National Revolution has begun!' A stupefied audience listened as the scruffy rebel declared:

> The Government of the November criminals and the Reich President are declared removed. A new National Government will be nominated this very day here in Munich . . . We can no

longer turn back; our action is already inscribed on the pages of world history.

It was a precipitate and poorly organized affair, so woefully supported that when the Nazis marched on Munich the following day, they were crushed by waiting police and troops. Yet the publicity generated by the Beer Hall Putsch and Hitler's subsequent trial did succeed in announcing the arrival of the Nazis on the political scene. Hitler devoted a significant proportion of the 13 months that he spent in gaol to dictating *Mein Kampf* (*My Struggle*). This turgid, rambling and undistinguished fusion of autobiography and political treatise failed to set literary tongues wagging, but it did provide an insight into Hitler's irrational mind, his ideology and his future ambitions – including his intentions for the Soviet Union.

Mein Kampf was not just about Hitler's struggle, but the ongoing struggle he perceived between strong pure races and mixed weak ones. It was a fight that, he argued, the strong would win, as was nature's way. Consequently, Hitler believed that if Germany developed into a pure Aryan race – 'the highest species of humanity on the earth' – it would defeat and rule over inferior races. Yet this destiny, he contested, was threatened by the 'corrupting influence' of Jews and Marxists. He wrote that 'Marxism itself systematically plans to hand over the world to the Jews' while 'The Jewish doctrine of Marxism rejects the aristocratic principles of Nature and replaces the external privilege of power and strength by the mass of numbers and their dead weight.' Once 'Jewish Marxism' had been identified as the cause of Germany's post-war ills, it was a simple step to pinpoint the elimination of Jews and Marxists as necessary. '[T]here are only two possibilities,' Hitler suggested, serving up a common enemy upon which Germany could focus its suspicions, concerns and distress, 'either victory of the Aryan or annihilation of the Aryan and the victory of the Jew.'

The ideas expressed in *Mein Kampf* did not have shocking implications just for Germany, but also for Europe and the wider world. Hitler emphasized that war was 'quite in keeping with nature' and should be 'embraced'. In seeking to abolish the Treaty of Versailles, reinvigorate German militarism, establish a Reich of German-speaking peoples and attain *Lebensraum* (living space) in eastern Europe for 'racially pure', self-sufficient Germans, Hitler did not shy away from the idea of a war in general, and a war against the Soviet Union in particular. The preparation of a nation fit and ready to undertake such a programme would need careful direction and, the Nazis argued, this should be done by an authoritarian government led by a dictator whose wishes would be obediently fulfilled. On his release from prison, Hitler immediately began to plan a route to power and the realization of his political ideals.

Throughout this period Hitler refined his political skills and two distinct sides to his personality emerged. In private he was awkward, undistinguished, irresolute and dull, but in public he became dominant, charismatic, decisive and prone to tirades. Hitler's rages were a political instrument that he turned on and off as necessary, but he was capable of completely losing control. Indeed, one party official suggested that Hitler had to work hard to 'conquer his inhibitions' and explained 'how necessary to his eloquence were shouting and a feverish tempo'. He had a horror of appearing ridiculous and began to spend considerable amounts of time practising his carefully choreographed speeches. Starting slowly, gently and quietly, he would increase the intensity, the volume and his gesticulations until he was shouting and thumping the lectern. Meeting Hitler for the first time, industrialist Paul Weber was surprised by the outward ordinariness of the small dark man who greeted him in Munich during 1928:

Here was an unassuming man with a weak handshake dressed in a slightly ill-fitting dark suit . . . We were ushered into a private meeting room where Hitler took an age to decide who should sit where. He seemed nervous, but as the room filled with 10 and then 20 others, his back straightened, he snapped orders to his acolytes and brought the meeting to order. He then embarked on a 20 minute lecture ... before inviting others to speak. Throughout the three-hour meeting I am not sure that Hitler was moved by one word that anybody said although he listened intently ... When he disagreed with an individual, his dark eyes bored into the speaker, which, I am sure, was most off-putting. Occasionally, he would hit the table and pace the room in frustration. I got the impression that Hitler entered the meeting with his mind already made up and that the evening was just a great act – but I am not sure. What I do know is that Hitler was a master of manipulating decisions and events to get what he wanted.

Dominating the Nazi Party structure and its decision-making process, Hitler resolved to seek popular support and use the democratic system to attain power. The tainted Weimar regime continued to produce governments that failed to grapple with Germany's manifold problems, and Hitler recognized that there was an opportunity for the Nazis to prosper if the party offered strong leadership, vision and vague yet inclusive policies. As Hitler was keen to point out, the Nazis provided the electorate with a new and unsullied option. He remarked, 'We are the result of the distress for which others were responsible.' It seems that the population reacted positively to this strategy for Nazi Party membership grew during the second half of the 1920s, although the number of seats they won in the Reichstag – the German parliament – was limited by a revival in the economy and the political stability that followed the election as President of Field Marshal Paul von Hindenburg in 1925. However, an economic collapse in 1930 during the Great Depression produced fertile ground for the Nazis to increase their parliamentary representation.

Protected by his fanatically loyal Schutzstaffel (SS) detachment,

Hitler's public profile continued to grow despite the setback of failing to oust Hindenburg in the presidential election of 1932. Yet with the jobless total reaching 5.1 million that year, the electorate seemed to be increasingly tempted by the Nazi message, and the party became the largest in the Reichstag. In such circumstances, Hitler was the obvious choice for the Chancellorship, although Hindenburg was concerned at his aims and ambitions. However, Hindenburg's worst fears were assuaged by the same leading businessmen and army figures whom the Nazis had spent a great deal of time and resources flattering. Hitler was appointed Chancellor on 30 January 1933. Although the President hoped that Nazi extremism would be suffocated by the more traditional right in the coalition government, this was not to be. Hitler was not going to be smothered by anybody, and he immediately set about ensuring that his political career continued unfettered.

The first shackle that Hitler planned to remove was Germany's hard-won democracy. The smashing of the Weimar constitution came in March 1933 with the introduction of an 'enabling bill', which freed Hitler from the legal restraint of the President, parliament and the voters. Having implicated the Communist party in a plot to burn down the Reichstag, he was able to ban the Communists' participation in the vote, and this critical Nazi legislation was passed to the intimidating sound of the SA and SS chanting 'We want the Bill – or fire and murder'.

Hitler then turned on his political opponents. First, he banned all other parties and then, during the summer of 1934, he purged his own party. He decapitated the Nazi left by removing the leadership of the socialist-leaning and dysfunctional SA and so protected his right-wing agenda. Executions were carried out by the SS, assisted by the Gestapo (*Geheime Staatspolizei*), the secret state police. Hitler personally arrested SA leader Ernst Röhm by bursting in on him in a hotel room and, with revolver in hand, shouting, 'You are under arrest, you pig.' The subsequent execution of Röhm and others was justified at a cabinet meeting on 3 July, where it was decided that murders without trial were 'lawful for the necessary defence of the state'. It was clear from that day forward that opposition to Hitler and the Nazis was best avoided.

On 2 August 1934, Hitler took the opportunity offered to him by Hindenburg's death to amalgamate the offices of Chancellor and President, a further step in his mission to consolidate power. As Führer and Reichskanzler, Hitler was determined to subjugate the population to his will and prepare them for his more ambitious political aims. He sought nothing less than total loyalty. 'The people are impotent, they cannot rule themselves; yet I cannot rule the people unless I am the soul of the people,' he said. He also demanded and received the soul of the Wehrmacht (Armed Forces) from Colonel-General Werner von Blomberg, the Minister of Defence, in return for the purging of the SA and promises of increases in its size and capability. After a long and proud history of the armed forces standing outside politics, from 2 August 1934 its members were required to repeat the following:

I swear by God this holy oath, that I will render unconditional obedience to the leader of the German Reich, Adolf Hitler, supreme commander of the armed forces and that, as a brave soldier, I will be ready at any time to stake my life for this oath.

To some, these words came easily, but to others they were worrying. Infantryman Alarick Lindner testifies:

We officers were particularly disturbed by the politicization of the army and concerned with where it might lead us . . . The change was forced on us and it happened quickly. Within weeks the German Eagle badge that we wore proudly was redesigned with a swastika [Nazi Party symbol] clasped between its talons, portraits of Hitler appeared in headquarters and a bust of Hitler appeared in the mess. We understood that we were servants to the politicians, but I abhorred being a servant to the person of Hitler. However, soon after, we were re-equipped and the battalion was strengthened by a new company ... Having been weak for so long, this turn of events made many – myself included – turn a blind eye to our 'Nazification'.

Having secured the loyalty of the armed forces, Hitler then turned to the German population and began to manipulate its attitudes and beliefs. Propaganda was given a high priority in this process and was overseen at a new ministry, which controlled the press, literature, music, the fine arts, theatre, radio and film. It was headed by the pinch-faced Joseph Goebbels, who argued:

It is not enough for people to be more or less reconciled to our regime, to be persuaded to adopt a neutral attitude towards us, rather we want to work on people until they have capitulated to us, until they grasp ideologically that what is happening in Germany today must be accepted but also can be accepted. Propaganda is not an end in itself, but a means to an end ... The new Ministry had no other aim than to unite the nation behind the ideals of the national revolution.

Hitler was portrayed as the personification of Germany's past, present and future, who deserved and demanded unquestioning compliance while applying the Nazi Party's creed. Just as Nazi imagery never allowed those in uniform to forget where their obligations lay, the civilian world also began to feel Hitler's omnipresence. Nobody could walk through city, town or village without setting eyes on a photograph of the Führer or a swastika-emblazoned flag. Newlyweds were presented with a copy of *Mein Kampf* and there was a legal obligation from July 1933 on all but the military to raise the right arm in salute and bark 'Heil Hitler.' Massive crowds gathered to listen to Hitler's speeches. During the early 1930s, the party faithful and threatened were bused from venue to venue in order to guarantee a large and passionate audience. By 1936 this was no longer necessary and American journalist Virginia Cowles wrote of one 200,000 strong rally:

> As the time for the Führer's arrival drew near, the crowd grew restless. The minutes passed and the wait seemed interminable. Suddenly the beat of the drums increased and three motor-cycles with yellow standards fluttering from their windshields raced through the gates. A few minutes later a fleet of black cars rolled swiftly into the arena: in one of them, standing in the front seat, his hand outstretched in the Nazi salute, was Hitler.
>
> Then Hitler began to speak. The crowd hushed into silence, but the drums continued their steady beat. Hitler's voice rasped into the night and every now and then the multitude broke into a roar of cheers. Some of the audience began swaying back and forth, chanting 'Sieg Heil' over and over again in a frenzy of delirium. I looked at the faces around me and saw tears streaming down people's cheeks.

Meanwhile, Goebbels – the holder of a doctorate in German philology – lashed out at 'degenerate tendencies' with highly orchestrated, public book-burning ceremonies, which consigned free thought to ashes. A witness of one such 'ritual' in central Berlin lamented:

> All afternoon Nazi raiding parties had gone into public and private libraries, throwing on to the streets such books as Dr Goebbels in his supreme wisdom had decided were unfit for Nazi Germany. From the streets Nazi[s] ... [had] picked up these discarded volumes and taken them to the square ... Here the

heap grew highter and higher, and every few minutes another howling mob arrived, adding more books to the impressive pyre.

The Nazi obsession with 'cleansing' was further manifested in the regime's policy towards the Jews. In its quest for 'racial purity', the government began to publish anti-Semitic propaganda, dismissed Jews from positions in government and excluded them from working in the media and entertainment industries. The victimization was taken up by sectors of the German population, which increasingly shunned Jews both socially and professionally. By September 1935, the Nuremberg Laws had removed citizenship from all Germans with one or more Jewish grandparent and forbidden the marriage of Aryans to Jews, but worse was to come. In November 1938, menacing anti-Semitism turned into murderous aggression when a nationwide pogrom was unleashed against Jewish-owned businesses and property. Scores of Jews were killed in a frenzy of violence, and thousands more were arrested and sent to SS-administered concentration camps where they joined other 'enemies of the state', including Marxists, criminals, homosexuals and vagrants. When it came to identifying and tracking down the 'undesirables and polluters of Germany', the security services were increasingly assisted by the public, who felt that it was their duty to do so. The more impressionable younger generation were particularly keen to provide information and the Nazis were equally keen to embrace them, the next generation of parents, workers and soldiers. Indeed, in a particularly sinister speech Hitler advised:

[W]hen an opponent says, 'I will not come over to your side,' I calmly say, 'Your child belongs to us already . . . You will pass on. Your descendants, however, now stand in the new camp. In a short time they will know nothing but this new community.'

In schools, the development of intellectual ability was replaced with practical skills and fitness. Textbooks were written to reflect Nazi ideology and the teaching profession was brought under close Nazi control. In higher education, pure research and traditional subjects went into sharp decline while new subjects, such as racial studies, were introduced to uphold Nazi concepts. Informal education was also controlled. Some popular youth organizations, such as the Boy Scouts, were banned and the Party took over others. The *raison d'être* for those groups that survived was to produce young men and women who were 'educated physically, mentally and morally in the spirit of National Socialism, to serve the nation and the racial community'. Boys aged 14 to 18, for example, could join the Hitler Youth, which offered a mixture of outdoor activities, physical fitness and careful indoctrination, while the League of German Maidens focused on directing girls to become good wives and mothers. Both sexes were lectured in their responsibility to provide a future generation of 'strong Germans ready to serve the Reich'. Some, it seems, lost little time in fulfilling their duty for in 1936, when members of the Hitler Youth and League of German Maidens gathered together at the annual NSDAP rally in Nuremberg, 900 girls returned home pregnant. Many parents were horrified by what the Nazi organizations turned their children into. Karla Kortig, the mother of two teenaged boys, recalls:

> The Hitler Youth ended my sons' childhood. They became loutish and spouted the Nazi mantra without thinking. Before they joined they were careful family boys who enjoyed being at the bosom of the family. Within weeks of joining that hideous organization they became distant, within months I hardly recognized them.

With such young men, Hitler sought to build a new warrior race, willing to make difficult sacrifices. If that meant Germany was becoming brutalized, then so be it. But in preparing Germany for war, Hitler needed more than just willing soldiers. He needed an economic and military infrastructure to support them.

Recognizing the close connection between the Reichsmark in the pocket and popular support for the regime, as well as the relationship between industrial output and his aim to prosecute a war successfully, Hitler was determined to 'reorientate' the German economy. Having immediately rejected any notion of restarting reparation payments to the Allies after they had been temporarily suspended in 1930, the Nazis sought to lower unemployment through a mixture of capitalist free-enterprise and public spending. Meanwhile, the nation began preparation for war with the regime's 1936 Four Year Plan, which sought autarky and the development of a *wehrwirtschaft* (war economy). Overseeing this critical project was Hermann Göring, a man with a severely limited understanding of the complicated issues involved but with unbridled ambition. Linking the plan with Hitler's desire for territorial acquisition, Göring said:

> We are overpopulated and cannot feed ourselves from our own resources ... we lack foodstuffs and raw materials ... The final solution lies in extending our living space, that is to say, extending the source of raw materials and foodstuffs of our people. It is the task of the political leadership one day to solve this problem ... I, therefore, set the following tasks: 1) The German armed force must be operational within four years. 2) The German economy must be fit for war within four years.

Yet as the German economy began to be reshaped to cater for the needs of war, the contradictory aspects of Hitler's economic plan began to reveal themselves. The quest to minimize imports, for example, was incompatible with the requirement for more raw resources to fulfil the rearmament programme. Although German industry was directed to produce synthetic oil, petrol, textiles and rubber, it missed its output targets by some massive margins. Thus, by 1939, Germany still had to import two thirds of its oil, one fifth of its food and one third of its raw materials. Göring failed to achieve autarky in four years and, therefore, Hitler had to add to his list of strategic objectives the requirement to plunder foreign assets. Germany had never embraced the idea of fighting another protracted and multi-fronted war, and six years after Hitler came to power it was clear that she was incapable of fighting either. It was a situation that neither diplomats nor generals could afford to ignore.

When the Nazis came to power there was no radical change in foreign policy, but there was a change in tone. While governments of the Weimar Republic initially sought concessions through 'passive resistance' and working in a constructive manner with the Allies (which led to Germany being accepted as a member of the League of Nations), from 1930 a far more aggressive posture was adopted. Hitler's regime added grit to international relations as it flagrantly set out on a course to destroy the Versailles agreement and regain 'Germany's rightful status as a great power'. Foreign affairs were Hitler's great interest and he spent an inordinate amount of time on how the military might be used to achieve his territorial ambitions. The destruction of the Treaty of Versailles was seen by Hitler as a means of accessing his wider foreign policy ambitions. Speaking to army officers in February 1933, Hitler said:

> The struggle against Versailles is the means, but not the end of my policy . . . we have to proceed step by step, so that no one will impede our advance . . . I must gain space for Germany, space big enough to be able to defend ourselves against a military coalition . . . We need space . . . to make us independent of every possible political grouping and alliance. In the east we must have the mastery as far as the Caucasus and Iran. In the west, we need the

French coast. We need Flanders and Holland. Above all we need Sweden ... We cannot, like Bismarck, limit ourselves to national aims. We must rule Europe or fall apart as a nation.

By October 1933, Germany had withdrawn from the League of Nations and its World Disarmament Conference in a calculated move to avoid their restriction. The French were understandably concerned and soon began to fortify their common border and build an alliance system against Hitler in Eastern Europe. It was overtures made by Paris to Moscow that led Poland, Russia's old enemy, to sign a non-aggression pact with Germany in 1934. That agreement erroneously implied that Hitler had no territorial ambitions in the East and accused France of mischief making.

Britain, meanwhile, felt safer behind the English Channel but hoped to avoid war by adopting a policy of 'appeasement' towards Germany. The teetotal Hitler was so delighted with a naval treaty between the two nations, signed in June 1935, that he celebrated with champagne. While pleased with the agreement that the German fleet could grow to 35 per cent of the size of the Royal Navy and build submarines, he was ecstatic to find that he was capable of pulling the weighty levers of international diplomacy. From this point on, Hitler gloried in manipulating international fears, leaving false trails and opportunistically manoeuvring Germany into advantageous positions. Yet although many of his diplomatic victories were completed legally – such as the January 1935 plebiscite in the Saar, which resulted in a 90 per cent vote in favour of the region returning to Germany – Hitler knew that he had to prepare his military for the moment when he was compelled to take what he wanted by force.

By announcing in March 1935 that a Luftwaffe (airforce) already existed, his army was 240,000 strong and conscription was to be introduced, Hitler ensured that Germany finally threw off its status as an enfeebled leper state. Evasion of the military provisions of the Treaty of Versailles had begun during the Weimar period when the intelligent and talented General Hans von Seeckt was Commander in Chief of the army. It was he who ensured that, although small, the army was a modern and educated élite that would prove a sturdy platform for later expansion. Seeckt turned necessity into a virtue and said: 'The smaller the army, the easier it will be to equip it with modern weapons, whereas the provision of a constant supply for armies of millions is an impossibility.'

It was also under Seeckt's vigilant and progressive stewardship that a stimulating debate began concerning the lessons of the Great War, how new technology might be harnessed by the army and the nature of future war. Interested in the potential for armoured warfare in cooperation with tactical air power, in 1922 the Germans began to conduct a series of military experiments in Europe's other pariah state, the Soviet Union. In exchange for industrial expertise and financial investment, the Soviets provided facilities for the Germans to build military aircraft and tanks and conduct manoeuvres away from prying eyes. This led to the publication of a radical new German doctrine: 'Leadership and Battle with Combined Arms'. During the Weimar period, the armed forces were inventive and resolute in the face of the Treaty of Versailles, but there is no denying that its restrictions, when combined with a lack of investment and weak political will, severely undermined what could be achieved. The Nazi regime, however, ushered in a new and explosive era in both foreign affairs and military development. From 1933 all three armed services were re-energized as Hitler made it clear that his agenda for Europe was inextricably linked to what the military could deliver. It was a clever move, for it deftly turned the officer corps' gaze away from politics and towards the fulfilment of their own pent-up ambition. Using the resources released by Göring's Four Year Plan, the armed forces grew, modernized and prospered.

A new generation of dynamic and innovative generals oversaw the rapid development of the army and the application of 'Army Regulation 300 – Troop Command', the 1933 doctrine with which the German army was to go to war six years later. An evolution of the theories expounded during the Weimar period, the German fighting method became known to the world as blitzkrieg (lightning war) and embraced manoeuvre in a balanced, all-arms approach to war fighting, centred around aggressive use of air power and the employment of tanks in panzer divisions. The aim, as would have been understood by the great nineteenth-century Prussian generals, such as von Moltke, was to encircle and physically annihilate the enemy in a *kesselschlacht* (cauldron battle) and through this achieve a *vernichtungsschlacht* (the annihilation of the enemy's armed forces through a single crushing blow). Blitzkrieg, therefore, presented Hitler with the means for a swift, efficient and decisive military victory, which avoided the protracted, bloody and resource-sapping fighting that he had experienced during the Great War. It was an exciting time for the professionals in the rapidly growing military machine, but as Major-General Heinz Guderian, an armoured warfare theorist and commander of one of the new panzer divisions, wrote in his 1937 book *Achtung – Panzer!*:

Little more than twenty years have passed since tanks first appeared on the bloody Somme battlefield; this is a short period in the span of history. But modern technical development has acquired storm force . . . On many issues [of their employment] there still exist differences of opinion of a sometimes quite fundamental nature. Only time will tell who is right. But it is incontrovertible that as a general rule new weapons call for new ways of fighting, and for the appropriate tactical and organizational forms. You should not pour new wine into old vessels.

During the late 1930s the Wehrmacht honed its fighting techniques as Hitler began his foreign policy experiments and flexed his new-found military muscles. First came the great gamble in remilitarizing the Rhineland in March 1936. Although both generals and diplomats feared that the action would lead to armed confrontation, in the event there were no moves to stop Germany and the episode raised Hitler's stock massively with the military. Next, valuable fighting experience was gained when both the army and airforce supported Franco's Nationalists in the Spanish Civil War, and then, in March 1938, came the Anschluss (union) with Austria. Although no fighting took place in this move to incorporate Germany's neighbour into the Reich, ground forces did roll across the border as a show of force and, in common with experiences to come, the staff learned a great deal from the opportunity to plan and organize a major military enterprise that required men, vehicles and resources to move considerable distances. As Hitler followed his troops into Vienna some 25 years after he had left the city, the success reinforced a feeling that Providence was on his side. Just after the war Albert Speer, the architect who became Minister for Armaments, wrote that Hitler: 'had pieced together a firm conviction that his whole career, with its many unfavourable events and setbacks, was predestined by Providence to take him to the goal which it had set him' and that continued boldness would reap reward. It seems Hitler's cult of personality was such that he was viewed as a messiah by his loyal circle who, when in his presence, were, according to Speer: 'insignificant and timid . . . They were under his spell, blindly obedient to him and with no will of their own.' Hitler relished the role and the adulation for, having found his life's meaning in politics, he believed that he was now on the verge of achieving greatness.

The Führer drew confidence from his early international successes and, no doubt, began to believe his own rampant publicity. He was willing to challenge any nation that blocked his way and did not shy away from using aggression to crush them. Indeed, Hitler announced enthusiastically to colleagues, while observing an army exercise during the summer of 1938: 'War is the father of all things; every generation has to go to war once.' Even so, with Britain, France and the Soviet Union actively seeking to avoid a conflagration, Hitler hoped that he would be able to soak up yet more territory before hostilities became necessary. Germany occupied the Sudetenland in October 1938, having achieved a diplomatic victory the previous month. Hitler stated that a region of Czechoslovakia, German-speaking Sudetenland, was his 'last territorial demand in Europe', and at a conference in Munich Britain, France and Italy endorsed its annexation. Neville Chamberlain, the British Prime Minister, returned to London to announce that the agreement had secured 'peace in our time'. Hitler, however, regarded such diplomacy as ample evidence that Europe was not willing to fight to protect Czechoslovakia and in March 1939 the Wehrmacht was ordered 'to liquidate the remainder of the country'.

It was a highly provocative act for this was not only Hitler's first attack against a foreign-speaking country, it was the invasion of a nation allied to both France and the Soviet Union. Faced with destruction, the Czech President capitulated without a fight and 'confidently placed the fate of the Czech people in the hands of the Führer'. France and the Soviet Union looked on aghast, but ultimately failed to act. Hitler, inviting his secretaries to kiss him, declared, 'Children, this is the greatest day of my life. I shall go down in history as the greatest German.' The betrayal of the Munich agreement meant nothing to Hitler, but it told all of those states willing to listen that appeasement had failed and Germany would be stopped only by a war.

It had taken Hitler just six years to demolish the Treaty of Versailles and redraw the map of Europe – but he was not finished yet. In April 1939, spurred on by his recent success and voracious appetite for territory, Hitler decided to invade Poland. This would be an unquestionably belligerent act, which would require Germany to use a military machine that was still to be fully tested, and would pull on an economy that remained poorly organized for war. Yet although advisers both in uniform and suits urged caution, Hitler's enthusiasm for the offensive was unbounded. But first he needed to ensure that he was not plunging Germany into a two-fronted war with Britain, France and the Soviet Union galloping to Poland's defence. Hitler therefore entered into some unlikely diplomacy. Led by Foreign Minister Joachim von Ribbentrop, a man who was thoroughly underwhelmed by Nazi philosophy, Hitler sought to reach an understanding with his ideological nemesis, Joseph Stalin. Under the non-aggression pact, which was signed in August 1939, the two states agreed not to attack each other and to remain neutral if either was attacked by a third power. A secret provision allowed for a dual invasion of Poland and its subsequent division between Berlin and Moscow. That agreement gave Germany the great advantage of allowing the Wehrmacht to deal with enemies one front at a time. In common with the pact with Poland, Hitler regarded this new deal as pragmatic, and without the prospect of longevity. Recalling his long-standing aim of 'slaying the Russian bear', he advised colleagues during the summer of 1939, before the pact was signed:

In a few weeks I shall stretch out my hand to Stalin at the common frontier and with him undertake to redistribute the world ... After Stalin's death – he is a very sick man – we will break the Soviet Union. Then will begin the dawn of the German rule of the earth.

Hitler was under no illusion that the German invasion of Poland would be resisted and so, for the first time, prepared to unleash his snarling armed forces. It was a new chapter for Germany, as Hitler made clear to his generals in May while they were in the midst of planning the campaign:

With minor exceptions German national unification has been achieved. Further successes cannot be achieved without bloodshed. Poland will always be on the side of our adversaries ... Danzig is not the objective. It is a matter of expanding our living space in the east, of making our food supplies secure, and of solving the problem of the Baltic states. To provide sufficient food you must have sparsely settled areas. There is therefore no question of sparing Poland, and the decision remains to attack Poland at the first suitable opportunity. We cannot expect a repetition of Czechoslovakia. There will be fighting.

The invasion began at dawn on 1 September 1939 and later that day Hitler announced to the Reichstag: 'I have put on the uniform which was once the most holy and precious to me. I shall take it off only after victory or I shall not live to see the end.' Hitler had every hope of achieving victory quickly, particularly as the Soviets were poised to attack from the east. Having destroyed the Polish airforce and won air superiority, the Luftwaffe was free to support the ground offensive. The two panzer-led pincers concentrated their forces to create local superiority, scything through the mal-deployed and thinly manned defences. The Poles conducted a fighting withdrawal and even launched brave counterattacks against some overextended attacking formations. But while the Polish army could make an attempt at defending against one enemy, the Soviet invasion – which began on 17 September – made their precarious position untenable. Polish capitulation on 5 October stunned observers. Germany had ripped through a nation of 35 million people with ease, using methods that quickly rendered the enemy's defences impotent. Yet it was a brutal campaign, which destroyed all before it, as explained by young SS officer Walter Schellenburg, who picked his way through the ruins of Warsaw:

I was shocked at what had become of the beautiful city I had known – ruined and burnt out houses, starving and grieving people. A pall of dust and smoke hung over the city and every-where there was the sweetish smell of burnt flesh . . . Warsaw was a dead city.

The invasion of Poland showed what Germany was capable of and it went beyond military accomplishment. Hitler was bent on destruction and said: 'We are ruthless. Yes, we are barbarians! We want to be. That is an honourable epithet. We are the ones who will rejuvenate the world. The old world is done for.'

The campaign in Poland provided the German high command with plenty of lessons to learn, but it seemed to vindicate blitzkrieg, the *kesselschlacht* and the *vernichtungsschlacht*. The Poles had been incapable of contending with the high-speed dexterity of the air-land invasion and a significant victory had been achieved at the cost of 50,000 German casualties. Hitler's belligerence, however, did finally lead to Britain declaring war on Germany, which surprised him. Paul Schmidt, a German government interpreter, wrote of the minutes after the British announcement:

> Hitler sat motionless, gazing before him. He was not at a loss, as was afterwards stated, nor did he rage, as others allege. He sat completely silent and unmoving. After an interval which seemed an age, he turned to [Joachim von] Ribbentrop, who had remained standing by the window. 'What now?' asked Hitler with a savage look, as though implying that his Foreign Minister had misled him about England's probable reaction. Ribbentrop answered quietly: 'I assume that the French will hand in a similar ultimatum within the hour.'

Moving to an anteroom, Schmidt broke the news to other members of the hierarchy:

Göring turned to me and said: 'If we lose this war, then God have mercy on us!' Goebbels stood in a corner, downcast and self-absorbed. Everywhere in the room I saw looks of grave concern, even amongst the minor Party people.

The British announcement was followed by a French declaration of war. Hitler had miscalculated. Germany had upset the balance of power in Europe and presented a threat, which in all likelihood would remain extant until the country had been destroyed. As a result, there would be much more fighting before Hitler could turn east. This situation forced the ultimate opportunist to acknowledge to a large group of senior officers that events had occurred 'not exactly according to the schedule which was envisaged'. The clock of war had been started and, since Hitler could not stop it ticking, he had to take the important decision concerning where and when to launch his next move.

While the Führer pondered affairs of strategy and grand strategy, clearly within his province as head of government, the army high command were becoming exasperated at his propensity to meddle in their province of operational and tactical affairs. Hitler had endeavoured to undermine the military's much cherished independence ever since he came to power and in February 1938 made a significant change in the military decision-making system. Having swept away the old system of command and a raft of unpalatable generals, he appointed himself Supreme Commander of the Armed Forces. For the first time since Frederick the Great, political and military powers were merged. The War Ministry was replaced by Oberkommando der Wehrmacht (OKW), which acted as the Armed Forces High Command and Hitler's own military staff. This gave the Führer a more effective means of directing the armed forces under the leadership of the loyal and subservient General Wilhelm Keitel. OKW took Hitler's ideas and translated them into orders that were passed on to Oberkommando des Heeres (OKH), the army high command;

Oberkommando der Marine (OKM), the navy high command, and Oberkommando der Luftwaffe (OKL), the airforce high command. Each then planned their own separate aspects of a campaign, but without any reference to a coordinating body. The system did not make best use of the expertise of the staffs, nor was it as efficient or effective as it might have been because it lacked any joint-planning headquarters, but it did allow Hitler to divide and rule the armed forces. The new Supreme Commander rarely let his service chiefs attend the same war conference at which he listened to reports, made decisions and issued directives. There were no 'checks and balances' and limited consultancy over strategy aims and how they were to be realized – Hitler took the decisions and it was Hitler's strategy that was pursued.

Yet it was not just in the upper echelons of decision making that Hitler involved himself, but also the conduct of war fighting. With the navy carefully toeing the Nazi Party line, and Hermann Göring – a fervent Nazi and former Great War fighter ace – commanding the Luftwaffe, it was the army that needed to be watched. Hitler did not trust the army high command's temperament, loyalty or decision-making ability and found them too class-conscious, negative and cautious. He was irked by their protest at his decision to reoccupy the Rhineland, their 'squirming' over the occupation of Czechoslovakia and their insistence that the army was still years away from being ready for war when he ordered the invasion of Poland. Their 'lack of vigour' led to Hitler's interference in OKH's planning and conduct of operations against the Poles, and his insistence on viewing orders down to regimental level for the first three days of the offensive, which kept him abreast of likely military developments – albeit at an obsessively low level – and gave him control. He listened to advice from experienced professionals, such as Colonel-General Franz Halder, who oversaw planning as Chief of the Army General Staff, and General Walther von Brauchitsch, Commander in Chief of the German Army, but did not necessarily act on it. As a former corporal, Hitler certainly did not have either the experience or qualifications to pass judgement on the physical application of force, but that did not stop him. The fact that the revisions made by Hitler to plans for Poland proved astute led him to think that his triumphant intervention was exactly what was needed to put pompous senior officers in their place, and encouraged even greater meddling.

The piqued and undermined generals believed that Hitler's interference was dangerous, his military thinking reckless and his lack of consultation gratuitous. Under pressure from his colleagues, Brauchitsch confronted Hitler about the situation, saying, 'OKH would be grateful for an understanding that it, and it alone, would be responsible for the conduct of any future campaign.' A chilling silence was followed by a response that was to become increasingly common when Hitler grew exasperated by the military – carpet-biting rage. For 20 minutes he fumed about the 'treacherous and cowardly General Staff' before leaving Brauchitsch alone to ponder the wisdom of ever having agreed to raise the subject. OKH had naively believed that the army carried more influence within the regime than it actually did, and had failed to recognize the new relationship that existed between the executive and the military. There was no longer a team, but a master and a servant. Brauchitsch and the army high command had been firmly put in their place, and to underline this Hitler announced to the General Staff that he would smash the West within the year.

Although Hitler's determination to attack the Soviet Union remained undiminished, his need to fight on a single front made him turn west first. With Stalin currently pacified by the non-aggression pact, Germany had engineered an opportunity to knock France and Britain out of the war without the threat of Stalin becoming involved. As Hitler said to his senior officers:

Russia is at present not dangerous. It is now weakened by many developments. Moreover, we have a Treaty with Russia. Treaties, however, are only kept as long as they serve their purpose . . . We can oppose Russia only when we are free in the west.

Although originally scheduled for November 1939, the German attack on France and the Low Countries did not take place until the following May due to various planning, logistical and weather considerations. In the intervening period Hitler sought to secure his northern Scandinavian flank, acquire coastal bases for the navy and protect the supply of iron ore from Norway and Sweden. Germany overwhelmed Denmark just hours after launching an invasion on 9 April and on the same day struck at Norway. The offensive began well, with Oslo and several other towns and cities falling quickly to German airborne and amphibious forces. Despite British and French troops landing at northern ports in mid-April, the Luftwaffe defeated attempts to resupply them and forced their evacuation just two weeks later. A subsequent Allied landing in mid-May eventually took Narvik, but met the same end just two days before Norway finally succumbed on 10 June.

Germany had notched up another comprehensive victory, but it did nothing to ease the growing tension between OKW and the service high commands. The campaign revealed an easily flustered Supreme Commander who had begun to exhibit huge mood swings as he bulldozed his way into operational matters. Moreover, Germany's achievement in Scandinavia had three significant detrimental strategic effects: in Britain it led to the feeble Neville Chamberlain being replaced as Prime Minister by the pugnacious Winston Churchill; it tied Germany to the provision of a large occupation force; and it so denuded Germany's surface fleet that it forced Hitler to rethink his future plans.

Yet by the time Norway fell, German forces were already surging through France. Beginning on 10 May, an audacious plan pinned the

Allies with a secondary attack into northern Belgium and Holland, while the main armoured force undercut them with a surprise thrust through the 'impenetrable' Ardennes, heading towards the English Channel. Hamstrung by their reliance on an outdated, static, defensive strategy – grinding the enemy down in attritional, positional warfare – the Allies were outflanked and completely dislocated. By 4 June, 338,226 British, French and Belgian troops were trapped on the Dunkirk beaches, allowing Hitler's forces to turn on Paris. The French capital fell on 14 June, four days after Benito Mussolini's Italy allied itself with Germany, and the nation yielded eight days later. Elated and acutely aware of the historical significance of the French submission to Germany a generation after Versailles, Goebbels wrote in his diary: 'The disgrace is now extinguished. It's a feeling of being born again.' Hitler had presided over one of the most complete victories in history and accomplished in six weeks what the Central Powers had failed to achieve during the entire 1914–18 war. Even so, the campaign revealed a number of ongoing problems and weaknesses that were to affect Germany's operational and strategic effectiveness.

While the rapid fall of France and the Low Countries seemed to reaffirm the military's approach to defeating an enemy quickly, there had been no plan to encircle or annihilate the enemy in one campaign. Even if events in France were used to validate the *vernichtungsschlacht* in retrospect, in fact the Germans simply took the opportunity that arose during the campaign to achieve it. Mindful of the old adage that 'no plan survives first contact', commanders had a responsibility to be flexible and seize fleeting chances quickly. As a consequence there had been no plan for the German armoured force after it had penetrated the Ardennes, but although this encouraged initiative, it also created the potential for vacillation and space for enemy reaction. Hitler's own intrusions began during the planning phase when he overrode the fears of some of his more conservative generals (who preferred a pared down mechanized re-run of the 1914 Schlieffen Plan through central Belgium) and authorized the intrepid move through the Ardennes. Later, during the campaign itself, as armoured commanders (including Heinz Guderian and one Erwin Rommel), having passed through the Ardennes, took their chance and plunged for the coast, Hitler lost his nerve. Fearing that the armoured force was vulnerable since it had out-run its logistic support and the non-motorized infantry, which followed, he ordered a halt. Guderian later wrote:

> The Supreme Command intervened in the operations in progress, [the] results of which were to have a most disastrous influence on the whole course of the war ... The order contained the words: 'Dunkirk is to be left to the Luftwaffe ...' We were utterly speechless.

The inability of the Luftwaffe to prevent an evacuation of Allied forces from Dunkirk gave Britain hope and an experienced rump upon which to build a new army. As Guderian reflects, the decision was to haunt the Germans in the years to come, but the euphoria of victory choked any attempt to ask challenging questions about the experience – perhaps because Hitler knew that he would not like the answers. Hitler was, in the words of the obsequious Keitel, 'the greatest commander of all time', which, it seems, was to make up for various strategic and operational weaknesses. Those weaknesses were pushed out of sight by ambition, but as they festered some of the clearer-thinking generals remained concerned about how the armed forces would fare against stronger opposition with greater resources that allowed them to undertake protracted attritional warfare over great distances – the Soviet Union, for example. But Stalin's empire would have to wait a while yet. Britain still had to be defeated.

Hitler had expected Winston Churchill to submit to German threats after the ease with which France had been despatched, but he did not. Reflecting the defiance of the nation and, as a student of history, recognizing how difficult it was to mount a successful invasion across the narrow English Channel, the new Prime Minister was determined to fight on. This caused Hitler a problem for he had no invasion plans and there were not the naval resources to undertake the effort. He could ignore Britain, but he anticipated that if left undefeated, the islands would become a staging post for an Anglo-American invasion of the Continent at some point in the future. Britain had to fall, but the Luftwaffe's inability during the summer of 1940 to create the conditions under which an invasion could take place was a major setback. The Führer was furious but on 17 September the invasion was postponed and plans were never to be revived.

And so Germany's hastily prepared war caravan raced on with its blinkered driver gripping the reins ever more tightly as he headed towards a storm. The clock was ticking and Hitler was heading east.

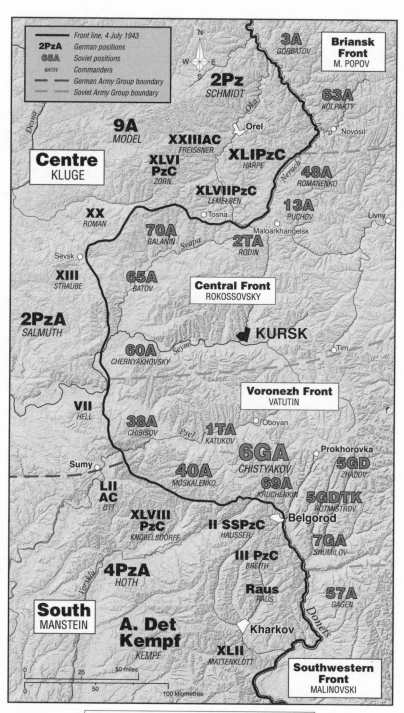

Map 3: The Eve of Battle, 4 July 1943

CHAPTER 2

The Origins of Annihilation II

(The Soviet Union and the Soviets 1918–41)

In May 1937, Marshal Mikhail Tukhachevsky was to have the honour of representing the Soviet Union at the coronation ceremony of George VI in London. He never arrived. Although the British Embassy was informed that the soldier had been taken ill, the truth was that Tukhachevsky had become a victim of a new phase in the Kremlin's 'cleansing operations'. His fate had been sealed in Moscow at a reception held after the May Day Parade when an ebullient Joseph Stalin remarked to his extravagantly moustachioed confidant, Marshal Semyon Budenny, that it was time 'to finish with our enemies because they are in the army, in the staff, even in the Kremlin . . . We must finish with them, not looking at their faces.' Budenny had been imploring Stalin to undertake a purge of 'difficult' senior officers for several months because he believed that it would remove the final threat to the General Secretary's power outside the secret police. Those senior officers included 44-year-old Tukhachevsky, the Deputy Commissar for Defence, a bug-eyed womanizer who happened to be the most talented soldier of his generation. Arrested by the secret police (NKVD) along with seven other high-ranking colleagues, the men were driven to Moscow's notorious Lefortovo Prison where they were tortured.

The officers' trial was held on 11 June and was overseen by a secret special military tribunal of the Supreme Court, which included Budenny. The fictitious charges levelled against Tukhachevsky and his fellow (grotesquely bruised) accused included involvement in treasonable contact with unfriendly powers, espionage, sabotage and assassination. Proceedings were a mockery. The critical evidence amounted to little more than the blood-spattered confessions extracted while the accused were being beaten. Stalin had already directed that the 'traitors' be shot, so there was only one possible outcome and all eight were sentenced to death. Just after midnight the senior executioner, Captain Vasili Blokhin, fed eight rounds into his pistol's magazine and politely asked his prisoners to kneel on the dirt floor and bow their heads. Then, walking behind his prey, he cocked his pistol and proceeded to shoot each in the back of the neck. Stalin was not present at the trial as he had been attending his mother's funeral, but he insisted on hearing all the gory details on his return. 'What were Tukhachevsky's final words?' he asked Nikolai Yezhov, the NKVD's sadistic chief. 'The snake said he was dedicated to the Motherland and Comrade Stalin,' came the reply. 'He asked for clemency.' Stalin was silent for a moment – and then belched.

The circumstances leading to the Soviet military being so savagely treated by a paranoid dictator go back at least as far as 1917. As in Germany, the route to totalitarianism and war started with revolution that had its roots in the Great War. Although pressure for change had been building for decades, the ongoing demands were ignored by the ruling Romanov dynasty, which eschewed modernization as much as it deplored the concept of democracy. The Romanovs presided over a backward nation. An unproductive economy, massive peasant population, pitiable levels of literacy, autocratic political system, corrupt bureaucracy and ineffectual military combined to ensure a poorly motivated and underdeveloped Russia was ill-prepared for the rigours of a protracted total war. Lieutenant-Colonel Edward Leigh was a British liaison officer working in the Russian capital, St Petersburg. Writing to his brother in February 1914, two weeks after taking up his appointment, Leigh remarked:

> Russia is a squalid place with a population that cares little for other than scraping a living from the soil. Poverty abounds, government is shambolic and I have quickly learned not to trust any officials ... An army reflects the society from which it is drawn and the Russian army is disordered and lacking in modern weaponry ... All of this and the weather is appalling cold!

Three years later Russia was deeply embroiled in the Great War and on the verge of revolution. In February 1917, having suffered months of heavy casualties and military disappointment, cold, hungry workers began to strike and to express their discontent. In the capital, renamed Petrograd in 1914, the police reported that the government's heavy-handed attempt to quell public meetings arranged to discuss the situation had caused 'workers, led by the more educated and perhaps the more revolutionary among them [to] adopt an openly hostile attitude to the government and protest against the continuation of the war.' Some violent unrest followed and Colonel Leigh, now heading an office concerned with the 'evaluation of Russian operations', wrote home:

> The authorities seem to be losing control. I have heard reports of troops firing on demonstrators in the city ... Last week I witnessed a march with banners and singing. The Romanovs seem to be the target, but so are factory owners and employers ...

There is a tension in the air which could very well develop into something very nasty indeed.

Leigh was correct. The dissatisfaction did initially focus on the monarchy for the Tsar, Nicholas II, not only led Russia into the war, but in making himself Commander in Chief of the army, he tied himself personally to failure.

The abdication of the Tsar on 15 March 1917 provided the impetus for further change. An indecisive, liberal-socialist provisional government struggled to deal with the myriad problems facing the nation, but the Soviets – workers' councils comprising delegates elected by the people – began to make progress on some local issues. Increasingly dominated by extreme, left-wing socialists (Bolsheviks), the Soviets agitated for more fundamental changes through a Marxist revolution. One of the loudest Bolshevik voices was that of Vladimir Lenin. He called for 'peace, bread and land' and raged, 'Down with Provisional Government: All Power to the Soviets!' The Bolsheviks' virtually bloodless seizure of power in a proletarian-based revolution on 7 November 1917 in Petrograd ousted the provisional government. There followed a series of measures that invested more power in the people. For example, workers' control was instituted in industry, private ownership of land was abolished and estates were handed over to the peasants. Some pronouncements had international ramifications – non-Russian states were offered self-determination, and in December, Russia dropped out of the war.

However, while superficially dealing in democratic ideals, the Bolsheviks – now officially titled the Communist Party and led by Lenin – broke up the Constituent Assembly when election results were not as favourable to them as had been anticipated. Furthermore, fearing a popular backlash, all other political parties were prohibited by the new Communist dictatorship, and in the early autumn of 1918, the 'Red Terror' began. This 'terror' struck a heavy blow against counter-revolutionaries and was used by Lenin to announce to the nation that there would be no return to the old Russia and that disloyalty to the regime would not be tolerated. Lenin said: 'We need the real, nation-wide terror which reinvigorates the country and through which the Great French Revolution achieved glory.' The Cheka – the security arm of the regime – immediately executed hundreds of members of the former ruling classes (including the Tsar and his family) and thousands more followed. Lenin justified his actions by saying: 'How can you make a revolution without executions?' Some 250,000 people were killed over the next four years. A teacher from Smolensk whose brother was arrested and later executed for 'seditious literature' (he wrote romantic poems during his lunch break) later recorded: 'It was as if the regime would not be satisfied until they had silenced every critical tongue.'

The bloodshed continued during a civil war that lasted until 1923. Beset by non-Russian, anti-Bolshevik forces and internal anti-Bolshevik 'White' forces, which sought to destroy the revolution, the mass conscript Red Army struggled on several fronts. In the end, the aggressors were undone by long lines of communication, disunity and half-heartedness in the face of passionate and resolute defence. Poland won its independence from Russia as did Finland and the Baltic states, but the revolution was secure. A thankful Leon Trotsky, the People's Commissar for War, told an appreciative party audience in October 1923: 'All the forces of the old world have failed to strangle the revolution in its cot. Now we shall grow and become strong.' Having suffered over 20 million casualties since 1914 and undergone fundamental political, social and economic change since 1917, it was clear that the nation needed to consolidate, revitalize and modernize. Thus, in the wake of the civil war a new nation was born, the Union of Soviet Socialist Republics. Its capital was Moscow and organizational reforms were instituted to ensure its governance. For the first time in a generation the nation could look to the future. But one question remained – with Lenin ailing, who was going to lead the youthful Soviet Union forward?

By the time of his death in January 1924, Lenin was perceived by many as an irreplaceable icon. Although the vastness of the Soviet Union, its poor communications and the limited education of its population meant that national politics were far from an obsession for the peasantry, the reach of the Communist Party was great. Daniel Vogel, a production manager from Berlin who had recently arrived in the country to advise Soviet industry as part of the regime's new understanding with Germany, wrote in his diary:

> The death of Lenin has been announced. People have taken it badly for they seem to view him as a father figure. Petrograd is to be renamed Leningrad in his memory. In the afternoon I travelled to a large farm to see some of our [machinery] at work. Here were people that work 18 hour days just to survive, but even they were talking about Lenin's passing . . . The peasants like stability and fear the unknown. I am surprised, but the country seems to have plunged into deep mourning.

The struggle to succeed Lenin was already a year old by the time he was laid to rest in a mausoleum on Moscow's Red Square. The front runners jostled for position, and carefully manoeuvring himself into position by marginalizing his opponents and gaining allies was Stalin. Born Iosif Vissarionovich Dzhugashvili in Georgia in 1878, his father was an unsuccessful cobbler prone to drunkenness and violence against his family. Iosif's was an unhappy childhood, but as biographer Robert Service points out: 'Not everyone beaten by parents acquires a murderous personality. Yet some do . . . [and] it is scarcely astounding that he grew up with a strong tendency towards resentment and retaliation.' At the age of six the young Iosif fell prey to the potentially fatal smallpox virus and later he was knocked down by a horse-drawn trap, which left his left arm permanently shortened and lacking flexibility. After school – where his intelligence and hard work were noted along with his occasionally furious temper – he attended an Orthodox seminary. It was here that the teenager came into contact with socialist ideas, and he eventually became a professional revolutionary. Changing his name to Stalin (which means steel) to convey a certain image, he worked for 15 years to bring down the Tsarist regime, and on several occasions was arrested and exiled. By this time, aged 36, he was described by a fellow revolutionary as 'thick-set, of medium height, [with] a drooping moustache, thick hair, narrow forehead and rather short legs . . . his speech was dull and dry . . . a narrow-minded, fanatical man.'

Playing a key role in the 1917 seizure of power as part of the inner circle of Bolsheviks, Stalin was rewarded with an appointment as People's Commissar for Nationalities. He had an active civil war, clashing frequently with Trotsky, organizing the defence of Tsaritsyn (which in 1925 was renamed Stalingrad in his honour) and ordering the executions of former untrustworthy Tsarist officers along with deserters, defectors and other 'counter-revolutionaries'. Following his elevation to membership of the Politburo (the governing and central policy-making body of the Communist Party) in 1922, Stalin was made the Party's General Secretary. This was not a significant position at the time, but as it gave him control of the party machinery and appointments – including the NKVD – he could build a base of support. Beginning to promote himself as a future leader, Stalin drew the attention of Lenin, who thought him 'uncouth' and was not convinced that he would 'always manage to use power with sufficient care'. But Stalin was politically astute, robust and highly determined. As other leadership candidates, such as the 'political simpleton' Leon Trotsky, dropped out of the demanding race, Stalin's power grew and by the end of the decade the Party addressed him as *vozhd* – leader.

Stalin was diligent and hard working. He rarely rose before noon but worked deep into the night. His spacious study in the Kremlin was panelled with stained oak and hung with portraits of Marx, Engels and

Lenin – minimalist and simply furnished. Alanbrooke, Chief of the British Imperial General Staff, compared it to the 'waiting room of an English railway station'. Stalin's desk, however, was piled high with documents that were covered in his trademark blue pencil notes, indicating the long hours he worked and how he exhausted those around him. He was an exacting boss who used his large personality to encourage his staff in their business but would not tolerate substandard work. Possessing a photographic memory, a quick brain and an eye for detail, he expected briefings to be thorough, clear and precise. Listening to reports while strolling around the room smoking his much-loved Dunhill pipe filled with cigarette tobacco, he had the disconcerting habit of standing face to face with a speaker if he wished to put that person under pressure. If he spotted a weak argument or received an inferior briefing, he would not fail to lambast the perpetrator and it was not uncommon for his short temper to burst. Hundreds were given 'the treatment' over the years, including one middle-aged propagandist, Pavlo Kulik, who incurred Stalin's wrath by misinterpreting some figures. Kulik has testified:

> It was an experience that I have never forgotten. It is seared into my memory . . . I had muddled two sets of numbers which thoroughly undermined the point that I was trying to make. Stalin approached me, his face ashen, his head jutting forward and his brow furrowed. His dark eyes seemed to reach deep into me and wrench out my stomach. He then exploded into a rage demanding to know why I had made a mistake, but not giving me time to provide an answer . . . It was the first and last time that I met Comrade Stalin.

By the age of 50, Stalin was undisputed leader of the Soviet Union and had cultivated the image of being tough but reasonable, a man to be obeyed, who demanded loyalty but was approachable and fair. In particular, he was seen as a man with the sort of ideas that would modernize the Soviet Union for, as Lenin had said, 'electrification and literacy equal communism'. It was a commonly held belief that educated, fit and healthy workers would not only be happier, but more productive. Stalin helped to ensure that education was made mandatory for children and supported a universal literacy programme, under which the number of people who could read and write grew from around 25 per cent of the population in 1917 to over 80 per cent in 1939. It was a process that developed the national intellect, but was also used by the Communist Party to ensure that its political message was read and understood by all. In this way, the population was gradually exposed to Marxist-Leninist ideology and learned compliance to the regime's will.

The young were further moulded by youth groups controlled by the Communist Party, such as the Little Octoberists (for the very young), Young Pioneers (for those aged nine to 14) and Komsomol (for 14- to 28-year-olds). These organizations aimed to fashion hard-working and loyal future generations – a mobile pool of labour that could be dipped into to carry out party projects. Komsomol, for example, provided teachers for the adult literacy programme and organized regional sporting events. The group was also used as the eyes and ears of the regime in remote towns and villages as the Party became increasingly intolerant of opinions that ran contrary to the official point of view. 'Enemies of the state' were to be uncovered and imprisoned, while published works and the arts were censored to ensure that they were 'ideologically safe'.

The Soviet Union's cultural life, therefore, became a sterile wasteland of the simplistic political settings so redolent of 'Socialist Realism'. Addressing the First Congress of Soviet Writers in August 1934, writer Yuri Olesha advised that working men and women be placed at the heart of novels where 'they strove and succeeded'. He recommended characters who revealed the virtues to which all good Communists should aspire for 'when you depict a negative hero, you yourself become negative'. The aim was to produce art that inspired the population, helped the masses become good socialists, motivated them to defend the revolution and encouraged the rejection of any thoughts and ideas that criticized the regime and its creed. Perhaps the best illustration of the sort of publication that the regime foisted on its people was *Pravda* (Truth), the official newspaper of the Central Committee of the Communist Party, which became a beacon for Communist ideology and could be relied upon to be unfailingly supportive of the government and present an upbeat interpretation of the nation's achievements.

It is within the pages of *Pravda* that the Soviet Union's economic rise was charted in considerable detail. Stories with strap-lines such as 'Oil Production Figures Soar' and 'Leningrad Factory Breaks Construction Record' were commonplace in the 1930s while strenuous efforts were being made to drag the economy into the twentieth century. However, the wholesale nationalization of industry in the wake of the revolution may have provided the regime with immediate control over proletariat urban workers and manufacturing output, but this would be for nought if the nation starved. Lenin's land redistribution among the peasantry – which formed 80 per cent of the population – had had a catastrophic effect on food production. Large, efficient farms that had provided a food surplus were carved up into smaller, uneconomical family plots. Moreover, seizure of grain to feed the cities had led to rural famine and a widespread turning against Marxism by the peasantry. The introduction of a New Economic Policy (NEP) in March 1921, however, encouraged peasants to produce a surplus by allowing them to sell their produce for the best price. It was not a panacea, but the NEP alleviated the immediate threat of a food crisis, and by restoring an element of market economy across the nation also stimulated industry. This was critical for the Soviet Union, because although successful in its defence of the revolution during the civil war years, both Lenin and Stalin believed that, having retired to lick their wounds and regain their strength after years of fighting, the capitalist nations would seek to annihilate the regime.

There is no doubt that the Soviet Union felt vulnerable after its recent experiences – Lenin called the country 'an oasis in the middle of a raging imperialist sea' – and, now cast as a pariah state, remained 'at risk'. In 1924, Mikhail Frunze, People's Commissar for Military and Naval Affairs (War Minister), politician, army commander and military theorist, wrote:

> In a conflict of first-class opponents, the decision cannot be won by one blow. War will take the character of a long and fierce conflict . . . Expressed in the language of strategy, this means a change from the strategy of lightning blows to a strategy of exhaustion. Thus the bond between the front and the rear in our days must become much more close, direct and decisive. The life and work of the front at any given moment are determined by the work and condition of the rear.

Having studied national performances during the Great War, as well as Russia's own civil war, Frunze felt impelled to call for the development not only of a strong economy but a nation, society and armed forces fit for the rigours of contemporary conflict. The idea was progressively taken up and the Soviet Union, very slowly but surely, prepared for 'total war'. There was a grand aspiration to develop significantly the capability of the economy and military while mentally conditioning the population for hostilities. Indeed, the regime saw the creation of an atmosphere of tension and apprehension as a useful means by which to galvanize the population to greater efforts in the work place and to expose traitors. There were regular war scares – often on the merest sliver of a pretext – which kept the nation on its collective toes. Propagandists depicted Stalin as the rock upon which enemy aggression would be broken. He said in 1927 that it was just a matter of time before there was 'a new imperialist war [aimed] against the Soviet Union in particular' and in the following year: 'Comrades, our class enemies do exist. They not only exist but are growing and trying to act against Soviet power.' By the early 1930s, and clearly pointing to Germany and at the rise of Hitler, Stalin warned: 'Again, as in 1914, the parties of bellicose imperialism, the parties of war and revenge are coming to the foreground. Quite clearly things are heading for a new war.' Stalin willingly tied himself to a new militarism just as Hitler did in Germany. As Richard Overy has written in his superb assessment of the two men, *The Dictators*:

> It was not mere accident that both Hitler and Stalin chose to be seen in public wearing simple military-style dress. Stalin's plain high-collar tunic and knee-length boots were modelled on the uniform of the new Soviet army, unadorned and braidless ... Wearing uniform was a deliberate choice, indicative of the two men's differing beliefs that revolutionary war, or the struggle for national existence, was in some sense a permanent state of being.

Thus, Soviet economic and social development programmes should be viewed through the prism of the regime's need to defend itself. Stalin, meanwhile, worked tirelessly to ensure that the population's energy was directed solely towards achieving this ambition.

Creating a nation fit for war could not be achieved quickly, but it was given structure under Stalin's direction in a series of Five Year Plans that covered all aspects of development, including heavy and light industry; communications; agriculture; transportation; the welfare system; health and education reforms. The First Five Year Plan, introduced in 1928, sought to make the nation industrially self-sufficient and militarily stronger. In February 1931, Stalin said in a speech to industrial officials and managers:

The history of old Russia consisted, among other things, in her being ceaselessly beaten for her backwardness ... For military backwardness, for cultural backwardness, for state backwardness, for industrial backwardness, for agricultural backwardness. They beat her because it was profitable and could be done with impunity ... We have fallen behind the advanced countries by fifty to a hundred years. We must close that gap in ten years. Either we do this or we'll be crushed.

The purpose of the First Plan, therefore, was to ascertain what needed to be produced and then to ensure that the requisite commodities were produced to the necessary quality and in the required quantity and got to where they were needed in time. It was the mother of Soviet mass production and the father of the nation's internal communications. By 1932, wagon loads of rapidly produced goods were leaving factories in Leningrad and Moscow and efficiently transported by road, rail and canal to distant regions of the country. The Plan was nominally overseen by Vyacheslav Molotov, a loyal supporter of Stalin and Chairman of the Council of People's Commissars (Prime Minister) since December 1930, and to fulfil it the regime put workers under tremendous pressure to work harder and longer than ever before. Posters on canteen notice boards and factory floors proclaimed: 'We Will Turn the Five Year Plan into a Four Year One' and 'Through Production Comes Strength'. Komsomol was mobilized to undertake construction projects, such as the huge Dneiper Dam, and prisoners were routinely worked to death in labour camps. The result was that, although Molotov's massively ambitious production goals were not met, industry developed markedly in the late 1920s and early 1930s with the nation's infrastructure dramatically improving and the production of coal and iron quadrupling. This success was not achieved without a price being paid, though, and with increasing numbers of peasants working in factories, that price was the spectre of a crippling food crisis.

The prospect of widespread famine finally forced the government to merge small, inefficient peasant farms in a process called 'collectivization', which took place between 1928 and 1935. It destroyed the peasants' much-cherished independence and rested the long arm of the state on the farm gate. The policy was met with derision in the countryside and its implementation led to great hardship. Government quotas were often unachievable, leading to a significant drop in the peasants' standard of living and the constant fear of requisitioning. Mikhail Batkin, who worked fields near Kursk with his father, testifies:

> We were told what each new farm had to produce. It was a frightening amount, much more than was possible on the land that we had. My father was very worried that whatever food we kept for ourselves would be taken to make up the deficit. There was a feeling that we were worthless . . . that the cities were sucking the life out of the countryside.

The result was not an increase in food production but a decrease in the three years after 1929 as the disincentivized peasantry struggled to produce what the burgeoning cities needed. Stalin blamed the slightly better off Kulaks (around four per cent of the population) for hoarding, resisting the changes and waging a 'silent war' against the Soviet state. 'They need to be taught a lesson,' he growled to a colleague in February 1932. 'This situation is undermining all that we have achieved. These people are holding us to ransom and it cannot continue.' His opportunity came later that year when crop failure led to a widespread famine – the *Holodomor* – in the major grain-producing regions, which Stalin exacerbated by requisitioning more grain for the cities and increasing its export. Seven million died (including one in eight of the Ukrainian population). Stalin was single-minded and received the figures coldly: 'Nothing can be allowed to stand in the way of our industrialization ... If there are obstacles, they will be overcome – and then crushed.'

The initial momentum created by the First Five Year Plan was maintained by subsequent schemes. The Second Plan, in 1932, placed a strong emphasis on heavy industry and the development of military hardware while a third, in 1938, pumped resources into developing armaments and ensuring that factories were beyond the reach of an attack from the West. It was a time of significant Soviet manufacturing development hammered out of workers who were expected to produce more each year. The press published stories of remarkable deeds to 'inspire' the proletariat. They included news on 31 August 1935 that miner Aleksy Stakhanov had exceeded the norm of 6.5 tons of coal per five-hour shift by producing 102 tons of coal, having worked non-stop through the night – double what a squad would regularly produce. On 19 September it was announced that he had set a new record by mining 227 tons of coal in a single shift. Stakhanov became a national celebrity and appeared on the cover of the December issue of *Time* magazine in the United States, which reported:

Commissar Ordzhonikidze [Commissar for Heavy Industry] saw to it that Comrade Stakhanov received a motor car and other luxuries unheard of for a Russian miner. After diligent search in other Soviet mines and factories, fresh Heroes of Labor were produced whose feats of 'Stakhanovism' as played up by the Soviet Press became more and more stupendous ... To the galaxy of correspondents and photographers gruff, iron-jawed Communist Party Agent Konstantin Giorgevich Petrov was introduced as 'the man who discovered Stakhanov.' Asked reporters of Stakhanov: 'Do you get many letters? Do people write to you asking about your method of work?' 'He gets letters from all over – hundreds of letters!' cut in The-Man-Who-Discovered-Stakhanov. 'All women want to know if he has really doubled his wages. All men want to know how he has improved technique. Hundreds of letters!'

Yet while some workers rose to the challenge set for them by the regime in spectacular fashion, others did not. The same *Time* article that revealed how Stakhanov was being lauded went on to say:

> In the Gorky automotive works the Brothers Ivan and Feodor Kriachkov assassinated their fellow worker Ivan Schmerov because he had speeded up his daily output 200%. Tried before a military tribunal, they were sentenced to death. In the coal mine at Stalino two assistant foremen, a check-weigher and an electrician, were arrested for the murder of a fast-working Stakhanovite who had peached on them to the Bolshevik labor boss as 'opposed to Stakhanovism.' In a nearby mine a worker shot at his Stakhanovite mine manager, and missed. The most spectacular blow against Stakhanovism is supposed to have been struck by Engineer S. Plotnikov, a member of the Communist Party up to the time of his arrest. According to the Soviet Press, Engineer Plotnikov became so vexed at Chelyabinsk by the boastful uppishness of the local Stakhanov gang that he ordered the fastest speeder-uppers to dig in an extremely dangerous pit of Mine No. 204. Sure enough, the pit caved in on them.

Workers were subjected to appalling day-to-day pressures and, in common with the peasantry, there was a growing sense of paranoia. Show trials in the late 1920s and early 1930s underlined the absolute necessity to conform to government requirements. The poor wretches who stood before the kangaroo courts charged with 'treason', 'sabotage', 'espionage' and the like were most likely merely bad time keepers, drunks and dawdlers.

Collectivization and the show trials reflected an increasing harshness towards the most vulnerable in Soviet society. Unfortunately for the terrorized population, Stalin could justify the excesses by pointing to productivity figures, which grew year on year. Steel output rose from 4.3 million tons in 1928 to 18.1 million tons a decade later, coal production more than trebled from 35 million tons to 133 million and truck production rose from a mere 700 vehicles to 182,000. Moreover, while in 1928 some 60 per cent of Soviet industry was light and 40 per cent was heavy, by 1941 the figures had been reversed. The Soviet Union possessed an economy far better configured for total war by the late 1930s than it had ten years earlier, but at the cost of the hope and liberty of a large proportion of the population. Yet if the population was disillusioned and angered at the situation, Stalin knew the reason for it – they were 'sworn enemies of Soviet power'. That the situation did not lead to peasants and workers rallying against the regime was testament to the success of the Party's propaganda and social programmes, which provided a growing 'mind control', but was also due to the fear that it engendered in the masses. Arms were manufactured as the standard of living slumped, and terror replaced altruism. In the Soviet leader, Hitler seems to have seen a kindred spirit for he said, 'That fellow Stalin is a brute, but you really must admit, he's an extraordinary fellow.'

The arming of the nation took place within the wider strengthening of the armed forces. Increasing funds were pumped into the military as the Soviet Union began its quest to 'develop a first-class military machine to destroy the forces of capitalist-imperialism'. The Russian military had recently been through a torrid time. The army had peaked at 5.5 million men during the civil war, but demobilization left a rump of just 600,000 men in the mid-1920s, which quickly became little more than an ill-disciplined rabble, unwilling and unable to contend with the demands of modern soldiering. A special commission established in 1924 to examine the nation's defensive situation concluded that the army was 'not a reliable fighting force' and recommended a radical overhaul. Mikhail Frunze attempted to grasp the nettle and instituted reforms linked to the Five Year Plans. These were to have a dramatic impact. He advocated a 'unitary military doctrine' under which the army would be trained for offensive operations and united by its resolve to carry out the Communist Party's aim of promoting world revolution. Compulsory peacetime military service was instituted, formations were reorganized, training improved, equipment improved, leadership strengthened, drills and uniforms standardized. Morale began to seep back into the force, which had previously felt undervalued and neglected. At a time when most other European nations sought to disarm and embrace peace, the Soviet Union rearmed and professionalized. In 1913 real defence expenditure had been about 5.2 per cent of gross national product, by 1933 it had risen to around 12 per cent and by 1940 it was at 18 per cent. At the beginning of 1928 the Soviet Union had 92 tanks and 1,394 military aircraft; by January 1935 the numbers had leapt to 10,180 and 6,672 respectively.

As the army's body was strengthened by Frunze, so its mind was improved by Tukhachevsky. Appointed in 1925 as Chief of the General Staff, the brilliant 32-year-old Mikhail Tukhachevsky began to examine how the Red Army went about its business and was not impressed with what he found. Assisted by Aleksandr Svechin and Vladimir Triandafillov, two other sparkling Soviet military thinkers, Tukhachevsky rewrote the army's doctrine. In May 1928 he published *Future War*, which not only further recommended the desirability of total mobilization of the economy and society for war, but also explored operational fighting methods. Clearly influenced by German theorists, Tukhachevsky advocated deeply penetrating attacks on the enemy with paralyzing, all-arms, offensive action, involving thousands of armoured vehicles and aircraft in massive quantities. He argued that recent history showed that modern, industrialized states were too powerful to be overcome in a single battle, and looked to strategic victory through the accumulation of operational success.

Although Tukhachevsky enjoyed political support when he launched into his doctrinal review, his demand for huge resources soon earned him enemies. Neither Stalin nor Frunze's replacement, the thoroughly underwhelming Kliment Voroshilov, were impressed and, having been removed as Chief of the General Staff, Tukhachevsky was sidelined. His replacement, Boris Shaposhnikov, was a safe pair of hands, but Tukhachevsky continued to lobby for investment in the colossal resources that he believed the Soviet Union required, and in 1930 he forwarded a memo to the Kremlin, pressing the case for '40,000 aircraft and 50,000 tanks'. He expanded upon his views in *New Questions of War*, published in 1932, and four years later wrote:

> The nature of modern weapons and battle is that it is an impossible matter to destroy the enemy's manpower in one blow in a single day. Battle in modern operations stretches out into a series of battles not only along the front but in depth.

By the time he wrote these words, Tukhachevsky's star was once again in the ascendancy. The foolishness of keeping his undoubted talents under wraps had been recognized and he had been made one of the first five Marshals of the Soviet Union. Moreover, aspects of his concept of 'Deep Operations' were refined and incorporated into PU-36, the last completed Soviet Army Field Regulations to be published before the outbreak of the Second World War. Tukhachevsky, however, would not live to witness that event.

Executions, imprisonment and 'disappearances' had become a fact of life in the Soviet Union by the 1930s, and Stalin did not hesitate to purge the Party and the armed forces – those closer to the heart of power – in his quest to protect the regime and his place in it. Indeed, Rodric Braithwaite has written: 'The fears of the Bolshevik leadership were more than a mere obsessive fantasy. But there was paranoia as well. In Stalin it reached the proportion of a monomania.' This political terror began in 1933 with the expulsion of 790,000 Party members on fabricated charges of corruption, careerism and plots to assassinate Stalin. Show trials were held during the middle of the decade leading, inevitably, to imprisonment and executions. Of the 1,966 delegates to the XVIIth Party Congress in 1934, for example, some 1,108 were executed. In the spring of 1937, Stalin said:

> The wrecking and diversionary-spying work of agents of foreign states has touched to one degree or another all or almost all of our organizations, administrative and party as well as economic . . . agents of foreign states, including Trotskyists, have penetrated not only into the lower organization, but even into certain responsible posts . . . Is it not clear that as long as capitalist encirclement exists we will have wreckers, spies, diversionists and murderers sent to the interior by agents of foreign states?

The political purge left the armed forces as the only major area of state to avoid the terror – but only until June 1937. Just at the moment when a new, large, modern, professional force was emerging, freer from political interference, the military leadership was swept away in a purge. It began with the execution of senior officers – including Tukhachevsky – and rolled on through the officer corps. Of the five marshals created in 1935, only two emerged from the cull with their lives, 15 out of 16 army commanders were killed, 50 out of 57 corps commanders, 154 out of 186 divisional commanders and 401 out of 456 colonels. One Russian source suggests that the total number of officers purged between 1936 and 1938 was 41,218, although most were dismissed rather than arrested or executed.

In their place, Stalin oversaw the advancement of young, talented and reliable soldiers, such as Georgi Zhukov and Konstantin Rokossovsky, who had made their names during the civil war. These men found that the glass ceiling previously thwarting their ambitions had been removed – but they were not allowed to forget their powerful political patrons. Stalin underscored this control by reasserting the role of political commissars at divisional level and below, along with their equivalent in army and front formations. These officers were appointed by the government to ensure political correctness and loyalty to the regime. They held a position equal to that of the commander but with the authority to countermand his orders. The commissars had had their wings clipped in the Frunze reforms and suffered heavily in the purges, but now their power returned. Their influence was exaggerated by the impact of the purges, which left the armed forces with inexperienced and compliant officers who were unwilling to show initiative and challenge the system.

Just at a time when threats to the Soviet Union were mounting, Stalin not only cut the heart out of the army, he also gave it brain damage. Fewer than 10 per cent of surviving officers had higher military education, and most had secondary education and nothing more. The military's cohesion was shattered, its modernization set back, its integration of new weaponry and technology hampered. Yet the impact of the purges must be seen in context, for the military was far from the finished article when the purges began and by 1941 around 80 per cent of the purged officers had been reinstated. Moreover, the armed forces continued to grow and between January 1939 and May 1941, 161 new divisions were activated. Thus, although it is true that 75 per cent of all officers had been in position for less than a year by 1941, that was because of the rapid increase in the creation of military units, not because of the purges. Indeed, it was the time it would take for the massive Red Army to mobilize that forced commanders in 1940 to explore an initial defensive phase in response to an invasion, not the recent decline in its fighting ability. The Soviet Union remained, resolutely, offensive in outlook but its military needed time to prepare itself.

The situation was similar in the field of foreign affairs. While Stalin's instinct was to act pre-emptively against the German threat to the Soviet Union, the nation needed more time to prepare. The understanding reached between Germany and the Soviet Union was mutually convenient but did not stop either pursuing relationships with other states. Feeling susceptible in the wake of the civil war, and still labelled an outsider in the wake of the revolution, the Soviet Union had a great deal to gain by making friends in Europe. By the end of the 1920s the Commissar for Foreign Affairs, Maxim Litvinov, had established friendly relations with most Western powers and acceptance by the international community.

The Soviet Union needed all the friends it could get in 1931 when a rabidly anti-Communist Japan with imperial ambitions moved up to its border, and occupied Manchuria. However, the threat posed by Hitler's Germany caused Stalin most concern and by 1935 he had overseen the signing of non-aggression pacts with Finland, Estonia, Latvia and Poland, joined the League of Nations and concluded a treaty of mutual assistance with France. Germany responded by signing a pact with Italy and Japan in 1936, which condemned international Communism as a movement that sought to 'disintegrate and subdue existing States . . . [and] not only endangers their internal peace and social well-being, but is also a menace to the peace of the world . . .'

This Anti-Comintern Pact was built on Hitler's obvious hatred of the Soviet Union, as stated in *Mein Kampf* and vocalized in his increasingly bellicose speeches against Moscow, to make armed confrontation increasingly likely. Both nations were militarized and both postured to make clear their willingness to use violence in support of a political cause – Stalin countered Hitler's 1937 jibe that 'the conquest of Russia will prove a straight-forward task for our forces' with 'German aggression is typical of weak states' – but Germany had the political, industrial and military momentum to make war first. Despite Stalin's disinclination to show goodwill towards Hitler, the resultant diminution in the Soviet Union's military prowess during the purges in 1937 necessitated that he swallow his pride. His overtures, however, were briskly rebuffed by Hitler, which forced Stalin to explore other options. Yet even with the threats to European security mounting, the Soviet Union's political ideology was not one that sent the West rushing to Stalin's side. Extremely limited military cooperation was agreed, but there was no integrated plan for defence against Nazi expansion.

The fragility of the relationship was thrown into stark relief during the summer of 1938. Although both the Soviet Union and France had treaty agreements with Czechoslovakia, pledging them to the country's defence, Stalin stood alone in his advocacy of concerted military action. Furthermore, no Soviet delegation was invited to the Munich conference at which the Sudetenland was ceded to Germany. The Soviet Ambassador to London, Ivan Maisky, astutely observed that international relations were entering an 'era of brute force, savagery and the policy of the mailed fist'. There was no 'collective security' in Europe and Hitler could exploit this.

Could it have been that the West used Nazism to keep Communism in check? Stalin thought so for when Hitler invaded Czechoslovakia, he condemned the appeasers as 'conniving in aggression, giving free rein to war ... The policy of non-intervention reveals an eagerness, a desire, not to hinder the aggressors in their nefarious work.' Yet although exasperated by the West, the Soviet Union was not in a position to give up on some sort of security agreement with it. Thus, on 17 April 1939, the Soviet Union offered Britain and France an alliance that would guarantee the integrity of every state from the Baltic to the Mediterranean and bring all three powers into war if any of the states were attacked by Germany. Despite Stalin's insistence that there was pressing need for an agreement, an Anglo-French delegation did not arrive in Russia to discuss a military pact until 10 August, and then Moscow was disgusted to find out that its delegates did not have the authority to sign official documents. A frustrated Voroshilov, unclear about whether the West would commit to plans to thwart Germany and apply military force, wrote 'without clear and unambiguous answers to these questions, further negotiations are pointless'. But Britain and France did not want to ally themselves with the Soviets and risk provoking Hitler. They had deep-seated fears that Stalin could not be trusted and would stand by as Germany made a push for Paris, using the time to mobilize. There is little doubt that Stalin did see the West as drawing at least some of the Wehrmacht's sting, but only as part of a two-fronted war. With no understanding having been reached, the Soviet Union was facing a precarious isolation.

Considering Berlin's rejection of his blandishments just months earlier, Stalin received Germany's reopening of the channels of communication in the spring of 1939 with some surprise. Negotiations began with the highly receptive Vyacheslav Molotov, the new Soviet Foreign Minister. On 19 August an economic agreement was signed in Moscow, which provided for the Soviets to send grain and raw materials to Germany in exchange for industrial machinery and finished products. Then, four days later, a non-aggression pact was sealed, which provided Stalin with the time he needed to make his defensive preparations while, critically, providing the potential to create a buffer against Germany if a large enough portion of Poland could be consolidated after the agreed joint invasion. This remarkable turn of events shocked the world and led Winston Churchill to write later: 'The sinister news broke upon the world like an explosion.' Once the necessary documents had been signed the deal was celebrated with a cocktail party. Having toasted the absent German Chancellor, Stalin turned to Ribbentrop and said, 'The Soviet Union is very serious about the new pact. I give you my word of honour that the Soviet Union will not cheat on its partner.' Hitler, meanwhile, sipped a glass of champagne and, turning to his private secretary, Martin Bormann, said, 'Europe is mine!' The Führer was convinced that the strategic momentum was with him, but Stalin believed that Hitler had slipped up. 'I know what Hitler's up to,' he smirked to Molotov. 'He thinks he has outsmarted me, but actually it is I who have outsmarted him.' The true victor of this positional shadow boxing was a matter of conjecture, but what both leaders recognized at the end of August 1939 was that war between Germany and the Soviet Union had been postponed, not cancelled.

The non-aggression pact was signed just days before Germany began its eastern expansion. It marked the beginning of a period during which Stalin increasingly tried to convince himself that Berlin's actions were reasonable despite evidence to the contrary. Thus, rather than viewing Hitler's invasion of Poland as a worrying development, he joined in, explaining to a colleague on 7 September that it was to the Soviet Union's advantage:

A war is on between two groups of capitalist countries . . . for the redivision of the world, for the domination of the world! We see nothing wrong in their having a good hard fight and weakening each other . . . Hitler, without understanding it or desiring it, is shaking and undermining the capitalist system . . . We can manoeuvre, pit one side against the other to set them fighting with each other as fiercely as possible . . . The annihilation [of Poland] would mean one fewer bourgeois fascist state to contend with! What would be the harm if as a result of the rout of Poland we were to extend the socialist system onto new territories and populations?

Giving the order for the Soviet troops to begin their part in the offensive, however, must have been difficult for Moscow. How would the purged army perform? Would the Wehrmacht and Red Army make a common border in Poland with equanimity? Stalin did not authorize his one-million-man advance until 17 September, late enough to ensure that the Poles were well beaten, but early enough to make a grab for the spoils. It was a sensible decision. The Red Army faced minimal resistance and, by 24 September, had reached the agreed demarcation line and brought their area under control for the loss of just 3,500 casualties. The successful operation reassured Stalin that his armed forces remained a useful political tool. Indeed, overlooking the many and various weaknesses of the enemy they were fighting, the relative ease with which the Red Army had completed its business may even have given Stalin an overly optimistic perception of what they were capable of achieving. Thus while Moscow reported a 'convincing performance . . . which revealed that the capabilities of the army were assured', Polish reports revealed 'poorly motivated' troops and officers with a 'low standard of intelligence and slovenly appearance'. A school report for the Soviet forces might have read: 'Steady, but with plenty of room for improvement', but Stalin was not content to allow them the time and space in which to absorb the lessons of the campaign. He threw them into another far more exacting test.

Keen to ensure that Finland could not be used as a launch pad for a German attack against him, Stalin requested that Helsinki allow him to station Soviet troops on Finnish soil. That highly provocative act reflected the confidence he had drawn from the Polish campaign, and from recent success against the Japanese in a border dispute battle at Khalkin Gol. The Finns' refusal led to an invasion, and although Voroshilov had assured Stalin it would be successful, within a week of being launched on 30 November, it quickly faltered. Attacking on a broad 1000 mile front with some 450,000 men, 2000 tanks and 1000 aircraft, the Soviets' offensive ability to conduct mobile operations was soon shown to be wanting. Running into well-established Finnish defences in the south, for example, they were stalled. The Soviets were poorly prepared for fighting against static defences in cold weather. Their equipment and weaponry were outdated, their fighting methods looked inappropriate and their political officers proved to be a hindrance. Soviet infantryman Georgy Uritski recalls:

It was a winter that I have tried to erase from my memory. A terrible experience. Many of us had received little training and had only the vaguest idea of what was expected of us. My company was wiped out. Attacking a Finnish position without artillery support, we were cut to tiny pieces. Again and again we attacked until we ran out of men . . . My life was spared, but I lost my right hand . . . The snow was steeped in the blood of the fallen. It was a travesty, a waste of so many young lives.

Stalin had overestimated the abilities of his forces and paid the price during that winter, when there was little forward movement. However, a new and successful offensive was launched by General Semyen Timoshenko on 11 February 1940 after a period of reorganization and a dramatic improvement in firepower. The Finns sued for peace on 6 March, but its acceptance by Stalin reveals what a struggle the campaign had been for the Soviet Union. The Finns suffered around 90,000 casualties, but it cost the Red Army over half a million men and achieved a small fraction of Moscow's territorial aims. In the first major post-purge campaign, the Soviet Union had revealed to the world a feeble offensive capability, and had been obliged to use brute force finally to overcome the Finnish defences. As Uritski noted:

Looking back – from a soldier's perspective – we were not prepared for what was to come. Events were moving too fast for us, we were pushed too far, too fast. In military affairs such mistakes are paid for in a very sad way.

The experience in Finland led to a series of military reforms in an attempt to mitigate some of the most obvious failings. Initiated by Timoshenko, the man of the moment, who was made a Marshal of the Soviet Union and replaced Voroshilov as People's Commissar for Defence, the improvements encompassed practical winter clothing and fighting equipment, more effective all-arms cooperation and enhanced military education. These were essential developments if the colossal Soviet military machine was to rediscover its fighting prowess, but in such a recently retarded organization it would take a couple of years before they bore fruit. Thus, while pursuing the skills and assets required for a more sophisticated way of fighting, the Soviets would endeavour to make the best of what they had and keep things simple. As Voroshilov explained in a memorandum: 'We must ensure that the tenacity and flexibility of the Soviet soldier is exploited and our frontier defences are strengthened. Together they form a formidable barrier to any aggressor.' This approach seems commonsensical, but it was founded on flawed logic. Using strong defences close to the new German–Soviet border to defeat enemy skirmishers may have given time for the mass of the peasant-worker army to mobilize before unleashing a massive counterattack, but what if there were no skirmishers? Blitzkrieg had no place for them, and recent events suggested that a Wehrmacht attack against the Soviet Union would open with a full-blooded armoured assault supported by air power.

The building of defences had started in the 1920s with the Stalin Line, which was developed close to the western border. In 1936 efforts were begun to update and strengthen the system by incorporating natural features, such as rivers, marshes and hills, as well as by the construction of camouflaged concrete emplacements, forts, field works, tank traps and killing zones. These improvements were not completed until the summer of 1940, by which time the Stalin Line was no longer on the Soviet Union's western border. The new Polish territory in the west was a useful defensive cushion but come that summer was not Stalin's only land-grab. Exploiting the ongoing redefinition of national boundaries, Stalin annexed Latvia, Lithuania and Estonia in the north along with Bessarabia and Northern Bukovina (part of Romania) in the south. In so doing, he provided the Soviet Union with extra width and depth but also denuded his frontier of defences as the

Stalin Line was rendered impotent. Indeed, one might argue that Hitler had cleverly drawn the Red Army out of its defences by enticing its leader forward with the prospects of Soviet aggrandisement. If so, then Moscow fell head-first into a brilliant trap for, in June 1940, Stalin demanded the fortification of these newly occupied areas despite the distinct possibility of a German strike before the defences' completion. The construction of the 800 mile long Molotov Line used resources from the Stalin Line, which became a fallback position, but there was no defence in depth to catch and slow the German thrust. Moreover, the Soviet strategy of static positional warfare followed by counterattack was not dissimilar to that utilized in northwestern Europe and thoroughly defeated by the Wehrmacht even as work on the Molotov Line began.

But in the early summer of 1940 the Soviets had decided on a course of action and the preparation of defences required every week that Stalin could buy them. In such circumstances, Moscow was extremely careful not to antagonize Hitler and went out of its way to ensure that their August 1939 trade agreement was adhered to. Between January 1940 and June 1941, Stalin supplied Hitler with 2 million tons of petroleum products, 648,000 tons of wood, 26,000 tons of chromium, 140,000 tons of manganese ore, 14,000 tons of copper, 100,000 tons of cotton, 1.5 million tons of timber, almost 1.5 million tons of grain and much more besides. The value of these resources to Germany's war-making capability is difficult to overexaggerate. The High Command's war economy staff went so far as to say that further campaigning was 'only possible with continued access to oil and mineral deposits'. Stalin's assets would allow Germany to fight beyond the summer of 1941 while any further campaigning would have to be sustained by seizing resource-rich territory. Hitler's timetable for attacking the Soviet Union was, therefore, largely dictated by the rate at which he could accumulate Soviet resources with which to carry out the invasion.

Stalin could not have been anything other than aware that he was strengthening the German threat, but he was caught in another trap and chose to sacrifice the lesser for the greater. Time was the most precious commodity to the Soviet Union and so deliveries were made in full and on time despite the heavy burden this placed on the Soviet system. Moreover, it was done despite increasing German disinclination to fulfil its part of the deal and share its advanced military technologies. Sensing Stalin's predicament, Hitler did not feel the need to advantage his enemy, particularly as he had his own concerns about a Soviet pre-emptive strike.

Time was running out and with France defeated and the British sidelined, Stalin recognized that the Soviet Union would have to face the ideological and military wrath of Germany alone.

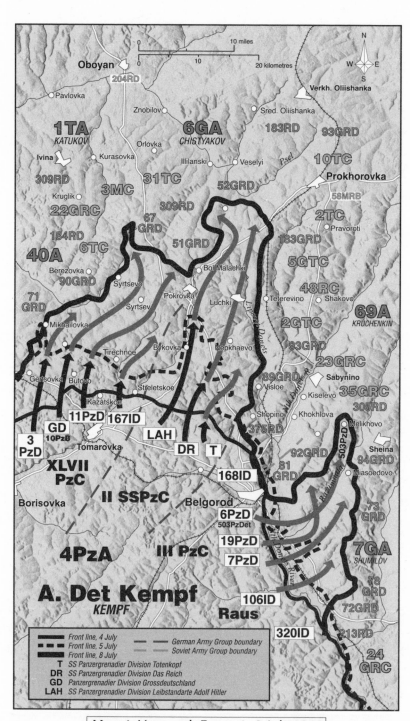

Map 4: Voronezh Front, 4–8 July 1943

Oboyan
204RD
Verkh. Oliishanka
Pavlovka
Znobilov
Sred. Oliishanka
1TA
KATUKOV
6GA
CHISTYAKOV
183RD
93GRD
Orlovka
Illilanski
Veselyi
Psel
10TC
Ivina
Kurasovka
Prokhorovka
309RD
3MC
31TC
52GRD
58MRB
Kruglik
2TC
Pravoroti
22GRC
67 GRD
309RD
58MRB
183GRD
184RD
6TC
51GRD
5GTC
40A
Berezovka
Boll Malachki
48RC
90GRD
Syrtsevo
Teterevino
Shakovo
71 GRD
Pokrovka
Luchki
69A
KRUCHENKIN
Syrtsev
2GTC
Mikhailovka
Bykovka
Nepkhaevo
93GRD
Tirechnoe
23GRC
Gertsovka
Butovo
Streletskoe
89GRD
Sabynino
35GRC
Kazatskoe
Visloe
Kiselevo
305RD
11PzD **167ID**
Shopino
Khokhlova
Melikhovo
GD
10PzB
LAH
375RD
503PzD
3 PzD
Tomarovka
DR **T**
92GRD
Sheina
94GRD
XLVII PzC
168ID
81 GRD
Miasoedovo
Borisovka
II SSPzC
Belgorod
6PzD
503PzDet
73 GRD
4PzA
III PzC
19PzD
7PzD
7GA
SHUMILOV
A. Det Kempf
KEMPF
106ID
78 GRD
72GRD
Raus
320ID
213RD
24 GRC

Front line, 4 July — German Army Group boundary
Front line, 5 July — Soviet Army Group boundary
Front line, 8 July
T SS Panzergrenadier Division Totenkopf
DR SS Panzergrenadier Division Das Reich
GD Panzergrenadier Division Grossdeutschland
LAH SS Panzergrenadier Division Leibstandarte Adolf Hitler

0   10 miles
0   10   20 kilometres

CHAPTER 3

Invasion

(Barbarossa: December 1940–September 1941)

The news that the Germans were attacking along the western frontier and bombing cities did not at all surprise General Georgi Zhukov when he was told in Moscow at 0330 hours on 22 June. Even so, as Chief of the General Staff, he did not relish fulfilling the order of Marshal Semyon Timoshenko, the Commissar for Defence, to inform Stalin. After several failed attempts to raise somebody on the telephone at the General Secretary's dacha, a drowsy duty officer picked up and said that Stalin was asleep. 'Wake him up immediately,' Zhukov insisted. 'The Germans are bombing our cities.' A couple of minutes passed before Stalin took the receiver and was told the news. His silence was that of a man struggling to interpret the reality of an event that he had persuaded himself would not happen. 'Do you understand me?' Zhukov inquired, but the line remained quiet. Several seconds passed before Stalin seemed to regain his poise. 'Go to the Kremlin with Timoshenko,' he ordered. 'Tell Poskrebyshev [his secretary] to summon all Politburo members.' Stalin remained unconvinced that an invasion had begun even as he was sped through the deserted Moscow streets to his office. How could he have been hoodwinked? Yet shortly after his arrival, Foreign Minister Vyacheslav Molotov, having met with an ashen-faced German Ambassador, told Stalin, 'The German government *has* declared war on us.' Stalin sank down into his chair and after a long and thoughtful pause proclaimed, 'The enemy will be beaten all along the line.'

The shattering news was broadcast to the population at noon when the voice of a nervous Molotov trilled:

> Citizens and Citizenesses of the Soviet Union! Today, at four o'clock in the morning, without addressing any grievances to the Soviet Union, without declaration of war, German forces fell on our country, attacked our frontiers in many places and bombed our cities . . . an act of treachery unprecedented in the history of civilized nations . . . The Red Army and the whole nation will wage a victorious Patriotic War for our beloved country, for honour, for liberty . . . Our cause is just. The enemy will be beaten. Victory will be ours.

In failing to announce the full scale of the disaster and by calling upon the population's devotion to their nation rather than the Party, Molotov struck a patriotic chord while allowing a stunned people to absorb the information. As they did so, the decision makers reacted to the German invasion by mobilizing the armed forces and putting their faith in the Molotov Line and local counterattacks. Stalin had not been surprised by Hitler's invasion; he had been astounded.

Hitler's determination to destroy the Soviet Union was multi-faceted and all consuming. His ideological opposition to the Communist state verged on the maniacal: 'One day,' Hitler affirmed, 'the Russians, the countless millions of Slavs, are going to come. Perhaps not even in ten years, perhaps only after a hundred years. But they will come.' A

bove left: Making his only
isit to Paris, Hitler stands
efore the Eiffel Tower on
8 June 1940. One year later,
is troops would be beginning
heir invasion of the Soviet
nion. IWM HU 3266

Above right: Plagued by hunger and anger at Germany's
continued participation in the First World War, tens of thousands
of workers took to the streets during the spring of 1918. Here, a
Berlin delicatessen has been plundered by a mob. IWM Q 110881

Below right: The uncompromising
General Heinz Guderian (standing), a
pioneer of armoured warfare, directs
his Panzer group from a command
vehicle in France during the 1940
campaign. IWM MH 29100

elow left: Hitler, flanked by the brown-shirted SA, is
uded at a Nuremberg rally in 1934. One participant
alled the passion roused by the Führer at the event
varely containable'. IWM MH 11040

Above left: At the height of the Great Depression, Hitler reviews members of the SA from his car in the Bavarian city of Nuremberg. IWM NYP 68041

Above right: Vladimir Lenin addressing a large crowd in 1917. He was a first rate public speaker and galvanised his audience by demanding that they help 'turn the imperialist war into civil war' and, in so doing, bring down the old order. FPG/GETTY

Left: Joseph Stalin in typical pose for an official photograph. He made up for his lack of physical stature by force of personality. His simple dress drew those in his company to his eyes which, one official later noted, were 'dark and deadly'. IWM HU 10180

Bottom left: Marshal Mikhail Tukhachevsky in 1935, two years before his violent death. He had been awarded six bravery decorations before being taken prisoner by the Germans in February 1915. He eventually escaped and returned to Russia at the height of the revolution.

POPPERFOTO/GETTY

Right: A Soviet inter-war exercise in the Ukraine used to develop all-arms and inter-service cooperation. War Minister Mikhail Frunze wished to see a 'unitary military doctrine' for offensive operations that would create world revolution.

THE TANK MUSEUM, BOVINGTON

Below: With red flags attached to the bayonets of their rifles, Russian soldiers drive towards Petrograd during March 1917.

IWM Q 69408

Left: Jewish women are murdered in an open pit by members of an SS Einsatzgruppen (Special Operations Unit) during a 'cleansing operation' on 14 September 1941. IWM HU 86369

Above: Soviet Katyusha (multiple rocket launchers) in central Russia during August 1941. Cheap, mobile and feared by the Germans for their ability to deliver concentrated devastation at speed, they were, however, inaccurate and slow to reload. THE TANK MUSEUM, BOVINGTON

Right: An official portrait of Marshal Georgi Zhukov. Born into a peasant family and conscripted into the Russian army in 1915, he performed well on the Eastern Front with the cavalry until he was badly wounded. He remained in the army after the revolution and rose to the rank of Marshal in the wake of the Battle of Stalingrad. IWM RUS 1191

above: In scenes reminiscent of Napoleon's invasion of Russia, this image raises the armoured ~~fa~~cade of the Wehrmacht to reveal old technology. During the *rasputitsa* (time without roads) the ~~ra~~in and mud led to atrocious fighting conditions. BUNDESARCHIV, BILD 101I-289-1091-26, FOTOGRAF: DINSTÜHLER

below: One of the few Soviet T-34s available during 1941 rolls through a destroyed German ~~po~~sition. The T-34's speed and agility made it an outstanding weapon with a simple design that ~~w~~as relatively easy to produce and repair. The tank gradually asserted itself in ever-increasing ~~nu~~mbers on the battlefield from 1943 onwards. THE TANK MUSEUM, BOVINGTON

Left: With the Germans bearing down on Moscow and Leningrad, the Soviet propaganda machine churned out vast numbers of posters which became commonplace on the streets of towns and cities throughout the western Soviet Union. This example says: 'Soldier of the Red Army, save us!' IWM PST 6136

ВОИН КРАСНОЙ АРМИИ, СПАСИ!

Below: Awaiting the inevitable German onslaught: marines of the Soviet Northern Fleet crouch in hastily dug forward trenches in early 1942. In the foreground lies a PPD-40 submachine gun which had come into service in 1935. It was complicated to make and at this time was being replaced by the simpler and more effective PPSh-41. IWM RUS 35

Above: Carnage in southern Russia during operations to extract German formations from the Caucasus.

Right: Stalingrad, November 1943. General Chuikov said, "approaching this place, soldiers used to say: "We are entering hell." And after spending one or two days here, they say: "No, this isn't hell, this is ten times worse than hell."""

Above: Ground-based, static frame launchers fire 310mm rockets into German positions during the Battle of Stalingrad. These weapons were commonly used to prepare the battlefield before an attack. THE TANK MUSEUM, BOVINGTON

Below: A film still from footage shot by a Soviet cameraman in early 1943 showing German prisoners of war being escorted away from Stalingrad. IWM MH 9701

pre-emptive strike to destroy Bolshevism would remove the threat while also providing the land and other resources that the Nazis so coveted. These 'immeasurable riches' were not only essential for the Reich to expand but also, by the end of 1940, to maintain previous gains and remove a military threat. Hitler fervently believed that the invasion of the Soviet Union was not a whim, but a necessity, and later said: 'For us there remained no other choice but to strike the Russia factor out of the European equation.' Irresistibility and need came together to make an invasion the critical aim of the Nazi regime and the focus of German strategy. In 1939 Hitler announced to a League of Nations official:

Everything that I undertake is directed against Russia. If those in the West are too stupid, and too blind to understand this, then I shall be forced to come to an understanding with the Russians to beat the West, and then, after its defeat, turn with all my concerted force against the Soviet Union.

To the blinkered Führer, the defeat of the Soviet Union was a panacea that would make Germany unassailable in Europe.

In late July 1940, while Germany was still basking in its success in Western Europe, Hitler announced to colleagues that he wanted to launch an invasion of the Soviet Union in the spring of the following year 'to smash the state heavily in one blow'. The High Command had more time to prepare for the invasion than for any other offensive of the war. Preliminary planning began immediately and led to Hitler publishing Directive No. 21 on 18 December. Announcing that preparations were to be completed by 15 May 1941, the Directive stated that '[t]he mass of the Russian Army is to be destroyed in daring operations by driving forward deep armoured wedges, and the retreat of units capable of combat into the vastness of Russian territory is to be prevented.' The final objective was to be 'the general line

Volga–Archangel' and was to be achieved within five months. Hitler believed Moscow itself to be 'of no great importance' in the defeat of the Soviet Union; he sought a victory to the west of the capital, having denuded Stalin of both defenders and resources. The Red Army was to be encircled and liquidated within 250 miles of the start line and in around eight weeks. Speed was the essential ingredient in the plan and the military placed their faith in blitzkrieg to catch Stalin cold and ensure that Germany was not dragged into a protracted struggle for which she was ill-prepared.

The offensive was codenamed Barbarossa after Frederick I Barbarossa (Red Beard), the twelfth-century German emperor who led a crusade against Saladin's Muslim armies. In 1941, Hitler's crusade against Bolshevism, Jews and other 'radical elements' would show no mercy as his soldiers occupied captured territory and exploited it, having subjugated the useful 'inferior population' and exterminated the rest. Yet the wide-ranging nature of German ambitions provided ample potential for confusion, inefficiency and contradiction in their pursuit. There was no one single, achievable aim identified by Hitler, no tri-service planning, and plenty of opportunities for Clausewitzian 'friction' to unhinge the best efforts of the Wehrmacht to deliver the aims in the timeframe. Barbarossa was a smorgasbord of an operation, a mixture of ideological, military, economic and territorial aims upon which Hitler could feast but which his planners would struggle to pull together and his field forces would struggle to carry out. Senior commanders, such as Colonel-General Franz Halder, Chief of the Army Staff, were aghast at the scope of the operation and feared that Hitler had eschewed practical considerations for 'a mystical conviction of his own infallibility'.

Barbarossa was to open with 3.8 million German forces, supported by 3,350 tanks and 7,200 artillery pieces, attacking in three army groups to a depth of between 500 and 900 miles across a 1000 mile front. Army Group North, commanded by General Ritter von Leeb, was to push through East Prussia and the Baltic states to Leningrad; General Fedor von Bock's Army Group Centre was to encircle Minsk, Smolensk and then Moscow; Field Marshal Gerd von Rundstedt's Army Group South, separated from Bock by the Pripyat Marshes, was to cross the plains of southern Russia and the Ukraine to Kiev and then to Rostov. Bock's formation was to provide the main effort along the best roads, and while plunging towards their own 'vital objectives', the army groups on either side were to provide flank protection and ensure that the enemy, naturally drawn to the defence of the capital, was defeated before the advance reached Moscow. Army Group Centre would, therefore, benefit from two panzer armies while Leeb and Rundstedt received one each. Bock was also supported by 1,500 of the 2,770 available aircraft from the Luftwaffe, which was trained and configured specifically for ground-support operations. Blitzkrieg was to be given the opportunity to deliver Hitler another remarkable victory.

German strategy and operational methods were based on the rapid defeat of the Soviets, specifically to avoid the protracted campaign that Hitler was not prepared to fight. The Soviet Union had a population of 190 million compared with Germany's 80 million in 1941, so there was no desire to become involved in an attritional conflict, although planners struggled to see how the Soviets could be defeated in a matter of a few weeks. They feared that the difficult terrain, vast distances and inhospitable Soviet autumn and winter weather would have a far larger part to play in the outcome of the campaign than Hitler wanted to acknowledge. The logisticians fretted about the feeble Soviet communications infrastructure, the roads of compacted earth, the incompatible railway lines that rendered German locomotives and rolling stock useless, and the general lack of essential resources ranging from spare engine parts to attacking formations. There were too few panzer divisions for such an ambitious offensive, for example, and so in typical 'make do and mend' style Hitler merely halved the number of tanks and supporting assets in each existing formation in order to double their number. Yet even this drastic move did nothing to attend to the lack of motorization in the vast majority of the army – less than 17 per cent of the German ground forces were motorized – which would cause it to lag behind the spearheads. Hitler's army was one that, despite its close relationship with fast-moving armoured warfare, relied extremely heavily on boot leather and horse-drawn transport to advance east. Some 625,000 hungry and thirsty horses were consequently prepared for Barbarossa and just 600,000 vehicles, consisting of a toe-curling 2000 variants. These vehicles were also hungry and thirsty, but the lack of spare parts, petrol, oil and lubricants did not bode well for the Wehrmacht's ability to keep them moving. Barbarossa was a logistical nightmare. Indeed, in December 1940 Major-General Frederich Paulus, the head quartermaster, conducted a wargame which demonstrated that the operation's logistic arrangements would collapse before they reached the upper Dnieper. Hitler was unmoved. The army was admirably imbued with flexibility and opportunism, and the necessarily 'Gradgrindist' planners were under such pressure that they had to fudge critical issues and ignore unhelpful information.

The generals were justifiably concerned at Hitler's lack of consultation about the application of force, his oversimplification of a whole series of massively complicated issues. It seemed that the Führer's mind was already made up and no experts or documents were likely to change it. Fritz Wiedemann, a member of Hitler's personal staff, recalls: 'Hitler refused to let himself be informed . . . How can one tell someone the truth who immediately gets angry when the facts do not suit him?' However, recalling their previous deep-seated concerns about earlier successful campaigns, the generals offered very little resistance to plans that they instinctively believed to be flawed. Thus, when Hitler said that with the launch of Barbarossa 'Europe will hold its breath', the same was true of many of his senior officers. Colonel-General Heinz Guderian, commander of Bock's Second Panzer Army, received a map brief from his staff. 'I could scarcely believe my eyes,' he later wrote, '[and] made no attempt to conceal my disappointment and disgust.' Knowing history, Guderian was well aware that others had tried to overwhelm Russia and failed:

Renewed study of the campaigns of Charles XII of Sweden and of Napoleon I clearly revealed all the difficulties of the theatre to which we threatened to be committed; it also became increasingly plain to see how inadequate were our preparations for so enormous an undertaking. Our successes to date, however, and in particular the surprising speed of our victory in the West, had so befuddled the minds of our supreme commanders that they had eliminated the word 'impossible' from their vocabulary.

Far from believing that it was 'impossible' to defeat the Soviet Union rapidly, Hitler was confident of victory. His successful, large, well-educated, carefully trained and competently led military machine would, he was sure, prove too strong for its 'subhuman' adversaries. The Führer further fortified himself with the belief that the Soviet Union was economically, industrially and physically backward, a retard nation with a purged army equipped with obsolete weaponry. 'You only have to kick in the door,' Hitler declared, 'and the whole rotten house will come crashing down.'

The Soviet force that would have the task of stopping the German invasion amounted to nearly 5 million troops in 20 armies consisting of 303 divisions with 19,800 artillery pieces and 11,000 tanks. The Red Air Force had 9,100 aircraft. Although an awesome military machine on paper, it was riddled with inadequacies brought about by the effects of Stalin's terror, rapid expansion and lack of investment. Thus, although senior staff officers advocated a pre-emptive strike on Germany – Deputy Chief of Operations General Aleksandr Vasilevsky wrote in May 1941: 'I consider it necessary not to give the initiative to the German command under any circumstances, to forestall the enemy in deployment and to attack the German army at the moment when it is still at the deployment stage' – Stalin recognized that the army was not ready for any such move. Zhukov, who was appointed Chief of the General Staff in January 1941, wrote in his memoirs:

> Two or three years would have given the Soviet people a brilliant army, perhaps the best in the world . . . [but] history allotted us too small a period of peace to get everything organized as it should have been. We began many things correctly and there were many things we had no time to finish. Our miscalculation regard[ing] the possible time of fascist Germany's attack told greatly.

New mechanized corps were formed but industry and infrastructure struggled to keep pace with their voracious appetite for resources and so they were short of men, trucks and tanks. Zhukov argued that 16,600 of the latest tanks were required within a total force of 32,000 tanks to equip fully the mechanized corps, but just 7000 tanks were delivered between January 1939 and June 1941, and of these just 1,861 were new types, including the KV-1 and T-34. The 125 new infantry divisions were also undermanned and underequipped, the artillery lacked anti-tank brigades, communications remained antiquated, the airforce lacked modern aircraft, airfields and trained pilots, and air defence was disorganized and poorly armed. In the spring of 1941 the Soviet military was a gawky teenager made ungainly by a rapid growth spurt and desperate for some independence. On the eve of war, some 2.5 million men in 15 armies, and 20 out of 28 mechanized corps, were defending the frontier and organized into five fronts (approximately the same as the German army groups): the smallest was the Northern Front, commanded by Lieutenant-General M.M. Popov, which faced the Finns and the Germans in Norway; Colonel-General F.I. Kuznetsov's Northwestern Front faced Army Group North in the

Baltic states; Army Group Centre was confronted by General D.G. Pavlov's Western Front; the Southwestern Front under Colonel-General M.P. Kirponos was opposite Army Group South, and the Southern Front, commanded by Major-General I. Tiulenev, was waiting opposite Romania.

This first strategic echelon was arranged in three shallow and incomplete defensive belts, which would also be expected to carry out local counterattacks against the advancing Germans. A further five armies were assembled on the critical obstacles of the Dnieper and Dvina rivers to form the second strategic echelon, which was to carry out the decisive, crushing counteroffensive and push into Germany. Whether the half-equipped, rigid and unwieldy mechanized corps were capable of sustained operations deep into the enemy rear was unlikely. However, the longer the Soviets offered resistance, the more they could draw on their expanding resources, which included some 14 million men with basic training ready to move into the line. Even so, informed observers gave the Soviets little hope of lasting long enough to bring these troops into action. The British Joint Intelligence Committee was convinced that Moscow would fall within six months, while its US equivalent expected a German victory within weeks.

As the Red Army dug in on the frontier during the spring of 1941, the Germans began their deployments towards them. Hitler's preparations for Barbarossa were complicated by fighting around the Mediterranean in support of the Italians during the spring. Drawn into North Africa, Yugoslavia and then Greece, the Germans rounded off their successful sweep with an invasion of Crete. The diversion meant that the launch of Barbarossa had to be delayed until 22 June. It also added extra wear to vehicles, equipment and men, and pushed the offensive closer to the worsening autumn weather. The delay convinced Stalin that it was too late in the year for Hitler to attack. He also thought that Hitler would not consider taking on the might of the Soviet Union until his dispersed military machine had been brought together and was stronger. 'We have a non-aggression pact with Germany,' Stalin explained to a colleague. 'Germany is up to her ears with the war in the West and I am certain that Hitler will not risk creating a second front by attacking the Soviet Union. Hitler is not such an idiot and understands that the Soviet Union is not Poland, not France, and not even England.'

Unwilling to face the awful truth that he had placed the Soviet Union in a supremely vulnerable position, Stalin rejected intelligence that strongly suggested an imminent German attack. A German Communist spy in Tokyo, Richard Sorge, confirmed his frequent warnings with an invasion date of 20 June. Meanwhile, Head of Soviet Military Intelligence Lieutenant-General Filip Golikov, fearful of providing reports that ran contrary to what Stalin wanted to hear (for several of his predecessors had been shot for their explicit warnings), reported at the end of March:

The majority of the intelligence reports which indicate the likelihood of war with the Soviet Union in spring 1941 emerge from Anglo-American sources, the immediate purpose of which is undoubtedly to seek the worsening of relations between the USSR and Germany.

Thus threats were deemed 'imagined' or 'exaggerated' and Golikov dismissed Sorge's intelligence in a sentence: 'We doubt the veracity of your information.' Consequently, in a fit of remarkable optimism, Stalin chose to believe that the obvious German military build-up – together with more than 300 high-altitude reconnaissance aircraft sorties over Soviet territory – was an attempt by Hitler to extract more economic and political concessions out of him. Soviet passivity in the face of provocation led Goebbels to note in his diary that May: 'Stalin and his people remain completely inactive. Like a rabbit confronted by a snake.'

Timoshenko and Zhukov made efforts to shake Stalin out of his stupor and mobilize, but to no effect. In mid-March they asked the General Secretary to authorize the call-up of reserve personnel 'so as to update their military training in infantry divisions without delay', but were told that 'calling up reservists on such a scale might give the Germans an excuse to provoke war'. Undeterred, the two men continued to badger Stalin, whose patience reveals his considerable respect for the two soldiers. Timoshenko's stock remained relatively high after his success in Finland and Stalin rated Zhukov as a battle-field commander, particularly after his success at Khalkin Gol. Dynamic and unconventional, ruthless and focused, former NCO Zhukov had supreme confidence in his own ability and excelled when put under pressure. By the end of the month, the tenacity shown by Timoshenko and Zhukov was partially rewarded when Stalin made a concession and gave permission for them to call up some 500,000 men for border military districts to augment infantry divisions, and 300,000 more were called up in early April – but their deployments would not be completed until 10 July. The military hierarchy continued to make discrete preparations for war, but on 14 June Timoshenko and Zhukov were again refused authorization for full mobilization. This time Stalin lost his cool; the pressure was beginning to tell, and after his Commissar for Defence had left the room he ranted, 'It's all Timoshenko's work. He's preparing for war. He ought to have been shot . . .'

By Saturday, 21 June, the longest day of the year, Soviet troops were enjoying the warm weather and looking forward to their day off. The Western Front headquarters were relaxed and General Pavlov enjoyed an evening at a Minsk theatre. Even when his head of intelligence sidled up to inform him of stories about an imminent German attack, Pavlov remained unperturbed, replied, 'It can't be true,' and stayed in his seat. He received a full briefing later, in which it was explained that 'considerable activity along the front line' and intelligence from deserters pointed to a German attack 'within hours'. The information came from Wehrmacht soldiers with Communist sympathies, including Sapper Alfred Liskow, who crossed the lines and told of a dawn crossing of the River Bug with 'rafts, boats and pontoons'. Border guards reported hearing tank engines being started, vehicles moving and a flurry of activity by enemy troops, but Stalin remained unmoved and explained it as a deliberate German ploy to provoke the Soviet Union. Timoshenko, Zhukov and Lieutenant-General Nikolai Vatutin, the Deputy Head of the Planning Division, did not agree and immediately went to see the General Secretary. Finding him pale and ill at ease, the triumvirate implored him to put the armed forces on full alert. While still hanging on to the last worn strand of hope that Hitler was merely sabre rattling, he agreed. The resultant directive announced:

A surprise attack by the Germans . . . is possible during the course of 22–23 June 1941. The mission of our forces is to avoid provocative actions of any kind, which might produce major complications . . . Disperse all aircraft . . . and thoroughly camouflage them before dawn on 22 June 1941 . . . Bring all forces to a state of combat readiness.

Few formations received this warning due to the shambolic state of Soviet communications. Pavlov, meanwhile, took matters into his own hands and checked on the readiness of his troops. To his dismay he found that they were dispersed on exercises, required vital supplies and were hamstrung by a lack of transport.

He did not sleep that night but minutes after Stalin retired to bed, the first German shells exploded on Soviet positions.

At 0315 hours on 22 June 1941, a shattering German barrage targeted Red Army defences along the entire front. It was followed by an immense ground advance, which was closely supported by ground-attack aircraft. Other elements of the Luftwaffe dropped their bombs on Soviet cities and attacked enemy airfields, destroying 1,200 aircraft. The German spearheads plunged forward, cracking open the enemy's defences. In certain sectors, however, there was no enemy to fight. In Army Group North's 6th Panzer Division, for example, Colonel Erhard Raus's 6th Motorized Infantry Brigade saw no enemy that morning and enjoyed 'the beauties of the landscape'. Recognizing that their luck could not last, his leading battalion probed ahead, expecting the worst. At around 1300 hours, they contacted the enemy. 'The first victim of the ambush,' Raus explains, 'was the company commander, who was driving at the head of his column. Before he even had time to shout an order, he was shot through the forehead by a Russian sniper from a distance of at least 100 metres.' The desperate fire-fight that ensued was replicated along the line as the border guards fought for their lives and German units sought to exploit gaps. Moscow garnered any scrap of information they could from the confusion, but Captain Ivan Krylov was told by a fellow staff officer:

Everything is going well ... The men have been ordered not to die before taking at least one German with them. 'If you are wounded,' the order says, 'sham death, and when the Germans approach, kill one of them. Kill them with your rifle, with the bayonet, with your knife, tear their throats out with your teeth. Don't die without leaving a dead German behind you.'

Such tenacity was not without its merits, but it could not stop the defenders from becoming thoroughly dislocated as their command and control was shattered – a process assisted by German Special Forces, which had infiltrated the Soviet rear to cut telephone lines, attack headquarters and seize key bridges. The Germans intercepted panicked Soviet transmissions – 'We are being fired on; what shall we do?' – followed by silence. Such was the psychological impact of the attack and the chaos that ensued that the defenders struggled to comprehend what was happening to them, let alone slow down or stop the Germans.

Announcing the invasion to the waking nation in a radio broadcast, Goebbels spoke Hitler's words in a triumphant tone:

At this moment a march is taking place that, for its extent, compares with the greatest the world has ever seen. I have decided today to place the fate and future of the Reich and our people in the hands of our soldiers. May God aid us, especially in this fight.

Later that morning an ebullient Hitler proclaimed to colleagues, 'Before three months have passed, we shall witness a collapse of Russia, the like of which has never been seen in history.' Meanwhile, in Moscow Stalin was struggling to understand the unfolding situation. At 0715 hours he had published Directive No. 2 to the armed forces, announcing the German invasion and ordering them to 'attack the enemy and destroy him in those regions where he has violated the border [and] mount aviation strikes on German territory to a depth of 100–150km [60–90 miles].' By the evening, however, as the scale of the impending disaster became clearer, Directive No. 3 authorized a general counteroffensive 'without regard for borders'. What followed was a gigantic clash, without restrictions, between two great nations. It would not end until one of them had been destroyed.

The Red Army threw itself at the Germans with nine mechanized corps seeking to bedevil the invaders as they fought through the first echelon's weak defences during the first two days. The Soviets fought with fury but without finesse and were no match for their adversary. Incapable of dealing with a fast-moving enemy, their cumbersome tank brigades were undermined by poor intelligence, supply difficulties and a tactical naivety that led to their destruction. Communications between units, formations, arms and services quickly disintegrated.

Relying more on insecure and inflexible field telephones rather than radios, commanders could not impose their will on the battle and were either forced into inaction or decisions based on unconfirmed reports. Speaking for the higher formations, Zhukov later wrote that 'commanding generals and their staff still had no reliable communication with the army commanders. Our divisions and corps had to fight in isolation, without cooperation with the neighbouring troops and aviation, and without proper direction from above.' The ensuing disorganization allowed the Germans to achieve the momentum that their armoured forces needed to break through. Blockages could be removed by the Luftwaffe but such was the call on its services that the ground forces usually made an attempt themselves first. Raus's brigade, for example, came upon KV-1 heavy tanks, which initially seemed unstoppable. He later wrote:

One of the tanks drove straight for the [150mm] howitzer, which now delivered a direct hit to its frontal armour. A glare of fire and simultaneously a thunderclap of a bursting shell followed, and the tank stopped as if hit by lightning. 'That's the end of that,' the gunners thought as they took a collective deep breath. 'Yes, that fellow's had enough,' observed the section chief. Abruptly, their faces dropped in disbelief when someone exclaimed, 'It's moving again!' ... [It] crashed into the heavy gun as if it were nothing more than a toy, pressing it into the ground and crushing it with ease as if it were an everyday affair.

The situation was eventually controlled by the armour-piercing shells of the superb 88mm gun – a powerful and versatile flak weapon, which proved a first-class tank killer.

Despite the continued German advance, the Soviets did not crumble but they did suffer heavy losses in men and material (by dusk on 23 June, 6th Panzer Division had destroyed 125 Soviet tanks). A German staff officer summed up the situation when he wrote: 'The Russian mass is no match for an army with modern equipment and superior leadership.' The skirmishing that had been expected of the Germans did not materialize and Zhukov admits in his memoirs that he and his colleagues severely underestimated the initial power of the attack:

> We did not foresee the large-scale surprise offensive . . . we did not envisage the nature of the blow in its entirety . . . to concentrate such huge numbers of armoured and motorised troops and, on the first day, to commit them to action in powerful compact groupings in all strategic directions with the aim of striking powerful wedging blows.

As Moscow struggled to get a grip on a situation that was rapidly developing into a national disaster, the world reflected on the implications of Hitler's invasion. Prime Minister Winston Churchill offered Britain's full support to the Soviet Union and broadcast to the nation:

> No one has been a more consistent opponent of Communism than I have for the last 25 years . . . But all this fades away with the spectacle that is now unfolding . . . We have but one aim and one single, irrevocable purpose. We are resolved to destroy Hitler and every vestige of the Nazi regime. It follows, therefore, that we shall give whatever help we can to Russia and the Russian people . . . His invasion of Russia is no more than a prelude to an attempted invasion of the British Isles . . . The Russian danger is therefore our danger and the danger of the United States, just as the cause of any Russian fighting for his hearth and home is the cause of free men and free people in every quarter of the globe.

Yet despite Churchill's laudable intentions, British politician Harold Nicolson wrote in his diary on 24 June: '80 per cent of the War Office experts think that Russia will be knocked out in ten days.'

Immune from grand strategy and concerns about anything much more than their immediate future were the troops at the front. Surging forward, ever farther from their loved ones, the Wehrmacht hoped and believed that the campaign would be a short one. In Army Group South, Eleventh Army infantryman Gottlob Bidermann was part of an anti-tank company that was armed with 12 37mm guns. From notes made in a small, leather-bound diary, he later recalled: 'Everyone was confident that this war against the Soviet Union, like the conflict with France and Poland, would pass quickly.' Since his 132nd Division was in reserve during the early stages, his memories of the first week of Barbarossa were dominated by images of recently finished battles. '[I was] struck by the lingering smell of smoke and ashes,' he remembered, 'and soon we could observe the large craters and scorched vehicles that depicted the handiwork of the German Stuka dive-bombers.' Marching through a parched landscape, Bidermann's first sight of the enemy did not fill him with fear:

The dusty road was lined with endless columns of Russian prisoners in ragged khaki-brown uniforms ... [m]any of those without caps wore wisps of straw or rags tied to their close-cropped heads as protection against the burning sun, and some were barefooted and half-dressed, giving us an indication of how quickly our attacking forces had overrun their positions ... They filed past us silently and with downcast eyes; occasionally several of them could be seen supporting another who appeared to be suffering from wounds, sickness, or exhaustion.

Such images are echoed by 20-year-old infantryman Herbert Henry, who testifies:

The sight of the line of retreat of their army, wrecked by our tanks and our stukas, is truly awful and shocking. Huge craters left by the Stuka bombs all along the edges of the road that had blown even the largest and heaviest of their tanks up in the air and swivelled them round . . . we've been marching for 25 kilometres past images of terrible destruction. About 200 smashed-up, burnt-out tanks turned upside down, guns, lorries, field kitchens, motor-cycles, anti-tank guns, a sea of weapons, helmets, items of equipment of all kinds, pianos and radios, filming vehicles, medical equipment, boxes of munitions and books, grenades, blankets, coats, knapsacks. In among them, corpses already turning black.

Bidermann and Henry were part of a well-oiled machine that drove the front forward remorselessly in a series of encirclements and thrusts. Punching forward towards Moscow, Army Group Centre made good progress against Pavlov's Western Front, which found it difficult to break contact and withdraw to regroup and take up better defensive positions. Within days, Guderian's Second Panzer Army and Hermann Hoth's Third Panzer Army were creating a double envelopment around Minsk in an attempt to remove the Western Front from the Soviet order of battle. The Luftwaffe made short work of those units that pulled back in disorder, and regularly attacked any Soviet concentrations. Arriving in a non-descript village with a Red Army unit, war correspondent Vasily Grossman later noted:

[T]hree Junkers appeared. Bombs exploded. Screams. Red flames with white and black smoke. We pass the same village again in the evening. The people are wide-eyed, worn out. Women are carrying belongings. Chimneys have grown very tall, they are standing tall amid the ruins. And flowers – cornflowers and peonies – are flaunting themselves so peacefully.

He had already witnessed the impact of a raid on Gomel as the Luftwaffe sought to disrupt Soviet westward movement, and made some notes in his journal:

> [H]owling bombs, fire, women . . . The strong smell of perfume – from a pharmacy hit in the bombardment – blocked out the stench of burning, just for a moment. The picture of burning Gomel in the eyes of a wounded cow.

Minsk was also heavily bombed as Army Group Centre surrounded it. 'The whole city was in flames,' Zhukov later wrote. 'Thousands of peaceful inhabitants hurled their dying curses at the Nazi brutes.' By the fifth day of the German offensive Pavlov was reporting to Moscow that he was powerless to stop the German tanks from creating their encirclement. Although of very limited military value, the Western Front was told to do all that it could to slow Bock's advance and was ordered to defend the city.

Even as Pavlov pondered his options, on 26 June Zhukov, Timoshenko and Vatutin were meeting with Stalin to discuss plans to defend Moscow. They were all tired and Stalin was irritable. Leading them to the table in his office on which lay a marked map, the General Secretary growled, 'Put your heads together and tell me what can be done in this situation.' Their proposal was quickly accepted: 'building up a defence in depth on the approaches to Moscow, continuously harrying the enemy and checking his advance on one of the lines of defence, then organizing a counteroffensive, by bringing up for this purpose troops from the Far East together with new formations.'

As the Soviet hierarchy moved to put this plan into action, on 30 June Bock's panzers completed their encirclement of Minsk and isolated the 10th, 3rd, 4th and 13th Armies. Guderian called it 'the first great victory of the campaign'. As the plodding infantry closed up to eliminate the pocket that had been created, the beleaguered Soviets were gradually overwhelmed. Some escaped through the porous German clinch to regroup and then join troops trying to stop the armoured spearheads from reaching the Dnieper in early July, but these attempts were doomed to failure. On 10 July, the day after resistance at Minsk had been crushed, Guderian had already begun his crossing of the Dnieper. In less than three weeks, Bock's Army Group Centre had advanced 360 miles and cost the Soviets 417,790 casualties, 4,799 tanks, 9,427 guns and mortars and 1,777 combat aircraft. Pavlov – a medal-festooned Hero of the Soviet Union – was executed along with eight other senior officers for 'lack of resolve, panic-mongering, disgraceful cowardice . . . and fleeing in terror in the face of an impudent enemy'. The regime had 'gripped' the situation in the only way that it knew how. Failure was met by death either at the hands of the Germans or the NKVD. It was now up to Pavlov's replacement, Timoshenko, to stem the German tide west of Moscow, the city Stalin referred to as 'the beating heart of the Soviet Union'.

The defence of the capital may have been regarded by the Soviets as critical to their survival, but the Germans were also planning to overrun Leningrad and the Ukraine. Army Group North's armour advanced to a depth of 60 miles on the first day of the campaign and was far too strong for Kuznetsov's Northwestern Front. Having raced through Lithuania, elements of Colonel-General Erich Hoepner's Fourth Panzer Army had pushed 270 miles to the Western Dvina by 26 June. The river was crossed on 2 July, after the infantry had caught up, and Leeb then focused on smashing the defences that Popov's Northern Front had hastily erected to protect Leningrad. In an attempt to stop the German juggernaut, Stalin despatched Nikolai Vatutin to provide Kuznetsov with trusted support. On his arrival from Moscow, Vatutin immediately asked for the Front's losses so far and was horrified to learn that they amounted to 90,000 men, 1000 tanks, 4000 guns and mortars and over 1000 combat aircraft. Turning to the dishevelled Front commander, he said, 'Leningrad must not fall. We must do everything in our power to defend the approaches to the city – even if it leads to the destruction of your formation.'

Army Groups Centre and North had made an excellent start to the campaign, but Army Group South had progressed less well. Advancing along the worst roads and facing the strongest Soviet formations in defence of the resource-laden Ukraine, Rundstedt's formation ran headlong into the Southwestern and Southern Fronts. The main attack emanated from southern Poland and, led by Colonel-General Ewald von Kleist's First Panzer Army, headed towards Kiev while 200 miles away a subsidiary attack sought to clear the southern Ukraine and the Black Sea coast. For the first two days of the offensive Rundstedt had little difficulty in overrunning the border defences, but then Kirponos – with Zhukov temporarily at his side, to ensure that he was resolute and bold – ordered armoured counterattacks. The huge armoured battle that developed involved more than 2000 tanks ranging across a 42 mile front. It failed to stop the First Panzer Army but stretched German resources, undermined Kleist's momentum and tested his nerve. By 30 June, Rundstedt's armour had reached Lvov and was closing in on Rovno. The Southwestern Front, having lost more than 2,600 tanks since 22 June, was struggling to extract itself from a rapidly deteriorating situation and feared encirclement. Colonel I.I. Fedyuninsky, commanding 15th Rifle Corps of 5th Army, has testified:

> Sometimes bottlenecks were formed by troops, artillery, motor vehicles and field kitchens, and then the Nazi planes had the time of their life . . . Often our troops could not dig in, simply because they did not have the simplest implements. Occasionally trenches had to be dug with helmets, since there were no spades.

Farther south, Tiulenev's Southern Front was also being pushed back and struggled to stay in contact with the Southwestern Front's left flank as Army Group South's secondary thrust sought to break the two apart. Retreat, again, was inevitable and was punishing for the Soviets. Gottlob Bidermann's formation remained the reserve but he continued to slog forward in ferocious heat and thunderstorms through 'an endless open space with only occasional clusters of sparse trees stretching to the horizon'. He wrote:

> For days great numbers of destroyed Russian tanks lined our path, and capsized prime movers with limbered field guns were scattered along the roadsides. In the fields one could see numerous abandoned Russian artillery positions that appeared to be intact, indicating how quickly our offensive had overtaken the Soviet defenders . . . The graves of German and Russian soldiers were now found to be close together.

The situation did nothing to dispel Bidermann's belief that the Red Army was no match for the Wehrmacht and he remained concerned that his unit would not see action 'before the inevitable surrender of the Soviet Union'.

The Soviets had been dealt a severe blow in the 'Battle of the Frontiers'. The invaders had pushed over 350 miles into their territory and inflicted on them some 172,323 casualties with the loss of 4,381 tanks, 5,806 guns and mortars and 1,218 combat aircraft. The German High Command felt confident that the whole business could be brought to a victorious conclusion quickly. Franz Halder wrote in his diary: 'The objective to shatter the bulk of the Russian Army this [western] side of the Dvina and Dnieper has been accomplished . . . It is thus probably no overstatement to say that the Russian Campaign has been won in the space of two weeks.' Hitler was so optimistic that he ordered massive new armaments programmes for the airforce and the navy in preparation to defeat the British and take the war to the United States. Yet those who were willing to strip away the euphoria surrounding the first weeks of success recognized that there was still plenty of fight in the Red Army. Many front-line commanders reported stiffening resistance and evidence of stretched lines of communication. But could the Red Army withstand the continued onslaught long enough to take advantage of German overstretch?

By the end of June, Stalin was physically and mentally drained. He had given his all to managing the crisis, and had done so, as a colleague later wrote, 'displaying confidence and calmness and demonstrating great industriousness'. Nevertheless, the General Secretary had been humiliated by Hitler's invasion. Less territory had been lost by Tsar Nicholas II during the Great War prior to the revolution, and recognizing this Stalin admitted, 'Lenin founded our state and we've fucked it up.' In what seemed like a fit of despondency, Stalin retreated to his Kuntsevo dacha on 29 June and suddenly stopped leading. Contrary to impressions, though, Stalin had not given up hope and had already directed organizational changes that, he believed, would streamline the Soviet response and help harness the nation's strengths. Before continuing the work, however, he wanted to test the foundations of his leadership. By taking himself away from the Kremlin, he paused not only to draw breath but also to draw political enemies out into the open. Yet rather than attempting to seize power on 30 June, Molotov, the only credible alternative to Stalin, led a delegation to the dacha. He recalled: 'Stalin was in a very agitated state. He didn't curse, but he wasn't quite himself. I wouldn't say that he had lost his head. He suffered, but didn't show any signs of this.' Molotov explained that the Politburo wanted Stalin to take up the reins of power once more and head a State Committee for Defence (GKO), a body with total power to conduct the war as it saw fit. The GKO would direct the activities of government departments and the General Staff, which concerned itself with strategy, as well as the Stavka (the Supreme High Command of the Soviet Armed Forces), which Stalin had activated on 23 June with responsibility to prepare and conduct military campaigns, coordinate operations and organize forces.

Stalin replied to Molotov's request with a modesty that was not out of character: 'Can I lead the country to final victory?' Kliment Voroshilov, the Deputy Premier, replied, 'There is none more worthy.' Stalin shifted uneasily, looked into the eyes of the waiting men, and finally agreed to take up the position. At that moment he became titular Supreme Commander of the Soviet Union and days later added the role of People's Commissariat of Defence to his already extensive portfolio of appointments. Stalin had cleverly used a national emergency to complete his quest to attain ultimate authority. By 10 July 1941, Stalin dominated the Party and executive, controlled the armed forces and directed all strategic decision making.

Stalin threw himself into work with renewed vigour and immediately took steps to ensure that the Soviet Union could sustain its war effort over the coming months and years. Using all of the organizational skills that he had developed in clawing his way to power, Stalin oversaw the raising of reserves, the evacuation of Moscow and measures to ensure that the Soviet Union's manufacturing infrastructure was kept out of Hitler's reach. He was absolutely insistent that the route to victory lay in out-producing Germany, and as a consequence some 1,523 factories had been moved more than 1000 miles east of Moscow by November. This forward thinking, along with a 'scorched earth' policy of destroying anything of use in the path of the rampaging enemy, provided the foundations for the nation's long-term resistance to the Germans. Indeed, Zhukov later declared, 'The heroic feat of evacuation and restoration of industrial capacity during the war, and the Party's colossal organizational work it involved, meant as much for the country's destiny as the greatest battles of the war.'

Stalin knew that this work would be for nothing if the fighting front collapsed, and along with spending considerable time overseeing the development of plans to thwart the Wehrmacht's march eastwards, he also attended to military discipline. He was concerned at the high desertion rates across the front in June (5000 men were caught running from one bloody Southwestern Front battle) and reports of self-inflicted wounds, which together not only led to denuded defences but also eroded the morale of those who were left to do the fighting. Wanting to ensure that each and every soldier felt the Party's hand on his shoulder, on 16 July Stalin reintroduced 'dual command', which required military commanders to work in harness with a political officer or commissar. Those caught with self-inflicted wounds were summarily executed by members of the NKVD Special Department. Deserters faced a three-man military tribunal, which could order the death sentence. Meanwhile, Levrentiy Beria, head of the NKVD, was ordered by Stalin to remove unreliable elements from military units and to arrest those spreading rumours and indulging in defeatist rhetoric. The result was another bloody, merciless purge in which nearly one million Red Army personnel were condemned by military tribunals and many more were shot on the spot without trial.

To stiffen further the resolve of the troops, Order No. 270 condemned all those who surrendered or were captured as 'traitors to the motherland', and branded any officer who retreated or gave himself up as 'a malicious deserter', liable to be shot in the field and have his family arrested. One of the first victims of this Order was Stalin's own son, Yakov, whose capture in early July led to his wife spending two years in a labour camp. Stalin did not intervene in the matter and refused to exchange his son for a high-ranking German prisoner. Yakov was eventually shot, having deliberately walked into the perimeter zone at his prisoner-of-war camp.

Stalin's 'terror' and harsh policies did little to deal with the cause of desertion and self-inflicted wounds. Morale was often very poor and it was not uncommon to find soldiers underweight, since their diets did not provide the calories that they needed. Breakfast was thick soup, lunch was buckwheat kasha, tea and bread, followed by more soup and tea in the evening. Sometimes they received nothing at all for days on end. One soldier wrote home: 'We're living in dugouts in the woods.

We sleep on straw, like cattle. They feed us very badly – twice a day, and even then not what we need. We get five spoonfuls of soup in the morning . . . we're hungry all day.' Gabriel Temkin observed a Red Army unit in his village: 'Some in trucks, many on foot, their outdated rifles hanging loosely over their shoulders. Their uniforms worn out, covered with dust, not a smile on their mostly despondent, emaciated faces with sunken cheeks.' These men did not look as though they were physically capable of giving battle and many were mentally fragile. Poor preparation and low motivation – many did not support the regime and half were non-Russian – undermined their capabilities while 'suicidal orders' and naive tactics often led to heavy casualties. The skinny Soviet infantry threw themselves at heavily armed enemy formations with fixed bayonets and cries of 'Hoorah!' but often without air or artillery support. They attacked in waves, which the Germans cut down with automatic fire, mortars and artillery until there were no more, leaving heaps of dead on the battlefield.

The truly horrific losses at the front were glossed over by the regime, which managed and manipulated the information released to the population. Stalin did not want the Soviet people to recoil in horror from the war, for as poet David Samoilov said, 'We were all expecting war. But we were not expecting *that* war.' Stalin wanted them to embrace the struggle with passion and resilience. Propaganda was therefore written by skilled writers, overseen by the Sovinformbiro (Soviet Information Bureau), which had been established in the first days of the war to 'bring into the limelight international events, military developments, and day-to-day life through printed and broadcast media'. Journalists and stories were carefully controlled by censors, and trusted officials inspected copy for ideological mistakes. Thrice weekly press conferences were held by the Deputy Foreign Commissar Solomon Lozovsky, who was also the Deputy Chief of the Sovinformbiro. His tone was always optimistic, lost territory was only temporary and major disasters were not mentioned at all. Front-line troops had their own press. The most popular was *The Red Star*, for which Vasily Grossman wrote. It was often read aloud to the troops, who were also shown carefully constructed newsreel re-enaction of their battles.

Radio was a great source of information, and millions listened to broadcasts by anchorman Yuri Levitan, who always started with the words 'This is the Soviet Information Bureau . . .' and provided considerable detail of heroic Soviet actions and successes. However, listeners soon learned that phrases such as 'fighting in the Minsk direction' meant that the city had already been lost, and that 'heavy defensive battles against superior enemy forces' meant a full and disorderly retreat.

On 3 July, radio listeners heard Stalin addressing the nation for the first time in the war. Erskine Caldwell, an American living in Moscow, wrote of the event:

At 6.30 a.m. practically every person in the city was within earshot of a radio, either home set or street loudspeaker. Red Square and the surrounding plazas, usually partially deserted at that hour, were filled with crowds. When Stalin's speech began, his words resounded from all directions, indicating that amplifiers were carrying the message to every nook and cranny of the city.

Delivered in an unusually clear, calm voice, Stalin spoke of Germany as an 'unprovoked aggressor . . . [a] vicious and perfidious enemy'. However, in calling for the country to defeat the invader, he did not try to tap into the nation's revolutionary zeal but, just like Molotov's announcement of war on 22 June, he called for a 'patriotic war . . . a war of the entire Soviet people' in an attempt to reach out to a wider constituency. Despite the excesses of his regime, Stalin's patriotic war demanded that the Soviet Union unite against a deadly common enemy. He ended his address with the words, 'Comrades! Our arrogant foe will soon discover that our forces are beyond number . . . Forward – to victory!'

Captain Ivan Krylov has said, 'the tone of [the speech] surprised me
... It had occurred to me that this new tone was due to exceptional
danger. He was afraid ... He was doubtful of the attitude of the
people in face of the German attack; he was afraid of a revolt against
the regime.' It was, according to journalist Alexander Werth, based in
Moscow to report for the *Sunday Times*, an 'extraordinary' performance,
and he later wrote in his history of the war that it was essential to a
'frightened and bewildered people' and meant that, after all the 'artifi-
cial adulation', they now 'felt that they had a leader to look to'. Erskine
Caldwell agreed and noted:

> As an observer, I had the feeling that this announcement imme-
> diately brought about the beginning of a new era in Soviet life.
> The people have heard for the first time since the war began a
> fighting speech by their leader. As a Russian said to me, you may
> be sure that from this moment a grapple with death has begun ...
> I would not be surprised if the entire population of Moscow
> suddenly besieged the military offices for permission to move *en
> masse* to the front.

During the first days of the war, a flood of Soviet men had poured into
hastily established recruiting stations to volunteer for service in a rush
of patriotism, panic, anger and duty. In Moscow, 3,500 men presented
themselves for service in the first 36 hours while in the Kursk province
some 7,200 people applied for front-line duty in the first month. One
man from the city of Kursk told a crowd: 'I lived through German rule
in the Ukraine in 1918 and 1919. We will not work for landlords and
noblemen. We'll drive that bloodstained Hitler out bag and baggage. I
declare myself mobilized and ask to be sent to the front to destroy the
German bandits.' Few volunteers had any idea of what they were
signing up for. Life in the military was brutal. The average front-line
tour of duty for an infantryman was just three weeks before he was

seriously wounded or killed. The regime had to ensure that they had bodies to replace the fallen and it did not take the Soviet propaganda machine long before it was churning out posters and literature to remind the population of their 'patriotic duty'. Alexander Werth reported from the capital:

> Posters on the wall were eagerly read, and there were certainly plenty of posters: a Russian tank crushing a giant crab with a Hitler moustache, a Red soldier ramming his bayonet down the throat of a giant Hitler-faced rat – '*Razdavit fascistskuyu gadinu*', it said: 'Crush the Fascist vermin'; appeals to women – 'Women, go and work on the collective farms, replace the men now in the Army!' . . . *Pravda* or *Izvestia* with the full text of Stalin's speech were stuck up, and everywhere crowds of people were re-reading it.

Women did take the place of men on the land and in factories – by the end of the year they made up 41 per cent of the labour force – but 800,000 were also accepted into the military as nurses and laundresses, and eventually as snipers, tank crews, gunners, infanteers and naval crew. It was not unusual for a small group of women to serve together in a section or a crew. In fact, there was a policy of keeping groups of volunteers together because it was deemed advantageous for morale. The result was 'The Sportsmen's Company', 'The Writers' Company', 'The Musicians' Company' and the like. During July author Konstantin Simonov came across one such unit filled with men aged between 40 and 50 years old in tatty tunics.

> I remember that they produced a gloomy impression on me at the time . . . [they] were thrown in to plug the gap, because something – anything – had to be thrown in, at whatever the price, to preserve the front, which the reserve armies were preparing

further to the East, nearer to Moscow, from being shattered to pieces . . . I thought: do we really have no other reserves besides these volunteers, dressed anyhow and barely armed?

There were reservists, of which 5.3 million were mobilized in the last week of June, but with the age of conscription soon lowered to 18 years and the volunteering campaign growing in scope, it was evident that everybody had a part to play in the rapidly developing total war. This included groups of partisans made up of civilians and those troops who had become separated from their units. Scant planning had been made for irregular warfare by the outbreak of war, but its potential was soon recognized by Moscow, and in July Stalin said, 'There must be diversionist groups for fighting enemy units. In the occupied areas intolerable conditions must be created for the enemy and his accomplices.' Within a year, an estimated 90,000 partisans were operating behind enemy lines. Many were directed by special NKVD units sent by Moscow for the purpose. These units were not only a means of unhinging the enemy through acts of sabotage, ambushes and attacks on their lines of communication, but also became the face of the Party in occupied territory. One German infantry officer, Karl Hertzog, recalls:

We feared the partisans. They were ruthless and difficult to track down. We expended considerable time, energy and resources trying to locate them, but we rarely did. On one occasion I led a patrol into a known partisan stronghold and just escaped with my life. My platoon was slaughtered. Ten were killed on the spot, 15 were taken prisoner and the remainder – myself included – managed to escape. Three days later we found the dismembered corpses of those men who had been captured by the side of the road.

The stoicism of the Soviet troops and the viciousness of the partisan action were based in a complicated mixture of factors, but chief among them was the defence of their homeland. There was a widely held belief that the invaders would take away the little that they had. Gottlob Bidermann has said:

> The individual soldiers of the Red Army evolved into fighters distinctly different from soldiers we had first encountered. The mentality of the soldier changed from one of apathy and indifference to that of a patriot. The idea of belonging to an élite army that was alone saving the world from Fascism was being instilled, and a sense of pride evolved that had long been absent from the ranks of the Soviet armed forces.

Indeed, an elderly Tsarist general told Heinz Guderian:

> If only you had come twenty years ago we should have welcomed you with open arms. But now it's too late. We were just beginning to get on our feet and now you arrive and throw us back twenty years so that we will have to start from the beginning all over again. Now we are fighting for Russia and in that cause we are all united.

The population's developing affinity with the cause was given substance by the Germans' often contemptible, ideologically motivated treatment of prisoners and civilians. The 'cleansing' of captured territories was primarily carried out by four SS Einsatzgruppen (Special Operation Units), which acted as paramilitary death squads. Jews and those elements deemed to be hostile to German interests were either arrested and used as slave-labour – the first of seven million who arrived from occupied territories – or were executed. The genocide was carried out not just by the SS. Before the invasion the army high command had issued a formal instruction, the 'Commissar Order', that captured 'political leaders and commissars' were to be shot on the spot. Moreover, Wehrmacht soldiers were expected to 'cooperate' in Hitler's stated ambition for the Soviet Union – 'Occupy it, administer it, exploit it' – and had been legally exempted from a whole catalogue of crimes. Some units and some soldiers had no compunction in crossing the moral line and complying with Hitler's most repugnant demands, which were treated as routine military operations. Others did it because they were weak and some conformed for an easy life. Mass executions of civilians followed the Wehrmacht's arrival in a town or village. The observer of one such act in Lotoshino told Alexander Werth:

> The first day the Germans came . . . they hanged eight people in the main street, among them a hospital nurse and a teacher. The teacher's body was left hanging there for eight days. They had called for the people to attend the execution, but few went.

The Wehrmacht were followed by the Reich Commissars, who administered the occupation with a heavy hand. Alana Molodin says, 'It was a difficult time. I was twelve years old and made to work for the Nazis. I became a servant at the administrator's office and counted myself as lucky . . . Friends were raped, beaten and disappeared. I was regularly hit. I witnessed one elderly lady shot as she shuffled in front of an impatient German's car.' It also became common for Soviet prisoners to be executed. Hertzog said that this first occurred due to 'a lack of resources to deal with the hundreds of men that we captured'. The Germans had not made adequate provision for the taking of prisoners and their extermination relieved units of their responsibilities for them. A German soldier testifies:

> Once a soldier had killed in combat and had friends die at their side, it was not so very difficult for some to shoot dead unarmed

prisoners. It is not an excuse, but we were barbarised by war. Moral boundaries became blurred and only the best officers made them clear. I am ashamed to say that I was the member of a unit that carried out atrocities. But at the time we saw it as our job. We did not think about it. We saw ourselves as dead men walking in any case.

By 8 September the murder of Red Army troops was given legitimacy by an OKH decree, which stated that Soviet prisoners of war had 'forfeited all rights'. The results were horrendous. One civilian recalled:

[T]he enemy locked captured Red Army men in a four-storey building surrounded by barbed wire. At midnight the Germans set fire to it. When the Red Army soldiers started jumping from the windows the Germans fired at them. About seventy people were shot and many burned to death.

Those who were not executed faced an awful ordeal in filthy compounds surrounded by barbed wire, without shelter, food, water or warm clothing. Some were killed at the whim of their guards; most suffered beatings and were left to die in squalor.

German excesses were not without their negative consequences. A German intelligence officer argued in a report about the root of Soviet fighting spirit: 'It is no longer because of lectures from the *politruks*, but out of his own personal convictions that the Soviet soldier has come to expect an agonizing life or death if he falls captive.' Heinz Guderian concurred. Describing a scene near Smolensk, he wrote:

A significant indication of the attitude of the civilian population is provided by the fact that women came out from their villages on to the very battlefield bringing wooden platters of bread and butter and eggs and, in my case at least, refused to let me move on before I had eaten. Unfortunately this friendly attitude towards the Germans lasted only so long as the more benevolent military administration was in control. The so-called 'Reich commissars' soon managed to alienate all sympathy from the Germans and thus prepare the ground for all the horrors of partisan warfare.

Although the Soviet regime put in place a number of measures to ensure that the Red Army soldier fought to the last round, increasingly it was German behaviour that proved the greater motivator. Far from tapping the significant anti-Stalin sentiment present in the Soviet Union in 1941, the invaders legitimized Stalin's rule in a way that he could never do. A Soviet officer told Werth:

This is a very grim war. And you cannot imagine the hatred the Germans have stirred up amongst our people. We are easy-going, good-natured people, you know: but I assure you, they have turned our people into spiteful *mujiks. Zlyie mujiki* – that's what we've got in the Red Army now, men thirsting for revenge. We officers sometimes have a job in keeping our soldiers from killing German prisoners; I know they want to do it, especially when they see some of these arrogant, fanatical Nazi swine. I have never known such hatred before. And there's good reason for it ... I cannot help thinking of my wife and own ten-year-old daughter in Kharkov.

Vasily Grossman found a locket on a dead Soviet soldier, Lieutenant Miroshnikov, with a note inside:

If someone is brave enough to remove the contents of this locket, could they send this to the following address ... 'My sons, I am in another world now. Join me here, but first you must take revenge on the enemy for my blood. Forward to victory, and you, friends, too, for our Motherland, for glorious Stalin's deeds.'

Death and destruction continued across the front during July as the Wehrmacht progressed towards Leningrad, Moscow and Rostov. While all three German army groups posed threats, it was Army Group Centre's advance towards the capital that caused Stalin most concern. Bock's formation grappled with the remnants of six Soviet armies while an army from the reserve was deployed behind them at Smolensk – 230 miles west of the capital – and a further two armies defended Moscow itself. Unable to do more than temporarily slow the onslaught, the Soviet formations fell back and by the middle of the month the German armour looked ready to encircle Smolensk. Despite the danger to the withdrawing forces posed by Bock's panzers, the fractured armies were ordered to defend the city for as long as possible in order to provide Moscow with time to prepare its defences. A tremendous battle followed, which caused Guderian great difficulty in sustaining his momentum as casualties mounted and his logistics buckled. The situation became so acute that the commander of the 18th Motorized Division, whose tired troops were fighting through intense heat and in choking dust, thought that a halt was required 'if we do not intend to win ourselves to death'. But the Second Panzer Army pressed on regardless while the infantry raced to catch them up. One of those trudging his way eastwards was 30-year-old German Signals NCO Helmuth Pabst. Footsore and sunburned, having marched 780 miles, Pabst wrote in his diary on 16 July that his 'knees were shaking' with fatigue.

Army Group Centre was visibly tiring but Hitler was entirely confident that it was in a prime position to take its goals, and ordered the Luftwaffe to begin bombing Moscow. The first raid took place during the night of 21 July and was met by a tremendous anti-aircraft barrage, 'shrapnel from the anti-aircraft shells clattering down on to the streets like a hailstorm; and dozens of searchlights lighting the sky'. Three rings of anti-aircraft defences surrounded the city and, during that first raid, just a dozen of the 200 German bombers managed to break through. Undeterred, similar operations followed as Hitler endeavoured to undermine Soviet defensive arrangements before launching a ground attack on the city.

Bock was on the point of taking Smolensk, although weakening, but Berlin did not take the option of downgrading the attacks on Leningrad and the Ukraine to reinforce Army Group Centre – quite the opposite. With a firm flank established from Velikie Luki 120 miles north to Lake Illmen, in early July Army Group North's Eighteenth and Fourth Panzer Armies struck out from the Western Dvina for Leningrad. Leeb's men, issued with obsolete 1:300,000 maps, immediately found the going tough with well-set defences situated on difficult ground. Reflecting on the 6th Panzer Division's progress, Erhard Raus has written:

> [T]he enemy offered stubborn and skilful resistance in the woods and thickets, time and again launching counterblows supported by tanks . . . [T]he road suddenly changed into marshland of the worst kind. Tanks and guns bogged down . . . Progress became increasingly difficult . . . [T]he first moor could only be traversed after hours of backbreaking work by every officer and man, tormented by swarms of mosquitoes as they employed tree trunks, boughs, planks, and the last available fascine mats to create a barely passable route.

Nevertheless, Leeb's unremitting pressure on the Soviet defences began to pay dividends and by 14 July the tenacious Army Group North's persistent panzers reached the River Luga, just 80 miles south of Leningrad. Here some torrid defence by the Northern Front forced the tired German spearhead to stall for several days while they waited for the infantry, who were far to the rear, fully committed in clearing operations. Leeb faced a dilemma. His stretched lines of communication and the difficult terrain were causing shortages and undermining the momentum of his attack, and with three defensive belts protecting Leningrad, he needed all the power he could muster to break through. These obstacles had been constructed under the orders of Marshal K.E. Voroshilov, commander of the Northwestern Direction, one of three short-lived Soviet strategic commands that had been formed on 10 July for greater control and coordination of resources. His orders were simple: defenders were to 'fight to the last round and the last drop of blood' to prevent Hitler from securing Leningrad, the former capital and the birthplace of Bolshevism. Some valuable factories were located in the city, and from Leningrad the Germans could swing around to approach Moscow from the north. Voroshilov demanded, therefore, that the city be held 'at all costs'.

As Leeb considered his options and reported to Berlin that he was facing 'considerable obstacles to his future offensive plans', Hitler urged Army Group South onwards into the Ukraine against the Southwestern and Southern Fronts. By 9 July, Rundstedt's First Panzer Army, heading for Kiev, was still 60 to 120 miles short of the Dnieper. The Sixth Army lagged over a week behind and the Seventeenth Army was making even slower progress towards the Crimea. Rundstedt spoke to Hitler on 15 July and blamed his difficulties on 'atrocious roads, intolerable heat and unexpectedly heavy enemy resistance'.

Gottlob Bidermann fought his first battle during this period. At the collective farm of Klein-Kargarlyk, his unit came under heavy fire as they worked to clear the position: 'The incoming rounds shook the earth beneath us, and only with great effort could we hear the shouted commands above the explosions.' An attack forced the enemy out into the fields, where they were immediately targeted. Bidermann recalled:

[O]ur forward machine-gun crews fired their MG-34s while standing on the waist-high wheat, each barrel resting across the shoulder of a crewman in order to maintain a clear field of fire. A number of Russians were struck by the bursts of machine-gun fire and tumbled to the earth, disappearing among the wheat stalks.

Having taken the objective, Bidermann and his colleagues rested – an advance of eight miles had taken six hours – and prepared for their next attack 'in an endless land, where unbroken fields stretched to the horizon before us from sunrise to sunset. I wondered how many more . . . battles lay ahead of us during our march away from the setting sun.' There was a great deal more fighting to do, and Rundstedt's formation was struggling to keep up with its campaign timetable.

On 19 July, with Army Group North on the Luga, Army Group Centre in the process of completing the encirclement of Smolensk, and Army Group South still short of the Dnieper, Führer Directive No. 33 was published. In it Hitler announced: 'The objective of future operations should be to prevent the escape of large enemy forces into the depths of Russian territory and to annihilate them.' Bock was to continue his push on Moscow but with infantry alone. His Third Panzer Army was to assist Leeb's assault on Leningrad and his Second Panzer Army was to drive south, linking up with Rundstedt's Army Group South to complete a massive encirclement in the northern Ukraine. The attack on Moscow was effectively postponed as these 'diversions' sought to link up the front and give Army Group Centre an opportunity to consolidate around Smolensk. Although the pincers of Army Group Centre's panzer armies met successfully east of Smolensk on 27 July, trapping 700,000 defenders, the success was marred by logistic turmoil and the strongest Soviet counterattacks to date. Moreover, 200,000 of those initially surrounded had managed to break out of their encirclement before the arrival of the German infantry.

Meanwhile, stubborn Soviet resistance against Army Groups North and South had raised questions in Hitler's mind about whether it was prudent to charge on to Moscow while Leningrad and the Ukraine remained in enemy hands. The aim had never been to break Soviet will by taking Moscow, but to destroy the Red Army *before* advancing that far. As such, Berlin had never placed a great emphasis on the capture of the Soviet capital. On the eve of Barbarossa the General Staff had argued: 'The occupation and destruction of Moscow will cripple the military, political and economic leadership as well as much of the basis of Soviet power. But it will not decide the war.'

The Germans were poorly placed to continue the advances to all three Army Group objectives. By the third week of July, although they had destroyed more than half of the Soviet order of battle, Soviet reserve and volunteer armies were being activated, over half of the German armour had been lost or was unserviceable, 40 per cent of all soft-skinned vehicles had been destroyed and lines of communication were overstretched, leading to shortages of critical supplies. The problems inherent in an operation that had multiple and competing strategic aims, and rested on inadequate campaign planning, short-term strategic preparation and a lack of resources, were now clearly visible. Hitler looked to the skill and flexibility of the Wehrmacht to overcome them.

In the wake of the Smolensk encirclement, Heinz Guderian was appalled to learn, at an Army Group conference, that his armour was being diverted away from Moscow. His anger remains palpable in the pages of his memoir that deal with the event. He wrote:

This meant that my Panzer [Army] would be swung round and would be advancing in a south-westerly direction, that is to say towards Germany . . . All the officers who took part in this conference were of the opinion that . . . these manoeuvres on our part simply gave the Russians time to set up new formations and to use their inexhaustible man-power for the creation of fresh lines in the rear area: even more important, we were sure that this strategy would not result in the urgently necessary, rapid conclusion of the campaign.

Führer Directive No. 34, published on 30 July, postponed the armoured diversions due to 'the appearance of a large enemy force before the front, the supply situation, and the necessity of giving the Second and Third Panzer [Armies] 10 days to restore and refill their formations'. However, there were some changes to the plan for rather than continuing its attack towards Moscow with infantry alone, the tired and vulnerable Army Group Centre was to 'go on the defence' and protect Smolensk.

As Guderian's Second Panzer Army made its preparations to link up with Army Group South, Rundstedt moved his Sixth Army towards Kiev. On 3 August meanwhile, Kleist's panzers completed the encirclement of 20 divisions from 6th, 12th and 18th Armies around Uman, south of Kiev. They captured 107,000 officers and men, including the two army commanders, four corps commanders, 11 division commanders, 286 tanks and 953 guns. Two corps commanders and six division commanders perished. By this time, the Second Panzer Army had left Army Group Centre and begun its diversion to create the Kiev encirclement. Zhukov had anticipated this move, having blocked Army Group Centre's route to Moscow with the new Central Front and given notice for a withdrawal: 'The South-Western Front must be withdrawn in its entirety beyond the Dnieper . . . Kiev will have to be surrendered.' Stalin disagreed, replaced Zhukov as Chief of the General Staff with Boris Shaposhnikov on 30 July, and sent him to command the newly activated Reserve Front. This Front was to attack Army Group Centre south of Smolensk at Yelnya, less than 200 miles from Moscow. Stalin's decision to sack Zhukov had as much to do with his need for an experienced and reliable man to undertake operations to stall Bock's advance as it had with his anger at the general's decision to abandon Kiev.

By 6 August, Guderian was successfully smashing his way through the Soviet formations, which Stalin had relied upon to hold him. Damage was being inflicted on the Second Panzer Army, but not enough to thwart its progress. Telegraphing the Supreme Commander, Zhukov stated that the enemy was 'throwing all of his shock, mobile and tank units against the Central, Southwestern and Southern Fronts, while defending actively against the Western and Reserve Fronts'. Time was running out for the Red Army in the Ukraine. Over the next two weeks, Guderian continued to chew his way forward and forced Moscow to take a decision about what to do next. On 21 August, at a critical Council of War, an exhausted Shaposhnikov recommended 'a withdrawal towards Kiev' and beyond to various lines of defence covered by rearguard actions 'in order to allow our troops to escape from the pincer movements the Germans are organizing everywhere'. Semyon Budenny, the commander of the Southwestern Direction, was not impressed and said, 'I have powerful defences at Kiev and I can hold them as long as I have a soldier to fire a rifle or a horse to carry a gun. I guarantee that their little joke will cost the Germans more than all the rearguard battles proposed by Marshal Shaposhnikov.' Stalin listened to both arguments and announced:

The Council of War orders the execution of the plan for a battle of attrition ... without losing sight of the necessity of prolonging the battle as long as possible in order to permit the evacuation of the Ukrainian key industries.

The decision was to stand and fight to destroy the Germans.

By late August, Guderian had reached the Desna River between Kiev and Briansk and it was at this point that Stalin ordered General Andrei Yeremenko, commander of the new Briansk Front upon which the Supreme Commander had pinned many of his hopes, finally to destroy the Second Panzer Army. Yeremenko signalled Stalin that he was confident of success. He received the reply: 'Guderian and his whole group must be smashed to smithereens. Until this is done all your assurances of success are worthless.' Anticipating Guderian's imminent breakthrough, Army Group South had crossed the Dnieper and closed up to the Southwestern and Southern Fronts from Kiev down to the Black Sea. As they did so, the Briansk Front was being mauled and in failing to stop the Second Panzer Army lost over 100,000 casualties and 140 tanks.

The trap was beginning to close in the Ukraine, and Kirponos was desperate to withdraw his Southwestern Front, reporting to Moscow: 'Delay could result in the loss of troops and a great deal of material.' Stalin was unmoved and on 11 September replied: 'your proposal to withdraw forces . . . we consider dangerous . . . Stop looking for lines of retreat and start looking for lines of resistance and only resistance.' Stalin was confusing military reality with pessimism and two days later Major-General V.I. Tupikov, the Southwestern Front's Chief of Staff, radioed Shaposhnikov: 'The catastrophe that is clear to you will occur in a matter of several days.' The airforce did what it could to help fracture the German attacks, but their lack of communications, skill and modern aircraft limited their chances of success. After a visit to an airfield, Vasily Grossman reported:

> There was a roar of engines starting up, dust, and wind – that very special aircraft wind, flattened against the ground. Aircraft went up into the sky one after another, circled and flew away. And immediately the airfield became empty and silent, like a classroom when the pupils have skipped away. It's like poker: the regimental commander threw his whole fortune into the air . . . He is standing there alone looking into the sky, and the skies above him are empty. He'll either be left a pauper, or will get everything back

with interest ... Finally, after a successful attack on a German column, the fighters returned and landed. The lead aircraft had human flesh stuck in the radiator. That's because the supporting aircraft had hit a truck with ammunition that blew up right at the moment when the leader was flying over it. Poppe, the leader, is picking the meat out with a file.

The Red Air Force lost 1,561 aircraft in the skies over Kiev but ultimately failed to do any more than inconvenience the German ground forces from time to time. The Soviets fought on, their commanders becoming more despondent with each hour that passed. Timoshenko, the new commander of the Southwestern Direction, could bear the situation no longer and gave Kirponos oral permission to withdraw to new defences along the Psel River line. Kirponos, however, had been told personally by Stalin to 'hold Kiev no matter what the cost' and so asked for the order to be confirmed in writing by Moscow. This was done rapidly, but due to a communications breakdown Kirponos did not receive authority to abandon the city until the early hours of 18 September. The delay was fatal. By that time, the First and Second Panzer Armies had completed their encirclement of the four beleaguered armies. The Soviets lost 440,000 men, 2,642 guns and mortars and 64 tanks at Kiev, making the battle the biggest defeat for the Red Army in the war so far.

Stalin's unreasonable decision to defend the Ukrainian capital had given Hitler's ambition to destroy his enemy before reaching Moscow a considerable boost. At Leningrad, however, the Supreme Commander's logic was far from flawed as he attempted to fix a large number of German formations on the city's outskirts. Army Group North launched its attack on the city from the River Luga on 8 August. It took the Germans nearly a week of hard fighting to overcome the Soviet defence, and not before Leeb had lost 21,000 men (the taking of Kiev accounted for 100,000 Wehrmacht casualties), 300 tanks and

600 artillery pieces. But as before, the Red Army was capable of slowing but not stopping their enemy and, by the end of the month, Army Group North was just 25 miles south of Leningrad. Three fresh Soviet armies were rushed to the sector to avert a catastrophe, and Popov took command of the Leningrad Front just as the Germans began their approach to the city. Among the attacking forces was a motorized corps that had just arrived from Army Group Centre's Third Panzer Army. The defenders' left flank was ripped open before the line was stabilized and, concerned at Popov's performance, Stalin wrote to Molotov on 29 August: 'I fear that Leningrad will be lost by foolish madness . . . I'm disturbed by the lack of activity of Leningrad's commander.'

By the first week of September, the Germans had isolated the city from the rest of the country, which made it dependent on supplies arriving from across Lake Ladoga, 20 miles to the east – its south bank was still in Soviet hands. Leningrad had been encircled. With the Finns threatening from the north, the situation looked so propitious for the Germans that Halder wrote in his diary: 'Leningrad: Our objective has been achieved. Will now become a subsidiary theatre of operations.' Popov was replaced by Zhukov in another crisis of command.

Arriving on 11 September, Zhukov immediately recognized that the situation required all of his organizational and motivational skills if the Germans were not to overrun the city. As shells began to scream in, the population raced to complete Leningrad's defences – an outer belt of concrete and earth bunkers, anti-tank ditches and natural obstacles, and an inner belt of heavily fortified positions, which encircled the city's perimeter. Leningrad itself was prepared in detail. Roads were barricaded, buildings were fortified, weapons were stored ready for distribution, factories, bridges and key buildings were prepared for demolition. By mid-September the Germans had nudged to within seven miles of the centre but here, facing torrid resistance, Leeb's offensive ground to a halt. The people of Leningrad continued to go about their business as shells landed in the parks and streets. 'I recall the day very well,' says Malana Ragulin:

I was walking with my mother along one of the main streets, past some shops, when there was a loud explosion. It was the first time that I had heard such a thing – although I was soon to become very used to it – and there was a white blast followed by red flame about 50 feet from us. We were thrown to the ground as windows were blasted out and covered us in glass. There were no casualties that time – but by the end of the day, as the shells continued to fall, there were many.

But there was no panic. Zhukov and the NKVD provided strong leadership. There was no dithering. The people were given direction, the military were given orders and the situation was brought under control as the Germans attempted to penetrate the city's defences. Soviet counterattacks were strong and, although some German regiments managed to edge a little farther forward, Zhukov's line held. Disappointed that Army Group North had not been able to storm the city, the High Command and Leeb decided that the best course of action was not to get involved in street fighting and house clearance, which would nullify their strengths and demand massive resources, but instead to conduct a siege. Leningrad was to be suffocated and on 22 September Hitler announced:

The Führer has decided to erase the city of Petersburg from the face of the earth. I have no interest in the further existence of this large city after the defeat of Soviet Russia . . . We propose to blockade the city tightly and erase it by means of artillery fire and continuous bombardments.

The German ability to tighten a noose around Leningrad was, however, undermined by determined Soviet action, which revealed that Zhukov was not willing to be a passive observer in the slow death of the city. By persisting with resource-sapping counterattacks, the Red Army pushed and pulled the besiegers around the perimeter while partisans attacked their lines of communication. Leeb struggled to apply his force as he wished and felt the consequences of having lost 60,000 men since 9 July. A combination of stretched lines of communication, resource difficulties and tiredness in the face of stubborn defence resulted in Army Group North being fought to a standstill. Even so, by the end of September, the city had food for just three more weeks and was totally dependent on its Lake Ladoga lifeline. So began one of the longest and most deadly sieges in modern warfare.

After Kiev had been taken and Leningrad contained, Army Group Centre could restart its operations against Moscow. In the meantime, Bock's formation defended its position and prepared itself for a renewed offensive by resupplying and reorganizing – albeit without the two armoured formations that continued to be employed elsewhere. The Soviets, however, did not allow the Germans to undertake this without applying intense pressure on the formation, and throughout the late summer they counterattacked Smolensk. In the resultant battle, large tracts of territory did not change hands, but it was important nevertheless. It was a passionate, destructive struggle after which, Werth reported, 'every village and every town had been destroyed, and the few surviving civilians were now living in cellars or dugouts'. During it, Zhukov launched what he called his 'first independent operation', an attack that was, he said, 'the first test of my operational-strategic ability in the great war with Hitlerite Germany'. The Yelnya Offensive in mid-August was one of the most noteworthy German reverses to date and the first successful planned Soviet offensive of the war.

Although hailed as a great victory, its impact was far from decisive but it did break the encirclement of Smolensk, made Bock react and upset his regeneration plans. More generally, the battle for Smolensk was a turning point in the grinding, attritional campaign that was unfolding. Casualties in the eight-week struggle around the city amounted to nearly 750,000 Soviets and 250,000 Germans. Arguing that the Wehrmacht was in a far poorer position to absorb these losses than the Red Army, Zhukov later wrote: 'The battle of Smolensk played a crucial role in the initial period of the Great Patriotic War . . . [as] the enemy striking groups had been exhausted.' The confrontation had exhausted and numbed the Germans, and gave them no cause to think that the coming attack on Moscow would be anything other than a bitter contest, which would stretch into the autumn and winter. The confidence of Halder, the man who had written that Russia had been all but defeated in two weeks, was draining away, as this diary entry reveals:

The whole situation makes it increasingly plain that we have underestimated the Russian colossus . . . [Soviet] divisions are not armed and equipped according to our standards, and their tactical leadership is often poor. But there they are, and as we smash a dozen of them the Russians simply put up another dozen. The time factor favours them, as they are near their own resources, while we are moving farther and farther away from ours. And so our troops, sprawled over an immense front line, without any depth, are subjected to the incessant attacks of the enemy.

Hitler's decision to halt Army Group Centre in order to seize the Ukraine and Leningrad has often been depicted as totally misguided. With Army Group Centre entering the autumn bloody and bruised, its armour further weakened by diversions, and the Soviets given the opportunity to strengthen their defences in and around Moscow, it is not difficult to see why. Yet it could be argued that Hitler's choice was inspired, for despite Zhukov's insistence that German losses were more detrimental to Berlin's ambitions than Soviet losses were to the defence of Moscow, this is not necessarily true. Red Army casualties sustained at Leningrad, Smolensk and particularly Kiev, amounted to another important step towards its defeat. It was only a step, however, and it remained to be seen whether the Wehrmacht could turn operational success into strategic victory. As Guderian later wrote: 'It all depended on this: would the German Army, before the onset of winter and, indeed, before the autumnal mud set in, still be capable of achieving decisive results?' Moscow beckoned.

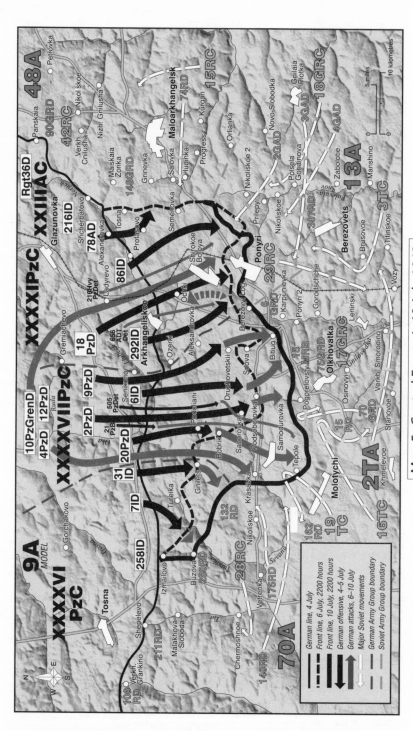

Map 5: Central Front, 4–10 July 1943

CHAPTER 4

Heading South

(Moscow to Stalingrad:
October 1941–early February 1943)

Alexander Werth was driven slowly along a frozen, debris-strewn avenue, which ran parallel to the Volga. He gazed at the line of shattered trees, the destroyed tramcars and jumble of crushed, burned-out buildings. His car passed Stalingrad's ruined railway station, which had changed hands so many times during the recent fighting, before entering the main square where he spied a badly damaged statue of smiling, dancing children around a crocodile.

Werth had just turned 41 years old. The Russian-born BBC correspondent had fled to Britain just after the revolution but retained a deep love and respect for Russia and her population. He had a wonderful ability to empathize with people, which encouraged him to view the war through the eyes of those involved and provide an insight into their hopes, their fears, their lives – and the circumstances of their deaths. In a corner of the square he rifled through a heap of letters, maps and books that lay discarded on the frozen ground. The images of a small child running through a sunny field and a smiling mother proudly holding her baby were tucked between the pages of a Catholic prayer book. Walking between pummelled apartments towards another square, Werth stumbled across the corpse of a German soldier lying across the pavement. 'His legs still seemed to be running,' he wrote, 'though one was now cut off above the ankle by a shell; with the splintered white bone sticking out of the frozen red flesh, it looked like something harmlessly familiar from a butcher's window. His face was a bloody frozen mess, and beside it was a frozen pool of blood.' Such horrors were not new to Werth. He had visited many battlefields, but he could not forget the particular savagery of the fighting at Stalingrad, and the corpses reminded him that Field Marshal Friedrich Paulus had surrendered just days before. Here was a city of the dead proposing that mankind was doomed having played out one last great act of self-destruction. Now it was silent, 'as though a raving lunatic had suddenly died of heart failure'.

Werth continued to roam the desolate streets, trying to make sense of 'Stalin's great victory'. He happened upon the skeleton of a horse in the forlorn porch of the Army Red House. 'Here one realized particularly clearly,' he later wrote, 'what the last days of Stalingrad had been to so many of the Germans.' He watched as a pathetic human figure crouched over a cesspool near a ragged pile of yellow, wax-like corpses. Hastily pulling up his pants, the emaciated body stole away through a door to a basement. As he passed, Werth says:

I caught a glimpse of the wretch's face – with its mixture of suffering and idiot-like incomprehension. For a moment, I wished the whole of Germany were there to see it. The man was perhaps already dying. In that basement into which he slunk there were still two hundred Germans – dying of hunger and frostbite . . . And there seemed a rough but divine justice in those frozen cesspools with their diarrhoea, and those horses' bones, and those starved yellow corpses in the yard of the Red Army House at Stalingrad.

As the Battle of Smolensk drew to a close in early September 1941, the Red Army was still fighting hard across the front, and continued to occupy Hitler's geographical objectives. With daylight hours shortening and a distinct chill in the air, the Germans had no time to lose. On 6 September Führer Directive No. 35 announced that an attack would be launched to capture Leningrad, the Wehrmacht would advance deeper into the Ukraine towards Rostov, take the Crimea and prepare for an attack on Moscow. The Soviet capital now became Berlin's focus and planners worked to develop an offensive that would realize Hitler's aim – that '[t]he name Moscow will disappear forever'.

Operation Typhoon sought to wrap up the Red Army defending Moscow – the Briansk, Western and Reserve Fronts – and as such followed the same pattern as those that had gone before. Moscow was to be encircled in a massive double envelopment. The Third and Fourth Panzer Armies were to envelop defenders west of Vyazma before swinging north of Moscow, while the Second Panzer Army was to create a pocket at Briansk before advancing south of Moscow via Orel and Tula. Yet although the Germans had husbanded two million men, 14,000 artillery pieces, over 1000 tanks and 1,390 combat aircraft during Army Group Centre's pause, two months had not been long enough to gather together all of the supplies required for the attack. Nevertheless, Bock counted on his forces being superior to the defending Red Army troops in both numbers and quality. It was a sound assumption. The Red Army consisted of 1.25 million men – a poorly organized mix of veterans, volunteers and reservists – armed with 7,600 guns and mortars, 990 tanks and 667 combat aircraft. The lack of equipment and weaponry was chronic. Indeed, one political officer remembers: 'After very severe battles we had to send our soldiers back into the field to gather the dead with their weapons so that we could use them again the next morning.'

Nevertheless, Soviet lines of communication were short, the troops' motivation was high and, critically, they were more used to operating in the colder weather that was setting in. The Soviets had also spent the two-month respite building strong defences to protect Moscow. The front-line positions were backed by the half completed Mozhaisk line, which stretched from Kalinin to south of Kaluga (some 60 to 80 miles from the capital). The area incorporated Borodino, site of a battle fought on 7 September 1812 in which Napoleon overcame Moscow's defenders, but he ultimately failed to destroy the Russian army.

Operation Typhoon opened on 30 September when the Second Panzer Army thrust into the Briansk Front and by the end of the following day had advanced nearly 50 miles. With the Red Army fixed to the south of the capital, the Third and Fourth Panzer Armies began their advance on 2 October. Believing that he was on the cusp of greatness, Hitler informed his troops:

Today begins the last great decisive battle of this year. In it we will destroy the enemy and, in so doing, England, the instigator of this whole war . . . We are thus lifting from Germany and Europe the danger that has hovered over the continent ever since the times of the Huns and later the Mongol invasion.

Within two days, the Third Panzer Army had advanced 30 miles and the Fourth Panzer Army a stunning 48 miles into the Western Front's defences. Despite Stalin's concerns, it was not until Hoth and Hoepner were approaching Vyazma on 5 October that he authorized a withdrawal. As at Kiev, it was too late – the Supreme Commander seemed to believe that he had an endless pool of trained troops – and the Germans trapped the 19th, 20th, 24th and part of the 32nd Armies. The Second Panzer Army, meanwhile, had penetrated to a depth of 120 miles and threatened Orel. Vasily Grossman witnessed the city's population trying to escape:

> There are aircraft over [Orel]. Trucks. People carry children in their arms. Children sitting on bundles. [There is a constant] rattling noise during the night: the city is on the move . . . vehicles and carts move without stopping. In the morning the city is gripped by horror and agony, almost like typhus.

Having had a steam bath, Grossman left the city and ran into chaos just hours before Guderian's reconnaissance force arrived. Grossman noted in his journal: 'I thought I'd seen retreat, but I've never seen anything like what I am seeing now, and could never imagine anything of the kind. Exodus! Biblical exodus!' Meanwhile, 17th Panzer Division captured the Briansk Front headquarters, although its commander, Lieutenant-General A.I. Eremenko, and his adjutant just managed to escape. The two men evaded capture and after several days reached the headquarters of the 3rd Army. Here, wounded in the arm, Eremenko fought until airlifted to safety after the 3rd and 13th Armies were encircled on 7 October.

The Germans had scored major victories at Vyazma and Briansk with perhaps 750,000 Soviet troops being overrun together with 6000 guns and mortars and 830 tanks. A 300 mile wide breach had been unceremoniously torn in the Soviet defences. Sensing this success, Hitler addressed an audience at the Berlin Sportpalast on 4 October. It was his first speech to the nation since the start of the invasion. He announced that in 'the greatest battle in the history of the world' the Soviet Union was beaten, and with cheers resounding around the hall, added that she 'would never rise again'. Six days later Hitler's press chief, Otto Dietrich, spoke to the foreign press corps in the Propaganda Ministry in Berlin. After a theatrical entrance, he produced a vast map of the Soviet front from behind a red velvet curtain and read Hitler's words to the eager correspondents. Dietrich explained that the last vestiges of the Red Army had been 'trapped in two steel vices', which were being tightened every day by the German forces. Beyond them was 'undefended space', which the German troops were preparing to fill. Neutral pressmen shook their heads in disbelief, their glum expressions revealing their horror, while others rose to their feet and gave Nazi salutes. Headlines read: 'CAMPAIGN IN EAST DECIDED! THE GREAT HOUR HAS STRUCK!'

However, the situation was not as predestined as the German people were being led to believe. Some Red Army troops remained in position, ready to lay down their lives in defence of Moscow, and they were not as downhearted by the drizzly rain that began to fall as were the over-stretched Wehrmacht soldiers. As Vasily Grossman said: 'everyone is happy once again. The Germans must get stuck in our hellish autumn, both in the sky and on the ground.' But first the rain washed in General Georgi Zhukov, fresh from his success in setting the Red Army's defences in Leningrad. Arriving on 6 October to do the same for Moscow, his energy, charisma and know-how immediately produced results. He took charge of a merged Western and Reserve Front command consisting of a mere 90,000 men (all that was left from the Battle of Smolensk), and as one of his junior staff officers, Captain Pavlik Boklov, testifies:

After the enormous set-back of Viaz'ma and the German encroachment on Moscow the headquarters was very low. We did not know how we were going to resist the enemy armour and felt despondent . . . Zhukov's arrival, however, immediately changed our mood. He was like a whirlwind through the place and made us believe not only that we could save Moscow, but we would save Moscow. A new energy filled the place and propelled us forward through days of great darkness.

Whatever concerns Zhukov had about the precarious Soviet situation, he left for Stalin. 'The main danger,' he suggested to the Supreme Commander on 8 October, 'lies in the weak Mozhaisk defence line. Because of this, enemy armoured troops may suddenly show up near Moscow. We must bring up forces from every place possible to the Mozhaisk line.' Stalin agreed, but although reserves were rushed forward from other fronts, the Germans were already engaging Zhukov's stretched Mozhaisk positions. The battle to break through was fragmented and confused, with heavy casualties on both sides, but German pressure eventually punctured and then breached the position.

Throughout the middle of October, villages and towns fell to Army Group Centre – Kaluga, Borodino, Kalinin and Mozhaisk – forcing the Soviets back behind the next line of defence, which stretched longitudinally from the 'Moscow Sea' through Naro-Fominsk down to Tula. After that, the Germans would have to overcome another set of positions 18 miles from the centre of Moscow, then a suburban defensive belt, a rear defensive zone and, in the city itself, a complex system of barricades and strong points. These defences were being frantically built by 600,000 office workers, factory workers and peasants. With younger men having already been taken for military service, much of the work was done by women, for whom Zhukov was full of praise:

> [T]housands upon thousands of Moscow women, not particularly suited for the arduous job of sapping, who had left their comfortable homes to dig anti-tank ditches and trenches, put up barricades, construct 'asparagus' and other obstacles and carry sandbags. Mud stuck to their feet and to the wheels of the barrows in which they carried earth. Mud stuck to the blade of the spade making it unwieldy in the feminine hands.

Embarking on their battles through these defences during the last week of October, Bock's men made fair progress in a narrow sector some 40 miles east of the capital, but as the rain continued to fall, attacks began to stutter elsewhere. Helmuth Pabst marched into Kalinin with his unit on 24 October and noted: 'The road bears the stamp of war: destroyed and abandoned equipment, tattered and burnt-out houses, enormous bomb craters, the pitiful remains of men and animals.' This northern sector proved particularly difficult to move through, while in the south Guderian's Second Panzer Army was targeted by counterattacks outside Tula. Soviet obstinacy was already undermining Typhoon by the time worsening weather robbed it of what little momentum it had left. The *rasputitsa* (time without roads) led to atrocious fighting conditions. Kit was permanently soaked, weapons rusted, hands were puckered, everything was covered in slime and illness was rife. Army Group Centre received 23 train-loads of food and equipment each day – a third of that required – but even this was difficult to transport to where it was needed because roads from the railhead became choked with mud and immovable vehicles. Guderian noted: '[the] roads rapidly became nothing but canals of bottomless mud, along which our vehicles could only advance at snail's pace and with great wear to the engines.' Erhard Raus concurred and later wrote:

[C]art and dirt roads became impassable, and major roads soon became mud-choked. Supply trucks broke through the gravel-topped roads and churned up the traffic lanes until even courier services had to be carried out with tracked vehicles. By the height of the muddy season, tractors and wreckers normally capable of traversing difficult terrain had become helpless, and attempts to plough through the muddy mass made the roads even more impassable . . . Eventually only horse-drawn vehicles could move.

By late October, Raus's 6th Panzer Division had suffered substantial vehicle losses, most caused by wear and tear on components that had seen his tanks across 700 miles of the Soviet Union but were increasingly difficult to replace. Indeed, a paltry 35 per cent of all Wehrmacht vehicles were operational across the front by this stage, and having sustained 686,000 casualties (one fifth of their original Barbarossa force plus all replacements received since 22 June) just 83 of 136 German divisions were up to strength. In some areas the offensive ground to a halt, and to add to the woes of the Wehrmacht in particular, snow fell increasingly heavily with every passing week. Although initially thawing, making the wet conditions even worse, by early November it was settling – the first blast of what was to be an extraordinarily harsh winter. When commanders demanded anti-freeze for their vehicles and warm clothing for their troops, there was silence from Berlin. Morale plummeted with the temperature and Guderian noted that the mood of his men was 'a contrast to the high spirits in evidence at OKH and Army Group Centre!' The poorly prepared Germans were hitting the wall as they entered the last stage of their marathon. Typhoon was running out of puff.

Whether Army Group Centre had the strength to push on around Moscow was highly debatable, but postponement or withdrawal at this point was inconceivable to the High Command when the prize was so close. Nevertheless, an operational pause was deemed prudent to regroup, resupply and reorganize, beginning on 1 November until the roads froze. Then, Hitler said – not for the first time – the tanks would roll and 'Soviet resistance would be broken'. Guderian was not so optimistic and, frustrated by the situation, wrote:

> It is miserable for the troops and a great pity for our cause that the enemy should thus gain time while our plans are postponed until the winter is more and more advanced. It all makes me very sad. With the best will in the world there is nothing you can do about the elements. The unique chance to strike a single great blow is fading more and more, and I do not know whether it will ever recur. How things will turn out, God alone knows.

The Soviets, though, were taking the German threat seriously, and with good reason. Throughout October the defences had continued to be strengthened while engineers prepared to demolish the city if the worst happened; civilians continued to be evacuated along with national treasures, archives and Lenin's embalmed corpse. The General Staff and government both headed for new billets farther east. During this period, new panic had gripped Moscow, and the *Red Star* exhorted defenders to 'stand firm and fight to the last drop of blood' as 'the riff-raff armour of ruined Europe is being thrown against the Soviet Union'. On 13 October Colonel-General Alexander Shcherbakov, apparatchik and the soon to be Director of the Soviet Information Bureau, spoke at a meeting to encourage the population to mount the barricades and increase production, saying, 'Let us not shut our eyes. Moscow is in danger.'

The panic reached its peak three days later when a communiqué broadcast in Moscow announced 'During the night of October 14–15, the position on the Western Front became worse' and noted the large number of German tanks breaking through the defences. Rumours were rife that Stalin had fled, that he had been arrested, that there had been a *coup d'état*. That day Alexander Werth witnessed 'black snow' in the capital caused by the incineration of government paperwork and a 'great skedaddle' as bosses left their factories. Roads out of Moscow were blocked, railway stations became dangerously overcrowded, there was a run on the banks and empty shops were looted. It was a potentially explosive situation that needed to be quickly and deftly controlled. Nevertheless, a declaration on the following day that Stalin remained ensconced in the Kremlin 'working towards victory' and would not leave immediately brought stability. The visible presence of NKVD teams further underlined the image that the regime wanted to portray: nothing had changed. A state of siege was declared – the flight and chaos *would* end, the fight *was* to continue and the Germans *would* be repulsed.

This new strength was underscored by Stalin's insistence – much to the chagrin of the generals – that the annual 7 November Red Square parade, which commemorated the anniversary of the Revolution, would still be held. It was preceded by the usual ceremony, not at the Bolshoi Theatre as customary but in the ornate hall of the Mayakovsky Square subway station on Gorky Street to protect it from air raids. Here on the evening of 6 November, Stalin once again called for support for a total 'Great Patriotic War' and for the Soviet people to give their all for the war effort. The Supreme Commander said: 'If [the Germans] want a war of extermination they shall have it!' When the echoing applause died down, he continued: 'Our task now will be to destroy every German, to the very last man! Death to the German invaders!' Warming to his theme, he continued: 'Let us fight to liberate the nations groaning under the yoke of Hitlerite tyranny! Long live our Red Army and Red Fleet! Long live our glorious Motherland!' Repeating the words of his July speech, which were fast becoming a national slogan, he ended by saying: 'Our cause is just. The enemy will be beaten. Victory will be ours.' The audience was exhilarated, even though Stalin had just committed his nation to a war of annihilation.

The Red Square parade the following day took place in heavy snow and to the sound of muffled gunfire from the front 40 miles away. It was not easy to find the troops, tanks and artillery to make a show of strength, but it was done. Indeed, their task completed, the units involved – all armed for battle – left the square and were immediately directed to the fighting front. The parade was a great act of defiance and reinforced Stalin's zealous words of the previous evening with a reassuring show of flesh and metal. But the military situation remained serious, so serious that the Supreme Commander asked Zhukov, 'Are you sure we'll be able to hold Moscow? It hurts me to ask you that. Answer me truthfully, as a Communist.' Zhukov replied, 'We'll hold Moscow by all means. But we'll need at least two more armies and another two hundred tanks.' 'It's good that you are so confident,' Stalin said, and authorized the force he needed. In reality, Zhukov was not at all confident.

In such circumstances, the difference between success and failure can be found in small decisions. It was with some concern, therefore, that in the midst of preparing to face a renewed German attack, the commanders received Stalin's fresh order. Perhaps buoyed by the arrival of 150,000 reserves, he demanded that a series of spoiling attacks be mounted on the Germans, so interrupting preparations to defend the city. Zhukov was extremely unenthusiastic. Konstantin Rokossovsky, talented young commander of the 16th Army – one of those formations tasked with the operation – later noted:

What [Stalin] was thinking when he gave the order to attack, I do not understand even today. Our forces were very limited, and we were given no more than a single night to prepare for the attack. My arguments for postponing or cancelling the attack, or at least for extending the period of preparation, were ignored.

Starting on 11 November, although there were some local tactical successes, the pre-emptive attacks failed. None of the panzer armies were damaged and the battered Soviet formations were left poorly positioned to repel the expected renewal of the German onslaught. The November fighting was intense and conducted in desperately cold conditions – temperatures dropped to -31°F (-35°C). Muddy roads and tracks were transformed into rutted nightmares, which shook carts, gun limbers and trucks to breaking point. Both sides abandoned attempts to hold a continuous line and groups of men huddled together for warmth in ruined villages, dreading the order to move out and attack through waist-deep snow. Pabst wrote at this time: 'The snow is falling thickly and silently; it no longer blows about so much. It deadens all noise and it blinds you.' German commanders, particularly those in motorized and armoured units, complained that their troops, machines and equipment were not designed for such low temperatures, and Bock reported that his men had still not received winter coats. In such conditions it was not uncommon for entire platoons, and even battalions, to be blighted by frostbite and cold-related illnesses. Indeed, Guderian lost twice as many men through the cold as he did from enemy action during this period. Harald Henry had complained bitterly about the heat and dust of the summer but now he had something very different to rail against:

> From a quarter to six until two in the morning, with only a short pause, we were out in a blizzard. It penetrated our coats, our clothing gradually got soaked through, freezing stiff against our bodies. We were feeling unbelievably ill in the stomach and bowel. The cold soon exceeded all bounds. Lice! Frost gripped my pus-infected fingers.

Karl Hertzog recalls:

> I could never get warm, but it was no use complaining. We were all in the same situation. It wasn't just the cold itself that caused the problem – nipped fingers and noses – it was the sleep deprivation that it caused. We snatched a few minutes' sleep here and there before having to stand up and move our limbs to get some warmth into them . . . On one occasion I awoke to find one man quite dead. Killed by the intense cold.

Grossman wrote of a deep, black Red Army humour that was displayed at this time:

> Germans, frozen to death, lie on the roads of our advance. Their bodies are absolutely intact. We didn't kill them, it was the cold. Practical jokers put the frozen Germans on their feet, or on their

hands and knees, making intricate, fanciful sculpture groups. Frozen Germans stand with their fists raised, or with their fingers spread wide. Some of them look as if they are running, their heads pulled into their shoulders . . . One of them is in his underwear.

The Germans found what they could to provide insulation for their lightly clad bodies. The dead were stripped of their clothing, newspaper was stuffed into boots and under jackets, strips of material were used as scarves, and civilian clothing was worn whenever it could be found. The Soviets were hardly better prepared for the cold weather, even if they were more used to it. One freezing infantryman wrote to his mother, with a notable lack of sensitivity: 'Seven of our lads have frostbite in their legs. They're in hospital now. We had to go seven days without a crust, we were exhausted and starved. I've done nothing since I got back but eat. My legs have started swelling up a bit at night. I eat a lot, and my stomach aches all the time.' Stalin and Shaposhnikov did what they could to supply the troops with the special clothing that they needed, but industry could not keep up with demand. Felt boots (*valenki*), padded jackets and trousers, white camouflage capes, fur gloves and warm hats saved thousands of lives during the war, but initially they were reserved for the new armies that were forming. Werth was kitted out with the best clothing, but even he found conditions barely tolerable.

Your breath catches. If you breathe on your glove, a thin film of ice immediately forms on it. We couldn't eat anything, because all our food – bread, sausage and eggs – had turned to stone. Even wearing *valenki* and two pairs of woollen socks, you had to move your toes all the time to keep the circulation going. Without *valenki*, frostbite would have been certain, and the Germans had no *valenki*. To keep your hands in good condition, you had to clap them half the time or play imaginary scales . . . As you sit there in the van all huddled up and feeling fairly comfortable, you cannot bear to move, except your fingers and toes, and give your nose an occasional rub; a kind of mental and physical inertia comes over you; you feel almost doped. And yet you have to be alert all the time.

The German attack on Moscow was reignited on 15 November. The Second Panzer Army made an initial surge forward but found it ever more challenging to keep the leading 50 tank brigade supplied with fuel. Deep snow and the exceptional resilience of the Red Army often slowed Guderian's advance to a crawl, but towards the end of the month his formation was attempting to encircle Tula from the east. Blizzards, local enemy counterattacks and troubling intelligence that Soviet reserves were moving into the area led Guderian to ask Bock for his offensive to be halted. His request was declined, and on 27 November, those reserves – 1st Guards Cavalry Corps – struck hard and quickly ended the Second Panzer Army's prospects of taking their objective.

The Third Panzer Army, meanwhile, deftly forced the 30th and 16th Armies apart and compelled a withdrawal. Klin was taken on 23 November and by the end of the month several small bridgeheads had been established over the Volga–Moscow Canal, just 21 miles from the Kremlin. Advancing on Hoth's right flank from an assembly point due west of the capital, the Fourth Panzer Army set about kicking in Moscow's front door. Hoepner's men made slow but costly progress against the 16th Army. It was during this time that 28 men of Major-General Ivan Panfilov's 316th Rifle Division, led by a political commissar, supposedly halted a German armoured attack and knocked out up to 18 tanks. The men were made 'Heroes of the Soviet Union' and were seen as the embodiment of the Red Army's bravery, even though it was far more likely that the panzers had been stopped by 350 men, albeit armed with just four anti-tank guns. By 30 November, the Fourth Panzer Army had battled its way through to Krasnaia Poliana, and the 6th Panzer Division's five remaining tanks were a mere nine miles north of Moscow. From here, the officers studied the city's spires through their field glasses.

General von Bock had achieved a remarkable feat of arms in getting two of his panzer armies to the gates of Moscow, but remained some distance from achieving the aims of Operation Typhoon. The Red Army had tottered and swayed as the Wehrmacht's punches crashed into its battered frame, but did not collapse. The Soviet troops' toughness bought precious time, and the pressure on hideously taut German lines of communication ensured acute shortages in all formations as fatigue affected every limb. By early December, a frozen Army Group Centre had seized up. Hitler had to make a decision about what to do next. He was aware of increasing calls from commanders to withdraw their exposed forces to positions more conducive to defence to see out the winter.

Rundstedt asked for the same for his overextended Army Group South. During the autumn his Eleventh Army had pushed into the Crimea and, after some extremely bloody fighting, occupied it all except for Sevastopol. The Sixth Army, meanwhile, had advanced against an enemy struggling to retain its cohesion after Kiev, and on 25 October had seized the city of Kharkov. Forging on, Rundstedt's force had surged 50 miles beyond the Northern Donets by the end of the month, while to its south, the First Panzer and Seventeenth Armies pressed on west of the Mius River and attained a position from which to capture Rostov, the gateway to the oil resources of the Caucasus. The subsequent push to the city, however, was far from convincing. In common with every other German formation on the front at the time, supply problems, tiredness and robust Soviet defence had combined to hamper their momentum. Rostov fell on 21 November but Kleist's First Panzer Army was incapable of consolidating its gain and a Red Army counterattack sent it reeling back. That shock prompted Rundstedt to ask Hitler for permission to withdraw his weak and vulnerable formation to winter defences on the Mius without delay.

Hitler's Army Group commanders had advanced up to 720 miles

and could go no farther. Having suffered 743,000 casualties since the launch of Operation Barbarossa, most panzer divisions were reporting fewer than 20 operational tanks by early December and there was a widespread lack of food, ammunition and fuel. Faced with the reality of his worn-out troops' parlous situation, a frustrated Hitler halted the offensive on 5 December and authorized the limited withdrawal of Army Groups Centre and South. Guderian later wrote: 'Our attack on Moscow had broken down. All the sacrifices and endurance of our brave troops had been in vain. We had suffered a grievous defeat . . .' Hitler's gamble had failed, Barbarossa was dead – tripped up and ground down by its over-ambition and Soviet resilience.

The next stage of the battle caught the Germans completely by surprise. Believing that the Red Army was on its knees, the Army Group Centre commanders, although unable to inflict the *coup de grâce*, did not think their enemy was capable of much more than licking its wounds. On 1 December an OKH assessment read: 'The enemy facing Army Group Centre is at present incapable of mounting a counter-attack without bringing forward substantial reserves' and Commander in Chief of the German Army Brauchitsch said that the Red Army possessed 'no large reserve formations'. But as Typhoon choked, new Soviet forces *were* in place. Stalin had been canny. Resisting the temptation to feed his reserve armies into the battle for Moscow pell-mell, he cautiously husbanded them for a massive counterattack. At the end of October the Stavka had ordered the formation of nine reserve armies, including nine tank brigades, 49 tank battalions and more than 100 ski battalions along with 90,000 individual replacements for the Reserve and Western Fronts, all to be ready by the end of November. The individual replacements had fortified Moscow's defences during November, but the remainder were not released until the end of the month with the majority slated for the counter blow. Zhukov believed that the timing of the retort was perfect:

The enemy is exhausted. But if we do not liquidate the dangerous enemy penetration, the Germans will be able to reinforce their forces in the Moscow region with large reserves at the expense of their northern and southern groups of forces, and then a serious situation can result.

The aim was to remove the threat to Moscow, nothing more, for as Marshal Shaposhnikov astutely observed, the Red Army still had many lessons to learn: '[we need] to assimilate the experience of modern war . . . Neither here nor today will the outcome of the war be decided . . . the crisis is yet far off.' Even so, Bock did not know what was about to hit him.

On 5 December, attacking through swirling snow, Soviet artillery targeted known German weak points. The Germans were torn from their positions and forced to withdraw, pursued by winter-clad infantry, vehicles adapted for all-weather driving and aircraft that benefited from being kept in heated hangars. The German soldiers, looking for shelter, found it difficult to dig in to the iron-hard ground. Erhard Raus directed his men to use their explosives:

I ordered the engineer battalion commanders to disregard the frost and to blast enough craters into the solidly frozen ground along the tentative main battle line to provide shelter for all the combat troops . . . The noise of the 10,000-pound explosive charges somehow gave the impression of a heavy artillery barrage. Fountains of earth rose all around, and dense smoke filled the air.

Others sought refuge in ruined villages, which were immediately targeted by Soviet guns and screaming multi-barrelled rocket launchers. The Katyusha (Little Katie – from a song made famous by forces sweetheart Lidiya Rusanova, who reportedly paid for two batteries herself) delivered a fearsome amount of explosives all at once and had a great psychological impact. Mikhail Alexeyev, a Russian infantryman, wrote of his first encounter with them:

I had heard about the Katyushas, but never seen them in action. And so when I heard that hideous screech and hiss coming from somewhere behind me I couldn't help hunching down into my shoulders. I guessed what the noise meant, so I looked round and saw a majestic and awe-inspiring spectacle. It was as if . . . [they] let loose fountains of fire all at the same time. Then we saw something no less terrifying ahead of us: a line of flaming tornadoes, a good half a kilometre wide.

Bock was stunned. Caught cold, lacking manpower and with an airforce that strained to get airborne, the Germans initially struggled to react. The Third Panzer Army was hit hard and pulled back to Klin without orders, exposing the flank of the Fourth Panzer Army on its right. By the evening of 7 December the situation was so poor around Klin that Bock called 'even for the last bicyclist' to help him.

There was chaos, but it was quickly brought under control, and the ensuing battles say as much about the Red Army's limited offensive capability as they do about the Wehrmacht's inherent professionalism. The Red Army still preferred the control offered by straightforward frontal attacks rather than more tactically sophisticated fire and manoeuvre methods. The advance was slow and ponderous (two to 12 miles in the first two days) and where the enemy line was briefly broken, there was no exploitation. Over a period of 11 days, Zhukov's Western Front, on the Soviet left, managed to penetrate between 28 and 39 miles while Colonel-General Ivan Konev's Kalinin Front, on the right, covered a mere six to 13 miles.

However, the Second Panzer Army was also pushed into full retreat, despite having come close to encircling Tula, and several of its rearguard divisions were severely mauled. Guderian was despondent and, perhaps taking a swipe at the High Command, later argued:

> Only he who saw the endless expanse of Russian snow during this winter of our misery and felt the icy wind that blew across it, burying in snow every object in its path: who drove for hour after hour through that no-man's land only at last to find too thin shelter with insufficiently clothed, half-starved men: and who saw by contrast well-fed, warmly clad and fresh Siberians, fully equipped for winter fighting: only a man who knew all that can truly judge the events [that] occurred.

Soviet territorial gains achieved by the winter offensive were initially modest, but by the time the initiative petered out in early January 1942, it had succeeded in removing the immediate threat to Moscow from Army Group Centre, particularly around the northern and north-eastern approaches to the capital. Army Group Centre had been forced to withdraw in unprecedented disorder to new defences. Bock's force had lost 55,825 battle casualties, not a great number, but the experience was a chastening one for the German High Command and for the Wehrmacht. Front-line soldiers had been led to believe that it was just a matter of time before Moscow fell but after the events of winter 1941–42 many began to wonder whether the Führer's goals were still attainable. Bidermann went so far as to say that colleagues, 'regardless of rank or education, now believed that only the greatest skill and luck could bring us total victory'. Hitler had planned for the Red Army to be destroyed in 1941 and the failure to achieve this condemned the Wehrmacht to enter a new year not only with unfinished business in the West, but in the East as well. To make matters even more difficult, on 11 December 1941 Hitler had declared war on the United States in the wake of the Japanese attack on Pearl Harbor. Germany was now at war against two colossi, leading a despairing Guderian to write: 'The war was now really "total" enough for anyone. The economic and military potential of the greater part of the globe was united against Germany and Germany's feeble allies.'

The pressure was beginning to tell and Hitler was in the mood to replace those senior officers whom he perceived had failed him during Barbarossa. The ailing Rundstedt was replaced with General Walther von Reichenau, Bock by Field Marshal Günther von Kluge, and Leeb was retired on health grounds after handing command of the North to Colonel-General Georg von Kuechler. Brauchitsch suffered a heart attack, and found his appointment absorbed by the Führer himself. The army had failed to fulfil Hitler's wishes and would now be gripped and brought to heel. Guderian, a general who knew his own mind and would stand up to Hitler, was also sacked amid claims of an unauthorized withdrawal. He signed off with an order to his troops, which read in part:

> At this time when I am leaving you I remember our six months of battle together for the greatness of our land and the victory of our arms, and I recall with honour and respect all those who have bled and died for Germany . . . Good luck to you! I know that you will continue to fight as bravely as ever and that despite the hardships of winter and the numerical superiority of the enemy you will conquer. My thoughts will be with you in your hard struggle. You are waging it for Germany! Heil Hitler!

By the first week of January 1942, the total number of senior generals sacked by Hitler had reached 35.

On 5 January, as the Soviet attacks ran out of steam, Stalin called a meeting in his study to decide what to do next. It was not in his nature to relinquish the initiative having seized it, and buoyed by recent success he argued:

[Hitler has] prepared badly for the winter. This is the most favourable moment to go over to a general offensive. The Germans hope to hold our offensive until the spring so that they can resume active operations when they have built up their strength . . . Our task is therefore to give the Germans no time to draw breath, drive them to the West, and force them to use up all their reserves before spring comes because by then we will have new reserves and the German reserves will have run out.

The Red Army was to attack along the length of the front, from Leningrad to the Black Sea, with the main blow falling on the massive salient bulging towards Moscow and occupied by Army Group Centre. The Leningrad and Volkhov Fronts – established in December 1941 – would seek to liberate Leningrad and destroy Army Group North, while the Southwestern Front liberated Kharkov, the Donbas and the Crimea. Zhukov argued that it was an incredibly bold plan, considering Red Army weaknesses, but Stalin, inevitably, won the argument. Beginning just days later and foundering in the mud of the thaw at the end of March, the spring offensive proved both costly and unsuccessful.

The offensive against the Rzhev–Vyazma salient to the west of Moscow began on 10 January. The Soviets came close to trapping the Third and Fourth Panzer Armies but, once again, the Red Army was unable to finish the job and, having managed to survive the initial onslaught, the Germans hung on to both Rzhev and Vyazma, even though the bulge was reduced. Attempts to relieve the siege at Leningrad and destroy Army Group North also failed when the Volkhov Front tried to batter its way through the German defences only to become bogged down and then stall. The Southwestern Front, meanwhile, struck out to regain Kharkov and the Soviet Union's industrial heartland. Timoshenko pushed Army Group South back 50 miles beyond the Donets south of Kharkov, but German reserves arrived to stabilize the situation. Kharkov remained in German hands and the

Ukrainian offensive achieved little more than heavy casualties and a large exposed salient in the Soviet line. Further offensive action to the northeast of Kharkov merely established a second, smaller bridgehead across the Northern Donets. While this was going on, an amphibious assault by 40,000 men had re-established the Soviets on the Kertsch peninsula of the Crimea but, ultimately, the troops failed to encircle part of General Erich von Manstein's Eleventh Army, even though they frustrated German attempts to force the Sevastopol defences.

As a consequence of all this, Stalin's ill-founded spring offensive could be said to have achieved little, and had quickly degenerated into an unwieldy slogging match. It was a ham-fisted disaster, which led to the loss of another 444,000 Red Army troops but inflicted just 80,000 casualties on the Germans. Zhukov later summed up the Soviet mistake in one sentence: 'We had overrated the potentialities of our troops and underrated the enemy – he proved to be a harder nut to crack than we believed ...' But, he added, the experience was not wholly negative:

In severe, often unbelievably difficult, conditions our troops matured, accumulated battle wisdom and experience, and as soon as they received the minimum necessary technical means they turned from a retreating defensive force into a powerful offensive one.

Pausing to catch their breath after months of unrelenting fighting, both Hitler and Stalin planned their next moves. Soviet intelligence identified a renewed attack on Moscow from the Rzhev salient as most likely. The city remained an important centre and offered the Wehrmacht the opportunity to destroy large numbers of defenders. But Germany badly needed Soviet resources to maintain its war-fighting ability. Thus it was announced in Führer Directive No. 41 of 5 April: 'As soon as the weather and the state of the terrain allows, we must seize the initiative again . . . All available forces will be concentrated on the main operations in the Southern sector, with the aim of destroying the enemy before the Don, in order to secure the Caucasian oilfields and the passes through the Caucasus mountains themselves.' Hitler had deprived Stalin of millions of skilled workers, one third of his rail network, the rich grain-lands of the Ukraine and the industrial Donbas region, and now wanted to deprive him of the oil that the Germans so desperately needed.

Moscow, meanwhile, was wedded to the idea of launching offensive action whenever possible, but recognized that the Red Army was in no position to sustain another major attack that summer. Even so, Stalin believed that another attempt to regain Kharkov was both possible and desirable. Thus, gambling that Zhukov would be able to hold any renewed German attack from the Rzhev salient, a grateful Timoshenko prepared his Front for another Ukrainian operation. If Hitler could be denied the resources that he needed to prosecute a protracted war, Stalin fervently believed that the Wehrmacht would wither. In his May Day speech, the Supreme Commander made reference to the coming months being critical: 'The whole Red Army is to make 1942 the year of the final defeat of the German-fascist forces and the liberation of Soviet soil from the Hitlerite villains.'

Just before the renewed attempt to take Kharkov began, bad news arrived from the Crimea. The Soviet assault force had tried unsuccessfully to break through the German defences in the spring, and built up their numbers on the Kertsch peninsula to 260,000 men supported by 350 tanks, but in early May the Eleventh Army had struck back. By 21 May, the Red Army had lost its foothold on the peninsula and, with it, the only prospect of relieving Sevastopol. Three Soviet armies ceased to exist and the important naval base of Sevastopol was isolated and doomed. Bidermann took up position on a cliff opposite the emplacement Maxim Gorki before the ground assault to seize the city began:

The artillery, rockets, flak, and assault guns pounded the enemy positions for five days prior to the attack. Thirteen hundred guns opened fire on predesignated targets and field positions ... Never before or never again during the war would the German forces mass such artillery ... The barrages served to demoralize the enemy troops as well as to physically destroy their defensive capabilities.

The assault began on 8 June and a month later the last vestiges of resistance in Sevastopol had been wiped out. Manstein, the victorious German commander, was immediately elevated to the rank of field marshal by a delighted Hitler. For the Soviets, defeat in the Crimea was significant due partly to the loss of 280,000 men, but also to the release of the Eleventh Army for the Wehrmacht's next offensive drive.

The Soviet attempt to take Kharkov began on 12 May with a concentration of 640,000 troops, 1,200 tanks and 13,000 guns. Despite the selection of realistic objectives and a superiority of 3:1 in armour and infantry and 2:1 in artillery, the attack still failed. Basic errors included a lack of surprise, guns that were out of range of their targets and second echelon troops held too far behind the lines. Starting from the salients that had recently been created either side of the city, the attacks penetrated 12 miles to the north and 25 miles to the south. Nevertheless, the Germans retained their cohesion and their counterattacks became increasingly profitable as the Red Army's momentum waned. Zhukov later wrote:

Looking into the causes of the failure of the Kharkov operation, one can easily see that it stemmed from the underestimation of the grave situation in the South-Western strategic direction where sufficiently strong General Headquarters reserve should have been concentrated.

The Red Army was not well enough prepared for the operation while the Germans had recovered their poise far more quickly than Stalin had anticipated. The cost was enormous: 275,000 casualties, 650 tanks and 1,600 guns. Failure at Kharkov was another setback for Moscow. A total of 600,000 casualties had been sustained across the front in May, making 1.4 million since the beginning of the year. German losses for the same five months were around 190,000. Such a disparity was of considerable strategic concern to Stalin. Even with his greater depth of resources, at the current rate of attrition the Soviet Union would run out of manpower before Germany. To make matters worse, the losses in the eastern Ukraine handed Berlin the initiative in the area that had already been identified by Hitler as the sector in which the Wehrmacht would launch its next offensive action.

The tempo of operations for many of the German troops was extremely challenging. Here were young men whom their families would barely recognize. They lived in a brutal world where, as Karl Hertzog says, 'lives were a military currency that were traded and death was often seen as a blessed relief'. Helmuth Pabst found himself gradually hardened to life in the front line, and reflected:

On the whole, war hasn't changed. Artillery and infantry still dominate the battlefield. The increased fire-power of the infantry – automatic weapons, mortars and all the rest – it's not so bad as it's supposed to be. But you have to accept the basic fact, you're after another man's life. That's war. That's the trade. And it isn't so difficult. Again, because most weapons are automatic, most people don't realize the full implications of it: you kill from a distance, and kill people you don't know and don't see.

Pabst thought less and less about the likelihood of peace as the months passed, and became ever more fatalistic:

It's a strange life on this island in a foreign country. We have come to accept anything, no matter how strange, and nothing surprises us any more . . . It's a serious war – serious and sober. It's probably different from what you imagine; less terrible – because for us the things that are supposed to be terrible have not many terrors left. Sometimes we say: 'Let's hope it'll soon be over.' But we can't conceive that it'll be over tomorrow or the day after. So we shrug our shoulders and get on with the job.

By mid-1942 Pabst felt a comradeship with the fighting:

We are part of this war. It's a natural phenomenon. It was born and grew up, and when it wears out it will die. At first it was we who carried it along; now it's the war which carries us. We gave it a start, but in the end it has entered into us and made us its creatures. It has burnt out many things that were in us, and it will go on taking them away from us until we are reborn by it. It is wrong to fight against it; you mustn't look back, it only makes you sad and sick at heart. The only thing is to yield your soul to its power and make your peace with it. It's still stronger. But it will pass, like the rain.

Soviet civilians watched from their doors as Red Army units passed by. They occasionally nodded an acknowledgement as their gaze caught the eye of a soldier. Travelling at the rear, in search of a story, Grossman observed one forlorn figure eagerly scanning the faces of passing troops:

An old woman thought she might see her son in the column that was trudging through the dust. She stood there until evening and then came up to us. 'Soldiers, take some cucumbers, eat, you are welcome . . .' And they cry [these women], they cry, looking at the men walking past them.

Infantryman Fedor Tiomkin found the kindness of strangers both endearing and difficult.

> We were marching towards a river where we were to take up a defensive position in June 1942. We passed through a small non-descript place and it seems as if the entire population had crowded onto the road to stare at us. There was no cheering although one or two shouted encouragement for they knew that we were doomed. They also knew that if we were taking up positions close to their village, that they were doomed as well . . . As we were leaving the village a middle-aged woman ran up to me and handed me a loaf of bread and kissed me on the cheek. She had a tear in her eye and sobbed, 'For my son – my lovely boy.' I never saw her again but in that moment realized what terrible pain the nation was suffering as families were being torn apart. It reminded me of my family so far away. I tucked the bread into my jacket and began crying myself. I did not realize the stress that was building up in me. It was a release.

It did not matter what army a soldier served with, life in the front line was a stressful occupation – the fear of death and wounding; the loss of friends; the sights, smells and sounds of combat; sleep deprivation; the impact of the weather; the nutritionally deficient food; the responsibility; the unknown. The physical and mental strain all mounted up and sometimes, as Gottlob Bidermann wrote, men broke:

> A member of my gun crew, who had bravely served through all our previous engagements, suddenly scrambled to a far corner of our trench, pulled his helmet from his head, and screamed over the roar of explosions, 'I can't take it any more!' Foaming at the mouth and his eyes wide with terror, he struggled to his feet in an attempt to spring from the trench. I threw myself on him and

wrestled him to the ground as another shell exploded near the edge of the earthwork, sending white-hot splinters whistling through the air. Grinding his teeth, clawing and struggling wildly, he fought to escape. Rising quickly, I struck him hard across the face and threw myself on him once more. He lay motionless, staring wide-eyed at me, and I released him to seek shelter beneath the edge of the trench.

The man eventually sprang up and headed for the rear only to return to the unit later that evening as if nothing had happened. The incident was never mentioned again. Although rest and recuperation would have helped soldiers to cope with the lives that had been forced upon them, opportunities for home leave were rare and so any duties that took them away from the front line were savoured. Battalion commander Alarick Lindner testified:

> Time spent behind the lines was precious, although the men were often worked hard to cart supplies from place to place, dig trenches, relay roads or whatever, but they were safe. They slept, washed, wrote letters, laughed, relaxed a little ... We were given home leave for perhaps 10 days twice a year. Most men found it difficult. Their families were alien to them after the front, and their concerns seemed trivial compared to the life and death decisions that they had to make at the front. Some did not go home, but instead headed to a city where they got drunk and found the company of women.

Bidermann's excellent memoir does not demur from this view – the war consumed the men of the front line:

> The soldiers returned to the front [from home leave] dissatisfied, and sometimes disillusioned, as they came to realize that their

experience in war had altered them forever. They had learned that in Germany they were no longer at ease, that the friends and comrades of their units had become their family, and that the war had become their life.

The war dominated Hitler's life and he took a particularly close interest in the Eastern Front. Indeed, on 16 July the Führer moved from his Wolfsschanze headquarters at Ratenburg, East Prussia, to a new Führerhauptquartier near Vinnitsa in the Ukraine to oversee his summer offensive. This 'Wehrwolf' complex, constructed in the woods, proved muggy during the day and chilly at nights. It was a damp, mosquito-infested place. Occupants required daily doses of medication to ward off malaria. Log cabins and concrete bunkers were connected by underground tunnels, and defended by barbed wire, mines and sentry posts. All that its small community required was there: offices, conference rooms, a tea house, barber's shop, cinema, sauna and even an open-air swimming pool. Here the Führer's staff lived, worked and put up with his demands and his increasingly erratic moods. Hitler's daily routine differed little from that followed at the Wolfsschanze. He breakfasted alone before holding his 'noon' war conference, which could last for several hours. He ate a late lunch during which he often treated his companions to impromptu lectures and, therefore, ruined any respite that the break offered. Conferences and briefings continued after lunch and deep into the evening. Dinner, as a result, was rarely served before midnight – often a plate of vege-tables followed by apples (Hitler was vegetarian). He ate alone or with his long-suffering secretaries. Further meetings and discussions were held with his bleary-eyed staff into the early hours of the morning before he retired to bed at around 0400 hours.

Hitler's relocation was not unrelated to the deteriorating relationship that he had with his generals – a state of affairs underlined by his refusal to eat with them at Wehrwolf – and his desire personally to guide the 'politically reactionary' army to operational success in the Caucasus. By the early summer of 1942, OKH had been excluded from strategic decision making and become a voiceless administrative office that existed merely to effect Hitler's orders. In so doing, the commander in chief further distanced himself from pragmatic, professional advice and based his decisions on the advice of 'yes men' whom he had selected. The upshot was a Führer who was stretched extremely thinly across his burgeoning responsibilities, to the detriment of Germany's ability to function efficiently. As H.P. Willmott has argued, Hitler was 'head of state, executive, judiciary, party, armed forces and the army, and without the ability to trust competent subordinates sufficiently to delegate authority and without a cabinet system to plan, implement and supervise policy and to coordinate the various aspects of stagecraft, Hitler's direction of the war became increasingly arbitrary and erratic with the passing of time'. In the military sphere, Hitler's obsession with the war in the East was at the expense of other theatres, and his 'something will turn up' strategy, supported by an inefficient economy, was not conducive to long-term success. The result was that by mid-1942 Germany was no more prepared to fight a total war than it had been a year earlier. Russia had not fallen, blitzkrieg was fallible and Hitler was desperate for the resources with which to sustain his war effort.

Even as Hitler tightened the military's reins, Stalin was carefully loosening them. This did not mean that he relinquished control, far from it, but the Supreme Commander did offer his senior commanders greater scope to reveal their talents and experience. As historian Catherine Merridale says in her excellent insight into the Red Army during the Second World War, 'A new pragmatism was apparent everywhere . . . a new culture was slowly taking shape. Its key values were professionalism and merit.' There was a realization that the Red Army had to become more modern, to address its weaknesses by strengthening operational techniques and improving tactics. Here was the Soviet Union engaging in a 'dual strategy' that was developed for long-term success – the learning of lessons from previous battles to improve the performance of the armed forces and wear the enemy down. This was backed by growing industrial output as evacuated Soviet factories became productive once more. In 1942 they constructed 24,000 tanks and self-propelled guns, 127,000 guns and mortars and 25,000 aircraft. Over the same period the Germans produced 9,000 tanks, 12,000 guns and mortars and 15,000 aircraft.

Army Group South began its push to the Caucasus with half the strength that it had the year before – 68 weak infantry divisions and the equivalent of 10 panzer or motorized divisions attacked on a 400 mile front against the Southwestern and Southern Fronts, which consisted of a similar number of infantry divisions plus six tank corps. Even so, expecting operational surprise to unhinge a demoralized Red Army with the assistance of the majority of the tactical aircraft on the front at the time – some 3000 machines – the Führer again relied on blitzkrieg being successful. Hitler had been concerned for some time that the Soviets were able to escape from his forces' attacks and so undermine German operations, and he wrote in Directive No. 41:

> We must avoid closing the pincers too late, thus giving the enemy the possibility of avoiding destruction. It must not happen that, by advancing too quickly and too far, armoured and motorized formations lose connection with the infantry following them; or that they lose the opportunity of supporting the hard-pressed, forward-fighting infantry by direct attacks on the rear of the encircled Russian armies. Therefore, apart from the main object of the operation, in each individual case, we must be absolutely sure to annihilate the enemy by the method of attack and by the direction of the forces used.

What was fudged, in Hitler's desperation to destroy the Soviet defenders and take their oil, was supply. First, the Red Army had to be cleared along the Don south of Voronezh, then between Rostov and Stalingrad. Having taken those two cities, Army Group South would push south hundreds of miles into difficult terrain to seize the oil at Maykop and Astrakhan. Had the Soviets been prepared to grapple with the German offensive in a meaningful manner, Hitler's hopes could have been dashed extremely quickly but, true to form – both sides seemed hell bent on making the same mistakes time and time again – the Soviets disregarded solid intelligence gleaned from captured enemy plans and British interceptions of German signals. Instead, Stalin placed his defensive weight against Army Group Centre around Moscow while dismissing reports of 'German activity in the south' as 'a mere diversion'. The result was that, despite the Germans' befuddled and illogical plan for its summer offensive, which repeated many of the planning errors found in Barbarossa, the Red Army was unable to take the initiative because it was as underprepared to meet the German offensive as it had been 12 months earlier.

Operation Blau began on 28 June, and the Army Group South attack achieved some early success by crossing the Donets and pushing on towards the Don. On 23 July Voronezh was secured on the left and Rostov on the right, the latter providing a pivot upon which Reichenau's formation could swing through 90 degrees to advance through the Rostov–Stalingrad gap. The amount of ground that the Germans had taken was immense, but the opening of the offensive had not resulted in the major encirclement of Soviet forces that Hitler had demanded. The greater part of eight Soviet armies escaped encirclement west of the Don and Donets. Such had been the panic that the German offensive had engendered in the defending Red Army formations that, rather than standing and fighting, they had fled. Although this was later explained in Soviet histories as a calculated 'withdrawal from the punch' – a ploy that was used later in the year – the tactic was not being used deliberately at this stage. It was a worrying situation for Stalin, who had assumed that his army had matured into a reliable defensive instrument, and on 28 July he felt the need to reaffirm, in his Order No. 227, 'Not a step backward! . . . Each position, each metre of Soviet territory, must be stubbornly defended, to the last drop of blood. We must cling to every inch of Soviet soil and defend it to the end!' Ill-discipline had lost the Red Army critical parts of the Don and Donets coal basin and handed the Germans the strategic initiative.

An outbreak of influenza at Wehrwolf had claimed Hitler as one of its victims and by the time that Rostov had fallen, he was suffering from deliriously high temperatures. He had ordered that Army Group South be split into two separate commands. Army Group A on the German right was to destroy the enemy south of the Don and then 'occupy the entire eastern coastline of the Black Sea . . . force a passage of the Kuban, and occupy the high ground around Maykop and Armavir'. This was to be followed by an advance 'towards and across the western part of the Caucasus . . . as a force composed chiefly of fast-moving formations will give flank cover in the east and capture the Grozny area . . . Thereafter the Baku area will be occupied by a thrust along the Caspian coast'. Army Group B on the left, meanwhile, was to develop a 'thrust forward to Stalingrad, to smash the enemy forces concentrated there, to occupy the town, and to block the land communications between the Don and the Volga, as well as the Don itself'. Initially, the capture of Stalingrad had not been a key aim, but now Hitler had become drawn to the city as the Soviets had begun to build up forces in the area. Kleist said after the war:

> The capture of Stalingrad was subsidiary to the main aim. It was only of importance as a convenient place, in the bottleneck between the Don and the Volga, where we could block an attack on our flank by Russian forces coming from the east. At the start, Stalingrad was no more than a name on the map to us.

Ideally, Army Group B would have masked Stalingrad but since it was not strong enough, the plan had to be to neutralize the threat the troops concentrated there posed to its flank by entering the city. Hitler's ability to reinforce the attack in the south with Army Group Centre's resources was undermined by the Soviets' pinning them down north of Orel. Now Stalin tempted the Germans into the place that bore his name and so halved the force sent to capture the Caucasian oil.

The Sixth Army, its momentum thwarted by difficult lines of communication, reached the outskirts of Stalingrad on 23 August. Falling back into the city were the 62nd and 64th Armies, whose grimy troops looked shattered but ready to defend the city to the last. Grossman witnessed the preparation of defences, and later wrote:

> Those were hard and dreadful days . . . Men's faces were gloomy. Dust covered their clothes and weapons, dust fell on the barrels of guns . . . [t]hat was a terrible dust, the dust of retreat. It ate up the men's faith, it extinguished the warmth in people's hearts, it stood in a murky cloud in front of the eyes of the guns' crews . . . Trucks with grey-faced wounded men, front vehicles with crumpled wings, with holes from bullets and shells, the staff Emkas with star-like cracks on the windscreens, vehicles with shreds of hay and tall weeds hanging from them, vehicles covered with dust and mud, passed through the elegant streets of the city . . . And the war's breath entered the city and scorched it.

The Luftwaffe had already tried to flatten the city and left an inferno in its wake. 'Stalingrad is burned down,' Grossman continued. 'Stalingrad is in ashes. People are in basements. Everything is burned out. The hot walls of the buildings are like the bodies of people who have died in the terrible heat and haven't gone cold yet.' Nikolai Razuvayev recalled the heavy bombing: 'The ground under my feet was shaking. There was a continuous roaring on all sides, and fragments of bombs and broken stone were falling from the sky.' The more Hitler committed to the battle, the more he seemed to be fixated and blinkered by it. Taking the city became a personal challenge into which he was willing to throw more resources than its value demanded. Hitler justified his actions by advising the High Command that 'world opinion and the morale of our allies' demanded Stalingrad's capture, which was 'essential for Germany's ultimate victory'.

The Wehrmacht's interest in Stalingrad was not seen by Moscow as a threat, but an opportunity. By diverting so much of the Germans' offensive power to take the city, the Red Army was given the chance to fix it in position, and grind Army Group B down in place. If any one decision underlines the strategic importance that Moscow attached to the city, it was Zhukov's appointment at the end of August as Deputy Supreme Commander in Chief with orders to take control of the 'developing situation at Stalingrad'. Writing about it in his memoirs, Zhukov noted:

I knew that the Battle of Stalingrad was of an outstanding military and political importance. With the fall of Stalingrad the enemy command would be able to cut off the south of the country from the centre. We could lose the Volga which was a very important waterway, carrying large freight from the Caucasus. The Supreme Command was sending to Stalingrad all that it was possible to send.

Supplied by ferries across the River Volga, the 62nd and 64th Armies were hemmed in and forced apart by Paulus's Sixth Army during September. Attempts to reinforce them from the west side of the Volga were repulsed. The city's rubble-strewn streets ensured that the Fourth Panzer Army was forced to sit on the sidelines, protecting the southern approaches of Stalingrad, and the use of air power and artillery was limited by the close proximity of the protagonists, so the Battle of Stalingrad became an infantry action. Oberst Hans Doerr, Chief Liaison Officer with the Romanian Fourth Army, reported:

> The time for conducting large-scale operations was gone forever ... The mile as a measure of distance was replaced by the yard. Headquarters' map was the map of the city. For every house, workshop, water tower, railway embankment, wall cellar and every pile of ruins a battle was waged – one without equal even in the First World War ... The Russians surpassed the Germans in their use of the terrain and in camouflage, and were more experienced in barricade warfare for individual buildings.

It was what the commander of the 62nd Army, Lieutenant-General Vasily Chuikov, called 'The Stalingrad Academy of Street Fighting' in which a series of small actions were fought over tactically important points. The railway station, for example, changed hands many times and on one occasion was lost and retrieved several times in one day. Resource-sapping attacks quickly lost their shape in the crushed streets and counterattacks often succeeded. Troops picked their way through the debris and the shells of buildings in an attempt to dominate the ground, but attempts could be frustrated by a single sniper. These ruthless killers might lay in wait for hours – or even days – before pulling their trigger, and they became the scourge of the troops in the city. Fedor Tiomkin has said:

> It was not uncommon for German snipers to slow our attacks ... My platoon would be moving towards an objective – a slow process at the best of times – and a rifle round would crack. A man would fall to the ground. Another shot, another man down. We would throw ourselves to the ground trying to spot any movement which might give the sniper's position away. We rarely saw

them and had to try and work out where he was. Sometimes the attack stalled for so long that a man was sent forward to draw the sniper's fire so that we could spot it. If that man was lucky the sniper had moved or missed, but often he was hit ... On one afternoon three men were shot through the head in this fashion before we located the sniper. We hunted him down to a ruined office on the second floor of a building but he took his own life when he had him cornered.

Soviet sniper Anatoly Chekhov found his job difficult at first but quickly discovered that taking life was not as hard as he had expected:

When I first got the rifle, I couldn't bring myself to kill a living being: one German was standing there for about four minutes, talking, and I let him go. When I killed my first one, he fell at once. Another ran out and stooped over the killed one, and I knocked him down too ... When I first killed, I was shaking all over: the man was only walking to get some water! ... I felt scared: I'd killed a person! Then I remembered our people and started killing them without mercy ... I've become a beast of a man: I kill, I hate them as if it is a normal thing in my life. I've killed forty men, three in the chest, the others in the head. When you fire, the head instantly jerks back or to the side. He throws up his arms and collapses.

It was not uncommon for a soldier to be killed or seriously wounded on the day he arrived in Stalingrad, and a man who survived more than three days had earned the right to call himself a veteran. New and inexperienced troops were particularly vulnerable because they had yet to learn what Tiomkin called 'Stalingrad's rules of survival: how to move, how to react, how to live and how to kill in terrible conditions'. Casualty rates were appalling. German officer Joachim Wieder wrote in his memoir: '[T]he units of our corps suffered tremendous losses repelling fierce attacks ... The divisions occupying this sector were bled white and in most companies only about 30 or 40 men remained.' Chuikov found that the troops who were ferried across the Volga and into the city were understandably apprehensive. Interviewed by Grossman on the subject, the general said, 'Approaching this place, soldiers used to say, "We are entering hell." And after spending one or two days here, they say, "No, this isn't hell, this is ten times worse than hell."'

As the Sixth Army fought on in Stalingrad, Field Marshal Wilhelm List's Army Group A struck south towards the Black Sea, the Caucasus and Baku. During August, it conducted blitzkrieg across the Kuban and took the Novorossisk naval base (which allowed elements of the Eleventh Army to cross from the Kertsch peninsula and join the action), Stavropol and Maykop. By now the Red Army was deliberately 'trading space for time' and destroyed everything that might be of use to the First Panzer Army, including bridges, oil installations and the water supply. By the end of August, although the 1st Mountain Division had claimed Mount Elbrus (the highest mountain in Europe) for the Reich, Army Group A was left whimpering on dusty tracks that seemed to lead nowhere. Counterattacked by Red Army units, ambushed by partisan groups and made unwelcome by the local population, the advance of Army Group A stalled some 600 miles south of Stalingrad in the vicinity of Mozdok and well short of Baku. One junior officer, Elbert Hahn, who had served with distinction at Kiev, wrote in his journal:

We were relying on donkeys, mules and our few surviving horses for support. When there is no water, and often there isn't, the beasts die and the equipment that they are carrying is either crammed onto other animals or it is destroyed. The partisans use anything we leave against us and so we have to be careful ...

Further and further we go into the dusty recesses of this god-
forsaken land . . . We feel a long way from home and I have long
since forgotten why we are here.

The offensive was fast turning into a disaster and on 9 September Field
Marshal List was sacked, and Hitler asked whether the Führer was the
only man left with any 'loyalty to Germany [and an] aggressive fighting
spirit'. Taking personal command of Army Group A from his
Ukrainian headquarters, the former Western Front corporal ordered
further attempts to batter the formation through to its objectives
during the autumn. They met with stubborn resistance and very little
success. Colonel-General Franz Halder, the head of the Army General
Staff and a critic of the Caucasian adventure, could contain his fury no
longer. He was replaced by General Kurt Zeitzler.

By early November, Hitler was not a happy man. Stalingrad had not
fallen and Operation Blau had failed. Moreover, failure in the
Caucasus followed by the Allied occupation of French North Africa
had shattered his dream of linking up two parts of the German
armies in the Middle East. With Germany's offensive ambitions for
1942 in pieces, the Führer quit his Wehrwolf headquarters and
returned to the Wolfsschanze to direct a second winter of fighting in
the East. But first he needed to shore up his left flank on the Volga to
remove the threat of Army Group A being cut off between the
Caspian and Black Seas. The prospects of achieving this looked good
on 11 November, since Paulus's troops held 90 per cent of Stalingrad,
but the Wehrmacht had underestimated their enemy. The Soviets were
about to spring a trap.

Zhukov had been planning a counterattack since mid-September
when he listed his priorities: 'First, to continue wearing out the enemy
with active defence; second, to begin preparation for a counter-offensive in order to deal the enemy a crushing blow at Stalingrad to reverse
the strategic situation in the south in our favour.' For Operation

Uranus, Soviet pre-war operational methods were unpacked from storage and reinvigorated. Overseen by Zhukov, deception, security, camouflage (*maskirovka*), the concentration of overwhelming force at decisive points and all arms cooperation were highlighted as essential to an operation that sought to drive hard and fast into the enemy's rear. Forces secretly positioned either side of Stalingrad amounted to 1.1 million men, 13,500 guns and mortars, 900 tanks and 1,414 combat aircraft. They were to by-pass the bulk of the German armour and exploit the flanks held by inferior allied Romanian, Italian and Hungarian formations. The aim was to attain success at the operational level and in so doing offset German tactical mastery. The Soviets were becoming more savvy and that involved recognizing their own modest capabilities and limiting their converging attacks to a depth of just 90 miles. The Red Army had also learned that it needed to reconfigure its fighting power and so made its standard armoured formation the corps rather than the brigade, which doubled or trebled its clout. Moscow had great hopes for Uranus and if it was successful, there were plans to exploit it with operations to the Black Sea coast to isolate and then destroy Army Group A.

Operation Uranus stunned the Germans. The Red Army advanced their northern pincer against the Third Romanian Army in a heavy snowstorm on the morning of 19 November. Preceded by a devastating 80 minute bombardment from 3,500 guns – including 100 multiple rocket-launcher batteries – the onslaught shattered the enemy's communications, cohesion and morale. The Soviets broke through the Romanians in the early afternoon, and by the end of the day the defenders were being routed. Joachim Wieder, an intelligence officer in the Sixth Army, recalls:

The 19th of November will live in my memory as a day of black disaster. At the break of dawn on this gloomy, foggy day in the late autumn, during which lashing snowstorms were soon to appear . . . Russians attacked like lightning from the north and the following day from the east, pressing our entire Sixth Army into an iron vice.

The following day, the southern pincer struck against the Fourth Romanian Army with a similar result. Alfred Jodl, Chief of the Operations Staff at OKW, later admitted: 'We did not have the slightest idea of the Russian strength in that area. Previously there had been nothing there and suddenly a powerful blow, which proved decisive, was struck.' By 23 November, Zhukov's pincers met at Kalach. Some 290,000 troops from the Sixth Army and elements of the Fourth Panzer Army had been encircled in an offensive that was an ominous sign for the Wehrmacht. Joachim Wieder wrote: 'We have never imagined a catastrophe of such proportions to be possible.'

The Sixth Army was in dire straits. Caught with no winter clothing and little food and fuel, it was too weak to try to break out of its confines. But Hitler did not want Paulus to break out and instead directed him to establish 'Festung Stalingrad' – Fortress Stalingrad – and to 'dig in and await relief from outside'. Although he was placing this formation in a desperate situation, Hitler demanded that the Sixth Army pin and fix as many Soviet troops as possible around the Volga in order to give Army Group A the best possible chance to extract itself from the Caucasus. In the meantime, Field Marshal Erich von Manstein, the commander of Army Group Don – Paulus's new superior formation – would beg, borrow and steal whatever resources he could to try to effect a relief. However, Paulus was desperate for supplies and signalled:

Fuel will soon be exhausted. Tanks and heavy weapons then immovable. Ammunition situation strained. Food provisions sufficient for six days. Army intends to hold remaining area from Stalingrad to Don. Supposition is that closure of the

Southwestern Front succeeds and adequate provisions will be flown in.

The hapless Reichsmarschall Göring guaranteed that the Luftwaffe could provide the Sixth with what it needed to survive and fight, but it couldn't. Tasked with the job of resupplying the surrounded army, Luftflotte 4's commander, General Wolfram Richthofen, noted in his diary: 'The Sixth Army believes it will be supplied by the air fleet . . . Every effort is being made to convince the army that it cannot be done.' Attempts to resupply the formation were undermined by the lack of transport aircraft, appalling weather, Soviet fighters and dense concentrations of anti-aircraft guns – 266 Ju-52s and 222 other aircraft were lost in attempts to assist Paulus. He received an average of just 100 tons per day for the duration of the siege when he required prob- ably 15 times as much. Yet the Sixth Army fought on, its units ravaged by cold, starvation and disease as well as Red Army bullets, and its hope bound up in the arrival of Manstein's relieving force.

Army Group Don's Operation Winter Storm was doomed from the outset. Resources for the attempt were not plentiful as the Soviets began to further stretch the Germans with offensive action along the front. Beginning on 25 November and lasting into late December, Operation Mars sought finally to remove the Rzhev salient opposite Moscow and, possibly, provide a springboard for an attack on the German rear. Consisting of 800,000 Soviet troops and 2,350 tanks, the attack was anything but minor but it was clumsily handled and quickly deteriorated into a bloody slogging match. The 'Rzhev meat-grinder' eventually cost Stalin 500,000 men for little territorial gain and a mere 40,000 German casualties. But it did result in the Winter Storm strike force being limited to just two panzer divisions. One of them was Raus's 6th Panzer Division, whose commander, Lieutenant-General Erhard, later wrote: 'A task of historic magnitude was to be attempted, and the further conduct of the campaign hinged on its successful completion. Officers and men down to the lowest-ranking private were fully aware of this . . . all ranks were prepared to do their utmost to master this difficult assignment.' Although the Soviets were caught by surprise on 12 December, the first day of Manstein's thrust, torrid defence and poor weather caused the panzers to slow markedly thereafter.

Nevertheless, the Sixth Army heard about the push and its increasingly enfeebled troops were given another reason to resist the Soviet operations that were seeking to finish them off. Indeed, one infantryman in 376th Division wrote home: 'We're hoping to be out of this cauldron by Christmas . . . Dear parents, the war is soon going to be over. Once this battle is over, the war in Russia will be finished.' But there was no breakthrough by the relief column – the closest it got was 25 miles from the perimeter on 23 December – and the divisions were forced to withdraw in the face of a new Soviet offensive emanating from the Don, which blew a gap more than 100 miles wide in the German line. Zhukov called Winter Storm 'an absolute flop' and on the last day of 1942 looked forward to the development of his surge towards Rostov – and to the imminent elimination of the Sixth Army.

Paulus's Sixth Army fought in *Der Kessel* (cauldron) at Stalingrad, but the resilience of the troops was waning. Their hopes of relief had been dashed, supplies were exhausted and Soviet operations were choking the trapped Germans. General Chuikov later noted:

[U]p to the end of December, they continued to live in hope and put up a desperate resistance, often literally to the last cartridge. We practically took no prisoners, since the Nazis just wouldn't surrender. Not until after von Manstein's failure to break through did morale among the German troops begin to decline very noticeably.

Several Sixth Army officers shot themselves and the Nazi leadership made desperate attempts to extract members of their own family and friends. Their efforts often failed, not least because the crews of the few remaining aircraft that managed to land on Stalingrad's one remaining airstrip, ostensibly to evacuate a handful of the 50,000 wounded, were stormed by desperate men demanding to be flown to safety. The unassuming and softly spoken Paulus had no compunction in authorizing the execution of 364 men for cowardice in just one week. All able-bodied men were expected to fight, but without ammunition and sustenance they were useless. Some men turned to cannibalism and some even thought about eating their own body parts, as Wilhelm Beyer recalls: 'Even those accustomed to hunger, who knew how much pain the disappearance of the last small cushions of fat on the toes or elsewhere caused, seriously considered taking this action in defiance of orders.'

On 9 January, Paulus rejected a condition-riddled offer to surrender and directed that flags of truce were to be fired on. Remarkably, even as the remnants of the wrecked Army fell back to the city centre, some local counterattacks were delivered with considerable venom, but they could not stop the inevitable. Paulus capitulated on 31 January, just one day after his promotion to the rank of field marshal. He understood that no German field marshal had ever surrendered, but refused to commit suicide saying to one of his generals, 'I have no intention of shooting myself for this Bohemian corporal.' Of the 91,000 souls taken prisoner by the Soviets at Stalingrad, just 6000 survived the war to see Germany again.

The Battle of Stalingrad had been a titanic struggle, one of the bloodiest battles of the war, costing the most casualties – some 800,000 for Germany and her allies and some 1.1 million for the Soviets. According to Zhukov, the confrontation was comparable only to the Battle of Moscow. It was a major German defeat, a catastrophe that proved to be a vital turning point in the war, and a calamity so great that it could not be concealed from the German population. Most Germans knew of somebody who had perished there. The announcement of the defeat was greeted with despondency throughout the Reich and three days of national mourning were declared. On 2 February, German radio repeatedly played Siegfried's Funeral March from Wagner's *Götterdämmerung*.

The whole sorry episode raised questions about what Germany was doing in Russia. Soviet journalist Ilya Ehrenburg wrote: 'Up till then one believed in victory as an act of faith, but now there is no shadow of doubt: victory was assured.' Marianne Koch from Germany was a 26-year-old machine operator at the time of the battle. She recalls:

I had not questioned what we were doing until the end at Stalingrad. The defeat fell on us very hard. We had all been told that the war was going well and then this. It made me think whether what we were being told was true. No, I knew it was not all true, but Stalingrad awoke me and many others from our optimism, our ignorance. We began to see Germany and the war as it really was. Germany was fallible. Had Hitler's luck run out? We were frightened from that moment.

Marianne Koch had never met her father, who had been killed by a shell blast in the last days of the Great War, but cherished a letter that he had written to her just days before his death. Now she cherished a letter from her brother, who had written on 19 December from Stalingrad: 'The end is near. This cannot go on. Give my love to Mother for I cannot bring myself to write to her personally. We will all meet again in heaven. Always yours, Peter.' His body was never found.

To the Soviets, Stalingrad was a much-needed victory, which engendered pride in the Red Army, faith in the leadership and gave hope to a careworn people. In the space of just 12 months the Wehrmacht had been relegated from a threat to Moscow to a thinly stretched, resource-deficient force that had withdrawn in the face of Soviet offensive action. Although far from beaten, this was a remarkable turnaround in events and led to Stalin being selected as *Time* magazine's 'Person of the Year 1942'. The portrait that adorned the cover of the January 1943 issue showed a solid and dependable man, bearing the hint of a smile and a sparkle in his eye. It was captioned 'All that Hitler could give he took – for a second time', and its accompanying article read:

Only Joseph Stalin fully knew how close Russia stood to defeat in 1942, and only Joseph Stalin fully knew how he brought Russia through. But the whole world knew what the alternative would have been. The man who knew it best of all was Adolf Hitler, who found his past accomplishments turning into dust . . . Only Stalin knows how he managed to make 1942 a better year for Russia than 1941. But he did. Sevastopol was lost, the Don basin was nearly lost, the Germans reached the Caucasus. But Stalingrad was held. The Russian people held. The Russian Army came back with offensives that had the Germans in serious trouble at year's end.

Could this embryonic Soviet success be nurtured into something of greater strategic significance in 1943?

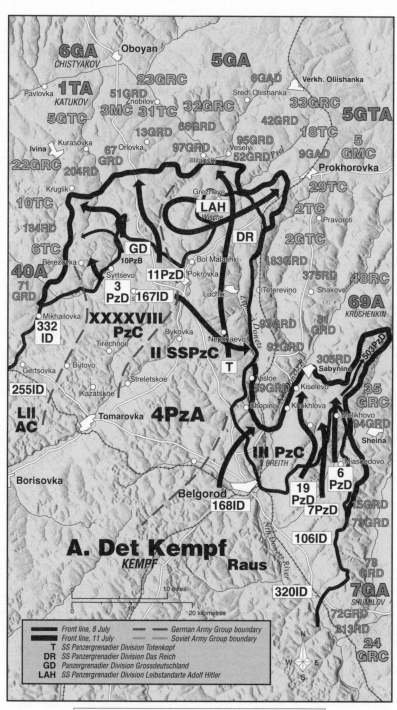

Map 6: Voronezh Front, 9 –11 July 1943

CHAPTER 5

Uneasy Calm

(Zitadelle Preliminaries: February–July 1943)

Recently arrived SS-Untersturmführer Roger Hoch was determined to get his 25 men through the battle. He was responsible for them and even though he did not know the platoon well, they deserved his best efforts. Hoch developed an immediate rapport with his platoon sergeant, Ebbert Zahn, and was careful to ask for his advice. He knew the value of an experienced, professional, reliable NCO, having been a platoon sergeant himself a year before. Now, fresh from officer school at Bad Tölz in Bavaria, the new officer had to try to win the respect and trust of his charges. He need not have worried. His face told the story of his war with the élite Leibstandarte Adolf Hitler (LAH), the men of the Führer's personal bodyguard – deep wrinkles were already etched on the face of the 23-year-old while a pair of white shrapnel scars stood proud on his tanned forehead. The canny Zahn had done a good job, for when Hoch took command of the platoon in early June 1943 as they moved into position for Operation Zitadelle, the men already knew that he had been at the front since the beginning, the very beginning, and had seen action in Poland, the Netherlands, Greece, Kiev, the Crimea and Rostov. His regiment had grown into a division and he had been selected as an officer candidate after his leadership potential had come to the attention of headquarters.

He had not wanted to become an officer, but he had stopped riling against the system long ago and went wherever it took him. His tattered photograph of the Führer remained in his left breast pocket, next to that of his parents and his childhood sweetheart. Adete was a flaxen-haired beauty whom he intended to marry just as soon as the war allowed, but he was concerned at her coolness towards him at their last meeting six weeks earlier. The war had changed them both.

So now he threw himself into preparing his men for their part in what the divisional commander had called 'the decisive offensive'. He honed their skills in training exercises and went to great lengths to pass on the benefit of his hard-won experience, which would not only make them a more effective unit, but would keep them alive. They practised picking their way through minefields, overcoming obstacles, attacking anti-tank gun positions, clearing trenches and cooperating with tanks. The days were long but Hoch had no difficulty in motivating his men to be as mentally and physically ready for the coming challenge as they could possibly be. Now, on 1 July, it was clear that it would not be long before they would be called upon to test their skills against the equally well-prepared and deeply entrenched Soviets. Hoch stole away to the front line with his company commander and scanned the enemy's positions 65 miles south of the city of Kursk. Nothing moved, but having memorized the aerial reconnaissance photographs of the sector, he knew that the camouflaged knolls and gentle folds in the ground before him contained the enemy. On his return to his waiting unit he took up the stub of a pencil and in his small diary wrote: 'Now I shall prepare for death.'

The Red Army's victory at Stalingrad ushered in a period of optimism for the Soviet Union. As Zhukov later wrote, the battle was fundamental to the military's continued development:

[O]ur troops received great schooling in the art of war. The commanding personnel gained great experience in organizing cooperation between infantry, tanks, artillery and airforce. The troops learned how to put up a stubborn defence inside a city, combining it with an outflanking manoeuvre. The morale of our troops had considerably risen, all that preparing a good soil for a counter-offensive.

But lessons took some time to filter through an organization the size of the Red Army and the counteroffensive to which Zhukov referred was workmanlike rather than scintillating. Having initially cracked the German front open on the Don, the attack rippled up and down the line, including a strike to the north from around Voronezh and south from the Stalingrad sector. Thus, during December and January, the Soviet front line in the south lurched forward to put the Red Army on the Lower Donets and just 50 miles short of its upper reaches. Although stubborn German resistance around Rostov allowed the First Panzer Army to escape through a narrow corridor to rejoin Army Group Don, the momentum was clearly with the Red Army, which had created an excellent platform for further advances. The troops sensed this. One young Soviet engineer recalled:

There is always a sense of anticipation with spring. The success at Stalingrad had been greeted by cheers in the regiment and there seemed to be a run of small victories in the early months of 1943 which added up to a definite movement of our line westwards – towards Berlin ... It was the best news that we had heard for 18 months and we did not expect it to stop. The army was filled with a sense of expectation.

Stalin was similarly optimistic about events, perhaps overly so in view of what his tired formations with their stretched lines of communication were capable of achieving at this time. But with the enemy on the back foot and Ukraine before him, he ordered the Germans to be pushed out of western Russia without delay. The resultant offensive featured drives for a bridgehead over the Lower Dnieper and to a line beyond Kharkov, Belgorod and Kursk, which was to be gained before the spring thaw when, in the words of one German general, 'Marshal Winter gave way to the still more masterful Marshal Mud'. Kursk fell on 8 February, Rostov on the 14th, Kharkov on the 18th, and significant progress was also made towards the Lower Dnieper. But with every step the Soviets became weaker and more vulnerable to their still formidable foe, who had not only been making plans to stop the rot, but also to strike back.

Late January and early February 1943 were dark days for the German army in the East. Just hours before the fall of Kharkov, a severely perturbed Hitler flew to headquarters – now redesignated Army Group South – at Zaporezhe where the men discussed the unravelling situation to the distant rumble of artillery fire. This was likely to be a critical meeting. An OKH officer admitted: 'Among his closest associates, Hitler has recently been given to loud outbursts of rage whenever the name Manstein is mentioned.' Indeed, Goebbels' diary suggests that Hitler intended to sack Manstein for withdrawing from Kharkov without orders. Nicholas von Below, the Führer's Luft-Waffenadjutant, explains:

Hitler forbade retreats from the front, even operational necessities to regain freedom of manoeuvre or to spare the men in the field. His distrust of the generals had increased inordinately and would never be quite overcome . . . he reserved to himself every decision, even the minor tactical ones.

Whatever Hitler's agenda at headquarters, he listened to Manstein's argument for his command to launch an immediate counterstroke, aimed at exploiting the Soviets' overstretch. The bulge in the Soviet line would be destroyed by retaking Kharkov and then Kursk. It was an audacious plan, but that was Manstein's forte and, if successful, would give the Wehrmacht just the boost it required before the spring. Opening on 19 February, the attack was led by SS-Obergruppenführer Paul Hausser's three-division SS Panzer Corps, which had been sent to the East by Hitler to give the Eastern Front some backbone. A brilliantly conceived and executed strike first stabilized the front by demolishing the Soviets' probing spearhead, then encircled and demolishing the main body of the attacking troops before retaking Kharkov on 15 March and Belgorod three days later.

Considering that Manstein's counterstroke took place just weeks after Paulus's capitulation at Stalingrad and within a fierce Soviet maelstrom, it was a remarkable feat. By destroying around five Soviet armies, restoring the line and wresting the initiative from the enemy, Manstein had single-handedly revived Hitler's fortunes in the region. Moscow had once again revealed its propensity to overestimate the offensive ability of its own army while underestimating the Wehrmacht's professionalism and capacity to reinvent itself. But it would be easy to overemphasize the strategic importance of the episode, which was merely a temporary reverse for the Red Army. As historian Evan Mawdsley has observed:

The early months of 1943 were not a period of German victory, despite the recapture of Kharkov. Manstein only made the best of a very bad situation. The destruction of the German army at Stalingrad continued to have deep and terrible reverberations.

The whole German line was creaking, as the OKH and OKW scavenged for reserves to throw into the southern gaps.

The Red Army had, after all, just achieved several back-to-back operational victories in the south and in so doing advanced 435 miles across a 750 mile front. Although Soviet over-ambition had presented Manstein with the opportunity to deliver his brilliant attack, which recovered one third of the ground that the Germans had just lost, it had failed to take Kursk and left a massive bulge in the Soviet line surrounding it. Moreover, the Wehrmacht remained badly damaged, overstretched, shaken and poorly placed to undertake a general offensive. In many respects, its general situation mirrored that of the Soviet forces. Both armies were therefore glad of the pause in fighting necessitated by the spring thaw, using the time to assess the impact of the last few months' campaigning, regroup, resupply, learn lessons and ready themselves for the summer.

What the two sides planned for the new campaigning season depended on what they could realistically achieve with the resources available to them. Germany's options were limited by the success of consecutive Soviet winter offensives, which had removed the threat from Moscow and the Caucasus. The recognition that the capital and oilfields were no longer within his grasp led Hitler to take two difficult but logical decisions: the phased withdrawal of Army Group Centre from the Rzhev salient to create a more economical front line, and the removal of the Seventeenth Army – the remnant of Army Group A that had been left in the Kuban to reignite a southerly thrust – to the Crimea. With the German army and its allies having lost 85 divisions to recent Soviet offensive action, this strategic housekeeping was timely. In 1941 there were 136 divisions manned by 3.8 million men; in 1943 there were 179 divisions but they were manned by just 2.7 million troops. At the same time, the Soviets could muster 6 million men, so while the Red Army was able to replace those men it lost, the Germans could not. The level of the Wehrmacht's early 1943 losses meant that Hitler was now the one likely to run out of manpower first. He had been drawn into a protracted industrial and economic struggle (*materialschlacht*) and by 1943 he was losing. There was a growing disparity in the two nations' capacity to produce the requisite manpower, weapons, ammunition, vehicles and equipment to sustain their war efforts, which fundamentally affected their plans. General Friedrich von Mellenthin, Chief of Staff of XLVIII Panzer Corps, has observed: 'In Russia the moral comfort of Manstein's latest victory could not obscure the fact that the whole balance of power had changed, and that we were faced by a ruthless enemy, possessed of immense and seemingly inexhaustible resources.'

Stalin was clear – 'The war will be won by industrial production' – and Moscow's strategic thinking was increasingly based around the relevant application of their numerical advantage. By the spring of 1943, that superiority could not only be seen in manpower figures, but also hardware. At the time of the spring pause in operations, the Germans had 2,209 tanks and assault guns (of which only 600 were operational) and 6,360 field guns while the Soviet Union had gathered 12–15,000 tanks and assault guns and 33,000 field guns. With all the resources taken in military conquests, the Germans should have been able to outproduce their enemy, but signally failed to do so through chronic mismanagement. The Soviet war economy was efficient and deftly handled by men who had experience in the role, but Hitler's economy was run by the incompetent Hermann Göring and was inefficient, bureaucratic and corrupt. The result was that in 1942, despite the trauma of invasion, massive loss of resources and the relocation of industry, the Soviets produced 25,436 aircraft, 24,446 tanks and 127,000 artillery pieces; the Germans managed only 15,409, 9,300 and 12,000.

In 1943 the gap was to widen even further and was exacerbated by the British and United States Lend-Lease scheme, under which commodities including agricultural machinery and industrial plant as well as thousands of tanks, aircraft, jeeps, trucks, boxes of ammunition and other military essentials arrived through the ports of Murmansk, Archangel and Vladivostock. When the scheme was agreed in the United States during October 1941, Maxim Litvinov, the Soviet ambassador to Washington, leapt up in delight and shouted, 'Now we shall win the war!' Stalin disliked having to rely on 'the charity' of the Western Allies, but later secretly confessed, 'If we had had to deal with Germany one-to-one we would not have been able to cope because we lost so much of our industry.' The plan was slow to get going, but by 1943 it was providing 17 per cent of Soviet aircraft, nearly 16 per cent of guns and ammunition and 14 per cent of vehicles.

More 'destructive' support was offered by the Western Allies in the form of developing Mediterranean operations and the prospect of an invasion of northwest Europe, which had the effect of stretching Hitler's resources far further than he had anticipated. Meanwhile, an Allied strategic bombing campaign undermined Germany's industrial output and demanded the diversion of valuable resources into the production of fighter aircraft and ammunition-hungry anti-aircraft batteries. The consequence of failing to defeat both the United Kingdom and the Soviet Union had grown to strategically damaging proportions by February 1943 as Hitler's scant resources were diluted across Europe while his economy was set to self-destruct.

The strategic situation had certainly affected Hitler by the time he returned to Wehrwolf to oversee the Manstein counterstroke. The complex seemed to reflect his mood, for as David Irving writes, it was not a welcoming place: '[Wehrwolf] in winter was a bleak and dreary site. Battle-scarred aircraft stood around the local airfield; the countryside was neglected; impoverished Ukrainian peasants with starving horses trudged the fields and forests collecting wood to warm their wretched hovels.' On 20 February, Guderian, who had not seen the Führer since December 1941, thought him much changed: 'In the intervening fourteen months he had aged greatly. His manner was less assured than it had been and his speech was hesitant; his left hand trembled.' Hitler had not taken a single day off work since 1939 and was clearly suffering from the strain. He was increasingly reliant on Dr Theo Morell, his personal physician, who produced a number of dubious potions to get his patient through the day. At Wehrwolf Hitler contracted what Morell diagnosed as 'brain-inflammation', which, he suggested, might have come on as a result of the acute stress that the Führer had suffered due to the loss of Stalingrad. He began dragging his leg, complained of splitting headaches and could not sleep without having taken a sedative. For a time, Irving has written, 'he tried to induce sleep by secretly drinking a glass or two of beer, but fearing fatness even more than insomnia, he soon stopped.' His moods became blacker and his temper shorter, and Morell tried to control them with injections of Prostakrinum hormones – a concoction made from a young bull's testes and prostate.

Hitler returned to the Wolfsschanze in mid-March much cheered by Manstein's success. According to General Alfred Warlimont, the deputy chief of OKW, he arrived 'with the air of a victorious war-lord, clearly considering himself and *his* leadership primarily responsible for the favourable turn of events in the East ...' Yet *en route* Hitler had been the target of an assassination attempt. A bomb had been hidden on his aircraft by a young officer during a visit to Kluge's headquarters. The lieutenant was not acting alone for he shared the views of his boss, Major-General Henning von Tresckow, chief operations officer of Army Group Centre, that Germany would be destroyed if Hitler remained alive. The failure of the bomb to detonate (probably due to the extreme cold in the luggage compartment where it had been placed) condemned the nation to fight on, but military opposition to Hitler's rule continued to grow as faith in his strategic abilities waned and defeats became more frequent. As Richard Overy has written: 'Hitler refused to accept his limitations, perhaps because he saw his calling as Germany's warlord as the central purpose of a dictatorship based on the ideal of violent self-assertion of the race, where for Stalin supreme command was above all a political necessity.'

Stalin had already begun to recognize his limitations as a military strategist and increasingly encouraged alternative opinions. Hitler would never have countenanced the appointment of an expert Deputy Supreme Commander, but in Zhukov the Soviet military machine had a professional who was capable of challenging his boss's ideas and offering alternatives. Stalin remained firmly in control, but his staff understood that he was increasingly persuaded by firm, clear and convincing arguments. Moreover, he delegated the responsibility for numerous decisions to trusted subordinates – although he insisted on being informed of those decisions so that he could overturn them if required. In doing this, he fixed the nation's future on men who were experts in their field and so long as they were successful, they would prosper. Good examples of such appointments were the Chief of the General Staff, General Aleksandr Vasilevsky, and his deputy and Chief of Operations, General Aleksei Antonov. These committed, hard-working professionals were cool under pressure and trusted by Stalin to provide him with the unvarnished truth while offering their views on key issues.

The Soviet regime was adapting to the requirements of total war far better than its German counterpart and was consequently well placed to make balanced strategic assessments and to develop relevant operational techniques. While the Germans kept faith with blitzkrieg despite evidence of its severe limitations after nearly two years in the Soviet Union, the slowly improving Red Army refined their use of the pre-war 'deep operations' doctrine under Zhukov's tutelage. To achieve this, various arms were reorganized within the services. In the army, the fighting power of the new, fast-moving Tank Corps had been seen during Operation Uranus at the end of 1942 for example. Their 228 tanks, anti-tank battalions, Katyusha rockets and anti-aircraft units provided the armoured formations with greater versatility, and when two came together with an added infantry division to form a Tank Army, the Soviets had just the powerful, self-contained and flexible formation in which they had been deficient. Moreover, the establishment of Mechanized Corps, with more infantry but less armour than the Tank Corps, provided the Red Army with the mobility and punch that the regular divisions lacked. In the airforce, meanwhile, aircraft that had been spread out across the front in support of each army unit were concentrated into air armies of up to 1000 aircraft for each of the 13 Fronts. This change, together with superior training, the construction of new airfields and stronger communications, imbued the airforce with greater tactical sense, flexibility and firepower with which it could win air superiority and support the ground forces.

These reforms would not transform the Soviet military into an organization that was capable of applying Tukhachevsky's complex manoeuvrist method overnight, but they did move it in the right direction. There was a definite structure to the modifications. Everything the military chiefs did was with the aim of defeating the Wehrmacht through a series of operational successes that could be stitched into a strategic victory. The performance of Armies and Fronts improved accordingly, a process assisted by the neutering of political representatives in their headquarters along with the abolition of all units' political commissars. Once again, commanders were encouraged to use their initiative, take responsibility and lead without fear of incurring the wrath of inhibiting minders. By the spring of 1943, the Soviet Union was not only out-producing Germany, but the modernization of its military and updating of its fighting methods meant that Stalin could fight on more equal terms with Hitler than he could before. 'The gap in organization and technology between the two sides,' Richard Overy argues, 'was narrowed to the point where the Red Army was prepared to confront German forces during the summer campaigning season in the sort of pitched battle of manoeuvre and firepower at which the German commanders had hitherto excelled.'

The summer of 1943 was primed for a monumental clash of arms. Hitler had realized that the Soviet armed forces were improving and, desperate to achieve strategic objectives as soon as possible, decided to seize the initiative and go on the offensive as the ground hardened. Although confident that the Wehrmacht would rediscover its old power, he was aware that it was too weak for a general offensive. The Führer was therefore tempted by a plan presented to him by Manstein on 10 March to remove the Kursk salient. The largely agricultural area was demarcated by the towns of Orel to the north and Belgorod in the south, had a frontage of 250 miles and was 120 miles from north to south and 60 miles across. By releasing the formations holding the bulge and destroying the Soviet armies defending within it, Hitler would gain not only the city of Kursk – a valuable communications hub with a population of approximately 100,000 – but also an excellent springboard for further offensive action.

However, another body of opinion argued that even a limited operation in the salient was precipitate, and that resources should be husbanded during a defensive period in order to concentrate on the threats in western and southern Europe. Heinz Guderian argued that the priority for 1943 should be 'the strengthening of our armoured forces in preparation for the many challenges to come . . . Their over hasty application in operations risks their future health and could lead to heavy losses that we would find difficult to replace.' Guderian had just been returned to Hitler's fold with his recent appointment as Inspector General of Armoured Troops. He advised that, having been rested, overhauled and refitted, the panzer divisions would be ready for offensive duty in 1944. Manstein did not disagree with the logic of this but was anxious that Hitler end the war within months, not years, for as he later wrote: 'We could clearly bury any hope of changing the course of the war by an offensive in the summer of 1943. Our loss of fighting power had already been far too great for anything of that order.' He rather naively (and secretly) hoped that success at Kursk might provide the prelude to peace talks without which, he was convinced, Germany would be destroyed.

The High Command did not want to give the Red Army the opportunity to develop its strength any further, and advocated a battle of annihilation with the main force of its most formidable foe in order to free itself to deal with the other threats. The Soviets seemed intent on defending the salient and had begun packing it with troops and tanks – OKH estimated some 60 divisions and six armoured corps (a total of 600,000 men) – which presented the opportunity for a significant victory. In any case, OKW opined, there were too few divisions for a static passive defence and it was essential to maintain the initiative. Hitler talked of the importance of offensive action for high morale and impulsively rejected any options – no matter what their pedigree and reason – that smacked of weakness. It was also critical that Hitler re-establish the credibility of his own leadership to doubters. A great military victory would reassure the Wehrmacht, the German people and his allies. Thus, when Hitler signed Operational Order No. 5 'Orders for the Conduct of War during the Next Months on the Eastern Front' on 13 March, it stated: '[I]t is necessary for us to attack before the Russians ... and take the initiative into our hands.' It outlined the intention to launch various attacks, including Operation Zitadelle (Citadel), the reduction of the Kursk salient by Kluge's Army Group Centre and Manstein's Army Group South, which was to begin in mid-April.

The proposed start date soon proved far too ambitious, partly due to the ground conditions but also because more time was required for preparation. By mid-April the size of the challenge presented by Zitadelle had been more fully recognized by the planning staff, and the offensive became the Wehrmacht's 1943 centre piece. Kurt Zeitzler, the bald Chief of the Army General Staff, who had the look of a local government officer and wore a Führer moustache, headed the planning team. After many operational concepts had been considered and discussed with Hitler, a plan was eventually published. Operational Order No. 6, dated 15 April, announced:

> The objective of the attack is to surround the enemy forces in the Kursk sector and destroy them with concentric attacks ... The moment of surprise must be preserved and, above all, the enemy must be kept in the dark about the date of the attack ... The attack must be conducted so rapidly that the enemy can neither withdraw from contact nor bring in strong reserves from other fronts.

Zitadelle was to be launched on 3 May, because it was deemed more important to attack before the Soviets had a chance to dig in or launch their own offensive than to take advantage of an extensive preliminary phase. An early strike, Mellenthin advised, had a greater chance of success for 'the Russian defences around Kursk were by no means adequate to resist a determined attack ... [but] a delay of one or two months would make our task far more formidable.'

The operation was to be classic blitzkrieg, eschewing a grinding advance for a swift and efficient strike, the kind of attack at which the Wehrmacht had excelled and which would preserve panzers for future operations. A double envelopment with pincers directed at the city of Kursk would surround the majority of the defenders and seal off the salient along the Maloarkhangelsk–Kursk–Belgorod line. It was a bold plan, audacious even, considering the physical condition of the Wehrmacht and what it had just been through, but Hitler and OKW were confident that Zitadelle would revitalize German strategic fortunes in the East. As Manstein said in a letter to Zeitzler on 18 April: 'Everything now depends on the success of Zitadelle. A victory at Kursk would also make up for the temporary setbacks elsewhere ... the sooner Zitadelle begins, the less danger there is of a prior enemy attack on the Donets region.' Hitler concurred and with every passing

day began to understand that the operation had more strategic significance than he had previously expected:

Our offensive is of decisive importance,' he suggested to OKW.
'[I]t must achieve its objectives swiftly and provide us with the
initiative during the spring and summer. We must prepare diligently but with discretion and ensure that the best formations,
weapons and leaders are positioned at the points of main effort
with access to plentiful supplies of ammunition. Every officer
and every man must recognize the significance of this attack.
Victory at Kursk must serve as a beacon to the world.

In common with the Germans, the Soviets had both offensive and
defensive options open to them in the spring of 1943. Obvious
German targets, such as the vulnerable Kursk salient, were naturally
readied for defence during the spring, but no decision had yet been
made regarding the Red Army's next move. In the meantime, the
General Staff made an assessment of likely German goals and developed options for a renewal of their own operations. During this
process it quickly became apparent that by far the most attractive
option open to Hitler was an attack on Kursk – a belief given further
credence by German troop concentrations spotted at Orel and
Kharkov. An intelligence picture was soon built up from reports
supplied by partisan groups, ground units and photographs produced
from aerial reconnaissance. The Soviet General Staff Study of the
battle in 1944 said: '[A]s early as March the Stavka of the Supreme
High Command had not only made a completely accurate prognosis
with respect to the overall nature of the forthcoming operations but
had also determined the deployment regions of his main groupings
and the probable attack axes.' With this information, and nearly two
years' experience of German methods, it was not difficult to deduce
their plan. By 8 April, Zhukov had enough information to make a

report to Stalin, which stated that the Germans would attack the Kursk salient with a strong armoured force. It read in part:

> We can expect the enemy to put greatest reliance in this year's offensive operations on his tank divisions and air force since his infantry appears to be far less prepared for offensive operations than last year ... In view of this threat, we should strengthen the antitank defences of the Central and Voronezh fronts, and assemble as soon as possible.

However, the Deputy Supreme Commander warned against a pre-emptive strike, saying:

> I consider it would be unsound to go over to an offensive with our forces in the very near future with the aim of pre-empting the enemy. It would be better if we were to wear down the enemy on our defence, destroy his tanks, and then, throwing in fresh reserves we go over to a general offensive [and] decisively defeat the basic concentration of the enemy.

Stalin's instinct, like Hitler's, was to attack the main enemy but his understanding that a general offensive would spread his forces too thinly made him interested in a pre-emptive strike at Kursk. The Supreme Commander pondered the report for another two days before calling for a major Stavka conference to discuss the situation. At that meeting on 12 April there was discussion about German intentions and capabilities, and reports from front-line commanders. Zhukov, who reiterated the points of his recent report, later said: 'The Supreme Commander listened to our views as never before.' By the end of the meeting the Stavka had made a decision, which, in the words of the 1944 General Staff Study on the battle, was to 'meet the enemy attack in a well-prepared defensive bridgehead, to bleed attacking German groupings dry, and then to launch a general offensive'. The Deputy Supreme Commander later commented that although going on the defensive, the Stavka's decision did not relinquish the initiative to the Germans: 'Appropriate orders were to be issued to the front commanders. The troops were to dig in deeply . . . The plan for our defence was thus not forced upon us by events but was prepared well in advance, while the timing of our offensive was to depend on the situation at the given moment.' The Germans were going to have the tables turned on them. They were to be drawn into a carefully devised trap, which aimed to destroy the Wehrmacht's armoured power and create the conditions for a major Soviet offensive.

At the heart of Stalin's plan was the careful use of intelligence, which would be allowed to guide the military's actions in a way that had yet to be seen in the war. Aleksandr Vasilevsky said that, compared with 1941 and 1942, there could be few criticisms made about Soviet intelligence that year:

> [O]ur intelligence was able to determine not only the general intention of the enemy in the period of the summer of 1943, the [intended] direction of his attacks, the composition of the striking groups and of the reserves, but also to establish the time of the beginning of the fascist offensive.

There were a number of important intelligence sources. The British had broken Wehrmacht signals traffic transmitted using their 'unbreakable' codes, which were encrypted on Enigma cipher machines. The decryption process, known as Ultra, was carried out at the Code and Cipher School operating under the Special Intelligence Service at Bletchley Park in Buckinghamshire. It produced some remarkable material, but this had to be used extremely carefully in order not to alert the Germans to the fact that their code had been broken. Some was sanctioned by Churchill to be released to the Soviets to assist them, and also in the hope of gaining helpful information about new German systems that were being encountered on the Eastern Front.

Ultra received its first evidence that the Wehrmacht was readying itself to launch an attack on the salient during 22 March. This was forwarded to Moscow and regular updates followed until May. It included a detailed German estimate of Soviet dispositions and information that not only gave an insight into their offensive thinking, but also revealed that they expected a heavily defended line and strong motorized and armoured counterattacks. Much of the intelligence could be verified by Bletchley Park agent John Cairncross, who handled data from decrypted Luftwaffe Enigma intercepts from the Eastern Front. The material that he passed on also allowed Moscow to construct a detailed picture of enemy formations, which developed into a complete German order of battle for Zitadelle.

The Red Trio Network, a Swiss-based organization run by Sándor Rado, also provided important intelligence. Rado's key agent was Rudolf Rössler (codenamed 'Lucy') who in the spring of 1943 was being asked specific questions to help Soviet planning at Kursk, including queries about the new Tiger and Panther tanks. The information that he provided often lacked detail, but it fulfilled the critical function of corroborating the intelligence provided by other sources.

Knowing the vital parts of Operational Order No. 6 allowed the Stavka to feel more confident in the decision it had made concerning Kursk. Nevertheless, the plan remained a great leap of faith. Moscow had chosen to ditch the main principle of their military philosophy, 'offensive action', in order to defend. But ensnaring the Wehrmacht in the Kursk salient presented a great opportunity to destroy German offensive power in one place rather than having to wear it down across the front in numerous actions. 'The Red Army,' as Evan Mawdsley has described, 'would gain an advantage by letting the Wehrmacht impale itself on the Soviet defences at Kursk . . .' Orders flowed out of the Stavka to make the salient a fortress. Commanders were briefed on the challenging concept of operations. Waiting for an attack was not an easy undertaking for anyone and Stalin remained concerned that he had handed Hitler the initiative and was fearful that his forces would not be able to withstand another blitzkrieg. The lead-up to Zitadelle would test Soviet nerves in a way that they had not been tested before. Stalin was learning that placing faith in one's senior officers was not easy.

Moscow's painful wait was unknowingly exacerbated by the Germans when Zitadelle's start day was postponed several times due to Hitler's concern over general preparations and the arrival of new weapons. Having annulled the 3 May launch date, a conference on the following day decided upon 12 June as the next target. Starting a summer offensive on time seemed to be a massive German stumbling block, but the Führer was insistent that the developing Soviet defensive works in the salient were crushed by a force of strength and vigour. He could not allow it to be any other way, for with his troops about to be overwhelmed in Tunisia, the prospect of Italy dropping out of the war and the growing threat of Allied invasions in the Mediterranean and France, Hitler could not risk the destruction of the Wehrmacht's prized armoured assets. Although the delay in the launch of the offensive gave the Red Army more time to ready itself, Hitler placed great faith in the gathering of his panzer divisions and, in particular, the delivery of three new 'wonder weapons', which he considered 'essential to Zitadelle's success': the Panzerkampfwagen VI 'Tiger' heavy tank; the Panzerjäger Tiger (P) 'Ferdinand' heavy assault gun; and the Panzerkampfwagen V 'Panther' medium tank. Only when his force was replete with these 'armoured miracles' would the order be given for Zitadelle to begin.

Heinz Guderian not only argued that the offensive was 'pointless' but advised OKW that 'heavy tank casualties were bound to be incurred and would ruin his plans for reorganizing the armour'. He also repeated an earlier warning that the Panthers had 'many teething troubles inherent in all new equipment'. On 10 May he took his argument a stage further and, having been informed that morning by the Reich Chancellery that the expected 324 Panthers would not be delivered until the end of the month, he confronted Hitler. The general tried to persuade him that Zitadelle was doomed: 'Do you believe, my Führer,' Guderian began, 'that anyone even knows where Kursk is? The world is completely indifferent as to whether we have Kursk or not. I repeat my question: Why do you want to attack in the east, particularly this year?' Hitler replied, 'You are quite right. The thought of this attack makes my stomach queasy.'

Despite the reservations of both men, the operation was not cancelled. Indeed, the Führer's obsession with the new weapons became even more intense as the challenge offered by Zitadelle increased, and he revealed a growing inability to distinguish between the essentials and the peripherals. For although the Ferdinand, Tiger and Panther were fine (if flawed) weapons, OKH was also desperate for infantry, ammunition, stores, junior officers and NCOs as well as a Luftwaffe fit for the critical task of close air support and battlefield interdiction. Walter Model, the commander of Kluge's Ninth Army, continually badgered his superiors with requests for 'More tanks! More officers! More artillery! Better training for the attack troops' and, according to General Mellenthin, 'produced air photographs which showed that the Russians were constructing very strong positions at the shoulders of the salient and had withdrawn their mobile forces from the area west of Kursk'. Indeed, Model went so far as to suggest that the longer the preliminary phase continued, the less justification there was for launching an offensive, and he recommended awaiting a Soviet push and then defeating that.

The start date for Zitadelle was consequently wrapped in strategic angst but when the promised Panthers failed to arrive and the operation was postponed for one final time to early July, even Hitler and the optimistic Zeitzler became concerned. With each passing day the Führer and senior commanders alike knew that Zitadelle was becoming more of a gamble. As Mellenthin later wrote:

For two months the shadow of Zitadelle hung over the Eastern Front and affected all our thoughts and planning. It was disquieting to reflect that after all our training, our profound study of the art of war, and the bitter experiences of the past year, the German General Staff should be dabbling with a dangerous gamble in which we were to stake our last reserves. As the weeks slipped by it became abundantly clear that this was an operation in which we had little to gain and probably a great deal to lose.

Devoid of alternatives, the High Command pressed on and the operation gained an unstoppable momentum, gradually welding Germany's fate to its muscular but lean body.

The final operational order for Zitadelle was published on 14 June and with that framework set, the Army Group commanders made the final adjustments to their plans, a process replicated in subordinate formations and units. The attacking forces amounted to 777,000 men, 2,451 tanks and assault guns (70 per cent of German armour on the Estern Front) and 7,417 guns and mortars. It was a formidable array of resources, which led Mellenthin to comment: 'From the strategic aspect Zitadelle was to be a veritable "death-ride", for virtually the whole of the operation reserve was to be flung into this supreme offensive.'

The face of the salient was to be held by four corps of the Second Army but the strike forces were built on either side of the salient. The northern attack, administered by Kluge's Army Group Centre, was to be undertaken by the Ninth Army commanded by the uncouth, pro-Nazi and ambitious Colonel-General Walter Model. The formation was to break the Soviet defences along the line of the Kursk–Orel highway and railway before driving southwards to Kursk where it would meet up with forces from Army Group South that had advanced from the south.

Model's main effort was to be made in the centre by General of

Panzer Troops Joachim Lemelsen's XLVII Panzer Corps, consisting of four panzer divisions with 331 tanks and assault guns – including 45 Tigers of Heavy Tank Battalion 505 – 178 field artillery pieces and 54 Nebelwerfers (high-explosive launchers). Providing cover to its left flank was XLI Panzer Corps under General of Panzer Troops Josef Harpe, consisting of one panzer division and two infantry divisions and with 304 tanks and assault guns – including 83 Ferdinands – 180 field artillery pieces and 54 Nebelwerfers. On Harpe's left was XXIII Corps under General of Infantry Johannes Friessner, consisting of a reinforced assault infantry division and two regular infantry divisions. It had no tanks, but it did have 62 assault guns, 214 guns and 57 medium and heavy werfers. Protecting Lemelsen's right flank was General of Infantry Hans Zorn's XLVI Panzer Corps, again with four infantry divisions and just nine temporarily attached tanks and 31 assault guns.

Model had a strong armoured force but decided not to employ the body of it at the outset because he did not want to break it on the dense Soviet defences and be unable to exploit any breakthrough. His initial strike force, therefore, would consist largely of infantry and artillery with Luftwaffe support and was tasked with breaching the first defensive line. That done, three panzer divisions would be released – Model's main offensive grouping – to smash the remaining defences along the primary attacking axis, followed by an infantry division and the two panzers from the reserve to achieve the final breakthrough to Kursk. It was a risky plan, considering the lack of infantry and artillery in the Ninth Army and the fact that just one of Model's infantry divisions was classed as at 'the highest offensive level' and four were deemed capable of only 'limited offensive action'. If they failed to make a breakthrough, the operation's timetable – to reach Kursk within a week to 10 days at the most – would be thrown into disarray. It was critical to succeed before the Soviets had an opportunity to launch heavy counterattacks and before casualties – particularly in the armour – began to mount.

From the southern salient the offensive was to be delivered by Manstein's Army Group South. Here, in the hands of one of the Wehrmacht's most respected exponents of manoeuvre warfare, the Germans were to unleash their main attack to smash through the Soviet defences. For this, Manstein was given almost double the armour provided to Model along with more infantry and artillery. The antipathy between Hitler and Manstein remained. Despite the field marshal's successful counterstroke, Hitler regarded him as 'too independently minded', while Manstein emerged from one situation briefing with Hitler, saying, 'My God, the man's an idiot.' Even so, the most powerful armoured formation yet assembled under one German commander, Hoth's Fourth Panzer Army, was placed in the hands of the commander of Army Group South.

The experienced, slight, silver-haired, shrew-like 'Papa' Hoth had developed a strong relationship with his superior, and they shared concerns about the operation and its 'lingering preparations'. Hoth's Army was directed by OKH to destroy the Soviet defences along a 30 mile front between Belgorod and Gertsovka, drive a wedge through to the town of Oboyan and then push on to Kursk. But Manstein and Hoth agreed that, having fractured the Soviet defences using a brutal mixture of armour and firepower from the outset, the unforgiving terrain and heavy Soviet defences south of Oboyan should be by-passed by swinging northeast to Prokhorovka. Here Hoth expected to meet and defeat the Soviet reserve, which was advancing west before crossing the Psel east of Oboyan. Then he would continue with all speed, joining the Ninth Army at Kursk.

Manstein's strike was to be delivered by XLVIII Panzer Corps commanded by General of Panzers Otto von Knobelsdorff, consisting of two panzer divisions, a panzer grenadier division – the ferociously strong Grossdeutschland Panzer Grenadier Division – and an infantry division. This gave the formation a total of 595 tanks and assault guns, 244 field artillery guns and 59 Nebelwerfers. On Knobelsdorff's right flank was II SS Panzer Corps commanded by SS-Obergruppenführer Paul Hausser, whose three panzer grenadier divisions were armed with 494 tanks and assault guns, 179 field artillery pieces and 138 Nebelwerfers. Protecting Hoth's right was Army Detachment Kempf commanded by General of Panzer Troops Werner Kempf. This consisted of III Panzer Corps, commanded by General of Panzers Hermann Breith, with three panzer divisions and an infantry division armed with 375 tanks and assault guns, 200 field artillery pieces and 54 Nebelwerfers; XI Corps (Corps Raus) commanded by General of Panzer Troops Erhard Raus, consisting of two infantry divisions; and the three infantry divisions of General of Infantry Franz Mattenklott's XLII Corps. The reserve, which could only be released on Hitler's authorization, was XXIV Panzer Corps commanded by General of Panzer Troops Walter Nehring, which totalled 181 tanks and assault guns and 123 field guns.

To a frustrated Manstein, Operation Zitadelle represented the antithesis of the way in which armoured formations should be employed. By attacking at Kursk, Hitler had chosen the unwieldy bludgeon rather than the finesse of a rapier. But with little option other than to make the most of the powerful hand he had been dealt in uninspiring circumstances, Manstein set out to ensure that the expected heavy armoured losses were as light as possible, and that Hoth reached Kursk in line with the operation's tight schedule. Manstein and Hoth put considerable faith in the aptitude of the élite II SS Panzer Corps, whose 'ideological warriors' offered experience, resilience and remarkable fighting ability. Hausser was extremely proud of his formation and supremely confident in its skill, but having been briefed on his corps' role in the operation, he felt bound to say that 'our success will demand all of our talent, experience and ruthlessness'. He also said that his corps was 'but one small part of a complex machine for this operation. We have put our faith in armour and must pray that that faith has not been misplaced.'

Hausser was concerned about whether, despite the armoured power husbanded for Zitadelle, it was capable of achieving what was asked of it – an anxiety that he shared with Hitler, Guderian, Model, Manstein and Hoth. The average number of tanks in the panzer divisions assembling for the operation was just 73, half of what it should have been, and most of these tanks were as jaded as the Wehrmacht's operational methods. The lightly armoured and armed Panzer IIIs and IVs, which made up the majority in the divisions, were not only time expired but not designed to be used in a frontal break-in battle against well-set defences. A plethora of self-propelled guns had been gathered to give the Germans extra punch, but having been plundered from defeated nations, they were so great in their variety that they were a maintenance and logistical nightmare.

The lack of armoured punch was why Hitler placed so much hope in the Tiger, Ferdinand and Panther. The Tiger was destined to become one of the iconic weapons of the Second World War and carried one of the greatest guns, the 88mm, which was sufficient to penetrate a T-34's armour up to about 1,800 yards. Its own armour was thick enough to withstand a Soviet 76mm gun except at very close range. The Ferdinand was a turretless Tiger carrying an 88mm L71 PAK 43 gun, which could penetrate enemy armour up to 3,300 yards. The Panther had been designed specifically as a reaction to the T-34. This 50 ton machine could reach speeds of nearly 30 miles per hour. It had sloped armour and its powerful, high-velocity 75mm gun was as adept at armoured penetration as anything else on the battlefield other than the 88mm. To one commentator, '[i]f any one tank deserves the distinction of being described as the best tank during the war, it has to be the Panther.' Guderian, on the other hand, while recognizing the strengths that these additions to the German armoured order of battle offered, believed that Hitler was expecting too much of them. The Tiger and Ferdinand were very heavy, slow, cumbersome and unreliable, and had a short range. The Inspector General of Armoured

Troops declared that he was impressed by their presence but said, '[T]he power of their guns and thickness of their armour meant little if they lacked battlefield mobility. For an army based around speed, these heavy beasts were a leap of tactical and technical faith.' The Panther had not been subjected to full trials, and numerous mechanical problems remained to be ironed out. It should also be noted that these new weapons were not numerous. The Fourth Panzer Army, for example, had 309 Panzer IIIs, 285 Panzer IVs, just 194 Panthers and 57 Tigers. Kempf and Model had no Panthers and only 45 Tigers each. Model had 90 Ferdinands, but there were none in the southern sector. The tired German panzer arm had just begun a process of transition, but it was not quite sure what it was being turned into and whether it would work. Operation Zitadelle, therefore, placed a great deal of emphasis on the acquisition of air superiority.

German commanders conducting offensive operations had come to expect excellent air cover, and with the Wehrmacht's lack of emphasis on ground-based artillery, the firepower that aircraft provided remained essential to the army's chances of success. The result was that 1,830 aircraft (equivalent to 70 per cent of the Luftwaffe's front-line strength in the East) were allocated to Zitadelle. Model was supported by 730 aircraft from General Otto Dessloch's Luftflotte 6; Manstein was backed by 1,100 aircraft from Colonel-General Robert Ritter von Greim's Luftflotte 4. In the final days before the attack, these aircraft were concentrated on airfields around Orel, Kharkov and Belgorod. It was a remarkable sight, said Luftwaffe engineer Ludwig Schein:

> I worked with the Heinkel 111 medium bomber and rarely saw other types. However, just before Kursk our airfield was inundated with different aircraft for different roles. We had been anticipating this as the bombs and ammunition that was being stored nearby had increased in variety, but I was not expecting such great numbers of ... Junkers 88s, Henschel Hs-129s,

Focke-Wulf 190s, Stukas and fighters of which most were Messerschmitt Bf 109s. We even had reconnaissance aircraft . . . All I can say is that there was organized chaos.

The German pilots and ground crews still held the qualitative edge over their Soviet counterparts, but their technical edge had been blunted with every passing month, because their aircraft were showing their age. Moreover, from the outset Dessloch and Greim were concerned that their operations would necessarily be curtailed by a lack of fuel, oil and lubricants. As Schein has testified:

> Our job was made immeasurably more difficult for the want of basic commodities. Considering the intensity of the missions that we had been led to believe were imminent, the lack of fuel and oil at the airfield was lamentable . . . The days went by in a blur of activity and most of us slept by our aircraft so that we could work on them in shifts over 24 hours. We did what we could with what we had to get the aircraft running as efficiently as possible because we knew how much the army boys relied on them.

Stuka dive bomber commander Major Frederich Lang left a briefing at which it had been made clear that the success of his aircraft was imperative to the operation:

> It was stated that the breakthrough of our troops depended on the effect of our first attacks. Each crew must be fully aware of the decisive importance of their effort. Our relatively weak army units had to rely fully on the support provided by the Luftwaffe and expected every aircrew to do its best.

Although the most efficient way of achieving air superiority was to attack the enemy's airforce on the ground, a lack of resources, clever

Soviet camouflage and the sheer preponderance of Stalin's aircraft precluded that. The plan, therefore, was to rely on the skill of the German fighter pilots to intercept any Soviet aircraft that attempted to enter the air space over the Kursk salient, while close air-attack aircraft went about their business in support of the troops on the ground. It was another risky strategy in a concept and design riddled with jeopardy, and the Luftwaffe commanders knew it. Schein recalls, '[O]ur superiors told us that the skies held the key to the success in Zitadelle, but that our success was not assured and to expect no end of hard work. We were told to expect a massive air battle.'

Confronting the German offensive were extensive Soviet defences, which would test the Wehrmacht's men and machines like they had never been tested before. Providing opposition in the northern salient was the Central Front commanded by General Konstantin Rokossovsky. Born in December 1896 to a Polish father and Russian mother, he suffered during the purges in 1937 when Beria's torturers subjected him to mock executions, broke several of his ribs, knocked out nine of his teeth, shattered his toes with a hammer and pulled out his fingernails. In March 1940 he was retrieved from a Siberian Gulag and commanded a mechanized corps during the following summer. Promoted in August 1941 to command the 16th Army, Rokossovsky went on to become chief of the Briansk Front and then the Don Front. Having defended against Army Group B's advance to Stalingrad, he commanded the northern wing of Uranus and went on to take charge of the reduction of the Stalingrad pocket. In the spring of 1943, when the Don Front was retitled the Central Front, Rokossovsky found himself in the way of the great German offensive against Kursk. Tall, physically fit and handsome – he had an eye for the ladies and kept a mistress throughout the war – Rokossovsky was an extremely capable general with an exceptional, analytical mind.

His Central Front consisted of the 13th, 4th, 65th and 70th infantry armies, and the 2nd Tank Army under Lieutenant-General A.G. Rodin, and was supported by the 16th Air Army commanded by Lieutenant-General S.I. Rundenko. In total, the Front had 711,575 men, 1,785 tanks and self-propelled guns, 12,453 guns and mortars and 1,050 aircraft. The expected main axis of German attack was defended by the 13th Army commanded by Lieutenant-General N.P. Pukhov, and covered 20 miles of front laced with 51,000 anti-tank mines and 29,000 anti-personnel mines. The 13th was deployed in three echelons nearly 20 miles deep and could be reinforced with tank and anti-tank units from the Central Front reserve. It was assigned 223 tanks and 47 assault guns – 44 per cent of the Front's artillery.

The Voronezh Front in the southern part of the Kursk salient was commanded by the moon-faced, 41-year-old General Nikolai Vatutin, who came from a village near Belgorod. He had served on the General Staff for the three years prior to the German invasion and became Chief of Staff to the Northwestern Front in 1941. Rejoining the General Staff briefly as deputy to Vasilevsky, Vatutin was given command of the Voronezh Front in October 1942 before a spell as chief of the Southwestern Front. He was returned to the Voronezh Front for the coming battle in March 1943 on Zhukov's recommendation and played a central role in the Soviet planning during the spring.

His Front was comprised of the 6th Guards, 7th Guards, 38th, 40th and 69th Armies, 1st Tank Army, 2nd Air Army and elements of the Southwestern Front's 17th Air Army. In total, it consisted of 625,591 troops, 1,704 tanks and self-propelled guns, 9,751 guns and mortars and 881 aircraft. Not entirely sure where the enemy would place his offensive weight, Vatutin organized his defence between the 6th Guards and 7th Guards Armies, each in two echelons with a third composed of front reserves. Lieutenant-General I.M. Chistyakov's 6th Guards Army on the right covered nearly 40 miles of the front line with 682 guns and mortars, 88 Katyushas, 135 tanks and 20 assault guns. Its first line was protected by 69,688 anti-tank mines and 64,430 anti-personnel mines; another 20,200 anti-tank and 9,097 anti-personnel mines protected the second line. Lieutenant-General M.S. Shumilov's 7th Guards, meanwhile, covered 35 miles of front with 1,573 guns and mortars, 47 Katyusha rocket launchers, 224 tanks and 22 assault guns.

In deeper reserve, to bolster the defence if necessary and provide the 'sword' of the counterattack behind the defensive 'shield', was the Steppe Front commanded by 45-year-old Colonel-General Ivan Konev. Like Rokossovsky and Vatutin, Konev was a widely respected commander who had made his reputation during the first two years of the war as chief of the 19th Army on the Western and then the Northwestern Front. He took command of the Steppe Front in June 1943, leaving him time to do little more than gain a broad under-standing of the capabilities of his formation and to strike up a working relationship with his subordinates. His 4th Guards, 5th Guards, 27th, 47th and 53rd Armies and 5th Guards Tank Army consisted of 573,195 troops, 1,639 tanks and self-propelled guns, 9,211 guns and mortars and the supporting 5th Air Army of some 563 aircraft. This made the total Soviet forces at Kursk 1,910,361 men, 5,128 tanks and self-propelled guns, 31,415 guns and mortars and 3,549 aircraft. The combined strength of the Central and Voronezh Fronts alone was 1,337,166 men. The Soviets had close to double the strength of the German troops, tanks and aircraft and four times the number of guns and mortars. Moscow was keen to ensure that the Red Army was as ready as it could be to meet Zitadelle. Zhukov later wrote:

The General Staff took steps to improve the army command structure. The organization table of fronts and armies was reviewed and improved. They were reinforced with additional artillery, antitank and mortar units. The troops were also strength-ened in the communications field. Rifle divisions were equipped with improved automatic and antitank weapons and combined into corps to give greater efficiency to the command structure and more power to the armies. New artillery and mortar units were formed and equipped with weapons of higher quality. Artillery brigades, divisions and corps were formed within the Supreme Command reserve to provide a high firing density on the principal sectors. Anti-aircraft divisions began to join the various units and the nation's air defence forces, greatly enhancing our over-all air defence. The Central Committee and State Defence Committee gave particular attention to tank production. The front also received the first self-propelled guns designed and produced by Soviet industry.

However, such statements and statistics emphasizing Soviet numerical superiority should not necessarily be taken at face value. In general terms, there was still a qualitative gap between the Soviets and the Germans in both soldiers and airmen, and also weaponry. The Red Army, despite improvements, remained crude. Training was rudimentary for the masses of replacements who were required to make up for heavy casualties; weaponry was utilitarian, built to last a matter of months and with few variants, which made logistics simple. There were, for example, just a handful of Soviet tank designs in production. The best and most numerous was the T-34, which was extremely mobile for a medium tank, but its 76mm gun had a low muzzle velocity, which limited its penetration and offered poor accuracy over longer ranges. This meant that it could not penetrate the Tiger's frontal armour even at very close range, and the armour of a Panzer IV presented difficulties. Yet it remained superior to most German tanks and had proved itself in battle and during the most trying of weather. But Tank Armies were not wholly armed with T-34s. Up to 40 per cent of some corps consisted of the lightly armoured T-70s with their 45mm gun. The 2nd Tank Army was totally reliant on T-70s. This meant that around one third of all Soviet tanks at Kursk were light T-70s.

The KV-1 heavy tank had the same gun as the T-34 but thicker armour, which made it heavier and slower. One young tank commander who had experience of both machines has said: 'I much preferred the T-34 because it offered speed and agility. The KV-1 was better protected but made a good target as it lumbered across the battlefield. It was no match for the Panther and Tiger with their excellent guns and optical sights.' The KV-1's limitations were well known and it was being phased out of production. Just 100 were allocated to the Central Front and 105 to the Voronezh Front.

Meanwhile, the Soviets had developed their airforce with the aim of using it to provide the same sort of support for the ground forces as the Luftwaffe provided for the Germans. Thus, of the 881 aircraft from the 2nd Air Army allocated to the Voronezh Front, 390 were fighters (such as Yak types 1, 3 and 9); 276 were ground-attack aircraft (Il-2 Shturmovik and Pe-2 dive bombers); 206 were bombers (medium Il-4 and heavy Pe-8); and the remainder were reconnaissance. With these aircraft, and with the aid of anti-aircraft teams, the Soviet airforce had the critical role of stopping a still technically superior enemy from commanding the skies and of dominating the air space themselves. This was the way in which the Soviets chose to fight their war. Mass – albeit with a modicum of budding sophistication at the operational level – was entrusted to overcome a smaller but more capable opposition. It might not have been pretty, but it was simple and increasingly effective.

The pause prior to the Battle of Kursk was one of the longest in the German–Soviet ground war. Having taken their decision to defend, the Soviets immediately began to organize under the watchful eye of Zhukov, who spent his time with the two Fronts, 'studying the situation and making preparations for the anticipated operations'. Helping in this task was the procurement of local intelligence from a variety of sources – partisans were ordered to locate enemy forces and ascertain their identity; railways were watched to identify cargo types and the frequency of its arrival at railheads; radio traffic was intercepted; soldiers were captured for interrogation; and detailed aerial surveys were carried out to discover the depth of the German positions. Unit movement, equipment recognition and other useful information was provided by a network of local spies for whom Erhard Raus had a grudging respect:

> We had to remain aware of the fact that the Russians made considerable use of the civilian population for intelligence missions. A favourite practice was the employment of boys eight to fourteen years old, who were first trained for this work and then allowed to infiltrate at suitable front sectors. Immediately before the offensive opened, more than a dozen such children were picked up in the Belgorod area alone. They gave detailed reports on the kind of training they received and their *modus operandi* . . . Their talent for observation and skill at spying was remarkable.

From their many intelligence sources, the Soviets gained a full and well-rounded picture of their enemy and his intentions. But they made a concerted attempt to disguise this from the Germans, allowing them to think that they had maintained operational surprise by leaving them to go about their business unmolested. Despite knowledge of supply columns advancing down roads to assembly areas, which could have been targeted by air or artillery strikes, they were left alone. Disruptive action was the domain of partisan groups alone. By the late spring of 1943, some 250,000 irregulars on the Eastern Front tied up approximately 500,000 German personnel (army, SS, police and security units) whose role it was to hunt them down. Despite the retribution carried out on the population for attacks on German forces – often at a rate of 100 executed for every one German soldier killed – the frequency of attacks reached new heights. Controlled and coordinated through the Central Partisan Headquarters, the irregulars pitted their local knowledge and ability to spring a surprise against their enemy's weaknesses, and consequently targeted rail communications, bridges, soft-skinned vehicles and any soft target that disrupted German plans, caused logistic difficulty and tied down personnel to guard duties. In Army Group Centre's area, 300 trains, 1,222 wagons and 44 bridges were destroyed during this period, and around the Kursk sector there were 1,092 partisan attacks against the railways in June alone. Although it is difficult to judge exactly what impact partisan activity had on German readiness, Kluge was disturbed enough to launch several operations to clear his rear area of partisans, and he used five divisions slated for Zitadelle. As Karl Hertzog testifies: 'Irregular activity meant that we were never safe and put us on our guard at all times. I did not experience an attack, but we heard stories of those that had. We had to be on our guard. It was part of the Soviets' strategy of wearing us down – and it worked.'

Both sides were engaged in often frantic efforts to ensure that they had the provisions they required, and where they required them, in time for the battle. Tanks, vehicles, guns, stores, equipment and the enormous paraphernalia of war were moved into position. The Ninth Army, for example, was supplied with 12,000 tons of ammunition, 11,182 cubic metres of fuel and 6000 tons of feed for the 50,000 horses in service for the divisions. In anticipation of heavy casualties, the Soviets established or revamped 450 hospitals and field treatment stations. The build-up of Soviet resources was remarkable and on one day alone a 6th Guards Army inventory reveals that the formation received 8000 rifles, 3000 bombs, 6,500 mines and 500 tons of ammunition. Werth noted in his diary on 11 June: 'I recorded a conversation with a Russian correspondent who had just been to Kursk. He said the Russian equipment there was truly stupendous; he has never seen anything like it.'

It was tiring work for all concerned. German troops undertook the heavy task of unloading trucks as colleagues endeavoured to keep the traffic moving along roads and tracks that crumbled under the strain. To this end, Mellenthin wrote:

> For nights on end the staff officers responsible for the movement of troops and munitions stood by the roadside and at road crossings to ensure that everything would go off without a hitch. Rain and cloudbursts did not allow the timetable to be adhered to in all respects.

Often the men were so busy that they could not look after their own equipment. Max Sulzer, an infantryman in XXIII Corps, recalls:

> In mid-June we spent much of our time off-loading wagons – ammunition and stores mainly – in preparation for the attack. I built up some muscles during that time, but it exhausted us and a number of men were injured in the process: several received back injuries and one man, a corporal, was killed when a stack of heavy wooden boxes fell on him . . . Our own equipment was left under guard in our harbour area but after one period away we returned to find that our baggage had been interfered with. Personal effects had been stolen. I found one of my kit bags in a ditch with its contents soaked . . . and our rifles had been poorly stored and were covered in rust.

For the experienced Sulzer, who had looked after his equipment assid-uously since the beginning of the invasion two years before, the event was a body blow. It was, he said, 'the very last thing that tired soldiers needed just before they went into battle. Morale plummeted.' Some troops, however, could not get away from their weapons. Panzer gunner Ludwig Bauer, for example, has said that his unit were with their tanks 'day and night'. During the day the crews were engaged in servicing and maintaining them; at night, they slept in or under them.

Soviet sapper Fyodor Onton found that he could get no respite from his task of bridging the various rivers and streams in the salient. He recalls:

> We divided our sector into zones and then prioritised those water obstacles that were in greatest need of a crossing. You must remember that we were not entirely sure when the Germans were going to attack and so this was important. However, as the days and weeks passed, all of the vital bridges had been built and so [we] had the luxury of erecting crossings over less important obstacles ... There was no lack of bridging equipment or manpower for these jobs. Each was erected quickly and efficiently with demolition charges attached for their destruction should they fall into enemy hands.

The Soviet preparation of the Kursk salient was stunning. Positions were established in great depth and with noteworthy attention to detail. The aim was to catch the German blitzkrieg in a cobweb of defences, where it would struggle and tire before the Soviets attacked. Defences were based on eight deeply echeloned zones and ran for 70 miles along the main enemy attack axes, which stretched 175 miles to the rear. A State Defence Line was designated along the River Don in case of another catastrophe, like the one in 1942. Utilizing *maskirovka* techniques to mask the flow of men and equipment, the Soviet defences were rapidly developed.

The first zone extended from the front line rearwards to a depth of three miles and was based on five parallel lines of deep entrenchments. The forward edge was protected by very deep and extensive barbed-wire fences, wide ditches, mines, steel anti-tank teeth, dammed rivers and some 503,663 anti-tank mines and 439,348 anti-personnel mines. Once into the defensive zone, the Germans would be confronted by strongly constructed, mutually supporting and very carefully disguised anti-tank resistance points, trenches full of riflemen, bunkers containing machine guns, saps, gun pits, more barbed wire and dug-in armour. More than 3000 miles of trenches were dug, laid out in a criss-cross pattern to allow defenders to move easily from one firing position to another. If the first defensive line was breached, the Wehrmacht would be confronted with a second and then a third line. Mansur Abdulin, an infantryman in the 66th Guards Rifle Division and veteran of Stalingrad, describes how after careful selection of their firing positions in blistering June heat, his section was detailed to dig a trench: 'At last, we had some heavy rain,' he later wrote, 'but we kept on working until it got dark . . . We also made a dugout with a thick layer of earth over the roof. It was a dry and pretty comfortable dwelling.' Nikolai Litvin was a 19-year-old anti-tank gunner in the 4th Guards Airborne Division, situated near Ponyri Station in the second line of defence. His 45mm gun had a PP-9 optical sight, which he describes as being so accurate that it was possible to hit a specific spot on a tank at over 500 yards. He recalled:

> The basic plan was that when the German tanks advanced, only the antitank guns and their crews would remain above ground, while the infantry and submachine gunners would remain concealed and under cover. When the tank battle concluded, our infantry and submachine gunners would emerge . . . We wanted to bleed the attacking Germans dry.

The firepower ranged around Litvin was considerable – some 11 dug-in tanks and 200 anti-tank guns per mile.

The aim was to meet the German attack with a curtain of fire and then to negate the panzers' momentum, mobility and capacity for effective command and control. The salient was made into one vast tank-killing ground, and the terrain was deftly incorporated into the Soviets' defensive system. The southern salient was predominantly flat, open, steppe land. The black fertile earth was divided into large fields of crops with the occasional ancient man-made burial mound (*kurgan*). The northern salient contained more varied terrain. Its fields ranged across gently rolling hills and were punctuated by collective farms, villages, orchards, copses and woods, which were worked into the defences. The Ninth Army's assembly area was covered by one such wood but the Soviets occupied the Olkhovatka hills, which were the dominating physical feature in the salient. Although neither high nor steep, they overlooked the low ground across which the Ninth Army was to advance. Their slopes were made into a pre-surveyed killing zone, and their heights were developed into a complex system of mutually supportive positions. Elsewhere, the abundant rivers and streams that ran from east to west throughout the salient were made into potential death traps – mines laced their banks, batteries of artillery had them in their sights and some were dammed to flood. Numerous dried river beds (*balkas*) were occupied by various headquarters, utilized as dumps for fuel, ammunition and stores, primed as troop concentration points and identified as useful for battlefield reorganization and night-time laagers for tanks. There were very few roads and most of these were merely tracks of compacted earth. The forward movement of heavy vehicles and tanks was, therefore, expected to be difficult and likely to become tortuous during high summer when thunderstorms commonly turned the roads into rivers of mud, fields became glutinous morasses and low-lying areas had to be redefined as marshland.

With the construction of such measured and strapping defences under way, Zhukov was not about to waste them with poorly set troops. Thus, as Moscow's 1944 study of the battle reveals: 'Staffs, units, and formations of all Central and Voronezh Front combat armies were intensively involved in combat training ... Staff and force exercises were conducted under real conditions which approximated to all impending defensive combat.' This was a rigorous process, the purpose of which was not only to instruct the troops in the latest tactics and hone their technique, but also to integrate new equipment and give units confidence against their feared enemy. A considerable amount of time was spent on communications. The Red Army had been working hard to improve its command and control performance, and the arrival of increasing numbers of radios helped enormously. During 1943, Lend-Lease supplied 35,000 radio stations, 380,000 field telephones and 956,000 miles of telephone cable, and formations in the Kursk salient were given priority in their distribution. By late May, Soviet units were deeply involved in mastering their new equipment, and exercises soon revealed much quicker reaction times and allowed commanders to use their initiative with greater success. The radios certainly assisted unit and formation tactics, and cooperation. Dimitri Trzemin worked extensively with the infantry, as his T-34 unit endeavoured to become more integrated in the forthcoming battle than it had been in previous fighting:

> Before Kursk we went into action and fought our own battles. If we could help the infantry, we would but it was difficult to find out exactly what they wanted us to do. As soon as we received a radio – I think that it was in the April [1943] – we were much more useful. Not only could we co-ordinate our actions with other tanks, but we could assist our infantry directly . . . Infantry commanders also helped us to stay safe by sending us warnings of enemy anti-tank guns and heavy armour. Radios transformed the way we fought.

The T-34 crews also worked hard to improve their levels of competency and received pamphlets advising them on how to 'Survive and Succeed'. This short *aide-mémoire* guided much of the training that tank crews undertook in the spring of 1943. It included encouragement to 'use speed to your advantage', 'move quickly between firing positions', 'not remain still for more than a minute', 'take routes providing most cover from enemy observers – avoid ridges where possible' and 'be bold – offensive action will unbalance the enemy'. Nikolai Litvin and his anti-tank team worked diligently, rehearsing their battle drills. He recalls:

> Whenever there was a lull, our gun crews trained. In the eight-man gun crew, each member had his own role. The weapon commander selects the target, the type of shell, the number of rounds, and gives the order to open fire. The gunner aims the gun and fires the weapon. The breech operator opens and closes the gun's breech in case the automatic device fails. The loader loads the shell into the gun and removes the spent cartridge case after firing. The *snariadny* [shell-man] prepares the shells for firing and hands them to the loader . . . He sets the distance a shrapnel shell will travel before it explodes. The *iashchechny* [case-man] opens the caissons, wipes the dust from the shells, and so forth. The ammunition carrier carries the shells from the caisson to the gun. The eighth member of the crew is either a driver for horse-drawn guns or the chief mechanic for mechanized towed guns. I was the gunner on my gun crew.

The infantry was also put through its paces and was instructed on what to expect from other arms, including the artillery, which was to work off a detailed fire-plan and neutralize the enemy's guns with sustained counterbatter efforts. Units were 'thoroughly updated', as Mansur Abdulin puts it. In late June he wrote:

> It is very hot. Not a cloud in the sky, not a drop of rain. The air is motionless and dry. All day long our regiment is involved in tactical exercises. I am now commander of the first and main mortar gun crew and assistant platoon commander. We train our

new recruits, sharing our Stalingrad experiences, and also learn some new things which we didn't have time for at the Tashkent Military School. We knew all the technical characteristics of Tigers, Panthers, Ferdinands and other enemy tanks and self-propelled guns. Our gunners received new anti-tank weapons. We also became acquainted with the new self-propelled 152mm guns [SU-152]. The infantry had enough reliable anti-tank weapons: all the soldiers carried anti-tank grenades and there was an ample supply of Molotov Cocktails.

The Wehrmacht also worked tirelessly to ensure that their troops' skills were honed for the task ahead. As General Erhard Raus commented, 'considering Russian dispositions, defences, and terrain, German strength could be considered only minimally sufficient for the assigned missions'. Like the Soviets, Model and Manstein directed that all units and formations undertake as much training as possible. Commanders tended to prefer specific instruction in how to overcome the obstacles that threatened to stop Zitadelle in its tracks, as Raus explains:

XI Corps staff made a thorough study of crossing the extensive minefields ... [and the] best method was to thoroughly instruct all infantrymen in enemy mine-laying techniques and in spotting mines by using captured enemy minefields as training grounds. This procedure required that all infantrymen be sent to rear areas in rotation and was therefore rather time-consuming. [Also] the divisions committed in the narrow attack zone had moved two-thirds of their combat forces to the rear, where the daily training schedule featured tanks passing over foxholes and the crossing of Russian-type minefields. This training paid off since it helped the soldiers overcome their fear of tanks and mines.

The effect of the protracted spring pause, therefore, was to give both forces the breathing space they required to become well set to conduct the operations that their high commands demanded of them. The transitional Red Army hoped that its defences would hold and that it could move from defence to offence as part of the same operational process. The overstretched Wehrmacht placed its trust in superior technique and skills. The local population watched with growing horror. Tanya Vershvovski, who worked on a farm near Oboyan, observed the troops and military hardware as it spilled into the fields:

> We were used to the war by the summer of 1943, but not being so close to the front line. We were very frightened but were told to carry on with our business and to keep our mouths shut about what we saw. The soldiers were very kind to us and some helped with chores and we helped bury [signals] cable and dug some latrines. They told us that a big battle would soon break out and to leave the area as soon as we could. We explained that we were not allowed to leave and so they helped us reinforce the farm buildings, half of which were taken over by medical staff as we had fresh water. It was an exciting time looking back on events, but at the time we did not have any idea whether we would live or die.

Many of the local population were evacuated from an area extending 10 to 15 miles behind the front line. Those who stayed, like Tanya Vershvovski, assisted the troops with their defensive works. By April, over 100,000 people were fully employed in the task, ordered to dig up their carefully tilled fields and smash holes in their precious homes. The town of Kursk was protected by batteries of anti-aircraft guns. It thronged with traffic and was a vital communications hub for the Red Army, although it had long since become a ruin. In the 14 months that they had occupied Kursk, the Germans had plundered, looted, raped and murdered their way into the nightmares of the remaining inhabitants. By June 1943 the town had become a lawless husk of a place. Armed gangs and desperate deserters roamed the streets as frantic mothers eked out a pitiful living and their grubby children played in the debris, occasionally becoming victims of unexploded ordnance. The situation was hardly any better on the farms, as Catherine Merridale describes:

> The hardship in the countryside was indescribable . . . the areas of occupation had been plundered, the people's livestock slaughtered or driven away, their crops destroyed or looted. Suspected partisans had been hanged, and then their neighbours – entire communities – had been punished for good measure. A total of nearly 40,000 houses, over half the region's entire stock, had been burned to the ground. Many able-bodied adults had been dragged off to work for the Reich as forced labourers. There was no one left to rebuild the houses, dig the fields or gather what was left of last year's crop.

The whole region was plunged into a struggle for survival. 'The armies that would fight near Kursk,' says Merridale, 'trained and prepared in scenes of medieval brutishness.'

The troops of both sides, despite their heavy workload, had plenty of time to think about their lives and the impending battle that could end them in an instant. While eating their meals, stopping for a cigarette or just leaning on their shovels, the troops ruminated about life and death, their families, their hopes and fears. Many managed to keep their anxieties at bay during the day, by indulging in the black humour that helps sustain armies around the world, but at night when the men were finally left alone with their thoughts, their imaginations could run riot. Veterans tended to be more sanguine about their situation than men who had no experience of battle, but some who had suffered in previous actions were prone to nightmares and preoccupation. Few did not feel a growing anxiety prior to battle, but those anxieties differed depending on a man's unit, personality, experience and background. Indeed, one practised junior German officer commanding a Tiger said, 'Probably none of us was free from fear. Before some operations, I did not feel at my best.'

Typical concerns among front-line troops were the prospects of death, mutilation and personal failure. Tightly bonded groups who were loyal to each other and suspicious of outsiders – the typical 'band of brothers' – were fuelled by common experience and shared hardships to fight harder and longer than those who did not enjoy the same connection. To such men the prospect of letting their comrades down was unconscionable. Bonding was common in vulnerable infantry units at the sharp end, but was not unique to them. Tank crews, for example, were a special breed who lived and worked in a very small and tight-knit community. Moreover, the chance of these men succumbing to a collective death was high. This was particularly true in the Red Army where the average T-34 survived just six months after production and 310,000 tank men trained in the war (78 per cent of the total) were killed. Yet few wanted to take their chances anywhere else and tank crews felt at home in their claustrophobic steel capsule, which was prone to draw fire from every gun in range. As tank man Aleksandr Sacharov explains:

> Others from outside cannot really help us in a serious situation. You can only assist from within the confines of one's own crew to get people out if the tank has caught fire. Crew members are closer to each other than brothers. Tank soldiers are like family sticking very close together. One always watched out for the others and would never leave them in the lurch in a crisis.

In such circumstances, some light relief during the warm weeks of early summer was necessary. As the temperature rose, the days lengthened and the world seemed far more welcoming than it had during the bleak days of winter and early spring, the troops let off steam. Some officers organized sports events. Gerd Schmükle, a battalion commander in the 7th Panzer Division, managed to put together a party with music and dancers:

> It took place during a marvellous summer night. About 500 soldiers were sitting around the stage where the dance acts performed. We all felt this was a party between life and death, between hope and despair, because it was clear that at least one third of us would be killed in action in the next few days.

Indeed, many behaved in a manner that suggested they did not expect to see another summer. One Soviet soldier recalls:

> 21 June 1943 is a date that I will never forget. In the afternoon I lost my virginity to a nurse who took sympathy on me – and several of my comrades, it seems – and in the evening I got drunk, properly drunk, for the first time in my life. I had never lived so intensely and have not done so since. In a strange way, it was a magical time.

The wait for the launch of Operation Zitadelle was anxious for everyone concerned. In the Wehrmacht, each postponement was greeted with alarm as evidence of substantial Soviet defences grew and the High Command squirmed when they were made aware of it. In Moscow, it became increasingly difficult for Stalin to resist unleashing a pre-emptive blow against his exposed enemy. The Supreme Commander became especially twitchy as his intelligence sources – and 'Lucy' in particular – failed to provide a precise date for the launch of the operation. The intelligence emanating from Switzerland usually lacked detail and its generalized statements (often caused by German rescheduling) led to a number of false alarms. The Central and Voronezh Fronts were put on a nerve-racking state of high alert on several occasions during May and June, and it took all of Zhukov's and Vasilevsky's skills to soothe Stalin's rage and stay his hand.

A number of anticipatory air strikes were launched, however, but their breadth was deliberately non-Kursk specific. Utilizing information about the Luftwaffe supplied by John Cairncross, the first took place in early May after the Soviets became convinced that Zitadelle would start on 10 May. During two days of raids against 17 airfields situated from Smolensk to the Sea of Azov, the Soviets claimed that 500 enemy aircraft were destroyed. Then in early June, after the Germans had bombed railheads supplying the Kursk salient and strategic industrial targets, Stalin authorized his airforce to strike back by targeting airfields between Orel and Bryansk. In the intense air battle that followed, which lasted until the middle of the month, the Luftwaffe claimed to have shot down 2,300 Soviet aircraft for the loss of 300 of their own machines. Yet despite his impulse, Stalin did not launch a ground strike and at a conference on 12 June, having received evidence that Zitadelle would be launched within the month, he finally made a commitment to defend.

During these final weeks, there was a flurry of activity at the front as units and stores were moved forward and tactical plans were refined. Both sides undertook reconnaissance missions as junior officers sought to acquaint themselves with the ground before them and gather local intelligence. Small parties of specially armed and briefed troops slipped into no-man's-land – usually at night – to explore the enemy's forward defences. On the night of 30 June, Lieutenant Bernard Roth and a section of seven men were ordered up to the Soviet outpost zone to check the extent of a Soviet minefield in the southern sector. Roth recalls:

It was a truly worrying assignment. We had all heard rumours that the offensive would start within days and were aware that the might of the Red Army was waiting for us. To be sent towards them with a handful of men was not something that I would have chosen to do. Nevertheless, there we were after dark crawling on our bellies through the long grass that separated our two lines ... After nearly 90 minutes, we reached our objective and I moved forward to make an assessment of the minefield – not easy in the dark – with my sergeant whilst the remainder of our group stood guard. Just as I had begun to wonder whether I would be able to do any useful work in the circumstances, there was an indistinguishable yell immediately followed by a burst of MP-40 fire. An enemy patrol had been spotted just [100 yards] away and was just about to cut off our line of retreat ... A brief fire-fight ensued in which we blazed away at some shadowy figures but managed to extract ourselves without any casualties. The reconnaissance had taken five hours and I returned to the company headquarters exhausted but with no useful information whatsoever.

The Germans' intelligence picture was not as good as it might have been. They believed that the Soviets were preparing just for a defensive battle, and even then underestimated the Red Army's strength. For example, by mid-June OKH thought that there were 1,500 tanks in the salient, but this was over 3,600 fewer than the true figure, and they miscalculated Soviet manpower by one million. The Soviets were mastering *maskirovka* while the Wehrmacht was feeding on intelligence scraps. Yet even with its network of spies, agents and information-gathering operations, Moscow found it difficult to pin down the exact date and time for the launch of Zitadelle. Strenuous efforts continued to discover them – Stalin remained eager not only to put the troops on alert but also to launch a massive disruptive bombardment on the German positions as they reached their jumping-off positions just before they attacked. Signals traffic was carefully monitored and analyzed for any clue, spies were ordered to report on any sign of an imminent attack and scouts were sent over to the German lines to seize a prisoner ('grab a tongue') for interrogation. Deserters were also questioned, and there were a spate of these in June. Nikolai Belov wrote in his diary on the 13th: 'Today another two have gone over to the enemy side. That's eleven people already. Most of them are pricks.' But German security was good. Troops at the front were given no information that may have been of use to the enemy until the very last moment, and so the Soviets remained in ignorance.

It was not until 1 July that Hitler assembled his senior commanders at the Wolfsschanze and announced: 'I have decided to fix the start date of Zitadelle for the 5th of July.' With the final late-arriving units moving into position – including the Panthers – and the imminent threat of a landing on Sicily supposedly receding (it began just nine days later), the Führer believed that the time had come. Although apprehensive, Hitler was confident that Zitadelle would at least succeed in removing the salient, would retake Kursk and remove vital Soviet resources from the front. He had latterly stopped referring to the offensive as 'decisive' but still maintained that defeat was out of the question. Within 24 hours of the decision to launch the operation being made, 'Lucy' had passed a warning on to Moscow. Aleksandr Vasilevsky wrote later: 'On the night of 2 July, the information received at General Staff from our intelligence section told us that in the next few days, at any rate no later than 6 July, the enemy's offensive on the Kursk front was bound to begin. I instantly reported this to Stalin and asked permission to warn the Fronts at once.' Stalin agreed and, beginning a pre-arranged series of measures, the general left to join Vatutin in the Voronezh Front headquarters while Zhukov settled himself with Rokossovsky and the Central Front.

It was high summer in central Russia and the dry heat of June had been replaced by a sultry, damp weather system that had settled over the region, bringing torrential downpours and thunderstorms. The ground dried quickly, but at his airfield Ludwig Schein was concerned: 'Bad weather meant that our aircraft could not do their jobs, and I wouldn't have wanted to take on the Soviet defences without the protection offered from the skies.' Bernard Roth commented: 'Stuck under my cape with the rain running down my back and my feet in a pool of water, I feared for the attack. I had witnessed what mud could do to armour and it filled me with dread.'

The Soviets, on the other hand, found the rain reassuring. Dimitri Trzemin recalls:

We had a tarpaulin attached to the side of our T-34 and watched as it caught a deluge and bulged in its middle ... But we were confident that with our wide tracks we could cope with wet summer conditions without a problem, and we knew that soft going would trouble the heavier German tanks ... The first days of July passed slowly but we were keen for the battle to begin. To get things moving after the long wait.

He did not have long to wait. On 4 July a different atmosphere pervaded the front – the Germans were in their assembly areas and a calm had descended. The reported change was taken by the Fronts and Moscow as a clear indication that an attack was imminent. Briefings and equipment checks took place on both sides of the line as the sun warmed the waiting troops. When clouds began to gather over the salient, the Soviets were surprised by a sudden but limited lunge forward by XLVIII Panzer Corps. The aim was to gain the advantage of some higher ground for artillery observers before the main offensive began. Grossdeutschland moved forward through minefields cleared the previous night and by 1600 hours one of its regiments, working in cooperation with 3rd Panzer Division, had seized the village of Butovo where spotters immediately set to work. The village of

Gertsovka, however, did not fall to Grossdeutschland and 11th Panzer Division until after midnight.

The Fourth Panzer Army's nudge was confirmation that the Kursk salient was just hours away from being engulfed by a furious battle. SS-Panzerschütze Walter Lau and the Tigers of LAH began the evening bivouacked in their assembly area, a flattened wheat field, where his commander, Helmut Wendorff, 'had the entire platoon lay in the rest positions in a semi-circle on their bellies with heads facing the centre. As expected [he] called for a song. We spent the evening singing.' Then, after midnight, the tanks moved to their jumping-off point. By 0200 hours the Germans were in position. They were issued five days' cold rations and given their final briefings and orders. These included an 'Order of the Day' from Hitler, which read:

Soldiers!

Today you will launch a great attack, whose outcome will have decisive significance for the war.

Your victory must strengthen the conviction of the entire world that resisting the German Wehrmacht is useless . . .

The powerful strike, which you will direct at the Soviet armies this morning, must shake them to their roots . . .

The German homeland . . . has placed its deepest trust in you!

The waiting Wehrmacht formations had no idea that their great offensive had been compromised, and waiting for them in bunkers, trenches, fortified buildings, copses and folds in the ground were some 1.5 million men. Lieutenant-General N.K. Poel, the political member of the 1st Tank Army, recalled:

While German officers were reading out the Führer's Order of the Day, our defences made the final preparations for the reception of the enemy. We thickened our foremost line, moved more guns into position, once more coordinated and completed our firing tables and concerted our plans.

The combatants readied themselves. One Soviet tank veteran watched his friend slowly, lovingly, spreading fat over a hunk of bread. 'Don't rush me,' the man said, 'I'm going to enjoy this. It's the last meal I'll eat in this world.' Some troops were far too nervous to eat. Many could do little more than try to doze, indulge in chat or write letters. SS-Obergrenadier Günther Borchers wrote home: 'I am in a flame-throwing team, and we are to lead the company attack. This is a real suicide mission. We have to get within 30m of the Russians before we open fire. It's time to write the Last Will and Testament.'

The Soviet commanders had to decide when to launch their bombardment. That evening, intelligence poured into the Front head-quarters where teams waded through a blizzard of information concerning details of XLVIII Panzer Corps' attack, the appearance of German minefield-clearance teams, attempts to cut barbed-wire obstacles and enemy movements. The success of the Soviets' preliminary bombardment depended upon it causing the greatest physical and psychological damage possible, so timing was essential. At the Voronezh headquarters, Vatutin and Vasilevsky were certain that all indicators were pointing to a dawn attack and so, shortly after 2230 hours, more than 600 heavy and medium guns, mortars and Katyushas of the 6th and 7th Guards Army erupted along a 12 mile frontage of the SS Panzer Corps. It bit deep into the German lines and rolled over the assembly lines and artillery batteries. A second, shorter barrage was launched at 0130 hours and this also targeted Army Detachment Kempf.

Rokossovsky and Zhukov, however, continued to wade through the reports. It was after midnight before vital information was identified. A German engineer had been taken prisoner in no-man's-land and when questioned said that the attack would be launched at 0330 hours. Thus, at 0200 hours, Zhukov authorized the bombardment to begin.

The ground shuddered beneath the Red Army's feet as the guns opened up in an ear-splitting roar that ripped through the night and Zhukov dubbed 'a symphony from hell'. Model and Manstein were severely shaken by the news that the Soviets were laying down an accurate and heavy bombardment on their positions for it revealed that the enemy knew far more about the operation than had been anticipated. Bernard Roth's regiment was waiting to move up the line when the Soviets struck:

> The shells came plunging out of the darkness without warning and we were caught in the open. We had not expected the enemy to catch us at such a time. There were casualties, but most of us found some cover and waited for the bombardment to pass over us . . . When after several minutes it was safe to venture out, the scene was chaotic. Vehicles were on fire and there were several corpses lying in the grass, but we soon recovered . . . Had we been attacked [an hour later] whilst the regiment was marching forward, we would have lost far more men.

The Soviet artillery did cause shock, casualties and destruction but, as Zhukov later argued, its effect was limited: '[W]e had expected that its impact would be greater,' he wrote. 'When observing the course of the fighting and questioning prisoners, I came to the conclusion that the Central and Voronezh Fronts had started the counter-preparation too early. The German soldiers were still asleep in the trenches, dugouts, and ravines and the tank units were under cover in the waiting areas.' Consequently, the strike did not throw the German schedule into disarray as intended and most formations were delayed by just 40 minutes. By 0400 hours the commanders had made the necessary adjustments to their plans and their bleary-eyed troops awaited the order to advance. Sitting on his Tiger as the eastern horizon revealed the first grey light of dawn, SS soldier Wilhelm Roes was in a positive mood: 'I said to myself, nobody will be able to resist this might. We were so confident of winning, as we had always done before. It was a dead certainty for all of us.' It was time for the largest set-piece battle in the history of war to begin.

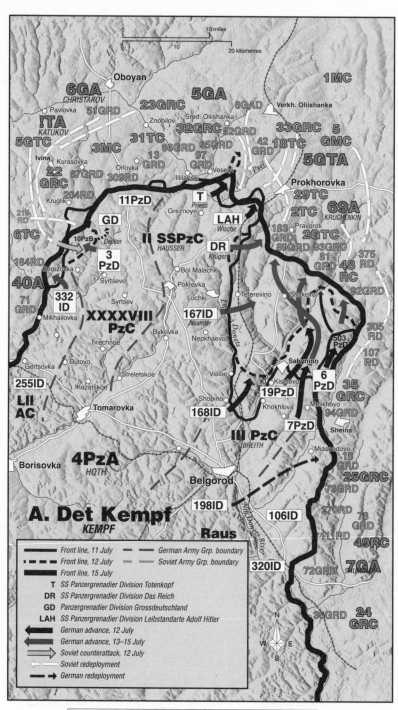

Map 7: Voronezh Front, 12–15 July 1943

CHAPTER 6

Breaking In

(Zitadelle Launched: 5 July)

Lieutenant Raimund Rüffer's previous experience with 78th Assault Division had been in a series of hastily arranged attacks during the winter, which had achieved mixed results. But the 20-year-old found Zitadelle very different.

Ivan bullets zipped around us, I could hear them flying past my ears. I expected to be cut down any moment or blown to smithereens by the shells that slammed about. This was not my first action, but it felt like it. We had been waiting. Oh, what a tortuous wait! As the day arrived our nerves jangled although we tried not to show it. By dawn I was cold, tired and – I don't mind admitting it – very frightened. We had not seen the enemy since March and in the meantime our bodies and minds had acclimatised to a war of training and fatigue parties. I enjoyed it. The comradeship in our platoon was sublime and, enjoying plentiful rations in the sunshine, it was easy to forget the coming storm.

But as the weeks passed it became increasingly difficult to ignore the inevitable and my thoughts turned increasingly to my parents back in Köln. I was concerned for their safety as Allied raids had been devastating. I had witnessed the destruction during my last home leave and had sobbed as I walked through shattered streets that were barely recognisable. At dinner my mother had tried to engage me in conversation about family matters, but it was clear that she was worried sick about me. She had good reason to be concerned for there were just 10 'originals' drawing breath in my 35 man platoon. She wanted to know about my war – which was understandable – but I grew angry at her questions which reminded me of the inquisitions that she had subjected me to after a day at school. I gave little away and altered the subject. She said that I had changed which made me furious, but my father calmed the situation saying that I was the same as ever, just tired. As a veteran of the trenches he recognised his son's reticence to talk about his life at the front. I sloped off to the garden and sat smoking – distracted. After a couple of hours my father found me. We sat together for a while and although we did so in silence and without our eyes meeting, a fresh connection had been made. Rising after a few minutes he put his hand on my shoulder, squeezed gently and left me to my thoughts. He understood.

Now, nearly nine months later with 78th Assault Division, I struggled on to the platoon objective, my muscles screaming and uniform drenched with sweat. We worked together without words, a glance was enough, covering the ground as quickly as possible. I heard my old friend Ernest panting seconds before his right arm was torn from his body by an explosion that flung his rifle at my feet. He whimpered as I moved towards him, but was silent by the time that I was at his side. A movement to my right. I twisted to see a camouflaged cover being thrown off a trench.

I instinctively yelled a warning, dropped to one knee and squeezed the trigger of my rifle. The butt kicked and a round was sent hurtling towards a faceless Soviet soldier. In that same instant I was knocked off my feet as though hit by a heavyweight boxer. A Soviet round had struck me in the shoulder, shattering the bone and leaving me gasping for air.

By 0500 hours on the morning of 5 July, despite the Soviet attempt to disrupt the opening of Zitadelle, the Ninth Army was attacking in the north, and the Fourth Panzer Army and Army Detachment Kempf in the south. The offensive began with the Germans' own preliminary bombardment, with the artillery and massed nebelwerfer batteries targeting the trenches and bunkers of the Soviet forward defences. The aim was not so much to destroy Soviet positions and kill the defenders – the 50 minute bombardment was far too short for that – but to dislocate and unbalance the enemy. Model and Manstein wanted to ensure that Soviet guns were neutralized, their command and control was disrupted and the infantry's heads were tucked firmly below the parapet as their tanks and infantry began to attack. Nevertheless, by the time the bombardment lifted, the artillery had fired more shells than they had during the campaigns in France and Poland combined. 'At last,' says heavy gunner Johan Müller, 'we were taking the initiative. After weeks and months of map work and firing tables, it was good to be in action again. We had plenty of shells to fire and got through them quickly. We were told that our work had been tremendously successful and its accuracy had been remarked upon by headquarters.' The attacking formations eased themselves forward, covered at first by the ground-based artillery and then by the Luftwaffe in the form of He-111 and Ju-88 medium bombers. Despite the best efforts of the Soviet Air Force to destroy the German aircraft on the ground that morning, ground-support missions were being flown in support of the offensive with near impunity.

The Luftwaffe had been alerted to the Soviet threat by the enemy's early preliminary bombardment, and then by seeing aircraft approaching their airfields on the radar. The 800 aircraft of Luftflotte 4 were spread over several airfields and in the process of being fuelled and loaded with bombs for their first sorties of the day when the sirens began to wail their warnings at 0330 hours. Many of the aircrews were in briefings or at breakfast but they immediately rushed to their machines and took off into the breaking dawn. Oberstleutnant Walter Lehwess-Litzmann, the commander of a German bomber group, recalls:

I had just gathered my commanders to assign them with their last instructions when I received an excited phone call which gave me revised orders. We were to take off immediately, although it was still dark, and attack the Soviet artillery positions.

The sky quickly filled with German aircraft. Over the radio, crews were told about the approach of a massive raid – it actually comprised 132 Il-2 Shturmovik ground-attack aircraft with a close escort of 285 La-5 and P-39 fighters. The German fighters were to intercept the Soviets, and the aircraft detailed to support the offensive were to start their missions immediately. So began the crucial battle for air superiority on 5 July. Within minutes, Miklós Keyneres, a Hungarian pilot of a Messerschmitt Bf-109, was locked in combat with Il-2s as German flak burst among the Soviet aircraft. He recalled:

In their great excitement, the flak gunners don't pay any attention to the close proximity of our own aircraft. But we ignore their fire. We have our eyes only for the four red-starred aircraft . . . The machine [a twin-seat Il-2 with a rear gunner] on the left side peels off from the rest, with me in hot pursuit. The hunt begins. The Russian pushes close to the ground and escapes, hopping over trees. But we remain clung to his tail. On my right hand side, three Germans are pursuing too. One of the Germans dives on it, but fails to bring it down. Now my turn has come. I pull up slightly and, from the far side, I aim ahead of the engine but hold my fire for another moment. The distance is still too great. Then I squeeze both firing buttons. I pull up in an instant to avoid colliding. I skid out to the right. I get on its left side again and from above and behind I shoot at the cockpit. By now the Russian gunner does not return fire. From a close distance I open up with the cannon. The machine shudders and hits the ground with its right wing tip. It slides along a creek, violently burning.

German anti-aircraft defences caused the incoming Soviets considerable problems, as Nikolay Gapeyonok, the pilot of a Pe-2 dive bomber, remembers, when they attacked an airfield west of Belgorod: 'We ran into a heavy AAA [anti-aircraft artillery] barrage, which disrupted our bombing. Two Pe-2s exploded in mid-air as a result of direct hits, and a third bomber was damaged.' It was a similar situation in the north where Senior Lieutenant T. Simutenkov, flying an Il-2, ran into a curtain of fire:

As we approached our target I could see the anti-aircraft fire ripping through the sky. I held my course and could just make out some enemy aircraft taking off. This was a shock as we were convinced that we would achieve surprise and record a major success, but before I had a chance to make my attack my aircraft was hit in the fuselage and then the right wing. Smoke began to seep into the cockpit and I struggled to remain in control . . . I feared that the engine would burst into flames but it did not, but it stuttered and lost power. I instinctively swung the aircraft south and within seconds was making a forced landing somewhere within our lines . . . It was still dark and I hit the ground with a fearsome crash which ripped the undercarriage off. But the aircraft skidded to a halt in a field and I was able to push back the cockpit and walk away shaken, but unharmed.

The Soviets had hoped to catch the Luftwaffe cold but instead took considerable losses in an air battle that developed into one of the greatest of the war. The Germans gained air superiority that morning and destroyed 176 enemy aircraft for, perhaps, as few as just 26 machines of their own fleet. Rather than removing a crucial element of the Wehrmacht's offensive ability, Stalin's airforce had provided the Germans with the opportunity to weaken the Red Army's defences. This meant that the Luftwaffe was able to fly nearly 4,500 sorties in support of the ground forces on 5 July, and despite flying 3,385 sorties of their own, the Soviets could not breach the German fighter screen in any numbers. A Moscow-sponsored report into the situation commented later in the year: 'Our aviation fought air battles primarily against enemy fighters along the approaches to the battlefield, while enemy bombers were operating almost continually against our defending forces immediately over the battlefield along the main axis.'

As the fight for the sky unfolded, Hitler's army began what was to become its own titanic attempt to crack the Red Army's defences. In the south, XLVIII Panzer Corps and II SS Panzer Corps threw themselves at the 6th Guards Army at the junction of the 22nd and 23rd Rifle Corps. Hoth expected the first two lines of Soviet defences – held by the 67th and 52nd Guards Rifles Divisions – to be broken that day, and by the end of the next day to have broken through the third line and advanced half the distance to Kursk. The Grossdeutschland Panzer Grenadier Division was the main attacking force, supported on its flanks by the 3rd and 11th Panzer Divisions. The Grossdeutschland's 384 tanks included the usual Panzer IIIs and IVs, but also a heavy company of 15 Tigers and 200 Panthers.

However, these new medium tanks had only just arrived at the front – Battalion 52 on 30 June and Battalion 51 on 1 July – and had had very little opportunity to orientate themselves and conduct the reconnaissance that they required. In line with Guderian's warning that the tanks were mechanically unreliable, two Panthers were lost to engine fires at the railhead and another six before they crossed the front line. To make matters worse, the two battalions not only lacked combat experience but had conducted just platoon-level battle training and had received no instruction in battalion level radio procedure. The situation led driver Gerd Küster of Battalion 51 to recall:

We arrived for the battle with just hours to spare. We were extremely tired and had to spend all the time available to us arming and servicing our Panther. We had received our tank just a week before and were still learning about its quirks. We were impressed with what we had learned but nervous as we had spent so little time training in her . . . It is very important for any soldier, but particularly a tank crew, to have faith in their weapons. We knew about the reliability issues – and were very aware that the engine could burst into flames – but what worried us most was a lack of 'feel' for the tank. How it would manoeuvre, where it could and couldn't go and the support that we would receive from the infantry and the air . . . In a sense, arriving at the front so late gave us little time to worry about such things. I spent the night [4–5 July] refuelling, lugging shells and trying to overcome a steering problem . . . We went into battle with weary eyes, splitting headaches and not the faintest clue what the battlefield had in store for us.

Backed by a heavy barrage from the artillery and led by 350 tanks supported by infantry, the Grossdeutschland Division advanced on a two-mile front towards the outpost villages of Gertsovka, Butovo and then Cherkasskoye in the first Soviet line. It was an awe-inspiring sight as the formation rumbled towards their enemy's defences. A German war correspondent described these as typical of the salient:

> The Guards Rifle Division [the 67th] dug in here believed that they were safe in their strong fortifications echeloned in depth. They were aware that swampy hollows and valleys, wide mine belts, wire entanglements, flamethrower barriers and tank ditches were in front of them. They also could see that they were deployed in a labyrinth of trenches and bunkers, anti-tank positions, rifle pits and mortar emplacements. Behind them a network of small strong points and defensive works were spread over the countryside.

Advancing into this web over open ground was the division's Fusilier Regiment, the bulk of the Panthers and a battalion from the panzer regiment. After an initial burst, the attack faltered when 36 Panthers plunged into a minefield. A series of explosions broke a number of tracks, which immediately halted the beasts and rendered them vulnerable to a wall of Soviet anti-tank and artillery fire. What little momentum the division had gained was taken from it as the battlefield was deluged with exploding shells and shrouded in a dense haze. The scene was observed by an officer in the division's artillery:

> Everything is shrouded in dust and smoke. The enemy observation posts certainly can't see anything. Our barrage is now over ... it has wandered from the forward trenches farther to the rear. Are the infantry there? We can see some movement, but nothing specific ... General depression! My high spirits are gone.

The mines needed to be removed and the tank tracks repaired before the advance could continue. Paul Carell, the pseudonym of SS

Obersturmbannführer Paul Schmidt, wrote of the mine clearers in his vivid history, *Scorched Earth*:

> The job needed a steady hand and calm nerves. Each anti-tank mine, when the earth had been cleared away around it, had to be lifted carefully just a little way because many of them were additionally secured against lifting by being anchored to a peg by a short length of wire. Yard by yard the parties crept forward – probing, clearing the mines with their hands, lifting them carefully, removing the detonators, and putting the death-traps aside. Down among the engineers crashed Soviet mortar shells. Over their heads screamed the deafening 8.8cm shells of their own Tigers.

The Germans had been trying to remove mines under cover of darkness throughout June. Henri Schnabel was section commander of a hastily trained team that had been specially formed for Zitadelle and sent to the southern salient at the end of May:

> The task was time-consuming and without end. The Soviets had sown thousands upon thousands of mines and we could never remove all of them and those that we removed were replaced. We worked at night up to the day of the attack. It was dangerous work because the Soviet mines were unreliable. Many of the mines we found were duds, but some were so poorly made that the slightest movement set them off . . . My team was set to work under heavy fire on the morning of 5th July. We were working with detectors under shell and machine gun fire with the tanks covering us the best that they could. A colleague lifted a mine . . . and it exploded killing him, and sent dirty fragments into my left leg as I worked beside him. I was attended to by a daring medic and continued my work . . . It was understood that each man

would continue in his task until he was physically incapable of doing so.

Such was the density of the minefield that clearing it took several hours. The infantry, meanwhile, tried to advance across it, keen to get to grips with the enemy who was delighting in causing the men of Grossdeutschland such distress. Their casualties were heavy and included the Fusiliers' commander, Colonel Kassnitz, who was leading the attack on the division's left. Those tanks and troops that could be pulled back to the start line were quickly withdrawn. For Lieutenant-General Walter Hoernlein, the Grossdeutschland's frantic commander, the situation was intolerable and yet he was powerless to do anything but look on and allow his subordinates to do their jobs. As one of his staff officers, Hauptmann Gunar Francks, has testified:

> We understood that this attack was going to be unlike our previous successes in France and Russia back in 1941 when we had moved far and fast. We had made many representations to Corps and Army that the defences were likely to sap our power, that for an armoured bludgeon to work it needs to be swung – it needs a run at the defences – but we were told that we had to make the best of the situation. I do not believe, however, that our superiors believed that the attack would be anything other than a bloody struggle.

Had the Red Air Force enjoyed air supremacy as expected, the carnage would very likely have been much worse. As it was, most Soviet aircraft seeking to target the German advance either failed to break through the Luftwaffe's fighter cordon or were prevented from conducting sustained attacks. Thus, although XLVIII Panzer Corps reported that morning: 'The entire corps sector is under heavy attack by Soviet Il-2 ground-attack planes and bombers', this was only relative to what it was used to facing. Moreover, many more enemy aircraft were repelled than managed to break through and those that caused initial concerns were swiftly chased away by the arrival of Bf-109s.

Nevertheless, Grossdeutschland endured a difficult morning, and the Wehrmacht was forced to confront a reality that they had not expected. The formation's official history – disparaging of the Zitadelle plan, although understandably fulsome in its praise for the troops – admits:

> It was enough to make one sick. Soldiers and officers alike feared that the entire affair was going to pot. The tanks were stuck fast, some bogged down to the tops of their tracks, and to make matters worse the enemy was firing at them with antitank rifles, antitank guns, and artillery. Tremendous confusion breaks out. The Fusiliers advance without the tanks – what can they do? . . . [and] walked straight into ruin. Even the heavy company suffered 50 killed and wounded in a few hours. Pioneers were moved up immediately and they began clearing a path through the mine-infested terrain. Ten more hours had to pass before the first tanks and self-propelled guns got through.

On the release of his division from the minefield's clutches, and desperate to regain impetus, Hoernlein ordered the Fusiliers and tanks forward to restart the attack on eastern Gertsovka. This time his force was halted below the village by the marshy ground surrounding the swollen Berezovyy stream. Sensing another opportunity, the Soviet airforce endeavoured to put pressure on XLVIII Panzer Corps, leading its commander, Otto von Knobelsdorff, to report to Manstein:

> Soviet air forces repeatedly attack the large concentrations of tanks and infantry near the crossings at Berezovyy. There are heavy losses, especially among the officers. Grossdeutschland's

Command Post received a direct hit, killing the adjutant of the grenadier regiment and two other officers.

As the stricken armour awaited rescue by recovery vehicles, the Grenadier Regiment on the division's right advanced more successfully towards Butovo. Leading the way were Tigers, which were employed in a classic arrow formation (*Keil*), with lighter Panzer IIIs, IVs and assault guns fanning out to the rear. They were followed by the infantry and engineers. These would support the armour by attacking anti-tank teams, destroying obstacles and clearing Soviet trenches. Near Cherkasskoe, Ukrainian machine-gunner Mykhailo Petrik waited in a bunker that he had constructed out of earth, wood and some metal sheeting:

Now was the moment that we had been waiting for. The Germans came. First, their shells and then their armour and infantry. Tanks and men across the front. With the noise of the shells exploding the sound of the attack was muffled. A fellow standing next to me looked over with a blank face, said something that I could not hear, and then looked back out over the parapet … We were nervous in our trench but readied ourselves. Ammunition and grenades at our elbow. We did not expect to survive and now we knew death was arriving and I could not catch my breath.

Striking the first blow and blazing a trail that others would follow placed a great deal of responsibility on the tank crews. Many panzer commanders preferred to use hand signals between themselves in battle to communicate, but on this occasion the dust and smoke obscured vision to such an extent that they had to rely on radios. Commanders listened to unit instructions and gave clipped orders to their own crews over the intercom. Each member of the team was addressed by his job title for clarity and was expected to remain silent unless he had something of importance to say. There was no time for distracting chit-chat in battle. The formation remained concentrated until the enemy was sighted, and then widened out but kept its shape. The commanders scanned the ground for threats. Dug-in armour was difficult to spot, and the low profile of anti-tank guns made them particularly tricky to pick up if covered by camouflage. Working in a minimum of pairs, and often in clutches of four or five, anti-tank guns could be devastating to most tanks at close range. The Tigers were well protected and had the critical role of winkling out and destroying these potentially destructive weapons. It was such a difficult job that, according to experienced tank commanders, the elimination of an anti-tank gun 'counted twice as much' as a tank kill.

Attacking ground troops would request an air strike while they were still a safe distance from the enemy. The request was radioed to a control centre by Luftwaffe liaison officers in the front line. It was an excellent system, for as Major-General Hans Seidemann, the commander of Fliegerkorps VIII, has testified:

Providing quick and effective ground support necessitated smoothly functioning communications between the attacking armies, corps, and divisions and the headquarters at Fliegerkorps VIII. The Luftwaffe had maintained a corps of liaison officers since the beginning of the war, composed of men who had strong experience in ground support operations. As usual during this offensive, we attached these teams directly to Army Group South's corps and division headquarters, and they accompanied their units directly onto the field of battle. There the Luftwaffe officers also acted as dive-bomber and fighter guides, using their radios to direct approaching formations to their targets indicated by the ground commanders, correct their fire, and provide updates on the current tactical air situation in the local area.

These arrangements were far better than the Soviet system, which depended on air-support signals being sent to an officer at a remote headquarters, where he had little understanding of the developing battle and could not assist the accuracy of any subsequent strikes. Thus while the Soviet airforce maintained its reputation for launching attacks on its own troops, waves of Stukas were expertly rolled on to their targets. They circled for around 20 minutes as each aircraft individually dived at 370 miles per hour at an angle of between 60 and 90 degrees and released its 550lb fuselage bomb and two wing-mounted 110lb bombs at around 1,500 feet. As one wave finished its work, another would arrive to replace it, and so it continued until the enemy had been neutralized or destroyed. Such attacks aided the advance of the tanks and grenadiers on the right of Grossdeutschland, which swept through Butovo in cooperation with Major-General Mickl's 11th Panzer Division and by the early afternoon was threatening Cherkasskoe. Chistyakov had reinforced the village that morning as soon as the Germans had shown their hand. His troops now engaged the approaching tanks and infantry with venom and the confrontation was brutal. Mykhailo Petrik fought for his life, his machine gun ripping through ammunition at an enormous rate, but his battle came to a sudden end:

We had the enemy pinned down, but there was little cover and they tried to attack. Every time they moved, we shot them. A small pile of casualties grew. But then we saw that they had a mortar and before I could open fire, we had been hit. That mortar round knocked me unconscious and, in so doing, saved my life. When I came to that evening my partner was dead and I was covered in blood from a bad head wound. I was a mess. Deaf, confused and unable to stand. Despite this I can still recall the mixture of damp earth, cordite and blood which filled my nostrils as I assessed my situation. Clearly the Germans had passed by thinking us both dead ... That evening, having gathered myself,

I headed north through the German lines and into the arms of comrades where I was patched up, given a rifle and sent to a trench. I did not last long. It was only hours later that I collapsed again. A shard of metal had, unknown to me, entered my neck from the mortar. My battle was over.

Cherkasskoe fell that afternoon. Swiftly redeployed Fusiliers and Panthers from Grossdeutschland's stalled attack advanced along with a detachment of Flammpanzer IIIs (flame-thrower tanks). Their blazing fuel oil suppressed the Soviet defences to allow combat engineers and the infantry to break in and mop up. Under intense pressure, the defenders buckled and the survivors fell back to the second line under covering fire, a 15 man rearguard fighting from the village's smoking ruins. The capture of Cherkasskoe, when added to the success of the 3rd Panzer Division on Hoernlein's left flank, which had managed to seize both Gertsovka and Korovino, meant that a considerable hole had been torn in the Soviets' first line of defence.

On XLVIII Panzer Corps' right, linked by 167th Infantry Division, which was held around Trirechnoe, was the second part of Hoth's main strike force – Paul Hausser's II SS Panzer Corps. Up against the 52nd Guards Rifle Division were the three SS-Panzergrenadier divisions: Leibstandarte Adolf Hitler (LAH), Das Reich and Totenkopf. All three were strong, élite, highly motivated divisions with fearsome reputations. Indeed, Lieutenant-General I.M. Chistyakov, commander of the 6th Guards Army, had warned his men: 'Be careful, comrades! Before you stands Hitler's guard. We must expect one of the main efforts of the German offensive in this sector.' Expecting Hoth's main effort to be towards Pokrovka (not to be confused with Prokhorovka 25 miles to its northeast) the Soviets sent considerable reinforcements south of the town in June, to add ballast. One of them, gunner Michail Khodorovsky, recalls:

I was not afraid of going into battle, but I did fear the SS or, rather, I feared being captured by the SS. Days before the battle we had received a lecture from our political officer warning us that the SS tortured prisoners and were likely to treat anyone that fell to them very badly. We were advised to fight to the last man, defend our comrades from these fascists. It fell to us, we were told, to stop Nazism rampaging across Mother Russia. We believed it. Every word of it, and so we fought like we had never fought before.

Confident in their business and utilizing tactics that were reminiscent of German stormtroopers in 1918, the infiltrating SS grenadiers had secreted themselves in no-man's-land during the night of 4–5 July. Having cleared lanes through the Soviet minefields, they sprang into action as their guns bombarded the Soviet front line at dawn, and they fell on the battered positions before the defenders had time to regain their poise. Led by a *Keil* of 42 Tigers, 494 tanks and assault guns attacked across a seven and a half mile front and slammed into the Soviet line. Totenkopf, the strongest of Hausser's divisions, screened the right flank of the attack with an advance to Gremuchii; LAH on the left advanced towards Bykovka and Das Reich moved in between via Berezov. Martin Steiger, commander of a Totenkopf Mark III, recalled the advance of the Tigers in front of him:

It was 4:15 am. A rustle, a hiss, a whistle! Columns of smoke rose like gigantic organ pipes into the sky. Artillery and mortars open the battle. A few minutes later heavy veils of smoke from the artillery explosions darkened the early morning sun. Stukas came and came, twenty-seven . . . eighty-one . . . we lost count. Stukas, heavy bombers, fighters, long-range reconnaissance planes; it was as if the air itself had begun to sing and hum. Finally, the order came: 'Panzers marsch!' Our attack was under way!

In LAH, SS-Untersturmführer Roger Hoch felt the tension in his platoon. After a busy evening in which he had little sleep, he was pleased to get into battle:

> I could not stand another delay and was delighted when we were told that the attack was on . . . The men looked relieved when I told them and there were a few brutish comments about what they would do with the enemy when they caught up with them. Much of it was bravado, I could tell that they were nervous. I would use the word 'frightened', but that was a concept that the men liked to see attached only to the others – the non-SS troops. But we all felt fear, I am sure, and the only way to banish it was to face it and defeat it by going into battle . . . As soon as we crossed the line, nerves vanished, anxious thoughts were dissolved, our minds were on the task in hand.

Although some of the tanks found the going difficult initially due to areas of wet ground, the corps gained momentum quickly. The main road to Bykovka was bordered by flat ground, which was covered by lanky, wavering, silvery-grey grass along with wheat and rye crops – the colour of the armour's recently prescribed yellow-olive-red-brown camouflage. The corps soon reached the cleared lanes of the minefield and as it advanced, the defenders' artillery, anti-tank guns and machine guns opened fire. As with XLVIII Panzer Corps, the three divisions were supremely well supported by the Luftwaffe, which sent high explosives and fragmentation bombs cascading into the Soviet positions. The Soviets did not panic, despite the speed of the onslaught and the razor-sharp metal splinters jagging through the air. Several guns took direct hits and lay in twisted heaps beside their mangled crews. Those gun crews who remained active found that their rounds failed to penetrate the Tigers' armour and, having given away their positions, they became victims of the tanks' 88mm guns.

For the Germans, it was crucial that the infantry moved quickly to clear the area, for as Wilhelm Roes, a Tiger radio operator, argues: 'The worst was the anti-tank hunting detachments which came in between T-34 attacks. You had to pay them particular attention – if they got through you were finished. An explosive charge and up you went.' Mansur Abdulin was a member of one such team, armed with magnetic mines, sticky bombs and Molotov cocktails. He advised: 'You should always act in pairs. The tank must ride over you, over your trench, then one soldier fires at the accompanying infantrymen, while the other throws the bottle or grenade.' The tanks defended themselves from the threat posed by these teams by rolling up to trenches, turning on the spot and collapsing the earth walls on to their occupants. Combat engineers and grenadiers undertook the gruesome business of demolishing obstacles and emptying trenches. This phase of the battle had something of 1918 about it as well, for the SS men often eschewed their rifles in favour of hand-to-hand fighting with entrenching tools, bayonets, knives, pistols and grenades. Where available, flame-thrower teams led the way, as Hans Huber testifies:

> [W]e worked our way forward into the trenches ahead of us. I fired a burst of flame as we approached every zig-zag in the trench and every enemy strong point. It was a strange feeling to serve this destructive weapon and it was terrifying to see the flames eat their way forward and envelop the Russian defenders. Soon I was coloured black from head to foot from the fuel oil and my face was burnt from the flames which bounced back off the trench walls or which were blown back at us by the strong wind. I could hardly see. The enemy could not fight against flame-throwers and so we made good progress, taking many prisoners.

When there were no flame-throwers available, the infantry jumped down into the traverses and cleared the trenches systematically, using well-rehearsed drills. SS-Mann Stefan Witte has said:

I left my heavier kit and advanced with a fighting knife and grenades ... Dropping into a trench system, my section threw grenades around the corners and into dug-outs which were then cleared out by men with sub-machine guns ... My knife was my only personal weapon and I used it once when I came across a Russian desperately trying to load his rifle. Without thinking I lunged forward and drove my knife into his stomach and twisted it, just as we had been trained. The man screamed, dropped to his knees and then fell onto his face. I moved on.

Slowly but surely, the SS divisions made their way through the first Soviet defensive line, but the defenders, recognizing that nothing was to be gained from surrendering, fought on. It was a violent tussle, as one observer describes:

The Tigers rumbled on. Anti-tank rifles cracked. Grenadiers jumped into trenches. Machine-guns ticked. Shells smashed sap trenches and dug-outs. The very first hours of fighting showed that Hausser's divisions were encountering a well-prepared and well-functioning opposition.

Even so, by 0900 hours the II SS Panzer Corps had cracked the Soviets' first line of defence. The final breakthrough occurred so quickly that Chistyakov, who was enjoying a 'second breakfast' of vodka and scrambled eggs in the open, was forced to flee to the relative safety of Lieutenant-General M.E. Katukov's 1st Guards Tank Army. By 1100 hours, the three divisions were busy engaging the positions between the Soviets' first and second main lines. It was a methodical advance –

the artillery was brought forward, the tanks reorganized and the infantry sent forward to skirmish, identify Soviet positions and begin eliminating them. A war correspondent who was attached to the Tigers that were leading SS-Gruppenführer Walter Kruger's Das Reich, wrote of the subsequent advance:

> This is the hour of the tank. Unnoticed we assembled at the bottom of a *balka*, the Tigers flanked by medium and light companies. Our field glasses searched the horizon, groping in the smoke that covers the enemy bunkers like a curtain. The leader of the Tiger half company, an Obersturmführer from the Rhineland whose calmness ennobles us, gives the order to attack. The tank engines begin to howl as we load the guns. The heavy tanks slowly roll into the battle zone. At 200 metres, the first anti-tank fires at us. With a single round, we blow it up. All was quiet for a while as we rolled over the abandoned enemy trenches. We waved to our brave infantrymen from our open hatches as we passed them. They were taking a short rest after having just stormed the enemy heights. We then moved into the next valley.

As the tanks continued their surge, isolated Soviet infantrymen scattered. The correspondent's report continued:

> Our machine gunners fired on [the enemy] and forced them to take cover. As both of our machine guns rattled, approving shouts of the crew accompanied the aim of the fire. A heavy enemy truck was seen in the woods on our right attempting to escape. We fired upon it and it burst into flames.

In this way, the divisions moved forward, carefully, but maintaining momentum. The tank commanders, their heads swivelling slightly as they scrutinized the terrain through open hatches, eventually spied the approach of enemy tanks. At 1300 hours Das Reich's armour came under fire from two T-34s, and although they were quickly despatched, 40 more appeared over the horizon, firing on the move. Several Tigers were hit but not damaged. Reacting quickly and taking up firing positions, the German armour selected targets and sent their armour-piercing rounds hurtling towards the enemy. Red Army tanks burst into flame as the panzers moved to new locations, stopped and repeated the process. After an hour of fighting, the field was covered in blazing hulks. Any survivors of the initial calamitous shell strike had just seconds to evacuate the tank before it was engulfed in flame, which threatened to ignite the fuel and ammunition. Nikolai Zheleznov was knocked to the turret floor when his T-34 was hit. The white-hot explosion had shattered his driver's head, torn the loader's arm from his body and sent scores of large metal shards into the gunner's unprotected body. A fire sucked the oxygen out of the compartment and set light to Zheleznov's uniform as he struggled to open the commander's hatch. Eventually pushing it free as the flames leapt up around him, he fought to pull himself out of the void but his left leg had been broken at the knee. Passing comrades pulled him clear of the tank just before it exploded but he had sustained horrendous burns.

Soviet tank man Vladimir Alexeev recalled that the panzers were very efficient: 'move, pause and fire – a very lethal combination'. Powerful guns, mounted on fast-moving, motorized turrets, gave the Tigers a considerable advantage while the thickness of their armour provided excellent protection. This led Ivan Sagun to suggest that any contest between T-34s and Tigers was unequal:

I had an encounter with just such a tank. He fired at us from literally one kilometre away. His first shot blew a hole in the side of my tank, his second hit my axle. At a range of half a kilometre I fired at him with a special calibre shell, but it bounced off him like a candle; I mean it didn't penetrate his armour. At literally 300 metres I fired my second shell – same result. Then he started looking for me, turning his turret to see where I was. I told my driver to reverse fast and we hid behind some trees.

The Soviets sought to negate the Tigers' advantages by fighting at close quarters, but without radios, keeping overall control was extremely difficult. Tactics had to be simple. Vladimir Alexeev told his T-34 platoon, 'Follow me – do as I do.' Yet without intercom, crews found it difficult to carry out their commander's orders – particularly in the heat of battle – and so they had to improvise a method of communication. Ivan Sagun developed a simple system: 'I directed the driver by tapping him on the shoulder with my foot. On the right shoulder meant go right, on the left shoulder go left. A prod in the back meant stop.' When battle was joined, he made signals to the gunner with his hands: 'A thumb up meant an armour-penetrating shell, two fingers for a shrapnel shell. The index finger also meant I needed a shrapnel shell; if we were facing another tank, he often knew which shell to use.'

Das Reich's battle with the T-34s lasted four hours. Although the 1st Guards Tank Army had failed to halt the division's advance, this had not been its aim. The tanks had been tasked with slowing the enemy's onslaught and, having achieved this, they withdrew. The 'armoured speed bump' had bought the time the second line of defence needed to prepare itself – the infantry was reinforced and more anti-tank guns were brought up – and plans were tweaked to take account of the challenge that now faced the 23rd Guards Rifle Corps. Das Reich, having had its sting drawn by the initial thrust, probed forward once more in the early evening, and was soon confronted by the minefield protecting the Soviets' second line.

Meanwhile, SS-Gruppenführer Wisch's LAH, operating on Das Reich's left, had taken Bykovka at 1610 hours and pushed on towards the Psel and Oboyan. Among the LAH Tiger commanders was SS-Untersturmführer Michael Wittmann. The 29-year-old Bavarian's skills had been honed during nine years in the army. He had seen action with LAH in Poland, Yugoslavia, Greece and Russia. A recent graduate of officer and tank school in Germany, he had returned to the Eastern Front and by the launch of Zitadelle was commanding a platoon of five Tigers. In common with Das Reich's armoured spearhead, LAH had been involved in intense tank combat throughout the day. Although Wittmann's tank had been hit several times during a battle in the late morning, it had not been immobilized and he had charged several anti-tank guns and crushed them before registering his first tank kill: 'The T-34's turret was blown clear of the rest of the vehicle, and flames enveloped the wreck.' Already drained by their efforts, Wittmann and his crew could not afford to rest and in the afternoon went to the aid of a fellow platoon, which had been cut off by several T-34s. One well-aimed shot smashed his Tiger's track and wounded his driver, requiring the replacement of both. Wittmann surged on and by the end of the day he and his crew had notched up eight Soviet tank kills and destroyed seven anti-tank guns.

By that time, the leading elements of LAH had moved up to the second line at Yakovlevo, just south of Pokrovka, but attempts to break through and make a dash to the Psel were rebuffed. The day's work had cost the division 97 dead, 522 wounded, 17 missing and around 30 tanks. But with Das Reich, the division had forced a wedge deep enough into Chistyakov's defences that it could, with care and some good fortune, be used to split the front wide open.

The limited success of SS-Gruppenführer H. Priess's Totenkopf on the right of II SS Panzer Corps, however, meant that Hausser's position was not as useful as it might have been. After taking Gremuchii, the division needed to press on to dominate the ground north of Belgorod and protect the corps' developing penetration. However, having detached the 155th Guards Regiment from the 52nd Guards Rifle Division, Totenkopf's attempt to drive it into the flank of the neighbouring 375th Rifle Division failed. Taking a stand on the Belgorod–Oboyan line, the regiment was reinforced by 96th Tank Brigade and held on. T-34 gunner Nicolai Andreev describes the scene:

We sped westwards to assist the right flank of the division [375th Guards Rifle Division] and fought a tough battle to stop the Nazis from enveloping them ... The battlefield was already littered with burning wrecks by the time that we arrived but we held them. By targeting the tracks on the Tigers we could at least stop them and their lighter tanks did not prove so much of a problem to destroy ... We worked closely with the infantry who seemed to be everywhere. That was our strength – numbers. Whenever the enemy thought that they were about to break through, we plugged the gap.

Its northern movement stifled by a tributary of the Lipovyi–Donets and movement farther east fiercely contested by the Soviets' armoured reinforcements, Totenkopf's attainments on 5 July fell far short of what had been expected of it. Hausser called on III Panzer Corps on his right flank to lend some support but was told that this was unlikely because Army Detachment Kempf had significant problems of its own. This formation had to cross the Northern Donets before it could engage the 7th Guards Army's defences. Although bridged overnight by engineers, the crossing points were targeted by the Soviet guns during Vatutin's pre-emptive bombardment, which was particularly punishing in this area. At the Mikhailovka bridgehead just south of Belgorod, the one place where Kempf had already established a crossing, eight infantry battalions from III Panzer Corps' 6th Panzer Division were subjected to a disconcertingly heavy bombardment. Then, when a company of Clemens Graf Kageneck's 503rd Heavy Tank Battalion – split one company per panzer division – began to cross the 24 ton Mikhailovka bridge, it too was targeted by the Soviet artillery. Kageneck watched aghast as the front exploded before him:

> [S]uddenly, a 'red sunrise' arose on the far side as hundreds of Stalin's organs hurled their rockets exactly onto the crossing site. The bridge was totally demolished and the engineers, unfortunately, suffered heavy losses. Never have I hugged the dirt so tightly as when these terrible shells sprayed their thin fragments just above the ground.

It became clear immediately that Kempf's plans had been compromised, and enjoying first-class observation from high ground on the east bank of the Northern Donets, the Soviets were in a strong position to unhinge his attack. The Tigers managed to cross and link up with the beleaguered battalions waiting for them on the east bank, but the remainder of 6th Panzer Division had to redeploy and try to use a bridge supporting the southern part of the bridgehead. The formation's commander, Major General Walter von Hünersdorff, was already anxious that he was falling behind the agreed timings but he became incandescent with rage when he found the designated bridge was already clogged with traffic. The formation went in search of another crossing, but failing to find one suitable, remained on the west bank of the river on 5 July.

Meanwhile, at the original crossing point, the Tiger-led attack on Stary Gorod (east of Belgorod) ran into a poorly cleared minefield and strong resistance, and stalled. It was a similar story farther along the line where the 19th Panzer Division crossed the river and ran immediately into Soviet mines, which ensnared a dozen of the attached Tigers. Kageneck was furious at what he deemed to be the 'widespread bungling' that had placed his tanks in such great danger. He cited unmapped Soviet minefields, commanders using inadequately marked maps and poor staff work. The division did recover to advance to a depth of five miles on its left, but the 19th Panzer Division's attack was not impressive and some aspects were indeed incompetent. The same charges could be levelled initially at 7th Panzer Division, whose bridges were strong enough to carry Mark IIIs and VIs but not the Tigers. Everywhere Kageneck looked, his assets seemed to be hamstrung by either enemy action or poor preparation. Attempts were made to drive the 60 ton monsters across the river to support the infantry and lighter tanks that were already taking a tremendous pounding on the opposite bank, but that plan was unsuccessful, as Tiger gunner Gerhard Niemann explains:

> The Russian artillery opens fire. We drive through a village. We are to cross a river via a ford near Solomino ... The leading tank has reached the ford. The others remain under cover. All around shells burst from enemy artillery. 'Stalin's Organ' also join in. It's a hellish concert. The lead Tiger, number 321, disappears to above its fenders. Slowly it pushes through the water. Then it becomes stuck on the far bank. Its attempts to get free fail. The marshy terrain is impassable for the sixty-ton tank. Widely spaced, the Tigers take up positions on the open plain before the Donets. The Russian artillery is concentrating on the crossing point ... The first wounded infantry are coming back. They can't comprehend that the Tigers are still here standing around inactive.

The company eventually crossed the river in the afternoon, following some swift work by engineers who constructed a bridge strong enough to take their tanks' weight. Engineer Rolf Schmidt 'worked like the devil himself' to ensure that the crossing was completed in 'record time':

> The Tigers were extremely anxious to cross and put us under tremendous pressure saying things like 'men are dying over there.

Faster, faster!' Some of the crews assisted us with some of the cables but on two occasions we were left waiting for sections that were held up in the rear. We later heard that enemy shelling had caused all sorts of delays ... In the end we finished the bridge extremely quickly considering the conditions. We lost two men to Soviet shells that afternoon ... When we gave the all clear to cross, the Tigers were all ready in a line, their engines running.

Once they had crossed the Northern Donets, the heavy tanks found the grenadiers pinned down by enemy fire and immediately set about destroying the Soviet bunkers. Niemann continues:

My foot presses forward on the pedal of the turret-traversing mechanism. The turret swings to the right. With my left hand I set the range on the telescopic sight; my right hand cranks the elevation handwheel. The target appears in my sight. Ready, release safety – fire. The target is shrouded in a cloud of smoke. 'Driver advance!' A slight jolt and already another picture presents itself. The first Red Army soldiers appear ahead of the tank. Masses of brown clad uniforms rise up. Standing and kneeling, they fire against the tank's steel armour. The machine-gun opens fire. One after another, high explosive shells detonate among them. They throw their arms in the air and fall. Only a few find cover in a depression in the earth. They are overrun by the following infantry.

Despite a poor start, the 7th Panzer Division eventually broke through the first defensive line and pushed on between Razumnoe and Krutoi Log. At six miles the division's advance was the best achieved by Army Detachment Kempf. On its right, the two infantry divisions of Corps Raus – spread over 20 miles and devoid of tanks – had little success. The advance began well with the river successfully crossed and the

spearheads of the 106th and 320th Infantry Divisions deftly negoti-
ating the cleared lanes in the minefield to fall hard and fast on the 72nd
Guards Rifle Division. With the two front lines so close together at this
point, the defenders had little time to ready themselves in the outposts,
as Erhard Raus later wrote:

> [T]he advancing infantry surprised them and had no difficulty
> ferreting them out. But when the infantry reached the two- to
> three-mile deep zone of battle positions prepared in the
> preceding months, they had to make extensive use of hand
> grenades in order to mop up the maze of densely dug-in trenches
> and bunkers, some of which were a dozen or more feet deep. At
> the same time, artillery and flak fired counter-battery missions
> against the enemy's heavy weapons that had resumed fire from
> rear positions, on reserves infiltrating through the trench system,
> as well as against Russian medium artillery.

The first Soviet line and the village of Maslovo Pristani were taken
after a fierce battle with some hand-to-hand fighting. The lodgement
was nearly lost when a Soviet counterattack supported by 40 tanks clattered into the tired Germans, but it was eventually rebuffed with the
assistance of divisional artillery and medium flak batteries. However,
still facing considerable resistance and having suffered 2000 casualties
during the day, the divisions could penetrate no farther and dug in for
the night.

By the end of 5 July, Manstein's attack against the Voronezh Front
had not achieved anything like the success it needed for the Soviets to
be psychologically damaged and their defences irretrievably dislocated.
In some places the attacking formations had barely breached the first
Soviet line, and although the two main attacking corps had blown gaps
in the defences, they remained short of the Soviets' second line, were
not joined up and displayed vulnerable flanks. The Germans had

significantly underestimated Vatutin's defences and this immediately undermined Manstein's timetable, despite Zhukov's displeasure at the results of the pre-emptive bombardment.

Across the front, Army Group South's thrust had been slowed, which allowed the Soviets time to react as soon as Manstein's intentions had been confirmed. Vatutin and his commanders were able to prepare their second echelons to meet the expected renewed German onslaught on 6 July. Shumilov's 7th Guards Army was reinforced with two rifle divisions from the reserve while the 15th Guards Rifle Division was moved into position behind the second-line defences opposite III Panzer Corps. The 6th Guards Army, meanwhile, moved two divisions in front of Pokrovka – the 51st Guards Rifle Division to the east, and the 90th Guards Rifle Division to the west – while 1000 tanks of the 1st Tank Army and the separate 2nd Guards and 5th Guards Tank Corps were brought forward to add an armoured backing to Chistyakov's rifle divisions. Behind them, the 93rd Guards Rifle Division was positioned astride the Pokrovka–Prokhorovka road. These deployments made Vatutin's priority extremely clear – the enemy would be denied the roads and communications hubs necessary to maintain his impetus, and reinforcements would be moved forward as needed to provide unremitting pressure on his main axes. Manstein's offensive was to be robbed of all momentum, ground down and snuffed out.

Even as Army Group South was attempting to deliver a strong armoured punch to the Voronezh Front's jaw, Model's Ninth Army began its attack in the northern salient with a series of lighter jabs. Here, nine infantry divisions, strengthened with assault guns and two companies of Tigers, were joined by a single panzer division to break through the defences of the Central Front's 70th and 13th Armies. Although this attack carried less armoured weight than Manstein's, the format was the same – a preliminary bombardment was followed by an airstrike against the Soviet defences in support of the ground attack. Without the mailed fist of armour, the first two phases of the attack were essential if the Ninth Army was to fracture Rokossovsky's defences. It was a gamble, as a junior officer on Model's staff recalls:

> We were not convinced that the choice of an 'infantry first' attack was wise. This was not just because the Soviet positions were known to be tough, but because – I was told – Model expected a breakthrough on the second day and possibly earlier. [The Corps commanders] thought this extremely unlikely and, even if it did occur, what was that success to be exploited with? The armour would take far too long to bring forward and charge through. The Soviets would fill the gap.

Major Max Torst, a company commander in the 6th Infantry Division, was unaware of the friction at headquarters concerning the plan, but in later life, as a student of the First World War, he noted distinct similarities between that plan and strategies employed in the battles of his father's generation:

> On the Western Front it was Germany that was defending and on the Somme [in 1916] we developed strong defences in depth to capture the British attack. This is what the Soviets had done to stifle our offensive [at Kursk]. We now played the part of the British and threw ourselves at those defences and bounced off . . . It does not take much imagination to transfer the scene from northern France to Russia. Put simply, defence was now stronger than the attack – and we were not used to that.

These astute observations are not at odds with the events that unfolded in the Ninth Army sector on 5 July, although German casualties were far lighter than those suffered by the British on the first day of the

Battle of the Somme, due to their accomplished tactics and the success of their aerial artillery.

The primary attack was by the two central corps – General Joachim Lemelsen's XLVII Panzer Corps and General Joseph Harpe's XLI Panzer Corps. Their flanks were to be covered by General Hans Zorn's XLVI Panzer Corps on the right and Johannes Freissner's XXIII Corps on the left. Zorn's 31st and 7th Infantry Divisions just managed to break the Soviets' first line by the evening of 5 July, as did Freissner's 78th Assault Division, but on the outer faces of the two corps, neither the 258th nor the 36th Infantry Division made any valuable penetrations. Despite the importance attached to these formations taking the Soviets' second line on the first day – including the key local communications hub of Maloarkhangelsk – the two corps were held several miles from it. Thus the anchors provided by the two formations ultimately lacked the depth required for XLVII and XLI Panzer Corps to advance unhindered by the concern about creating an obvious salient. Lemelsen's formation sought to crack the enemy's first and second lines between the Teploye and Olkhovatka axis using Mortimer von Kessel's 20th Panzer Division and Horst Grossmann's 6th Infantry Division with two panzer divisions being brought forward to exploit their success at the appropriate time. However, defences here were as strong as anything in the south. Minefields protected a mixture of carefully placed infantry, artillery and tanks in deep, mutually supportive positions. Indeed, the 15th Rifle Division's mines immediately slowed Lemelsen's strike divisions and it was not until 0800 hours that lanes had been cleared and the attack could progress.

From the outset, Soviet artillery pounded the advancing units, but unlike in the south, the fight for control of the skies above the battlefield was more even. The 16th Air Army suffered lighter losses in their pre-emptive airstrike than their 2nd Air Army colleagues. Indeed, Koba Lomidze, a rear gunner in an Il-2, recalls:

We made several sorties against the German panzers that morning although our fighters continually struggled to give us the time and space that we required. We were given specific orders to target the spearheads, but more than once we found Stukas dive bombing our artillery batteries trying to do the same ... The Stukas would mass above the target and our fighters would break them up. We did not have long before the German fighters arrived and so made our attack and left the area as quickly as we could. We were chased by Bf-109s on two occasions. The first winged us and the damage was not too bad, but on the second occasion, despite my best efforts, we were badly hit in the tail when he dived out of the sun. We limped home and made an ungainly landing. Overnight the damage was repaired and we were airborne again by dawn the following morning.

Meanwhile, on the ground, crossing through the minefield both divisions walked into what Max Torst has called a 'storm of steel':

I had not seen anything like it. It was a marvel that any of my company survived. Shells, bombs, mortars, machine gun fire and rifle fire fell on us like in a furious onslaught. Of my ninety men, six fell – two dead – but one of them was a young platoon commander. A softly spoken, gentle lad who hated the war and knew that he would not last the duration. It is perhaps because of that premonition that a senior NCO immediately stepped in to fill his shoes without a thought. He had been primed for the event ... And so we struggled on, desperate to get into a position where we could engage the defenders and dislodge them.

The two companies of 505 Heavy Panzer Battalion attached to the 6th Infantry Division, and leading the way, formed the largest single group of Tigers committed to battle on 5 July. Working well with the infantry, they stormed through the outpost zone in cooperation with the 20th Panzer Division and then pushed towards the first line between Podolyan and Butyrki. Airstrikes were called down when a stubborn obstacle was identified by a unit commander or when compelling information was obtained from the enemy. One intelligence officer feeding reports to the 6th Infantry Division testifies:

> We put an emphasis on taking prisoners, quickly interrogating them at battalion and passing important information up the chain as quickly as possible. This was critical [now] as it became clear that we knew far less about the Soviet defences than we thought we did . . . However, the skill was getting the information out of the prisoner and to where it was needed quickly. The material was time sensitive . . . Flooding headquarters with inappropriate material or providing it too slowly always led to lost opportunities.

One prisoner taken early that morning identified the boundary between the 15th and 81st Rifle Divisions as having suffered particularly badly during the preliminary bombardment. Within 40 minutes of the intelligence having left the man's lips, Stukas were *en route* to strike the area with Tigers following up. The arrival of German tanks immediately provoked the Soviets to send 90 T-34s to plug the gap in the line and block the heavy panzers' advance. During the resultant three-hour tank battle, the Soviets lost 42 tanks for two destroyed Tigers and five more with broken tracks. Even so, in common with events 100 miles to the south, the Red Army had successfully slowed the Wehrmacht's momentum. Here it was at the cost of the Germans breaching the 13th Army's first line of defence between Podolyan and Butyrki, which gave the Mark IIIs and IVs of the 20th Panzer Division the opportunity to push forward on the right while the 6th Infantry Division pushed forward on the left. But the Soviets did not disintegrate. They understood that each line was merely an obstacle and not a final defensive line. The aim was to wear the enemy out as they endeavoured to surmount each obstacle, and to stretch their lines of communication as exposed salients were created within their defences. Thus, almost as soon as Lemelsen's corps had reorganized in preparation for their attack on Bobrik, Stepi and Saborovka on the Sevana, the 29th Rifle Corps engaged them from positions along a low ridge in front of the second line. The bloody confrontation that took place here was witnessed by a Soviet observer, who wrote:

> The sky blackened from smoke and heat. The acrid gases from the exploding shells and mines blinded the eyes. The soldiers were deafened by the thunder of guns and mortars and the creaking of tracks ... All of the weapons of the infantry, and the anti-tank strong points and artillery groups supporting the [15th and 81st Rifle Divisions] entered the battle to repel the enemy blows. Soviet soldiers heroically struggled with the attacking groups of enemy. The infantry skilfully destroyed his tanks with grenades and bottles filled with mixtures of fuel. Under a hurricane of fire they stole up to the enemy vehicles, struck them with anti-tank grenades, set them on fire with incendiary bottles, and laid mines under them.

Here, up to six miles into the Soviet defences, XLVII Panzer Corps was held.

The Ninth Army's progress on 5 July was not limited to General Lemelsen's corps, though. The impression it made in the Soviet line was simultaneously broadened by Harpe's XLI Panzer Corps on Lemelsen's left flank. The 292nd Infantry Division supported by a detachment of Ferdinands from 656 Anti-Tank Battalion, together with the 86th Infantry Division, strengthened by a panzer regiment from the 18th Panzer Division and two Ferdinand detachments, aimed to advance to a line extending either side of Ponyri in the enemy's second line. The divisions breached the minefield in front of the 29th Rifle Corps' trenches with the assistance of demolition vehicles of Funklenk Company 313, comprising three command StuG IIIs and 12 Borgward B.IVs. These teams could clear routes through the area quickly, ameliorating the time-consuming and dangerous business of mass human involvement, and so speed the Wehrmacht on its way.

When mines were located, the first small, light-tracked demolition vehicle was driven forward to the launch spot. Attracting considerable fire, its driver then left the vehicle and by means of radio control delivered it to the target. On its arrival, a 500kg charge was dropped, the vehicle was withdrawn and an explosion produced via a delayed detonation. The percussion caused by that explosion tripped the mines and so created the first section of cleared path through the obstruction, which was immediately extended by the next demolition vehicle.

The breach having been made, the Ferdinands proceeded to engage the Soviet first line. In common with all Soviet front-line formations in the salient, the defenders here had received psychological as well as technical training to deal with the armoured threat and overcome the 'tank panic' that had been in evidence ever since the Germans invaded. Fyodor Onton recalled his instruction when, in June, he was ordered into a trench and a captured German tank was driven towards him: 'It was a frightening moment as the metal beasts came clanking and squeaking towards us but we were ordered to hold fast. A couple of my infantry colleagues looked grey and ready to flee but managed to keep a hold on their instincts. I heard later that the men had seen German tanks in action before and were the only survivors of one particularly desperate episode.' Nikolai Litvin had a similar experience and wrote in his memoir:

The tanks continued to advance closer and closer. Some comrades became frightened, leaped out of the trenches, and began to run away. The commander saw who was running and quickly forced them back into the trenches, making it clear they had to stay put. The tanks reached the trench line and, with a terrible roar, passed overhead ... it was possible to conceal oneself in a trench from a tank, let it pass right over you, and remain alive. Lie down and press yourself to the bottom of the trench, and shut your eyes.

This training seems to have worked. Paul Carell noted: 'Everything had been done to inoculate the troops against the notorious tank panic [and] the result was unmistakeable.' Both the 15th and 81st Rifle Divisions allowed the armour to clatter over their heads, popping up in the midst of the following infantry and separating the tanks from their support. With their thick armoured plate and large guns, the sluggish Ferdinands were most effective when supported by infantry who could protect them from close-quarter threats. As a battle erupted behind them, the armour was engaged by anti-tank guns and 'tank killer teams'. Thoroughly isolated, the weaknesses of the Ferdinands became obvious. Heinz Guderian had always understood that the clumsy tracked guns lacked not only the finesse that he would have liked, but also some basic technical features, and so they were left:

> [i]ncapable of close-range fighting since they lacked sufficient ammunition (armour-piercing and high-explosive) for their guns and this defect was aggravated by the fact that they had no machine-gun. Once [they] had broken into the enemy's infantry zone, they literally had to go quail shooting with cannon. They did not manage to neutralize, let alone destroy, the enemy infantry and machine-guns, so that our infantry was unable to follow up behind them. By the time they reached the Russian artillery they were on their own.

Crews were consequently forced to fire their stored MG-42s down the barrel of their 88mm guns. Some brave commanders used pistols to stave off the defenders' attacks. Trapped and exposed, the armour was picked off. The anti-tank guns scored some successes by penetrating the Ferdinands' rear armour, but often they targeted the tracks and by disabling them allowed teams to attach their demolition charges or turn the guns into giant fireballs with their Molotov cocktails. Onton says that these crude weapons were very effective:

We could make Molotovs extremely quickly. Each unit was issued with hundreds of glass bottles, gasoline, wadding and paraffin. Bottles were filled to the neck with the gasoline and the screw caps replaced. When required the caps were removed and the paraffin-soaked wadding was inserted into the bottle openings and ignited ... We had to be extremely careful how they were stored and where they were lit because these were very basic weapons and accidents were not uncommon ... When a tank or assault gun was identified as a target, the Molotovs were simply thrown at them. Ideally they would land on the engine compartment and gravity would send burning fuel into the vehicle. But if all we could do was throw them at the front of the turret, that was what we would do ... When the fuel's vapour ignited there was a boom sending black smoke into the sky and the tanks quickly caught alight ... It was amazing how those hunks of metal burned, but they did. The paint seemed to catch fire and, I assumed, the fuel entered the tank and set light to fabrics and ammunition. We knew that within a matter of seconds the crew would try to evacuate and we waited, picking them off as they appeared through the hatches. Sometimes our victim was finished off with grenades.

For much of the morning, tanks and infantry fought to regain the mutual cooperation on which the Wehrmacht depended. Although by noon the villages of Alexsandrovka and Butyrki had been taken and

Harpe's attack had broken the first line of defences across four miles, it lacked the energy to create a clean breakthrough. Thus both XLVII and XLI Panzer Corps were brought to a halt, resting on the outposts of the Soviets' second-line defences. Their fatigued divisions now had to reorganize, resupply and update their plans after their recent exertions. It was at this point that Model's armoured reserve might have been unleashed in order to exert pressure on the withdrawing enemy. Second-line defences could have been attacked before they were properly set. Indeed, Mortimer von Kessel believed that a fleeting opportunity was missed and later argued:

> Far ahead of the [20th Panzer Division] lay a massif [the Olkhovatka heights] on which we could see movement by the Russians. If the tanks had rolled through then, we would perhaps have reached the objective of Kursk, because the enemy was completely surprised and weak. Valuable time was lost which the enemy used to rush in his reserves.

As many on the Ninth Army staff had feared, the four panzer and panzer grenadier divisions that might have been able to burst through the Soviets at this stage were assembled too far to the rear to be of any use. Model had clearly not planned on the critical moment occurring so early in the battle.

The day's events left the Ninth Army with a broad but shallow lodgement in the Soviet defensive system, which did not cause Rokossovsky any undue concern. He had expected Model to make his main thrust towards Maloarkhangelsk, since its capture would have provided the Germans with access to the major roads in the sector, and his defences against the two strike corps sent to accomplish the task held firm. Moreover, the relatively weak showing of XXIII Corps allowed Rokossovsky to contain its threat comparatively easily, which enabled him to focus his attention on the stronger advance in the enemy's centre. Like Vatutin, the Central Front's commander had great faith in his second line of defences and did not believe that his plan had been endangered by the events of 5 July. He consequently ordered three armoured corps of General Rodin's 600 tank, 50,000 man 2nd Tank Army north to screen the approaches to his second line from Teploye through Olkhovatka to Ponryi, and backed them with the 17th Guards Rifle Corps. The 18th Rifle Corps was sent to reinforce the defences of Maloarkhangelsk. Model's offensive, in the same way as Manstein's, was to be robbed of all momentum, ground down and snuffed out.

Operation Zitadelle was finely poised by nightfall on the first day. The main German strike groupings were leaning on the outposts of the Soviet second-line defences in both the north and south, but their advance had not been as devastating as either Model or Manstein had hoped. The two men had carefully massed and prepared their forces for the great offensive, and they must have been disturbed that, having largely exhausted the element of surprise, the enemy had not been more fundamentally dislocated. They would also have noted that both Soviet Fronts were well prepared to meet their offensive and seemed more resilient than they had in the past. As Raus has written: 'Higher headquarters had been hoping the troops would encounter an enemy weakened in his power of resistance. This proved to be a delusion. The Russians appeared materially prepared . . . as well as morally inoculated against all symptoms of deterioration.'

The first day of Zitadelle had not resulted in the disastrous fragmentation of the Red Army, as had the opening of Barbarossa two years earlier, and Stalin must have been reassured by this, especially as he had handed the initiative to the Germans. Yet although the Supreme Commander was keen to learn about the progress of the ground battle, once he had been reassured about the steadfastness of the salient's defences, he wanted to know about the situation in the air. The Soviet airforce had lost around 250 aircraft to the Germans' 45, and he was anxious that the Luftwaffe had attained freedom of the sky. That evening, Lieutenant-General Sergey Rudenko, commander of the 16th Air Army, which was supporting the Central Front, explained to Rokossovsky that the air battle would be every bit as attritional as the Red Army's battle. When Stalin telephoned the headquarters to quiz Rokossovsky about the situation, he pressed the Central Front's commander for an unambiguous response, as Rudenko recalls:

'Have we gained control of the air or not?' That proved to be his main interest! Rokossovsky replied: 'Comrade Stalin, it is impossible to tell. There have been very hard combats in the air and both sides have suffered heavy losses.' But Stalin just retorted: 'Tell me precisely, have we won in the air or not? Yes or no?' Rokossovsky spoke again: 'It is impossible to give a definitive answer to that question, but tomorrow we shall solve this positively.'

The attention Stalin was giving to the aerial battle was not misplaced. He understood that the Wehrmacht's methods, and consequently their plans, were dependent on command of the skies. But no definitive pronouncement could be made on the air battle that evening, just as no definitive verdict on the ground battle had been reached – the Luftwaffe had the edge but the army was being held. The battle was still evenly balanced. Despite this, Stalin probably had more reason to sleep soundly that night than he'd had for many weeks.

At the Wolfsschanze, Hitler also had cause for optimism. Reports from the front confirmed that the Soviet defences had been pierced, and General Zeitzler said that the Führer was 'cautiously optimistic' – relieved, perhaps, that there was still hope after the first day. The German High Command expected its forces to deepen and widen their penetrations in the next few days, and to retain most of their cohesion and strength. Indeed, German losses had been relatively light for a break-in battle. The Ninth Army had suffered 7,295 casualties and lost around 150 tanks (although many were repairable) and the Fourth Panzer Army, its casualties unknown, had lost just 51 tanks. The Luftwaffe had been able to go about its business with confidence after the failure of the Soviets' early morning strike against its airfields.

Yet the opening day of Zitadelle had more in common with the grand set-piece battles of the First World War than with the dynamic manoeuvres that had marked out the Wehrmacht's greatest successes over the previous three years. In July 1943, the Germans had been forced to attack the enemy frontally, in a manner that demanded patient tenacity and plentiful resources – a style that crippled blitzkrieg and suited the waiting Soviets ensconced within their deep and complicated lair. The Wehrmacht needed a breakthrough and needed it fast.

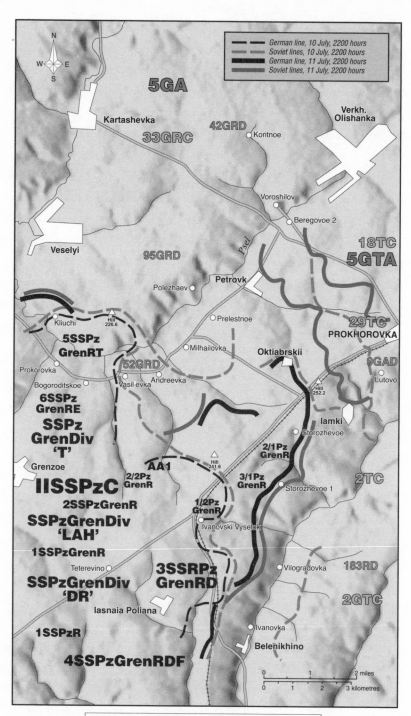

5GA

Kartashevka

Verkh.
Olishanka

42GRD

Koritnoe

33GRC

Voroshilov

Beregovoe 2

Veselyi

95GRD

18TC
5GTA

Psel

Polezhaev

Petrovk

29TC
PROKHOROVKA

Kliuchi

Hill
226.6

Prelestnoe

5SSPz
GrenRT

Milhailovka

Oktiabrskii

9GAD

Lutovo

Prokorovka

52GRD

Andreevka

Hill
252.2

Bogoroditskoe

Vasil evka

6SSPz
GrenRE

Iamki

Storozhevoe

SSPz
GrenDiv
'T'

2/1Pz
GrenR

Grenzoe

AA1

Hill
241.6

2/2Pz
GrenR

3/1Pz
GrenR

Storozhevoe 1

2TC

IISSPzC

2SSPzGrenR

1/2Pz
GrenR

SSPzGrenDiv
'LAH'

1SSPzGrenR

Ivanovski Vyselok

Teeterevino

3SSRPz
GrenRD

Vilogradovka

183RD

SSPzGrenDiv
'DR'

2GTC

Iasnaia Poliana

Ivanovka

1SSPzR

Belenikhino

4SSPzGrenRDF

0   1   2 miles
0   1   2   3 kilometres

Map 8: Prokhorovka, 10–11 July 1943

CHAPTER 7

Breaking Through

(Zitadelle: 6–8 July)

Nurse Olga Iofe dressed one gaping wound and immediately moved on to the next. There was no time to waste. Her skills were precious and she could not linger, despite the pleas of the young men to comfort them. One soldier – a boy really – with an awful head wound asked Olga to pray with him. Being a good member of Komsomol she should refuse, but being a first-class nurse she placed the palm of her hand on his brow and closed her eyes while he mumbled a few pious words. A doctor yelled for her assistance and she left her patient to die alone.

It was a busy day at the aid station, which was now just five miles behind the front line. Olga could not even begin to guess how many men had died there since the German attack resumed on the second morning of the offensive. The 22-year-old had qualified as a nurse in early 1941 and volunteered on the second day of the war. It was, she said, 'her duty to the Party and to the Motherland'. After a very brief induction into the army during which she learned to identify ranks and absorbed lists of 'forbidden activities', she was sent to the front where she had remained ever since. Yet Olga rarely took her full leave entitlement to rest and recuperate, despite the encouragement of her colleagues. If time away from the ward meant that men would die, then what right did she have to relax? In any case, she found it impossible to sleep away from her camp bed. A mattress was too comfortable and the quiet was intolerable. War had been a struggle at first, but now it filled her every fibre and she could not bear to be without it. Even the few hours that she had between shifts were spent strolling among the beds or storing the latest delivery of supplies that had been trundled along the salient's dusty roads from the east. She slept little and ate even less. Olga knew that she could continue like this for weeks and even months if necessary. She knew because she had worked without a break during the Battle of Moscow, and for a similar stretch during the advance from Voronezh to Kursk during the previous winter.

The day before had been frantic, despite a recent increase in the size of the medical team and many weeks of preparation. Six surgeons and 18 nurses worked as a tight unit in their well-provisioned hospital, which was attached to a farmhouse. They had running water, which had been connected courtesy of the engineers who had also cut a new access road, allowing trucks to deposit casualties quickly. Orderlies carried the wounded from the transport to a triage tent where they were assessed. Olga worked with a team who prioritized patients – walking wounded were attended to after the stretcher cases; head wounds, abdominal wounds and those bleeding heavily were rushed through. Surgeons operated in three 'theatres' established in the building's kitchen, parlour and only bedroom. Even so, casualties requiring treatment often exceeded the unit's resources, and those deemed 'without hope' were condemned to die in a sweltering, fly-infested tent through which Olga wandered during her breaks. The dead, meanwhile, lay festering in the scorching sun, awaiting burial in a massive pit dug during May.

Although unlikely to be the day when the outcome of Operation Zitadelle was decided, 6 July was, nevertheless, full of potential. The powerful Wehrmacht were poised to attack the Soviets' second-line defences, supported by a dominant Luftwaffe, and the defenders were facing the continuation of an intense and tormenting battle. Yet if the German forces could be contained, Rokossovsky and Vatutin recognized that, with time and resources on their side, they were well placed to weather the storm and provoke a devastating attrition. The two commanders also understood that their highly skilled and wily enemy remained capable of surprises. Just one slip could give Model and Manstein the opportunity to crack the front wide open and storm to their objectives.

The Voronezh Front was most vulnerable to being broken on 6 July after the Fourth Panzer Army's efforts the previous day. Hoth's advance may not have achieved all that Manstein had hoped, but it posed a distinct threat to Prokhorovka and Oboyan, if the 6th Guards Army were to be fractured. Indeed, it was now clear to the Soviet commanders that, although they had believed for weeks that the main German thrust would be delivered in the northern salient, this was not the case. As a consequence the 27th Army, which was to have been sent to Rokossovsky, was given to Vatutin instead. Even so, the immediate German menace would have to be faced by the overnight reinforcements, and much was expected of General Katukov's 1st Tank Army along with the 2nd and 5th Guards Tank Corps, which were brought up to bolster the second-line defences.

Overnight considerable discussion took place about whether these assets would be best used in a counterattacking role or in defence. In any case, the understandable fear was that they could fall prey to the enemy's powerful guns if they showed themselves on the battlefield. The decision was taken, therefore, to fix them in the defences by moving them into the emplacements that had been prepared for them weeks earlier. With just their turrets showing, they would not only prove an elusive target, but their guns would be a useful and reassuring presence to the infantrymen of the 6th Guards Army. Rifleman Sasha Reznikova recalls a T-34 arriving in his position near Syrtsev at around 0030 hours on 6 July:

> We knew that the Germans were assembling for an attack and were deeply concerned at being crushed by its armoured weight. Although we had a number of anti-tank guns in the area they could be crushed in an instant. The arrival of a T-34 helped to settle our nerves. We helped to camouflage the tank with grass and what branches we could find . . . The tank commander gave us faith with his defiant attitude. We would hold out!

This reinforcement was a highly successful endeavour. It was carried out efficiently and without the Germans realizing the precise nature of what was going on. A delighted Katukov later remarked: '[The enemy] did not suspect that our well-camouflaged tanks were waiting for him. As we later learned from prisoners, we had managed to move our tanks forward unnoticed into the combat formations of Sixth Guards Army.'

Paul Hausser's II SS Panzer Corps had also been busy during the few precious hours of darkness that early July offered. Fierce fighting continued in some areas as both sides used the cover of the night to improve their positions. At the tip of Das Reich, for example, acting Panzer Grenadier company commander SS-Untersturmführer Krüger spent six hours leading his unit in hand-to-hand fighting during which he was twice wounded. Remaining with the company, he continued to lead his men as they wrestled with several T-34s. Darting forward with a magnetic mine grasped tightly between muddy hands, Krüger was grazed by a round, which ignited a smoke grenade in his pocket and set his trousers on fire. Ripping the flaming cloth from his legs, he continued his attack on the T-34 in his underwear and succeeded in knocking out the tank.

Elsewhere, the front was quieter and the resupply of ammunition, fuel and other necessities took place without difficulty while commanders received their orders. Whatever the situation, and no matter how much sleep the tired troops had managed to snatch during the brief respite, at 0300 hours – accompanied by another strong artillery bombardment and streams of aircraft – the three divisions struck again. LAH and Das Reich pushed forward on a six-mile front northwards, led by 120 tanks with the Tigers at the point of the *Keil*. Their orders were to penetrate the heavily mined defences southeast of Yakovlevo and advance to the Pokrovka–Prokhorovka road. Hausser anticipated nothing less than the intense fight that ensued, but he also expected his men to break through the line and he was not disappointed. The Tigers, despite their lack of mobility, proved difficult for the Red Army to stop. Once again, well-aimed rounds achieved little more than shaking the tanks' occupants, although when Obersturmführer Schütz's Tiger took a direct hit and the driver's glass vision block struck him in the stomach, he needed more than a couple of minutes to compose himself.

The Soviet second line, despite its reinforcement, could not contain the power of II SS Panzer Corps, and after a desperate period during which 88mm guns picked off strong points, the defences were breached. A wedge of panzers prised open the gap and the armour dashed through while the grenadiers mopped up. The Soviets' plan to slow the corps while more substantial defences were readied came into play. Centres of resistance, which had been created in places conducive to tenacious fighting back, were supported by a counterattack. One such position, Hill 243.2 on the approach to Luchki (just south of the road to Prokhorovka), was covered by minefields, dug-in tanks, anti-tank guns, entrenched infantry and heavy artillery, which continued to pound the Germans engaged in breaching the second line. While the Germans were deciding how best to seize the position, based on information being supplied by reconnaissance units, the remnants of the

51st Guards Rifle Division and tanks of the 3rd Mechanized Corps from Yakovlevo, Pokrovka and Bolshie Maiachki launched successive counterattacks into the corps' left flank.

As panzer grenadiers were sent to deal with this destabilizing development, the armour pressed forward to batter holes in the Soviet defences. Michael Wittmann's LAH Tigers were ordered to destroy a battery of heavy 152mm guns that had been identified in a distant wood. The platoon advanced cautiously, utilizing whatever dead ground they could find and avoiding the enemy in order to maintain surprise. After two hours of careful infiltration, they finally took up firing positions several hundred yards from the target. On Wittmann's order, the five 88mm guns opened up simultaneously. The Soviet guns were shattered and their crews flung across the gun pits. Most of those who survived the initial salvo were caught by subsequent shells and the explosion of the battery's ammunition, which ripped through the position. The few gunners left alive fled the chaotic scene and were followed by the Tigers to a second battery, which was also destroyed.

Hill 243.2 was eventually taken after the arrival of LAH's towed artillery, assault guns and werfer batteries, which lent their support to the attack. Mikhail Katukov later wrote:

> Although it was noon, it seemed like twilight with the dust and smoke hiding the sky. Plane engines screamed as machine gun bursts rattled. Our fighter planes tried to drive the enemy bombers back and prevent them from dropping their fatal loads on our positions. Our observation post was only four kilometres from the forward line but we were not able to see what was happening in front because a sea of fire and smoke cut off our sight.

The Luftwaffe had indeed sent some Stukas and Ju-88s to assist but – as became common on 6 July across the salient – their impact was often not as great as it had been on the previous day because commanders could not fulfil all of the requests that they received for support. With too few aircraft for the job, a dearth of petrol, oil and lubricants and the increasing necessity to repair battle damage and conduct routine maintenance, the Luftwaffe was forced to prioritize calls upon their services. Moreover, because air-support missions took precedence over the ongoing attempt to win air superiority, German fighters were no longer in a position to intercept all Soviet airstrikes. The situation was not helped by so many flak weapons being diverted to ground duties. In such circumstances, the Soviet airforce could begin to assert itself more forcefully.

The Germans had not been stopped, but once again their thrust had been slowed to a crawl. Luchki fell in the early afternoon as Das Reich pressed forward on LAH's left flank, rebuffing various attempts made by the 5th Tank Guards Corps. That day, the LAH war diary admits to 84 dead and 384 wounded. By the evening, the nose of Hausser's penetration was almost touching the village of Teterevino, just seven miles southwest of Prokhorovka. However, the forward elements of the corps were extremely exposed, as one German LAH officer observed that evening: 'We could still capture Teterevino. But could we stay there? It was getting darker. We were worried about our flanks, so we set up defences.'

In fact, the flanks of the entire corps were exposed. During the day, the 49th Tank Brigade reinforced the men at Pokrovka and the 31st Tank Corps moved into Bolshie Maiachki to counterattack. However, it was the lengthening right flank that caused Hausser more concern, not least because its defence was robbing him of Totenkopf, which was lagging behind to protect it. One of Hoth's precious mobile divisions had to ward off the attentions of the 2nd Guards Tank Corps and the 96th Tank Brigade from across the Lipovyi–Donets River throughout the day, due to a lack of infantry to replace it. Indeed, by the evening of 6 July, more than 30 per cent of Manstein's armour was being used in the secondary role of flank defence. As David Glantz and Jonathan House have observed, across the front 'obscure battles along the flanks were already quietly assuming decisive importance'.

The reason why II SS Panzer Corps' right flank was wide open was the continued failure of Army Detachment Kempf to make adequate progress. Immediately recognizing the importance of stymieing Manstein's progress on the right of his attack, Vatutin placed considerable emphasis on undermining it and drawing its two corps eastwards, a task that General Shumilov's 7th Guards Army carried out with aplomb. Throughout the day, Corps Raus fended off counterattacks, which the commander called 'a considerable defensive victory'. He says that 'thanks primarily to the excellent performance of our infantry in permitting the Soviet tanks to roll over them ... which succeeded in separating the enemy tanks from their own infantry supports ... [t]he Russian infantry attack broke down in front of our lines, which now held without budging.' With the two infantry divisions on Kempf's right flank providing protection, III Panzer Corps would carry out the main attack. It was, Hoth emphasized to Hermann Breith, imperative that his armour find a way forward so that the 168th Infantry Division could move up to relieve Totenkopf. Thus, the 7th and 19th Panzer Divisions led the attack on the second morning of Zitadelle and were finally joined by the 6th Panzer Division in the afternoon, when it had finally crossed the Northern Donets. All three were thwarted by stout defence by the 81st, 73rd and 78th Guards Rifle Divisions, whose minefields, trenches and anti-tank strong points robbed the formations of the momentum that they needed. Panzer Grenadier company commander Leo Koettel noted in his journal:

6 July: Today we took [Kreida Station] but we have barely begun to move. We advance a few hundred metres, and then stop again due to a minefield, artillery, rockets and counter-attacks ... We have been roasting in the heat. We are only now managing to take

objectives that should have fallen to us yesterday morning. It is very disappointing.

The Tigers from the 503rd Heavy Tank Battalion supporting the divisions did what they could but found the going extremely difficult. Those attached to the 6th Panzer Division were constantly frustrated by the Soviet defences, as radio operator Franz Lochmann explains: '[we] came to a halt under heavy anti-tank fire in the midst of a minefield in front of an anti-tank ditch ... The combat engineers who advanced suffered fearsome losses. They were decimated before our eyes while they cleared entire belts of mines.' For the exasperated Clemens Graf Kageneck, the 503rd's commander, the day had been another bad one. He wrote:

Never before had a major German offensive operation had to master such a deeply echeloned and imaginatively organized defensive system. What von Manstein and von Kluge had feared since May, that with every week's delay the Russians would create a nearly impenetrable fortification, was what we now had to face.

In late afternoon, the 6th Panzer Division did manage to get the 73rd Guards Rifle Division's left flank to curl up, and force it to withdraw to a low ridge north of Gremiachii to Batratskaia Dacha, but it was backed by three more Guards Rifle Divisions and a fourth was *en route*. Thus, by the end of the day, although some progress had been made towards the Soviets' second line of defences, Army Group Kempf had been deftly contained and II SS Panzer Corps was denied the protection that it needed.

General Knobelsdorff's XLVIII Panzer Corps, meanwhile, recommenced its wrestle with the Soviet first line. Here the Panzer Grenadier Division Grossdeutschland, flanked by the 3rd and 11th Panzer Divisions, forced the 67th Guards Rifle Division to withdraw to the second-line positions held by the 90th Rifle Division and elements of the 3rd Mechanized Corps. Although its 167th Infantry Division struggled to keep pace – thus leaving the left flank of II SS Panzer Corps bare – the rest of the corps made excellent progress. Benefiting from some strong Luftwaffe support, it overcame various intermediate positions and achieved some impetus in its drive forwards. 'It was a hard slog, but ultimately successful,' wrote combat engineer Peter Maschmann to his father. 'We felt progress was being made and confidence washed over us.' Probing the enemy's second line for weak spots, 3rd Panzer Division's reconnaissance battalion reached the River Pena near Rakovo under heavy fire from the north bank. Here it found the river to be shallow, but the approaches were marshy and the banks were saturated, which would make it extremely difficult for armour to cross. Knobelsdorff had demanded that 'momentum be maintained whenever possible', but the division informed corps that the Pena should be avoided. In a deft move, Knobelsdorff quickly reorientated the corps northeast to more favourable terrain east of Alekseevka through Lukhanino and Syrtsevo. Grossdeutschland and the 11th Panzer Division were able immediately to set about the Soviet second line. An observer later noted:

> The entire area has been infested with mines, and the Russian defence along the whole line was supported by tanks operating with all the advantages of high ground. Our assault troops suffered considerable casualties, and the 3rd Panzer Division had to beat off counterattacks. In spite of several massive bombing attacks by the Luftwaffe against battery positions, the Russian defensive fire did not decrease to any extent.

Peter Maschmann and his team set to work removing the mines that were stalling the attack, and took heavy fire in the process:

It was not a job for the faint-hearted. I joined hoping to build great bridges – a passion of mine as my father was a civil engineer and I hoped to follow in his footsteps – but I ended up in a mine-clearing team! Life expectancy was not high. In a battle such as this, it could be measured in days, but there were a few of us that got lucky ... The belts before the Soviet line at Lukhanino were particularly dense and it was disappointing to be held up again after our excellent progress earlier in the day. But that was the enemy's aim. To slow us down and grind us into those never-ending, god-forsaken and blood-soaked fields.

The Grossdeutschland's history explains that, having carved their way through the mines, the division then had the usual Soviet defences to overcome:

[A] heavy tank battle developed in the broad corn fields and flat terrain there against the Bolsheviks grimly defending their second line of resistance. Earth bunkers, deep positions with built-in flame-throwers, and especially well dug-in T-34s, excellently camouflaged, made the advance extremely difficult. German losses mounted, especially among the panzers. The infantry fought their way grimly through the in-depth defensive zone, trying to clear the way for the panzers.

Although Grossdeutschland managed to pierce the line at Lukhanino, on its left the 3rd Panzer Division was held on the Pena, and on its right the 11th Panzer Division and the 167th Infantry Division's position framed a 52nd Guards Rifle Division salient, with its nose just to the west of the village of Bykovka.

Reflecting on the day, Hoth was doubtless pleased that the Fourth Panzer Army continued to show promise and was a step closer to freeing itself from the web of Soviet defences, but he had fallen significantly behind Zitadelle's timetable. By this time, his force should have been across the Psel rather than still smashing its way through the defences either side of Pokrovka. Mechanical losses had been high with at least 300 of his armoured fighting vehicles (AFVs) lost either to enemy action or mechanical failure. Grossdeutschland, for example, had only 80 of its 350 supporting tanks still operational. II SS Panzer Corps reported approximately 110 AFVs as 'fallen out' on 6 July and XLVIII Panzer Corps reported 134. These figures include many tanks and assault guns that were repairable, but losses to Manstein for the first two days of the battle were 263 machines from all causes and around 10,000 men. Richthofen's Luftflotte 4, meanwhile, had lost more than 100 aircraft over the same period, and its operations were further hamstrung by ongoing maintenance requirements and fuel shortages. As a consequence, the Luftwaffe launched 873 daylight sorties in the southern sector that day, while the Soviets' 2nd Air Army – having already replaced the aircraft lost in the opening air encounters – mounted an impressive 1,278. Luftflotte 4s Chief of Staff, General Otto Dessloch, was well aware of the increased Soviet air presence over the battlefield, but there was little he could do about it other than concentrate aircraft where they were most urgently required while eking out petrol, oil and lubricant supplies.

The Soviets were still strong on 6 July – far stronger than the Germans thought possible – but Vatutin had problems. There was a big hole in his defences and by midnight he had committed almost all of his Front reserves. The Voronezh Front commander dispatched a report to Stalin at 1830 hours and requested reinforcement. The Supreme Commander, having analyzed the situation with his staff in Moscow, was convinced of the seriousness of the position and released Lieutenant-General Pavel Rotmistrov's 5th Guards Tank Army (29th Tank Corps, 5th 'Stalingrad' Mechanized Corps and the additional 18th Tank Corps) from the Steppe Front reserve. The formation was provided with the stipulation that Vatutin must continue 'to exhaust the enemy at prepared positions and prevent his penetration until our active operations [counterattacks] begin'. There was to be no precipitate counterattack.

Konev was not happy about the piecemeal dismemberment of his reserve but a personal call from Stalin stopped his bleating and the formation was soon moving west. The aim was for the Army to be in the vicinity of Prokhorovka by 10–11 July, in time to deploy its 600 plus tanks, supporting artillery and infantry to prevent a decisive break-through by II SS Panzer Corps and XLVIII Panzer Corps. The Southwestern Front's 2nd Tank Corps and the 5th Guards Army's 10th Tank Corps were ordered to go immediately to the Prokhorovka area to provide the support that the Voronezh Front needed from 8 July. Vatutin's plan did not change – he would continue to wear down Manstein's force and use the reinforcements to finish off the process.

There was little time for rest that night, and in some places the fighting continued without a break through to the morning. The next day, 7 July, dawned dull, ushering in a period of cooler, wetter weather across the battle lines. XLVIII Panzer Corps and II SS Panzer Corps attacked out of a thin mist across a 30 mile front, the tank crews and infantry easing themselves forward once more, their tired, aching limbs yearning for respite and a warming sun. LAH surged towards Greznoye; Das Reich filled in the positions that it left behind on the road to Prokhorovka, supported by the inevitable Stuka formations. On this day, although half of Luftflotte 4 was temporarily reassigned to assist with Model's attack in the north, the remaining 500 aircraft had a great impact. One pilot, Captain Hans-Ulrich Rudel of III/Stuka-Geschwader2, was to become the most decorated German serviceman of the war and the only man to be awarded the Iron Cross with Golden Oak Leaves, Swords and Diamonds.

During February, the teetotal and non-smoking Silesian had become the first pilot to complete 1000 sorties, and in Zitadelle he flew the G-2 Stuka ('Kanonenvogel') armed with twin 37mm guns. Born on the second day of the Battle of the Somme in 1916, Rudel was much admired by Marshal Ferdinand Schörner, who later said, 'Rudel alone replaces a whole division.' The 'Stuka Ace' recognized in his autobiography that he was lucky to have survived so long, considering the vulnerability of the relatively slow and awkward Stukas. Zitadelle was a last hurrah for these dive bombers, which were being picked off with increasing frequency by Soviet fighters and flak. Yet, as Rudel argues, 'The aircraft had a devastating impact on the enemy and was irreplaceable.' He flew countless missions during the Battle of Kursk and claimed scores of tank kills. Rudel explains:

> We tried to hit the tanks in the weakest spots. The frontal part is always the strongest . . . It is more vulnerable along the flanks but the best aiming part is the rear where the engine is located, covered by thin armoured plating . . . This is where it pays to hit them, because where there is an engine there is always fuel! It is quite easy to spot a moving tank from the air, the blue engine exhaust smoke is a giveaway.

The salient that Hausser's corps was creating towards Oboyan and Prokhorovka was a clear threat to the integrity of the Soviet defences, and Vatutin re-emphasized his order for subordinates to put it under intense pressure to stop its expansion. This order was carried out throughout the day, and tenacious defence was mixed, wherever possible, with intrepid counterattacks. At Teterevino, for example, elements of LAH and Das Reich launched an attempt to break into the village after its defences had been softened up by Henschel Hs-129s and Focke-Wulf 190s. The Germans broke through the outer defences and then became entangled in the main defensive line. A protracted battle ensued, with T-34s from the 5th Guards Tank Corps, artillery and anti-tank guns. Tigers eventually managed to get through, and the village was seized during the late afternoon, along with the command post and entire staff of a rifle brigade. What had been expected to be a short, sharp smash and grab had turned into a bloody and gruelling battle. All the while, Totenkopf's great potential was nullified as it continued to be fully engaged in protecting the corps' lower eastern side. Thus, although Greznoye and Teterevino were taken by Hausser's division on 7 July, it turned out not to be a day of breakthrough and exploitation, but another day of slog and grind. In the circumstances, he had little option but to continue to plug away at the Soviet defences and hope that another day's offensive action would force them to succumb.

As Hausser's corps struggled on northeast of Pokrovka, Knobelsdorff's XLVIII Panzer Corps continued its attack on the Soviet second line with around 300 tanks, including just 40 remaining Panthers. By around 0600 hours a crunching battle was developing west of Pokrovka as the Soviets refused to give ground and retaliated against the Wehrmacht's violence with their own artillery bombardments and aerial attacks. However, the Grossdeutschland Division had ruptured defences the previous evening, and Walter Hoernlein was determined to batter away until he broke through, but progress was slow. The Panthers suffered heavy losses when they waded into a minefield, which had to be dealt with before the grenadiers could start to clear the bunkers, trenches and emplacements in close-quarter action. A Soviet observer noted: 'During repeated attacks, by introducing fresh forces, the enemy penetrated the defensive front and began to spread in a northern and northwestern direction. The brigades withdrew in bitter fighting.' Gradually, the Soviets were pushed back to the outskirts of Syrtsevo, leading XLVIII Panzer Corps' Chief of Staff, General Friedrich von Mellenthin, to write: 'The fleeing masses were caught by German artillery fire and suffered very heavy casualties; our tanks gained momentum and wheeled to the northwest. But at [Syrtsevo] that afternoon they were halted by strong defensive fire, and the Russian armour counterattacked.' Katukov did indeed unleash over

100 T-34s of the 3rd Mechanized and 6th Tank Corps to halt Grossdeutschland's surge, but despite air support provided by Pe-2s, Il-2s and fighters, the guns of the Tigers and Panthers and divisional artillery fragmented the riposte and forced the Soviets back. Yak fighter pilot Artyom Zeldovich recalls flying over the battlefield:

> The ground gradually lit up with flaring tanks. Some of them were German, but most of them were ours. The sky filled with a dense black smoke . . . We managed to keep the enemy's aircraft away for periods, but sometimes they broke through when we returned to base to refuel and rearm. When we returned, more tanks were burning and the battle had moved forward several hundred metres . . . It was clear that the Germans were heading for Syrtsevo and we had orders to stop them achieving this at all costs. Flying over the sector it was easy to see why. The road system was opening up, Oboyan was close by with Kursk not so far beyond it . . . The battle was a battle of resources, but it was also a test of wills. Looking down at Syrtsevo – an inferno – I wondered whose will would break first.

Neither side looked likely to crack on 7 July; both fought with no quarter given throughout the day. That evening, as the Soviets quickly reinforced Syrtsevo with elements of the 67th Guards Rifle Division and 60 tanks from the 6th Tank Corps, Grossdeutschland drew up towards the outskirts only to be confronted by yet another minefield. Even as work began to clear lanes through it in preparation for a renewed attack by the division the following morning, Hoernlein directed his Tigers to outflank the village. It was a bold move. The division needed a decent pause to recuperate after its exertions, but the commander was desperate to build up whatever impetus he could before darkness. His frustration must have been immense, therefore, when he learned that the manoeuvre had floundered due to the mechanical breakdown of Grossdeutschland's residual Tigers. It was not the first time in the battle that the technical frailties of these 'wonder weapons' had severely hampered promising tactical situations. Indeed, mechanical breakdown and temporary disablement were far more common causes of panzers being put out of the front line than tank kill. As a consequence, mobile field workshops had an important role to play in ensuring that the Germans' armoured fleet was inconvenienced as little as possible by minor ailments. Mechanic Karl Stumpp testifies:

We had to keep pace with the attack as much as possible which meant that vehicles were taken to a place of relative safety, camouflaged and guarded until we could arrive and do whatever we needed to do to get the vehicle back into battle again ... Occasionally the heavy tanks needed more specialist attention that would follow on behind us, but we could deal with most defects. We were targeted by Soviet aircraft because the tank was immobile, but we were protected by flak and this helped ... During this period in the battle mine strikes were common and we could repair suspension damage in just a few hours although it sometimes took longer ... Mechanical problems were not uncommon, particularly in the Panthers and Tigers. The Panthers had numerous faults which were not difficult to fix, but sometimes we lacked the spare parts. Problems with Tigers occurred mainly when the crews had not had a chance to undertake their own daily maintenance routines on their machine because of the intensity of battle.

Although just a few Tigers were destroyed during Zitadelle, the Soviets officially logged the destruction of hundreds. Indeed, on 7 July the Soviet Information Bureau made a remarkable announcement about the opening day of Zitadelle: 'The backbone of the German offensive thrust, the Tiger units, were singled out for special attention by our anti-tank units. They suffered heavy losses. At least 250 of these large tanks went up in flames on the battlefield.' A couple of days later the same agency declared that a further 70 Tigers and 450 other tanks had been destroyed on 7 July. Thus, by the end of the third day of battle, Moscow laid claim to an extraordinary 1,539 tank kills.

Although possibly just a massive over-estimation of their own destructive virility, the figure was probably plucked out of the air for propaganda effect. It might also reveal the grip that the Tiger had on the Soviet imagination. Built up to represent the power of the Wehrmacht on the fighting front, the Soviets would take delight in dismantling the image of invincibility that the machines engendered. If the Tigers could be defeated, then so could Zitadelle and with it Germany's offensive power in the East. What the official government statements did not say, of course, was that the Red Army was also haemorrhaging casualties and material losses. Operations to blunt the German advance were proving extremely costly. Vatutin was certainly aware of this reality and was sensitive to the fact that the High Command's attritional strategy was not without cost to his finite resources.

The Soviets were busy damming the front against a rising German tide, and if the dam burst, Manstein would gratefully send his forces to flood the rear of the Voronezh Front. The Soviets were feeling vulnerable in the south, which led Nikita Khrushchev, Stalin's political representative at Vatutin's headquarters, to declare to the assembled commanders that evening, 'The next two or three days will be terrible. Either we hold out or the Germans take Kursk. They are staking everything on this one card. For them it is a matter of life or death. We must see to it that they break their necks.' The battle was reaching a critical point in the sector. Vatutin issued a rash of orders and made strategic redeployments. He directed, 'On no account must the enemy break through to Oboyan.' The 40th Army was moved into the line from its duties defending the quieter face of the salient, and two counterattacks were to be delivered the next day against the Fourth Panzer Army. The Southwestern and Southern Fronts were directed to prepare for diversionary attacks, to take place before the counterattacks, to 'tie down enemy forces and forestall manoeuvre of his reserves'.

The operational situation in the southern sector of the Kursk salient remained finely balanced as darkness fell on 7 July. As a result, the battle continued to rage unabated in some areas. The Grossdeutschland history noted, for example: 'Night fell but no rest. The sky was fire-red, heavy artillery shells shook the earth, rocket batteries fired at the last identifiable targets.' In areas of great tactical or operational importance, units and formations did not differentiate between night and day as both sides sought to improve their positions. Pioneer Henri Schnabel did not get much sleep during this period and was finding it difficult to cope:

> This was the fourth night of our battle, because we had cleared minefields the night before the offensive began. We were exhausted because there was no let up in demands for our services. We lived on adrenaline and 10 minutes of sleep here, five minutes there. I had a crunching headache and often fell asleep standing up . . . Considering the nature of our job, this was hardly ideal. We were totally drained.

Red Army infantryman Feliks Karelin was also drawing on his last reserves of energy. He had been in the front line when the Germans struck on the 5th and had withdrawn back to a position near Pokrovka by the night of the 7th:

> I hardly recall the first days of the battle. They were a blur, but I remember that we did not sleep. Some men were in a worse state than I. One man I tried to wake as we moved back to a new

position but he was so tired that he decided to stay in his shell scrape and take his chances. The position was overrun an hour later ... The lack of sleep made it difficult to understand basic orders and to carry out simple tasks. I was confused and could barely operate as a soldier. However, we learned to take very, very brief naps which helped a little. I also found that enemy action was an excellent stimulant. I could be falling asleep on my rifle and with shells falling around me, but as soon as I was in danger from tanks or enemy [infantry] I would suddenly become alert. But as the days passed, this became increasingly difficult. My energy was being sapped.

Some of the troops had jobs that were so physically demanding that after the opening days of the battle, they could not carry on. One Tiger gun loader, for example, recalls: 'It was extremely hot and we had to rearm three or four times [a day]. This meant repeating the process of taking on forty to fifty shells, throwing out the empty casings and reloading three of four times.' Deemed physically incapable of continuing to fulfil his tasks, he was replaced. But for most there was no hope of relief and they had to make do with the few hours that darkness offered to 'recharge' before the next day's action.

The first job that most units undertook on halting for the evening was to replenish their ammunition stocks, refill magazines and machine-gun belts, and take up any other supplies, weapons and equipment that were needed. This would be followed by time spent finding shelter, reorganizing kit and cleaning weapons. Tank and vehicle crews would use the time not only to take on fuel, water and ammunition, but also to carry out some basic maintenance on their machines. Once this had been done, the men would eat – ideally, a hot meal from a field kitchen, but often from a box of cold, uninspiring rations that barely replaced lost energy.

Then, with their chores completed, the troops would settle down for some rest. Some might curl up in a trench, ditch or shell scrape; others might set up a bivouac in the woods. Tank crews always spent the night with their vehicles, either sleeping in the open or in tents close by. Sentries had the difficult job of keeping watch while their comrades slumbered. It was a task beyond SS Senior Corporal Pötter on the night of 7–8 July. He fell asleep within minutes of taking up his position. Shaken awake by his furious platoon commander, Michael Wittmann, Pötter was reminded of the seriousness of the offence that he had just committed, before being told to get some sleep. Wittmann personally took over the corporal's watch. Officers, of course, had responsibility for their men and so, in most cases, ate last, slept least and busied themselves with the day-to-day running of their units. Assisted by senior non-commissioned officers, they ensured that their men were in the best possible condition to fulfil their duties. Lieutenant Walter Graff, a panzer grenadier platoon commander, recalls:

My own tiredness was offset by the nature of my job. I had so little time to relax that I had little opportunity to feel tired. Of course, there were moments when I could hardly keep my eyes open, but I had responsibility for the lives of 30 men and so I could not afford to be anything other than completely focused. I also had to ensure that I was a role model to the platoon . . . As a result, I always tried to ensure that I was properly dressed, that I had shaved, that my boots were polished, my personal weapon was clean and that I conducted myself in a professional manner . . . Standards can slip very easily in battle, and that is when soldiers get into bad habits that can easily lead to casualties . . . I always ensured that I spoke personally to every man in my platoon every day about something unrelated to the war. I usually did this in the evening – if we were fortunate enough to be able to take a break – and would wander around the positions encouraging each, offering reassurance and a kind word.

Hardly refreshed, the men would be awoken, breakfasted, briefed and ready before the first light of a new dawn at around 0300 hours. Army Detachment Kempf's war diary reveals that it was fighting night and day to get III Panzer Corps moving north to support Hoth's advance, but despite its best efforts, it remained mired in a slogging match with the redoubtable 7th Guards Army. Immediately recognizing that he must ensure the Fourth Panzer Army was denied the support of Breith's formation, Shumilov poured resources into his defences northeast of Belgorod and continued to occupy Kempf with bone-crunching counterattacks. In this way, the Soviets stopped the three panzer divisions from gaining any impetus towards Prokhorovka. The result was that III Panzer Corps was largely held before Shumilov's second line, although by the evening of 8 July, the Tigers of the 503rd Heavy Tank Battalion leading the 6th Panzer Division had pierced their way in and helped develop a 10 mile deep, two and a half mile wide salient to Shilakhovo.

Meanwhile, both II SS and XLVIII Panzer Corps resumed their offensives with vigour at around 0500 hours on 8 July. LAH remained at the front of Hausser's corps, two panzer grenadier regiments from Das Reich held the line from Teterevino along the Lipovyi–Donets River, and Totenkopf (at last) began to transfer some of its flank protection duties to the infantry. Since III Panzer Corps had signally failed to provide the support expected of it, and Knobelsdorff's panzers had linked up with LAH at Yakovlevo, the 167th Infantry Division was moved from Hausser's left flank to his right. This allowed the leading elements of the relatively unscathed Totenkopf to support LAH's attacks on the 8th while the remainder of its units moved north to assume duties at the point of the attack on the following day. The reinforcement of II SS Panzer Corps' attack reaped immediate benefits because the two divisions worked in concert to expand the breadth of Hausser's attacking front. Caught by surprise, the Soviets were forced to relinquish Bolshie Maiachki early in the morning and to withdraw from Gresnoe back north to the Psel River.

The corps also managed to repel Vatutin's much-vaunted counter-attacks, which were unhinged by Hausser's own early advance, the late arrival of critical units and some poor coordination. First, 31st Tank Corps' strike was rebuffed as it emerged from Malye Maiachki, and then the newly arrived 10th Tank Corps was seen off as it pushed down the road from Prokhorovka towards Teterevino. The fighting was passionate and ferocious. One experienced German divisional gunner wrote in his diary that evening:

> We are under extreme pressure and the guns have been in action since 0430 hours. By noon we had run out of ammunition and had to wait two hours for resupply. It arrived with Soviet aircraft ... Enemy attacks have diluted our offensive ... This is the most intense fighting that I have experienced. We must break through soon or face the consequences.

Although the Soviet thrusts had failed to bring Hausser's advance to a halt, by fragmenting into a series of local actions that lasted for the rest of the day, they did ensure that the corps was burdened with the need to defend itself to the detriment of its forward momentum. A further attempt to hamper progress was launched against the corps' extended left flank and the newly arrived units of the 167th Infantry Division. Seeking to cut II SS Panzer Corps' lines of communication, the 2nd Guards Tank Corps had been ordered to attack westwards from some woods around the village of Gostishchevo (10 miles north of Belgorod). The impact could have been devastating because the Germans did not know that the formation was assembling for an attack, but it was spotted just in time by Hauptmann Bruno Meyer leading a flight of Henschel Hs-129s on a routine reconnaissance mission. Meyer's aircraft, together with some Fw-190s armed with SD-2 cluster weapons, proceeded to ravage the Soviet tank corps. The young officer later recalled: 'Wave after wave was emerging from the woods tugging gun mountings, mortars, anti-tank and anti-aircraft guns by hand behind them ... they came over a frontal area [five to six miles] wide. Then followed the tanks.'

The infantry were decimated by the cluster bombs but carried on marching forward despite the havoc surrounding them. It took the cannons and machine guns to rip through them before their stoicism was fatally undermined and they finally fled to the relative sanctuary of the woods. As they did so, their tanks were ripped apart by waves of Henschels sporting MK 103 30mm cannon. Within an hour some 50 T-34s had been rendered inoperable and two hours after that another 30 had been destroyed and thousands of dead lay across the battlefield. Although the bulk of the corps lived to fight another day, it was, nevertheless, an historic moment – the first time in history that a tank formation had been stopped by air power alone.

II SS Panzer Corps had managed to nudge forward beyond Greznoe on the fourth day of the offensive, but had once again failed to break the Soviet defences and was left battered and bruised by a string of Soviet counterattacks. The story of containment and counterattack was replicated in Vatutin's defence against XLVIII Panzer Corps. Knobelsdorff also attacked at dawn. Grossdeutschland took a line along the east bank of the Pena, the 3rd Panzer Division tucked in below its left flank and the 11th Panzer Division provided support on the right, advancing up the road to Oboyan. Grossdeutschland's thrust towards Syrtsevo was countered by Soviet armour, initially a cordon to slow the German advance, and then, later in the morning, General Krivoshein's 3rd Mechanized Corps unleashed a counterattack by 40 T-34s. It was another desperate encounter. Ten Soviet machines were destroyed by Grossdeutschland's eight serviceable Tigers and a collection of Mark IIIs and Mark IVs. Pulling back, having successfully inhibited Hoernlein's drive, the remaining Soviet tanks, guns and infantry organized themselves to protect the village once again. 'I have to say that the Germans were extremely tenacious – our equals in that regard,' says Sasha Reznikova. 'They did not give up and we knew that they wouldn't. They fought to the last when isolated and attacked until they could attack no more. I suppose they had no alternative. The enemy was desperate and had to drive forward at every opportunity.'

Inevitably, the Soviet defence began to crumble as Grossdeutschland launched a series of blows against Syrtsevo. Krivoshein's runner arrived at corps headquarters with regular reports: 'The 3rd Company of Kunin's battalion has lost all its officers. Sergeant Nogayev is in command . . . Headquarters of 30th Brigade has received a direct hit. Most officers killed. Brigade commander seriously wounded.' The defence began to waver and the Germans were not slow to exploit the confusion that affected the Soviet line as it began to lose its shape. By the early afternoon, units of Grossdeutschland had moved into the village and, after some close-quarters fighting, finally took their hard-won prize. They were immediately hammered by Soviet artillery firing from the west bank of the Pena.

Watching the fall of Syrtsevo with Katukov at the 1st Tank Army headquarters, with a sense of growing doom, was Lieutenant-General N.K. Popiel, the political representative, who later wrote:

We saw in the distance a large number of tanks. It was impossible to distinguish damaged tanks from those undamaged. The row began moving. Only a burned field a few hundred metres wide, nothing else separated us from the enemy. Katukov did not take the field glasses from his eyes. He mumbled: 'They're regrouping . . . advancing in a spearhead . . . I think we have had it!'

The men were witnessing Grossdeutschland's regrouping as the division began its next move northwards. As the 11th Panzer Division dealt with a number of Soviet tank attacks on the east flank, Hoernlein's formation pressed on, hoping to take some high ground to the east of Verkhopenye after a signal had been received declaring that the town had been taken in a daring *coup de main*. However, as the division's Armoured Reconnaissance and Assault Gun Battalions scouted ahead, they unexpectedly came across a Grossdeutschland panzer grenadier company in Gremutsch. It soon became apparent to the unit's embarrassed commander that he had not taken Verkhopenye as reported, but instead held a village several miles south of his objective. Even as the ramifications of the mistake were being digested, more than 40 Soviet tanks were attempting to retake the hamlet from the northeast. They were met by the assault guns, which had already been formed into a defensive perimeter by its 26-year-old commander, Major Peter Frantz. In a text-book action during which the enemy's armour was lured into carefully baited traps and destroyed piecemeal, Frantz systematically beat the Soviets away. Recounting the episode in some detail, Paul Carell concludes Frantz's story by dramatizing the final minutes of the battle:

[A] pack of T-34s and one Mark III were fast approaching the slope. Sergeant Scheffler had his eyes glued to the driver's visor. The gun aimer was calmness personified. 'Fire!' Tank after tank was knocked out by the 75mm cannon of armoured reconnaissance and assault gun battalions. The Soviet commanders attacked time and time again. Their wireless traffic showed that they had orders to break open the German line regardless of the cost. Seven times the Russians attacked. Seven times, they flung themselves obstinately into Major Frantz's traps. After three hours, 35 wrecked tanks littered the battlefield, smouldering. Only five T-34s, all of them badly damaged, limped away from the smoking arena to seek shelter in a small wood. Proudly the major signalled to the division: '35 enemy tanks knocked out. No losses on our side.'

By early evening, Grossdeutschland's armour approached Verkhopenye as yet more counterattacks struck the division's exposed flanks. Both the 3rd and 11th Panzer Divisions were also fending off strong enemy probes, so there was little that Hoernlein could do but absorb the blows and press on with his attack on the town. It was testament to the resilience of the division that the Soviets were not only held off, but a clutch of tanks and panzer grenadiers eventually penetrated their objective. As they did so, a furious contest developed around the perimeter, as one eyewitness describes:

> Ferocious, unparalleled tank battles ensued on the flats of the steppe, on hills, in gorges, gullies and ravines, and in settlements . . . The scope of the battle was beyond all imagination. Hundreds of panzers, field guns and planes were turned into heaps of scrap metal. The sun could barely be seen through the haze of smog from thousands of shells and bombs that were exploding simultaneously.

During mid-afternoon, a battalion of panzer grenadiers, a battalion of tanks and a handful of Panthers had assembled on the eastern approaches to the town and taken up defensive positions. Anti-aircraft gunner Lieutenant Haarhaus later recalled:

> The Russian ground-attack aircraft were quickly on the scene. They came sweeping in every two hours. Each aircraft dropped its 50 to 60 bomblets, strafed the infantry positions and then disappeared. For those of us in the Flak our mission had begun.

Sending up a stream of fire into the cloud-strewn sky, the muzzle flashes were soon spotted and their positions strafed. The gun teams instinctively cowered behind their weapon's flimsy armoured shield. Haarhaus continues: 'The rounds crack, whistle and crash around us. Only a few metres above us, the aircraft zoom over our guns, fly a broad loop and renew their attack. Those bastards have guts! Colossal!

That afternoon, we knocked three of them from the sky. But we also lost half of our crew to strafing.'

Verkhopenye was not taken on the 8th, but as dusk fell plans were made to seize the town on the next day. It was to be a busy night for the men of Grossdeutschland in their exposed positions. They not only refuelled and resupplied, but also had to ward off numerous Soviet counterattacks in the darkness, supported by low-flying Po-2s and Il-2s. The attention the Soviets paid to this inconspicuous town revealed Vatutin's fear that Manstein was on the verge of fashioning a breakthrough. Fearful of his remaining troops being destroyed unnecessarily in a fight to the last in Verkhopenye, the commander of the Voronezh Front ordered them to withdraw during the night of 8–9 July and establish new defences north of the town across the Oboyan road and along the Solotinka River, forward of Sukho-Solotino and Kochetovka to the Psel River. Here, the 31st Tank Corps and remnants of the 3rd Mechanized Corps would be joined by the 309th Rifle Division (from the 40th Army), the 29th Anti-Tank Brigade, two fresh tank brigades and three anti-tank regiments, which were to link in to established positions held by the 6th Tank Corps farther west. Along this line Vatutin hoped to halt Hoth's Fourth Panzer Army long enough to feel the force of the armoured counterattacks being mounted around Prokhorovka.

Manstein, meanwhile, believed that, although his offensive had fallen considerably behind Zitadelle's timetable, at last he was about to rent the Soviet defences asunder. 'The prospects for a breakthrough remain good,' the field marshal explained to Model on the night of the 8th. 'We must not fail to ensure that we give the enemy's defences no time to settle and yet retain the power to exploit our successes.' However, Hoth was concerned by intelligence that 'considerable Soviet armoured forces' were massing on his right flank, and Knobelsdorff's sources were telling him of the danger posed by the 6th Tank Corps on his left. The offensive could not continue without taking these threats into consideration. During the evening of 8 July, therefore, Manstein, Hoth, Hausser, Knobelsdorff and Kempf were locked in discussion about how to proceed. Although the Germans were making ground in the south, they were doing so slowly and suffering considerable losses in the process. In such circumstances, it would have been extremely beneficial to Zitadelle had the Ninth Army been powering through Rokossovsky's defences in the northern sector of the salient.

Model's advance had not been dramatic on the first day of the offensive, but the infantry-based attack had made progress towards the second line of defences. It was on these positions, stretching from Samodurovka to Ponyri and protecting the Olkhovatka heights, that XLVII and XLI Panzer Corps would focus their attention for the rest of the operation. However, 6 July began with a Central Front counterattack. Rokossovsky, while completing the reinforcement of his defences, which included two rifle corps and the 2nd Tank Army, unleashed 16th Tank Corps. Directed against the 20th Panzer Division in the area of the greatest German penetration, 100 T-34s and T-70s struck at 0130 hours. Within four hours, the thrust – which had been strengthened by 17th Guards Rifle Division – had developed into a major confrontation between Soborovka and Samodurovka. Taking advantage of the greater freedom over the battlefield that came with the mounting calls on the Luftwaffe's rapidly diminishing resources, the reinforced Red Air Force flew in close support. General Rudenko later explained:

I decided to change the tactics of the strike aircraft. I concluded that it would be more expedient to deal one devastating strike against a large force of enemy troops, so for this end I decided to dispatch our aircraft in massive strength. The idea also was that this massing of our aircraft would suppress the enemy's air defence and thus reduce our own losses.

Il-2s arrived in squadrons of eight and, having circled over the panzers and selected a target, took it in turns to dive down. They aimed at the rear end of their targets with bombs, rockets and cannon. Although it was beyond the Red Air Force to win air supremacy immediately, on just the second day of Zitadelle, it began to out-muscle the Luftwaffe, which gradually lost its aerial dominance. Although the Soviet air arm was not destined to be 'the decisive battle-winning instrument its numbers would suggest it should have become', Rudenko commented on the strikes that morning:

> The impact of their attack was powerful and obviously unexpected by the enemy. Smoke piles rose from his positions – one, two, three, five, ten, fifteen. It emerged from burning Tigers and Panthers. Despite the danger, our soldiers jumped out of the entrenchments, threw their helmets into the air and shouted, 'Hurrah!'

Although Rokossovsky's counterattack had run out of steam by mid-morning, it had successfully pre-empted Model's own thrust and allowed the Central Front time to conclude its defensive preparations. As German and Soviet aircraft continued to tangle overhead, General Lemelsen's XLVII Panzer Corps mounted an assault led by 300 tanks. To the right, pushing on towards Samodurovka, the 20th Panzer Division had now been joined in the offensive by two of the corps' reserve formations. On the opposite flank, the 9th Panzer Division advanced towards Ponyri Station, while in the centre, the 2nd Panzer Division, led by the 505th Heavy Tank Battalion's 24 serviceable Tigers, probed towards Olkhovatka against one of the most strongly fortified sections of the main defensive belt. The rumble of hundreds of guns mixed with the shriek of Katyusha and Nebelwerfer batteries in a shocking display of firepower. The battlefield erupted as bombs, shells, rockets and mortars exploded, each with a blinding flash, creating fountains of soil and palls of smoke. Tanks opened fire on enemy machines as the advancing infantry, denied any help across the featureless battlefield, was met by a hail of fire. 'It was Armageddon,' recalls one German survivor:

Every second that passed I expected to be my last. Men were falling around me but we just focused on our objective. Our officer was killed in an explosion, my section commander was shot through the neck shortly after . . . Soviet aircraft added to the hell as they appeared through the smoke without warning as we could not hear their engines over the noise of battle. They strafed us time after time, hour after hour . . . Death would have been a merciful release from that hell, but I came through. Those were the worst moments of my war, of my life. I am haunted by memories of it. Absolutely terrifying.

Gradually the two sides closed. Marc Doerr used his machine gun to suppress Soviet positions. 'I took up a position on the lip of a shell crater and concentrated my fire on a trench approximately 600 yards away where I could see movements . . . As the attack progressed I eventually moved into that trench and found it full of enemy dead. I believe that the Soviets called the MG-42 the Hitler Saw after the noise that it made. It was a fearsome weapon with a tremendous weight of fire.'

The panzers had destroyed numerous T-34s at long range, and then endeavoured to finish off the remaining tanks as the T-34s darted to within a couple of hundred yards of the German formations. The T-34s were pushed to their limits, engines roaring, and as the morning grew warmer, temperatures inside the cabins rose to excruciating levels. The perspiration dripped off the crews' noses and stung their red-rimmed eyes. Every time the main armaments were fired, the compartment filled with choking, blue-grey cordite fumes. Vladimir Severinov has said:

There was a lethal cocktail of vapours in a T-34 during battle. We once had a loader and then a driver pass out during action, which sent us into a panic as the tank was designed to advance when the throttle pedal was raised, not when it was lowered. We opened the hatch to let the worst of the foul air out and within a few moments the driver was aware enough to apply the brake. We were desperate to get out into the fresh air, but we could hear the rounds splatting against our armour and knew that we would be dead within seconds . . . Being in a tank in July 1943 was like being placed in a hot oven pumped full of toxins and suffocated.

Attacking units disappeared into a cloud of explosions and smoke never to be seen again. The Soviet second line ate up the Wehrmacht's young men hour after hour – but the divisions' commanders continued to hammer away. Infiltrations were made and snuffed out, assaults were mounted and crushed. Armour ran into minefields or fell pray to the anti-tank guns and tank-killer teams. Radios were alive with orders, and pleas for information about the progress of reinforcements and supplies. The Soviets hit back with local counterattacks, which sometimes stunned the Germans with their size and ferocity. At 1830 hours, for example, 150 tanks of the 19th Tank Corps struck the 20th and 2nd Panzer Divisions with such force that some regiments were sent reeling. Herbert Forman has testified:

The tanks came out of nowhere. Just as we were beginning to make a little progress. They clattered into us and made a mess of the positions that we had carved at such great expense. Within an hour our own armour had stopped the advance, but the battle continued until darkness and we were left back where we had started from that morning.

In this way, the offensive power of the Tigers was finally broken and the remaining six machines of the 505th Heavy Tank Battalion were withdrawn as the unit underwent a major overhaul and reorganization. Model's mailed fist, such as it was, had been denied its talisman.

XLVII Panzer Corps had been starved of its ability to manoeuvre and drawn into a cleverly executed slogging match by the enemy. Nowhere was this more apparent than at Ponyri Station, which was to develop into an encounter that became known to the troops as a 'mini-Stalingrad'. The village of Ponyri nestled in a *balka* a couple of miles to the west of Ponyri Station, which was a more substantial conurbation that had grown up around the local railway station. With its cluster of warehouses and sturdy buildings, the town, although small, was one of the largest in the area, and it controlled the roads and railways leading south. Its seizure was seen by Model as a means of breaching the Soviets' second line, rolling it up through Olkhovatka and opening a route to Kursk. Recognizing its importance, the 13th Army was determined to hold on to it at all costs. What resulted, therefore, was a fraught and bloody confrontation to which both sides committed copious resources over several days.

The Germans had already taken the northern part of Ponyri Station on the first day of Zitadelle, and at first light on 6 July, 292nd Infantry Division resumed its assault, supported by elements of the 9th Panzer Division on its right flank. Preceded by a heavy artillery bombardment and Stuka dive bombing, which reduced much of Major-General M.A. Enshin's 307th Rifle Division defences to rubble, the formations attacked. But the Germans stalled as they tried to pick their way through a protective minefield and over barbed-wire obstacles. These were covered by machine-gun nests and mortars, and the Soviet guns opened up. The Wehrmacht's attack was immediately stripped of its shape and stuttered forward with heavy losses. Some units managed to break into the town, but became entangled in a network of mutually supportive positions in streets of fortified houses. When the armour followed, they soon became aware of carefully positioned anti-tank guns, which quickly converted the unwary and unlucky into blazing wrecks that blocked the thoroughfares. The infantry endeavoured to clear buildings as they progressed southwards, but where successful they were soon overwhelmed by counterattacks. The Soviets seemed to glory in vicious hand-to-hand fighting.

A simultaneous attack was made to the east of Ponyri Station where the 86th and 78th Infantry Divisions sought to take Hill 253.5 and Prilepy. These positions would not only give the Germans an opportunity to undermine Ponyri's defences but also offered a means of outflanking the tenacious resistance of Maloarkhangelsk. Nikolai Litvin's battery was one of those that lay in wait for just such a move. They were situated in a field of uncut rye between two parallel ravines, which was deemed a likely area for a panzer attack. Having camouflaged their guns and established fields of fire, the gun crews prepared themselves for an onslaught. 'The morning of 6 July dawned cloudy, with a low, overcast sky that hindered the operations of our airforce,' the inexperienced Litvin says:

> At around 6:00 a.m., our position was attacked head-on by a group of approximately 200 submachine gunners and four German tanks, most likely PzKw IVs. The tanks led the way, followed closely by the infantry. The Germans were attempting to find a weak spot in our lines . . . but they didn't seem to see us. We felt a gnawing fear in the pit of our bellies as the German tanks rumbled toward us, stopping every fifty to seventy metres to scan our lines and fire a round . . . My knees and legs began to tremble wildly, until we received the command to swing into action and prepare to fire. The shaking stopped, and we became possessed by the overriding desire not to miss our targets.

The guns were ordered to fire when the enemy had reached within 300 yards of the line. Litvin continues:

Our Number One gun set a tank ablaze with its first shot, and then managed to knock out a second tank. The combined fire of our Number Three and Number Four guns knocked out a third German tank. The fourth tank managed to escape . . . [My gun] opened up on the advancing infantry with fragmentation shells. The German submachine gunners stubbornly continued to push forward. As they drew closer, we switched to shrapnel shells and resumed fire on them. Not less than half the Germans fell to the ground, and the remaining drew back to their line of departure.

A temporary lull followed during which the Soviet gunners breakfasted and celebrated their success with 100 grams of vodka, but a new push was heralded by a Stuka attack. These bombers were called 'musicians' by the Red Army due to their air sirens, which wailed as they dived on their targets. The first bomb exploded some 60 yards from Litvin's position. Another fell directly above his dug-out:

I saw my own unavoidable death approaching, but I could do nothing to save myself: there was not enough time. It would take me five to six seconds to reach a different shelter, but the bomb had been released close to the ground, and needed only one or two seconds to reach the earth – and me. During those brief seconds as I watched the bomb fall, my entire conscious life flashed through my mind. Everything seemed to happen in slow motion. I badly didn't want to die at the age of twenty . . . Just before the bomb struck, I rolled over face down in my little trench and covered my face with the palms of my hands . . . I heard the bomb explode. There was a repulsive smell of TNT, and I felt two strong blows to my head. It seemed to me that my head must have been torn off . . . The bomb had exploded very close to my trench, and I was buried in loose dirt.

Pulled unconscious from his entombment, it took three days for Litvin's hearing to return and another week before he could speak.

Subsequent pushes by the Germans did take ground but there was no breakthrough and Ponyri remained a hornet's nest in Soviet hands. As Zhukov later wrote: 'All day the roar of battle on the ground and in the air engulfed the area. Although the enemy kept pouring new tank units into the battle, here again he was unable to achieve a breakthrough.' On the flanks of the Ninth Army's front, meanwhile, neither XXIII Corps nor XLVI Panzer Corps could develop their modest first-day territorial gains in any meaningful way and failed to do so for the remainder of Zitadelle. As dusk fell on the 6th, therefore, Rokossovsky had been handed an opportunity to concentrate his defences against the centre of the line. With XLVII and XLI Panzer Corps still flailing through the 13th Army's main defensive line, the Central Front could feel content that they had managed to take the sting out of Model's initial blow. They had to remain wary of his reserves, though, and could not afford to relinquish possession of the Olkhovatka heights if they were to wear the Ninth Army down. By taking formations from the quieter areas of his Front – the 70th Army released one division and the 65th Army two tank regiments – Rokossovsky successfully managed to reinforce his defences with a minimum of disruption.

Even as the Central Front took steps to enhance their resistance, Model underwrote plans for his XLVII and XLI Panzer Corps to continue their frontal attacks on the Olkhovatka line. Like so many generals in similar situations down the centuries, when confronted with defences that were expected to break open at any moment, he felt compelled to throw more resources at them to complete the job. If, instead, Model had decided to concentrate his attack elsewhere, he would not only lose whatever momentum had been accrued but might also miss the opportunity to finish off a defence that was on the verge of collapse. Thus, on 7 and 8 July, the Ninth Army continued to pummel away at Olkhovatka's defences for, in the words of one

German observer, 'here was the key to the door of Kursk,' which could be seen 400 feet below. Model was convinced he could draw Rokossovsky's armour and defeat it on unfavourable ground. The fight for this part of the line, therefore, was never going to be anything other than a protracted brawl – the destruction of Soviet reinforcements was all part of the Ninth Army's plan.

Thus, on the morning of the 7th, XLVII and XLI Panzer Corps pushed forward once more. The attack was to take the form of three mutually supportive but distinct movements: one by the 20th Panzer Division towards the village of Teploe, the second by the 2nd Panzer Division (supported by the briefly rested Tigers of the 505th Heavy Tank Battalion) focusing on Olkhovatka, and the third into and around Ponyri by the 18th Panzer Division (released from the reserve), the 292nd and the 86th Infantry Divisions, supported by the 9th Panzer Division. The 6th Infantry Division was to continue plugging away in the middle of the line and provide a bridge linking the 2nd and 9th Panzer Divisions.

There was little finesse to Model's plan, which simply seemed to reflect the wider German desire to use brute force to smash holes in the enemy's positions. The application of the Ninth Army's force was, however, enhanced on 7 July by the temporary loan of over 500 aircraft from Luftflotte 4. He-111s and Ju-88s appeared over the battle lines at first light to soften the Soviets' defences, and were followed by Stukas operating just in front of the advancing panzers. As the ground formations once again became locked in combat, the Red Air Force sought to neutralize the Luftwaffe by smothering the front with aircraft. Although their losses were heavy – Stalin's pilots remained less capable than their rivals – the Soviets did succeed in denying the Luftwaffe freedom of movement in the skies above the battlefield. Indeed, as the Red Air Force's sorties increased and the Germans' declined for want of petrol, oil and lubricants and serviceable air-frames, it was the Soviets who achieved general and local air superiority over the Central Front, and this situation persisted throughout the rest of the operation. General der Flieger Friedrich Kless, Chief of Staff of Luftflotte 6, said:

By 7–8 July the Soviets were able to keep strong formations in the air around the clock . . . Unremitting air actions of extended duration necessarily caused the technical serviceability of our formations to decrease, therefore making it unavoidable that the quantitative Soviet superiority should temporarily be in a position to act directly against German troops during temporal and spatial gaps in the Luftwaffe fighter coverage . . . Russian air attacks began to hit the important supply roads of our spearhead divisions to an increasing extent, with raids striking points as far as [15 miles] behind German lines.

Often lacking the support of air artillery, upon which they had come to depend, the panzer formations felt vulnerable. Without the ground-based firepower, or boots on the ground to make up for this deficit, casualties mounted. Detailing the 20th Panzer Division's attack on Samodurovka, Paul Carell has written:

Lieutenant Hänsch rallied his small handful of men: 'Let's go, men, one more trench!' The machine-gun rattled. A flame-thrower hissed ahead of them. Two assault guns were giving them fire cover. They succeeded. But the lieutenant lay dead, twenty paces in front of his objective, and around him, dead and wounded, lay half his company.

Within an hour of closing with the enemy, all the officers of the 5th Company, 112th Panzer Grenadier Regiment, had become casualties. Other units suffered similar fates and with their attacks withering, some were forced to withdraw. Others, however, forged on and, in a series of local battles, managed to avoid the minefields, prise the Soviets from their trenches, overwhelm the anti-tank guns and perforate the defences. By noon, a two-mile gap had been created between the villages of Samodurovka and Kashara through which poured the Tigers followed by the 2nd and 20th Panzer Divisions. It was a critical moment in the battle for with the 6th Guards Rifle Division's left flank crumbling, XLVII Panzer Corps had gained a position from which they could make a direct assault on the Olkhovatka heights.

The situation had, however, been anticipated, and the Soviets were well placed to deal with it with the minimum of fuss. The 17th Guards Rifle Corps, supported by the 13th Army, had already acted to ensure that the ridge was well protected. Having surmounted one line of obstacles, the panzer divisions would have to do the same again if they wanted to gain the ridge. From their observation posts, the Soviet commanders peered through their field glasses at a scene of unremitting carnage as the tiring German thrust was subjected to the close attention of the Red Air Force. Valentin Lebedev, an infantry company commander, recalls:

> We could see the tanks assembling for an attack when they were attacked by Yaks and Il-2s. They were sitting targets and despite the best efforts of their anti-aircraft teams, wave after wave of aircraft flew in and did a great deal of damage. After about half an hour, it seemed as if the entire German army had caught fire. Unfortunately, that was not the case.

The Yak 9Ts, sporting 37mm cannon, and the Il-2s, carrying the new PTAB hollow-charge bomblets (which were being used for the first time), were well armed for their mission. The cannon were capable of ripping through 30mm of armour while the bomblets could penetrate 60mm. The turrets of the Panzer IIIs and IVs were just 10mm thick. Constantly moving to provide more difficult targets for the Soviet pilots to hit, the panzers were in poor order when the aircraft suddenly disappeared and dozens of T-34s were already at close range.

Feldwebel Günther Krause's Tiger took a round in its relatively lightly armoured flank, which set fire to the engine and badly wounded the loader. Krause wasted no time in ordering the crew to bail out and the loader's limp body was unceremoniously hauled out of the turret hatch as the tank continued to attract incoming small-arms fire. Throwing themselves into a ditch, the five men were then faced with the approach of enemy infantry, who had seen what had happened and were intent on denying the Wehrmacht the services of an experienced crew. Taking up their MP-40 sub-machine-guns and firing at the infantrymen in short bursts, Krause and his driver provided covering fire while the still unconscious loader was carried to the relative safety of a nearby copse. Once their three colleagues had successfully reached the trees, the two men joined them. As they did so, three Tigers came into view to rescue them – two occupied the enemy; the third rolled up by the patch of trees and took them on board.

The German attack on the Olkhovatka heights had been stopped before it even started. By dislocating the two panzer divisions with the airforce and following up with a well-timed counterattack, the Soviets had managed to maintain the integrity of the high ground for another day. Model had little more success at Ponyri. The 6th Infantry Division managed to take the village of Bitiug and the 9th Panzer Division advanced to Berezovyi Log, but overall the attack by the three divisions of XLI Panzer Corps on Ponyri failed to make much of an impression. Despite the additional firepower offered by the 18th Panzer Division, the 307th Rifle Division continued to hold out. Some parts of the town changed hands several times throughout the day but, critically, the Germans were deprived of the opportunity to make a concerted assault with a concentration of armoured vehicles by successful Soviet efforts to splinter their attempted drives. Assisted by battle debris, which included numerous burnt-out vehicles, the Soviets fought back. Tanks were dispatched by mines, guns and Molotov cocktails; the infantry were immobilized by field artillery, mortars and interlocking machine-gun fire. Any groups of Germans who did manage a degree of penetration into Soviet-held territory were ruthlessly hunted down by sections armed with sub-machine-guns, bombs and combat knives. There was little time for the combatants fighting in this arena to rest as the struggle played out within the narrow confines of Ponyri and its immediate surroundings. Assault after assault was launched into the town, and assault after assault was fended off as Rokossovsky flooded the area with guns. The unrelenting nature of the confrontation at Ponyri would never be forgotten by its participants on either side. For some the pressure was too much. Interviewing men who had fought in the battle weeks later, Vasily Grossman noted: 'Stories about 45mm cannons firing at [Tiger] tanks. Shells hit them, but bounced off like peas. There have been cases where artillerists went insane after seeing this.'

Disappointing though 7 July was for Model, since the Soviet defences had not collapsed and the Ninth Army was still stuck in the second line, the Soviets had been rocked. The Central Front was coping with the pressure of the offensive, but Rokossovsky's need for resources meant that he had to take units from less active parts of the front to reinforce his beleaguered 13th Army. The depth of the need can be gauged from the decision to draw on those units – such as IX Armoured Corps – that had been specifically positioned to defend the city of Kursk. It was a gamble, but at least these important deployments took place in the knowledge that Central Front intelligence ruled out a new German threat emerging elsewhere in the northern salient. Intelligence also told Rokossovsky that Model's reserves were running out. The Germans were offering a considerable challenge, but the Soviet defences were robust. The Ninth Army was being worn down and denied territorial advantage. As long as the Central Front could resource its operations for longer than the Ninth Army could sustain theirs, Soviet chances of success were good. Model's continued offensive action in the centre of the line over the next three days consequently played into Rokossovsky's hands.

On 8 July, the Ninth Army persisted with its attempts to take the Olkhovatka heights, focusing attention on Teploe and Ponyri. Model, offering more of the same, hoped that the Soviets would begin to wilt. Of the five panzer divisions that attacked that morning, only the 4th was fresh, drawn from the reserve. The 300 Tigers, Mark IIIs, IVs and assault guns advanced into a breaking dawn and were greeted by the Soviets as they had been on the previous three mornings of Zitadelle. Newly laid minefields stalled the tanks while artillery, Katyusha batteries and heavy mortars began the destruction. With poor weather severely limiting air operations on this day, it soon became clear that nothing less than heavy and sustained pressure on the Soviet defences would succeed in opening them up. By 0800 hours, some formations had begun to make progress. Although the 2nd Panzer Division was stalled as it began to climb the high ground towards Olkhovatka, the 20th Panzer Division had managed to overwhelm Samodurovka. In so doing, the formation had created the opportunity for the 4th Panzer Division to attack Teploe and, by exploiting the weakness inherent at the junction between the 70th and 13th Armies, gain access to the high ground beyond. The Soviets, of course, did everything in their power to stop the Germans from achieving their goal and were already moving reinforcements into the area as the first assaults on Teploe began. The series of attacks on the village were overseen by General van Saucken, 4th Panzer Division's commander, who later wrote of the first attack:

Artillery, mortars, Stalin organs, machine guns, and sharpshooters but especially extensive anti-tank guns spewed fire and doom. Packs of enemy tanks with all muzzles ablaze sallied forth again and again to counterattack. In the open terrain, our tanks, some of them Tigers, drove at full speed to make it harder for the enemy guns to hit them. The grenadiers could not keep up this pace and hung far back. The enemy strong points that our tanks had rolled over resumed firing, forcing us to give ground. Some tanks had to turn back to give them protection.

However, such was the unrelenting force with which the new division's 101 tanks struck the two rifle divisions defending the village that they fractured. The acting commander of the 4th Panzer Division's 33rd Panzer Grenadier Regiment recalls the final push into the objective:

At the head of my men, I stormed the village, which was already within reach. We could do it! With covering flanking fire from [1st Company], the men reached the edge of the village. In bitter hand-to-hand combat, one house after another was taken. My sub-machine-gun chattered along with those of the squad leaders as they stormed the houses and wiped out the Red Army soldiers firing from the window openings and the cellars. The fighting in the town lasted about an hour before the last Russian defenders were eliminated.

However, the Germans did not have the momentum then to take the high ground beyond Teploe. Observing the attempt to capture an elevated position later that day by 2nd Battalion, 33rd Grenadier Regiment, an officer later wrote:

The Russians laid down a curtain of defensive fire. After a few hundred yards, the German grenadiers lay pinned to the ground. It was impossible to get through the Soviet fire of a few hundred guns concentrated on a very narrow sector. Only the tanks moved forward into the wall of fire. The Soviet artillerymen let them come within five hundred, then four hundred yards. At that range even the Tigers were set on fire by the heavy Russian anti-tank

guns. But then three Mark IVs overran the first Soviet gun positions. The grenadiers followed. They seized the high ground.
They were thrown back by an immediate Russian counterattack.

The Soviet version of the same event came from the defending 3rd
Anti-Tank Brigade:

> At a little over 700 yards, the Soviet anti-tank guns open fire; in a
> little while the battery was left with only one gun and three men
> alive, who managed to knock out two more tanks. His remaining
> gun was destroyed along with its crew by a direct hit from a bomb
> and the battery was totally wiped out . . . The brigade commander
> [Rokuseyev] finally signalled Rokossovsky: 'Brigade under attack
> by up to 300 tanks. No. 1 and No. 2 battery into action. Request
> ammunition. I either hold on or will be wiped out. Rokuseyev.'
> The 3rd Brigade did both: it held on but was destroyed to a man.

By later writing that the anti-tank brigade had 'particularly distinguished themselves' in this battle, Zhukov was acknowledging that the
denial of access to the Olkhovatka heights on the 8th was critical to the
Central Front's continuing health. Indeed, such was the determination
of the Soviets to protect the position that, in a staggering effort, the
Germans were pushed back out of Teploe. It must have been another
moment of intense frustration for Generals Model and Lemelsen for,
yet again, after a supreme effort and some fine tactical work, the way
forward had been sealed by troops moving into pre-prepared positions
and striking back with assurance. Over the next five days, Teploe
changed hands several times as each side fought a battle that became a
sister to the ongoing struggle at Ponyri.

All along the line, the Ninth Army was held on the 8th and continued
to be held in the days that followed. Attempts to take Olkhovatka by the
concerted efforts of the 2nd Panzer and 6th Infantry Divisions were

broken on the slopes in front of the village with heavy losses. Even the arrival on the battlefield of the 3rd Company of the 505th Heavy Tank Battalion, direct from the railhead, failed to swing proceedings in the Germans' favour. By 12 July, the front line had barely moved in this sector, despite Lemelsen's dedication to the task of destroying the 75th Guards Rifle Division and its supporting formations. The same was true at bloody Ponyri, where the 292nd Infantry Division, supported by the 9th and 19th Panzer Divisions and eventually joined by the 10th Panzer Grenadier Division from the Ninth Army reserve, could not dislodge its redoubtable defenders.

However, by the end of the first week of Zitadelle, the Ninth Army had long since given up on the idea of reaching Kursk by means of a rapid breakthrough. As early as the evening of the fourth day of battle, Model, in his headquarters, had articulated serious doubts about the Ninth Army's ability quickly to develop the circumstances in which they could make a dash to Kursk. Having reached a maximum depth of just 10 miles for the cost of 50,000 casualties and 400 inoperable tanks, the German advance in the north had been anything but dramatic. Indeed, a Soviet report concluded 'after fierce battles along this axis, German forces were unable to achieve significant success'.

On 9 July, a conference held at the headquarters of XLVII Panzer Corps and attended by Kluge, Model, Harpe and Lemelsen agreed that they had no hope of achieving an immediate breakthrough but, in order to assist the southern attack, the Ninth Army would 'continue to maintain offensive pressure' on the Soviets. Model would attack, but as the context of his attack was changing so he moved inextricably towards more protracted operations along the Olkhovatka heights. On 11 July the *OKW War Diary* noted after another unfavourable day for the Ninth Army: 'it is now essential to inflict high losses on the enemy while keeping our own losses as low as possible.' There was to be, in effect, 'a rolling battle of attrition' aimed at maintaining pressure on the Soviets and, therefore, assisting Manstein's continuing attempts to penetrate Vatutin's defence in the south. This was a turning point in Operation Zitadelle for it was an acknowledgement that Model's attempt to reach Kursk had run into the ground, that his decision to drip-feed his armoured formations had backfired and given the Central Front the time and space that Rokossovsky needed to fend off whatever the Ninth Army threw at it.

The failure of the Germans to threaten Kursk severely from the north after nearly five days of fighting was, of course, not lost on Stalin. During the afternoon of 9 July, the Supreme Commander called his deputy and argued the case for launching the planned offensive into the German-held Orel salient towards Briansk. Zhukov agreed because he was confident that Model no longer posed a potent danger, saying, 'Here, on the sector of the Central Front, the enemy no longer has at its disposal forces capable of breaking through our defences.' Stalin consequently authorized Zhukov to launch Kutuzov on 11–12 July. Not only would the attack relieve pressure on the Central Front as Model would be faced with the enemy to his rear, but it would raise the morale of the Soviet troops in and around the salient while demoralizing the Germans. In the meantime, the Soviets continued to pin back the Ninth Army's increasingly desultory offensive, which, by locking itself into Rokossovsky's defences, played straight into their hands.

Zitadelle's continued potency, therefore, rested heavily on the shoulders of Manstein and the efforts of the Fourth Panzer Army in particular. If the formation could create a breach in the defences of the Voronezh Front and achieve the operational freedom that its commander so desired, the Germans could even yet unhinge the Soviets' defences and fall on Kursk. First, however, Hoth had to deal with Soviet armour that was massing on his flanks.

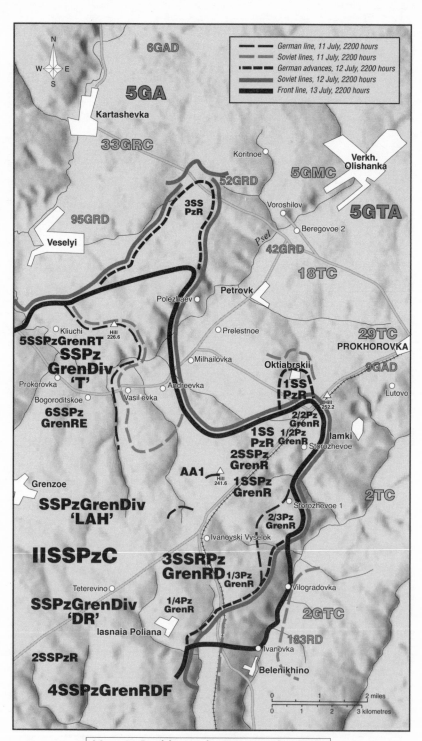

Map 9: Prokhorovka, 11–13 July 1943

CHAPTER 8

Anticipation

(Zitadelle: 9–11 July)

The partisans struck suddenly and with shattering effect. The light had already begun to fade when the commander of the convoy, Hauptmann Reinke, made his concerns known to his careworn superior but, having been told to 'get on with it', the 35 vehicles had rumbled out of the depot and towards the front. An hour later, the lead vehicle exploded, throwing a shower of sparks and debris into the gloom. An ambush had been sprung.

From the left side of the ragged dirt road, and making good use of the cover provided by a copse and shallow ditch, the irregulars poured a vicious barrage into the German flank from a range of 100 yards. Light mortar rounds burst among the stalled soft-skinned vehicles and immediately set them on fire. Machine gunners riddled the column with short, well-aimed bursts and automatic carbines joined the mêlée to target the forlorn crews. Reinke, travelling in the second vehicle, was killed by a round that entered his skull before he had an opportunity to open his door. Driver Johannes Erwin was at the wheel of the fifth truck, and he and his co-driver, Frederik Dexler, managed to extract themselves from the cab and take cover behind a wheel without being hit. Erwin drew and cocked his pistol as rounds clattered into the vehicle's thin metal bonnet and zipped through the canvas covering of its wagon. A tyre burst as small-arms ammunition popped and cracked in a blazing wreck nearby. Erwin shuffled to his right and took up a firing position by his dented front wing. He loosed off four unaimed rounds towards the trees and tried to comprehend the chaotic scene. Half a platoon of infantry was receiving orders from a gesticulating commander beside an adjacent truck. The man's voice was drowned out by the crump of explosions and the ripping of an MG-42, which had just begun to lay down suppressive fire.

Erwin watched as the two sections attacked, but by the time they reached the tree line, the partisans had long since melted away into the night. They left behind a battlefield. Cries for medics were carried on a gusting wind, which fanned the fires and sent smoke swirling across the road. Erwin ran a filthy hand across his sweaty brow as he walked over to Dexler, who was still lying prone, his head clasped tightly in his hands. He told his friend that it was safe to stand up, but Dexler had his eyes tightly shut and sobbed loudly into the Russian dirt. The stress and strain associated with two years' service on the Eastern Front was flooding out of him. Raising Dexler to his feet, Erwin led him past two corpses and inhaled the familiar aroma of fresh blood, charred flesh and burning rubber. The incident had lasted less than 10 minutes but had caused 35 casualties, destroyed nine trucks and left 21 more requiring recovery. It confirmed to Erwin what he already knew – survival was a lottery and reaching one's destination could never be guaranteed in the Kursk salient.

Such attacks by partisans complemented the Soviet aim of stretching the German forces and wearing them down wherever and whenever possible. 'They were a constant menace,' recalled infantryman Felix Dresener. 'They slowed our ability to supply the front line and forced us into clearing operations, which took troops away from the front line . . . Our platoon provided protection for several convoys, which kept us from the real battle for over a week. During that time we lost eight men and goodness only knows how many trucks. It was a simple Russian tactic, but effective.' The partisans and Red Air Force targeted the Wehrmacht's lines of communication with extensive and methodical attacks. Railway lines leading towards Kursk were systematically bombed and disrupted, as were roads from railheads and various depots. The Luftwaffe would ordinarily have offered protection, but its resources continued to decrease as calls on its support grew. By the fifth day of the battle, Zitadelle was being ground down from the outskirts of Kiev to the front line at Kursk. The whole operation was absorbing precious resources at an alarming rate as Model and Manstein continued to be confronted by complex defences, a tenacious enemy and some trying weather. On 7 July, for example, Model called on Zeitzler to supply 100,000 more rounds of tank ammunition '*immediately*'. On the following day, the Fourth Panzer Army lost another 125 tanks, taking Hoth's total of inoperable machines to 405 since 5 July.

Even so, the Wehrmacht continued to batter away at the Red Army in the salient, because it was still not clear who would emerge the victor. Nevertheless, Operation Zitadelle was rapidly moving towards its final act. Although Model's offensive in the north had been contained, rendering the Ninth Army capable of little more than maintaining pressure on the Olkhovatka heights, Manstein's attack in the south remained strong, and still had great potential. If the Fourth Panzer Army could overcome Major-General A.L. Getman's 6th Tank Corps south of Oboyan, it could then focus its attention on facing the massive Soviet forces that were beginning to assemble around Prokhorovka. Here, the 5th Tank Army and the 5th Guards Army – also released from the Steppe Front – were intent on stopping II SS Panzer Corps' advance, but if they were defeated, Hoth's armour could yet surge the 50 miles to Kursk. Thus, despite Zitadelle having fallen far behind its timetable and being weakened by days of heavy fighting, its threat remained alive. Manstein, therefore, was going to apply unrelenting pressure to Vatutin's formations, and on the morning of 9 July he attacked with 500 tanks across a 10 mile front. *Keils* of between 60 and 100 panzers, with Tigers at the point and panzer grenadiers following, moved against the 1st Tank Army and 6th Guards Army once more.

The day dawned grey and heavy rain showers drenched the combatants. 'If it was not bad enough to await the arrival of a monstrous armoured attack,' explains mortar man Igor Panesenko, 'but we did so with befuddled, tired minds and empty stomachs in the pouring rain. I had a fever and, in all honesty, did not care at that moment whether I lived or died. Many of us felt the same and it made us fearless and bold.' He listened for the sound of approaching tanks, which was a warning that an artillery and Stuka attack was about to begin. The first shells began to land at 0600 hours, and within the hour the front was alive with fighting. Verkhopenye did not succumb easily. Having been bombed by Stukas flying in appalling conditions, blasted by the division's artillery and probed by Mark IVs, Panthers and Tigers supported by infantry and assault guns, the defenders had to be cleared from every last building. Rushed into the line the previous evening, a soaked Igor Panesenko fought with his section in a ruined house:

> The forward positions eventually began to crack and were destroyed by tanks and infantry. We fought from house to house and room to room . . . As anti-tank guns were quickly destroyed by the armours' guns, the tanks were assailed by teams which used magnetic mines and Molotov cocktails. The supporting German infantry kept most away . . . [and we] took up a position in an upstairs room with half a floor and no roof. I was a good shot and managed to cause some trouble for the enemy as they stopped to check their position . . . I linked up with another couple of men and tried to stop the enemy from climbing the

stairs up to us. There was some hand-to-hand fighting and I grappled with a chap who grabbed my rifle. His teeth were clenched
and I could smell his breath as he shouted at me. Then he let go
and ran around a corner. A grenade! There was an explosion
which threw me to the floor. I came to seconds later with a large
German standing over me.

For all the barbarity of the Eastern Front and the ferocity of the
fighting that morning in Verkhopenye, Panesenko was helped to his
feet by the man whom he had been fighting just seconds before: 'It
reminded me of a football match before the war,' he continues, 'where
an opponent helps you up after a hard tackle! . . . It was extraordinary,
because we had seen what the Germans were capable of. Here I was
being led out into the street by a man who had been trying to kill me
moments before. He took me to a line of other prisoners. As he left –
I'll never forget this – he looked at me, nodded and smiled. There was
recognition in that brief gesture that we were part of something bigger
than both of us and that we needed to retain our humanity.'

The battle for Verkhopenye lasted throughout the morning, but
while that village was being beaten into submission, the 11th Panzer
Division continued up the road to Oboyan, linked up with II SS Panzer
Corps at Sukho-Solotino and advanced to the southern outskirts of
Novosselovka. The Fusilier Regiment of Grossdeutschland also
probed forward, heading to the west of Novosselovka, but was
brought to a halt by strong anti-tank guns and tanks. Eventually, more
German armour appeared as Verkhopenye was overcome, and the division's history records:

Our tanks soon ran into the enemy tank concentrations, however,
which were sighted from a distance of 2,500–3,000 metres. A
major tank versus tank battle developed with Stukas providing
continuous support. Hill 243.8 was reached after heavy fighting

and the panzers halted there initially. On the horizon were burning and smoking enemy tanks. Unfortunately three of 6th Company's tanks had been knocked out as well . . . In the further course of the engagement, Hauptmann von Wietersahm succeeded in carrying the attack as far as the anti-tank defences at the village of Novosselovka and reached [Hill 240.4].

However, Grossdeutschland found no way through the Soviet defences north of Novosselovka and it was at this stage that the *schwerpunkt* (focal point) of Knobelsdorff's XLVIII Panzer Corps was shifted from between the Pena and the road to Oboyan farther west. While the 11th Panzer Division was to continue its advance northwards, Grossdeutschland was to meet the enemy's armour on the formation's west flank. The aim was to deal such a blow to the defenders that they could no longer restrain the progress of the 3rd Panzer (with no Panthers or Tigers) and 332nd Infantry Divisions, held up at Berezovka, Alekseevka and Mikhailovka. It was believed that by plunging west Grossdeutschland could fatally undermine the enemy's defences, cutting the 6th Tank Corps' lines of communication along the Berezovka–Ivina road. Once the Soviet armour had been mauled, although Knobelsdorff's momentum would have been temporarily interrupted, Grossdeutschland could rejoin the 11th Panzer Division and restart its move on Oboyan – and then Kursk. Mark Healy argues that 'in hindsight the diversion would come to be seen as one of the major turning points in the battle in the south of the salient'.

Turning through 90 degrees, Kampfgruppe von Strachwitz – which started the morning with 19 Mark IVs, 10 Tigers and 10 Panthers – pushed towards Hills 251.4 and 247.0 and into the rear of the 6th Tank Corps. They were followed by the Reconnaissance Battalion and attached assault guns. These troops had spent the morning progressing up the road to Oboyan, supported by Stuka attacks that dispatched the defenders to 'commissar and Red Army heaven'. During the afternoon of the 9th, Grossdeutschland pushed west, but it was soon confronted by strong counterattacks, which denied Hoernlein his objectives that day. Thus, by nightfall, although XLVIII Panzer Corps was barely 12 miles from Oboyan, its chance of swiftly securing the town had suffered a blow due to the diversion of the élite Grossdeutschland Panzer Grenadier Division.

There is little doubt that where the Luftwaffe provided support, Knobelsdorff's corps profited, but on the 9th there was a notable drop off in support for the formation. The battle for the skies above the Kursk salient had continued to rage during the first five days of Zitadelle, but declining German air assets and rising Soviet resources made life increasingly difficult for the Luftwaffe. As a result, commanders continued to eschew the attainment of general air superiority over the battlefield in favour of local dominance. In this way, the Stukas could assist Grossdeutschland's attack towards Novosselovka, but that meant that the 3rd Panzer Division's requests for support were denied. Even worse, it meant that the division had to fight off marauding Soviet ground-attack aircraft using its own resources. To He-111 engineer Ludwig Schein, the problem was simple:

> We needed more aircraft, more fuel, more mechanics and more pilots. If we had as much and as many as the Russians, then we could have achieved air supremacy – not just air superiority – because our pilots were so much better than their Soviet counterparts. However, the sad fact was that we were under resourced and paid for it ... Our airfield was targeted three times on 9th July and we hardly paused in our maintenance on the Heinkels to take cover. We were under pressure to get the aircraft into the skies as quickly as possible – even if it meant cutting corners.

Over the period 7–8 July, German sorties fell from 829 to 652 while the Soviets' rose from 1,100 to 1,500. By the fifth day of battle, those inexperienced Red Air Force pilots who had survived their first brushes with the Luftwaffe found themselves far better prepared for aerial combat than they had been. Lieutenant Ivan Kozhedub, for example, had nearly been shot down in his La-5 fighter on the first day of the battle, but scored his first victory on the 6th and a second on the 7th. On the 9th he took to the air with four other aircraft and patrolled the front line on the Oboyan front. Kozhedub recalls:

> [W]e found the same scene as yesterday – a raging tank battle on the ground. Usually your attention is drawn to the sector where enemy bombers might appear. But aware of the tactics used by the 'hunters' [pairs of enemy fighters], I scanned the airspace above our heads. Almost immediately I discovered two aircraft high above. I recognized the sleek silhouettes of Messerschmitt 109s. They approached us from our own territory. Clearly these were a pair of hunters! The opponents started to turn towards us, obviously with the intention of attacking us from the front.

Leading the group, Kozhedub became the enemy's first target and prepared himself to kill:

> I also got the leader in my gunsight when they were at an altitude of 4000 metres. I waited for the distance to reduce before I opened fire. I was the first to shoot. I held the firing button, squeezed and blasted away a long burst, and it was sufficient! The leader turned over from his steep dive and I saw him hit the ground.

Oberfeldwebel Edmund Rossmann, a Bf-109 veteran with 93 victories, was in the same sector that morning when low cloud fragmented his small formation. Taking their opportunity, Soviet fighters attacked and hit two of the Messerschmitts. Rossmann explains:

Suddenly I saw [Feldwebel] Lohberg's aircraft pouring smoke, and it left towards the west. After a short while it belly-landed in a field about 20 kilometres to the west of Oboyan. When I saw Lohberg climb out of his aircraft and wave at me, I turned around and landed next to his belly-landed Messerschmitt with the intention of picking him up. He raced towards my aircraft, but just as he climbed onto the wing, he bent forward and fell to the ground. I unstrapped myself and jumped out to help him. In the next moment I received a terrible blow from a Russian rifle butt.

The Red Air Force's presence was growing but the Germans continued to dominate critical parts of the battlefield, as a post-operational report reflects:

[Our aviation] did not have air superiority over the enemy's main attack axis – along the Belgorod–Oboyan highway – until 10 July. Enemy aviation not only offered strong opposition to our assault aviation aircraft, it also gained air superiority over the battlefield relatively easily during the period necessary for his bomber operations.

Thus, it was not only XLVIII Panzer Corps that received Luftwaffe support where and when it was most needed on 9 July, but also II SS Panzer Corps.

Hausser's corps was engaged in heavy fighting during the night of 8–9 July as the 2nd and 31st Tank Corps sought to deny the division any respite. The Soviets made numerous local counterattacks in the driving rain, which necessitated rapid reactions. Even so, under the cover of darkness, Totenkopf continued to replace LAH in the nose of the salient while Das Reich held the corps' flank north of Smogodino and the 167th Infantry Division protected it to the south. Das Reich was destined to be fixed in place by counterattacks for another three days due to III Panzer Corps' continued failure to come up alongside, but LAH and Totenkopf endeavoured to push on. There is little doubt that II SS Panzer Corps was fatigued, but it had retained its morale and motivation while suffering relatively light casualties. LAH, for example, reported just 283 dead, 1,282 wounded and approximately 30 missing since the opening of Zitadelle. Moreover, although Hausser had lost 202 armoured fighting vehicles since the 5th, he still had 249 on the morning of the 9th and expected more to be returned to service shortly, having undergone repair.

However, the 9th was a frustrating day for the corps because it achieved minimal northward momentum. LAH began the day with an attack on the village of Sukho-Solotino, which it captured just before noon, but was subsequently pummelled by Soviet artillery for the rest of the day. 'The whole area was flattened by Russian gunners who had already ranged their guns,' says 11th Panzer Division's Arnold Brenner, who linked up with the SS troopers in the village that afternoon. 'We were caught like rats in a trap and could not move anywhere. The guns were eventually silenced by our bombers, but not before the place had been reduced to brick dust.'

LAH could not press on any farther, but on its right Totenkopf took Kochetovka – home to the 6th Guards Army headquarters – and assaulted Hill 241.6, which overlooked the Psel just three miles to the north. In several hours of fighting, Mark IIIs and IVs were accompanied by the last three working Tigers and drove forward behind a heavy barrage. The Soviet artillery responded immediately and as the supporting panzer grenadiers began to fall behind the *Keil*, T-34s were sent to intercept the panzers. As night fell the high ground remained firmly in the Red Army's hands, but Totenkopf readied itself for another attempt the following morning which SS-Brigadeführer Priess was confident would be successful.

During the 9th, Hoth's eyes were not only on Oboyan but also Prokhorovka as the 5th Guards Tank Army closed in on its destination.

The formation had undertaken a 240 mile journey to the salient and, in the words of T-34 commander Vladimir Alexeev, was expecting 'a very severe battle'. Vatutin received regular updates on the formation's progress, since he feared that the Fourth Panzer Army was on the verge of crossing the Psel and breaking into open country. With the 1st Tank Army and 6th Guards Army having suffered heavy losses, Rotmistrov's 593 tanks, 37 self-propelled guns and thousands of artillery pieces offered substantial reinforcement. Although the formation would ordinarily have moved only during the hours of darkness to mask its advance on a 20 mile front, Vatutin's situation demanded that it did not stop at dawn. Rotmistrov wrote in his memoirs:

> Even now, writing several decades later, I can see those country roads and the faces of the tank men blackened by dust and grease. Wherever you looked, you saw tanks, self-propelled guns, trucks and motorcyclists ... Along the roads motors roared, clouds of smoke hung in the air and everywhere hung the smell of diesel oil and burnt rubber.

Passing through towns, villages and forests and along dirt roads, throwing clouds of dust and grit into the faces of the commanders, the experience was an unpleasant one for the dog-tired crews. Alexeev explains: 'The move to Prokhorovka was a nightmare. It was really hot beneath the huge clouds of dust from the three columns of tanks.' Their situation would have been even worse had the columns been subjected to attack from the air, but although its movement had been picked up by reconnaissance planes, the Luftwaffe could not spare the aircraft to attack it. 'What a great advantage it was to us not to have the Stukas fall on us,' says driver Semen Berezhko. 'We were expecting them every minute. We had our own protection, but we were vulnerable to an attack ... As it was, we arrived at our positions untouched and in good order.' Berezhko began to move into his assembly area in the early hours of 10 July and before long the 5th Guards Tank Army, having suffered very few breakdowns, was deploying in an arc around Prokhorovka to attack the Fourth Panzer Army.

With Rotmistrov's men preparing themselves for battle, the 80,000 men and 185 armoured fighting vehicles of the 5th Guards Army expected to arrive at Prokhorovka by the morning of 12 July and a strike against the Orel salient imminent, Vatutin was reassured. But he could not afford to relax, as David Glantz has written: 'A panoply of former military disasters and dashed expectations had bred an air of realism in Soviet command channels. As comforting as developments seemed to be, Vatutin grimly awaited the verdict of the fickle gods of war.' That verdict, it seemed, would be reached after the launch of the counterattack planned for the 12th – the 5th Guards Tank Army and 5th Guards Army were to 'encircle and defeat the main German grouping straining towards Oboyan and Prokhorovka'. Although Vatutin believed that the initiative had shifted towards him, he did not know that Manstein and Hoth had *planned* to maintain XLVIII Panzer Corps' advance on Oboyan and shift II SS Panzer Corps' weight towards Prokhorovka to confront the developing Soviet threat to their flank. Indeed, before Zitadelle began, the Fourth Panzer Army was directed to 'anticipate an engagement with Soviet armoured forces near Prokhorovka prior to continuing the attack towards Kursk'. Thus, during the afternoon of the 9th, orders were promulgated for Hausser's formation to redeploy so that its divisions faced Rotmistrov's tanks to the northeast. II SS Panzer Corps was to attack Prokhorovka immediately and by seizing the town, unhinge the 5th Guards Tank Army's preparations while it was still moving into position.

Soviet intelligence picked up on the German reorientation and, during the night 9–10 July, Vatutin called a conference in Oboyan to discuss the situation. Believing that the German shift was a reaction to the Voronezh Front's tenacious defences, he declared to Vasilevsky and Rotmistrov: 'Having failed to penetrate Kursk through Oboyan, clearly the Hitlerites have decided to shift the axis of their main blow farther to the east along the rail line to Prokhorovka.' It was a false assumption based on a belief that the Fourth Panzer Army had so weakened itself on Soviet defences that it was seeking an alternative route to Kursk. In reality, Hoth's staff described Soviet defences before the Psel as 'hopeless', and II SS Panzer Corps, having finally wriggled free of the Soviet second-line defences, was only redirected due to the imminent arrival of the 5th Guards Tank Army. Moreover, the Fourth Panzer Army was far from a spent force. It still had nearly 500 operational tanks, and II SS Panzer Corps accounted for 294 of them. However, despite their skilful prediction of where the Soviets' reserve would enter the battlefield and their plans to stop it, Manstein and Hoth had not expected Army Detachment Kempf to have made such a stolid advance that II SS Panzer Corps would have to act alone. There was little that the commander of Army Group South could do but exhort III Panzer Corps, with its 116 serviceable panzers, to achieve a breakthrough and link up with Hausser's corps by 11 July for a drive on Prokhorovka.

While senior commanders dealt with issues pertaining to the days and weeks ahead, on the morning of 10 July their formations carried out their orders and manoeuvred for advantageous positions. The weather continued to hamper their plans. The Fourth Panzer Army reported: 'Under cloud covered skies and local thunderstorms, the roads were soft and in terrible condition for wheeled vehicles.' Desperate to maintain their impetus, Hoth and his commanders were frustrated by reports that vehicles had 'bogged', routes were flooded and visibility was severely reduced. Ralph Faber, a gunner with 11th Panzer Division, noted in his journal:

At last I have a moment to reflect on the last few days as rain continues to fall. We are currently awaiting the recovery of our [towed] gun which has become stuck after the road gave way under a wheel . . . I am covered in mud as rivulets run free down the track. The thunderstorms are so heavy that the ground does not have a chance to absorb the water before the next. It remains warm and steamy . . . We are all very tired after our recent efforts. It has been a hard battle with the gun in constant action but for the moment, we are going nowhere.

The low cloud base did not provide ideal conditions for air operations but the Soviets, always willing to use their superior resources in bold actions, sought to exploit the opportunity to target mired German units and attack their airfields. Il-2 pilot Boris Vassilieva recalls, 'We attacked a column south of Nechaevka which was reported as having become stuck between the Donets and a *balka* . . . I destroyed several vehicles and left the scene in flames just as another [squadron] arrived to finish the job.' Ivan Kozhedub, meanwhile, tackled a German airfield near Belgorod:

When we approached the target area, we saw dark thunderclouds that were building to the south, some of them reaching down to the ground . . . Our bombers had to go down to 400–500 metres, and this alerted the enemy. Suddenly a fierce AAA fire set in from all sides. Tracer bullets climbed up against us, and the sky, which was black with cloud, was lit up by flashes. By that time we had reached the target and the Pe-2s dropped their bombs all at once. The air base below was covered by smoke from exploding bombs. A few Junkers tried to take off, but our bombers and fighters attacked them and destroyed them all. Next our fighters strafed the AAA positions and silenced them. None of our aircraft was shot down, but many had been damaged by ground fire. My own La-5 had received a considerable number of 'extra holes'.

The Luftwaffe, meanwhile, focused its attentions on the front line and supported those formations that were encountering strong Soviet resistance. This included Grossdeutschland, which strove to 'finish off

6th Tank Corps' on Hoth's left flank. Advancing towards Kruglik under skies buzzing with Stukas – 'squadron after squadron of Stukas came over to drop their deadly eggs on the Russian armour' – and behind strong artillery barrages, elements of the division ground their way forward. In doing so, they cut the Soviet lines of communication that reached down to Berezovka, which, in turn, allowed the 3rd Panzer Division to move forward once more. It was an important success, but even if Grossdeutschland had landed a painful blow on the 1st Tank Army's weakening midriff, it did not provide XLVIII Panzer Corps with a free hand in the sector. The 6th Tank Corps was not destroyed and, having maintained its cohesion, the corps was destined to fight on and spite Knobelsdorff's operations. Reflecting on the formation's experiences, Getman later explained:

> Many of our soldiers and commanders fell heroically [during the first] five days of ferocious battle. Hundreds of the corps' soldiers were wounded and evacuated to the rear. We suffered especially heavy losses in equipment. By the end of 10 July, not more than fifty tanks, more than one half light, remained operational and three batteries of antitank guns . . . Nevertheless, the corps continued to resist the enemy. Having littered the field of battle with hundreds of his burned and destroyed tanks and guns and thousands of bodies, the enemy succeeded in pushing our lines back several kilometres . . . Meeting organized fire resistance, he ceased his attacks by nightfall. But, certainly, only so that he could renew the attacks in the morning with new force. Understanding this, we prepared for the new battle.

Major Peter Frantz experienced Soviet tenacity at first hand when, during the evening of 10 July, his assault guns came under Katyusha rocket attack:

I suddenly saw fiery arrows coming towards us from the outskirts of Kruglik. Before I would figure out what they were there were explosions directly in front of the mass of advancing assault guns. The vehicle next to me . . . began to stream smoke. Thank God it turned out to be one of the smoke candles that every assault gun carried. The vehicle had taken a direct hit in the bow plates but suffered no damage. The explosion and the effect of the projectile revealed that we were under direct fire from a Stalin Organ.

By the time that darkness fell, although the 3rd Panzer Division was moving forward once more, Soviet resistance before Kruglik was unyielding and the 6th Tank Corps fought on while the remainder of Grossdeutschland and the 11th Panzer Division were held on the road to Oboyan. XLVIII Panzer Corps took Hill 244.8 astride the road to Oboyan to the north of Novosselovka, but it would advance no further during Zitadelle. A German observer noted:

The highest point on the approaches to Oboyan had thereby been reached and, at the same time, the deepest penetration made into the Russian front. From the high ground one could see far into the valley of the Psel River, the last natural barrier this side of Kursk. With field-glasses the towers of Oboyan could be made out in the fine haze. Oboyan was the objective. It seemed within arm's reach. Barely twelve miles away. No distance at all under normal circumstances for a fast formation.

However, the diversion of Hoernlein's division had fatally undermined Knobelsdorff's northerly progress.

II SS Panzer Corps' advance towards Oboyan was also wrecked, but the cause of its distraction was the order to strike out towards Prokhorovka on 10 July. The primary offensive was to be conducted by

LAH advancing down the Teterevino–Prokhorovka road, supported by Das Reich on its right flank and Totenkopf on its left. The LAH commander, Theodor Wisch, expected to cover the nine miles to the town and capture it by evening. His troops, however, were rather more realistic. SS-Sturmmann Heinrich Huber recalled: 'After days of fighting we were feeling weak, although remained motivated by the important task before us. We did not underestimate the defenders before Prokhorovka for they were as motivated as we were. I did not expect the battle to be anything other than frenzied – I was not disappointed.' The fighting was ferocious that morning and the three divisions failed to make the impact that Hausser had hoped. Unit lethargy and an obstinate enemy do help explain the formation's sluggishness, but organizational turmoil caused by Totenkopf's redeployment from the right flank and the subsequent rotation of the corps through 45 degrees to face Prokhorovka in heavy rain were also responsible. The corps found it difficult to build up momentum from the outset.

Totenkopf opened the attack to anchor Hausser's northern flank and sought to cross the Psel and seize Hill 226.6 six miles west of Prokhorovka in order to cover LAH's exposed flank. Using 11 Tigers at the point of a *Keil*, which pushed towards the Psel in the early hours of the 10th, the division immediately ran into units of the 95th Guards Rifle Division. By mid-morning the Panzer Grenadiers were engaged in some close-quarters fighting with the Soviet defenders, who had withdrawn to the southern bank of the Psel as German engineers moved forward with bridging equipment. An infantryman of the 290th Guards Rifle Regiment, Anatoli Abalakov, says of the day, during which Totenkopf took 430 casualties:

The scene along the banks of the Psel was carnage, sheer carnage. We had been told to stop the Germans from crossing the water at all costs and we threw everything we had at them ... The bastards just kept coming at us. Our artillery gave some support and we fought with them between the falling shells. German artillery opened up, and then Stukas arrived. It was grim, remorseless stuff. The sort of fighting that a soldier hopes he will never be involved in because survival is very unlikely . . . When we were eventually overwhelmed, I swam to the north bank [of the Psel]. I was exhausted and still wore much of my equipment, but I was swimming for my life . . . I scrambled up the muddy bank and headed for a position that I knew existed in [a *balka*]. Shells, mortars and rounds were striking the ground all around me as I ran. How I was not hit I do not know. I was relieved to reach the position where I was pulled over some sandbags. Then, having fought with my bare hands against the SS monsters, swum a river and run the gauntlet through fire, an officer admonished me for withdrawing without permission and for losing my rifle!

This local battle had a considerable impact on II SS Panzer Corps' operations that day for by delaying Totenkopf's crossing of the Psel until noon, the Soviets not only gave themselves time to prepare their defences along the north bank of the river, but also delayed the start of the LAH attack until 1045 hours. Thus, by the time the corps was moving in the early afternoon, the Soviets were better set. Totenkopf was forced into a bloody struggle for Hill 226.6, and its southern slopes were taken by dusk, while LAH and Das Reich – which still had one of its panzer grenadier regiments holding the corps' flank to the south – were subjected to strong and destabilizing armoured counterattacks by Popov's 2nd Tank Corps. Das Reich's daily report noted:

There was lively enemy vehicle traffic and tank and infantry advances in front of the entire division sector. The enemy was particularly active in the area south and north of Belenichino and frequently directed heavy artillery fire and fire from tanks, especially on the northern division sector. The enemy repeatedly probed the positions of SS-Panzer-Grenadier-Regiment Der Führer with armoured attacks.

Since the flanking divisions were finding it impossible to make much headway, LAH's own attack suffered. Although Wisch's men took Komsomolets State Farm and then Hill 241.6, LAH remained five miles short of Prokhorovka by nightfall. Neither side got much sleep that night as they continued to fight for control of tactically important ground. Panzer grenadiers probed the Soviet line looking for weak points while Soviet teams replied with disruptive assaults and bombed German positions with skimming Po-2 bi-planes. Hausser, meanwhile, radioed orders to his divisional commanders, directing the attack to continue the next morning when Kruger's Das Reich would return to full offensive strength. Its second panzer grenadier regiment was being replaced on the lower flank by a unit of the 167th Infantry Division.

Throughout the 10th that flank had been put under considerable pressure by the 2nd Tank and 2nd Guards Tank Corps as III Panzer Corps endeavoured to advance and remove the danger that they posed. On the 9th, Breith's formation remained in the clutches of the Soviet second line, and that situation continued to cost its three panzer divisions energy and resources. The 6th Panzer Division's panzer regiment, for example, had begun Zitadelle with 105 tanks but by the end of the fifth day of battle had just 22 machines operational. The Tigers of the 503rd Heavy Tank Battalion had also suffered, largely due to mine impact and mechanical breakdown, but the efficiency of the workshops meant that Breith could still call on 33 heavies by the 10th. On that day, the 6th Panzer Division and 503rd Heavy Tank Battalion sought to break free of the Soviet defences around Shiakhovo and Melikhovo, supported by the 7th and 19th Panzer Divisions, but continued to be held. Corps Raus, meanwhile, had been reinforced by the recently arrived 198th Infantry Division and continued to stand firm against Soviet counterattacks on the right flank. On the left flank, the 168th Infantry Division did manage to take advantage of the withdrawal of the 81st and 375th Rifle Divisions, but was in no position to do anything other than nudge forward. The net gain of Army Group Detachment Kempf's efforts on the 10th, therefore, was territorially inconsequential and gave Hoth little hope that Breith's corps would be pulling up alongside II SS Panzer Corps any time soon. Combat engineer Rolf Schmidt, who had been working tirelessly in support of the panzers, felt frustrated:

> Each day we expected to break the enemy's defences, but there was line after line of trenches and minefields. It was extremely irritating. The panzers were straining to speed forward – it was what they had been designed to do – but were held up. Rather than moving to support the attack of the SS divisions, we were being worn down by lengthy battles within the Soviet lines . . . We knew what the corps had to achieve and had been told that a great attack [at Prokhorovka] could not take place until our panzers arrived. Great pressure was put on us to get the armour north as quickly as possible – but the enemy did everything in its power to stop us.

Twenty-two miles still separated III Panzer Corps from Prokhorovka, and intelligence received by Army Group South identified not only the movement of Soviet formations towards Prokhorovka, but also a major reorganizing of Soviet assets – confirmation for Manstein that he was in a race to grab the initiative. Major Leo Spiegel, a staff officer with the 11th Panzer Division, has described 'a tangible heaviness' hanging over Hoth's headquarters when he visited it on the evening of 10 July. Spiegel has testified:

> I was sent to see the operations staff at Fourth Panzer Army and found the place to be a strange mixture of frenetic energy and

resignation. It was clear that like [the staff at 11th Panzer Division] the team was extremely tired and tempers were frayed. I made my report – making sure that it was short and to the point – picked up some maps and was about to make my way out when I was invited by the Oberst to stay for a cup of coffee. We chatted about the unfolding operation and it became clear that whilst there was hope, there was also considerable concern that the enemy were bringing strong reserves into the sector. I was also informed, for the first time, that Model's offensive 'was dead in the water' and that the operation depended wholly on Fourth Panzer Army's ability to break through . . . I left the headquarters more concerned than I had been when I entered it an hour earlier. It was clear that Zitadelle was reaching its climax and that confidence was fragile.

The situation was discussed in detail at a conference conducted at Kempf's headquarters in Dolbino on the morning of 11 July. Manstein reflected the lack of optimism that Spiegel had picked up on the previous evening, and explained to the assembled commanders that Zitadelle was 'fragmenting'. According to General Busse, the Chief of Staff of Army Group South, Manstein posed the question: 'Should the attack be continued, considering the condition of the troops, the ever-increasing strength of the Russians, and – particularly – the fact that Ninth Army's assault had ground to a complete halt by 9 July?' Of course, it was not in Manstein's gift to bring the operation to an end, but by raising the question he made it clear that he did not expect to reach Kursk. The question remained, therefore, how best to proceed. What could be achieved in the time and with the resources still available to them?

Kempf was extremely negative and argued that his formation was exhausted and had suffered excessive casualties, and, even though Lieutenant-General Walter Nehring's reserve XXIV Panzer Corps (three divisions with a total of 112 tanks) was on its way to support him, his concern was that it was too little and would arrive too late. Hoth, however, was more optimistic and must have been irritated by Kempf's depressing summary. The Fourth Panzer Army's chief gave it as his opinion that, while undoubtedly tired and weakened by a week of hard fighting, his corps were still capable of dealing the Soviets a heavy blow. He lambasted Kempf for suggesting that Zitadelle should be brought to an end, and advocated the continuance of operations to destroy the enemy south of the Psel.

With little option but to continue with the offensive until Hitler instructed otherwise, and realizing that he needed to weaken the 5th Guards Tank Army if he was going to conduct a successful withdrawal from the salient in the near future, Manstein agreed. The plan, therefore, was to use II SS and III Panzer Corps to defeat the Soviet armoured reserve and, in so doing, achieve an OKW aim of drawing the Red Army's sting in the area. There was no doubt that by 11 July Zitadelle had failed but Manstein continued to make every effort to achieve what he could from a fatally flawed operation.

Despite Kempf's lack of enthusiasm for the continuance of the offensive, Breith was more sanguine about operations. Indeed, by the time that Manstein spoke to him in the early afternoon of the 11th, his formation had escaped the clutches of the Soviet second line, and the 6th Panzer Division, led by the 503rd's Tigers, had broken into open countryside. By the evening, after a titanic struggle northeast of Belgorod, the panzers were charging towards Prokhorovka. Rolf Schmidt's diary entry for the day simply states: 'Breakthrough.' The Germans had perforated the line at the junction held by the 107th and 305th Rifle Divisions, and immediately strained Lieutenant-General V. Kruchenkin's 69th Army's defences south of Prokhorovka.

It was a delicate moment for Vatutin's defences, but their task was clear – III Panzer Corps' offensive had to be stopped or, at the very least, drawn away from II SS Panzer Corps. Right across the front,

Vatutin juggled with his formations to create the time and space that he needed to assemble the troops for his counterattack and launch it before the march of the panzers became irrepressible.

Throughout the day, the Fourth Panzer Army continued to manoeuvre for position, and XLVIII Panzer Corps still hoped to make the leap to Oboyan. To facilitate this, units of Grossdeutschland continued to engage the 1st Tank Army in their thrust westwards. So successful were they on the morning of the 11th that by 1000 hours Hoernlein declared his day's objectives taken. Thus, with reconnaissance aircraft reporting that the enemy's infantry was withdrawing and intelligence from the front indicating that Katukov's formation was broken – 'Enemy infantry are retreating in long columns. They look to be in poor order and without heavy weapons' – Hoth concluded that the armoured threat to his flank had been vanquished. The 3rd Panzer Division was ordered to replace Grossdeutschland on the flank, enabling Hoernlein's men to attack northwards once more.

The attack was to be made in cooperation with 11th Panzer Division, which had spent the day trying to gain local tactical advantage. Arnold Brenner, a rifleman with the 111th Panzer Grenadier Regiment, recalls:

All day we fought for scraps of land. The entire division hardly seemed to move although by evening we may have advanced a further [mile]. It was demoralizing as our company lost 15 men that day with very little to show for it. Our advance seemed to have come to a grinding halt ... That evening we were told to expect a rapid advance the following day [12 July] but we all wondered how this could be. All day we noticed that the enemy were reinforcing their positions and we found ourselves under heavy and long aerial bombardments. It seemed to us that we had reached as far as we could go.

Although there may have been optimism that, with Grossdeutschland rejoining the fray towards Oboyan, rapid progress could be achieved, as Brenner sensed, XLVIII Panzer Corps had reached its culminating point. Far from having soaked up all of the Soviet reserves, Vatutin was husbanding forward elements of the 5th Guards Army – including the 10th Tank Corps, which had moved south of Oboyan – and a collection of other units with the purpose of striking Hoth's left flank. This force would target the fading 3rd Panzer Division, which had 23 remaining tanks, just as the 5th Guards Tank Army surged into Hoth's right flank. Indeed, T-34 loader Lev Drachevsky of the 178th Tank Brigade recalls:

> Having fought on the road to Prokhorovka on the 8th, by the 11th we were assembling to attack the opposite flank. Great efforts were made to keep the skies above us clear of snooping enemy aircraft – a job successfully done by our fighters and anti-aircraft guns – and we spent considerable time camouflaging our tanks. It was a great boost to our morale to be told that we were to strike the enemy in an attack which would bring an end to his offensive in the sector . . . We were still relatively fresh and knew that the Germans were tiring. I cannot speak for the others [in the crew] but I relished the opportunity to strike a blow for 'Mother Russia' and my family which had been wiped out by the German advance in 1941.

Throughout 11 July, the 5th Guards Tank Army was organizing itself in its new positions around Prokhorovka as II SS Panzer Corps continued its attack towards the town. Manstein put everything he had into the attack in the hope that he might catch the Soviets off-guard. Starting at 0500 hours, the 2nd Panzer Grenadier Regiment of LAH attacked along the axis of the road, heading into the settlement with armoured support. The defences were of the sort that all Wehrmacht troops knew so well by this stage in the battle, but it was the artillery fire from batteries ensconced in Petrovka and Prelestnoye in the Psel valley to the northeast that caused the majority of the division's casualties early that morning. 'From nowhere came a bombardment that shocked and stalled us,' wrote SS-Untersturmführer Alexander Simm. 'We threw ourselves to the ground as the shells landed among our ranks. We suffered a nasty few minutes before we got moving again.'

Meanwhile, exploiting the difficulties that Totenkopf and Das Reich were encountering on the flanks, companies of T-34s counterattacked the LAH column and ensured that the division's focus was not purely frontal. Nevertheless, Wisch's formation – nothing if not tenacious – managed to push within assaulting distance of Hill 252.2 by 0625 hours. Hausser sensed an opportunity to take the high ground and drive on to Prokhorovka, but his hopes were dashed when he received word that the armour had run up against a very deep and extremely wide anti-tank installation, covered by first-class defenders. Unbeknown to Hausser and Wisch, the Soviets had reinforced this critical area overnight with the vanguard of the 5th Guards Army – paratroopers from the élite 9th Guards Airborne Division – as armour from the 5th Guards Tank Army deployed rapidly behind them. After searching unsuccessfully for a way round, the panzer grenadiers called forward the pionere battalion to bridge the obstacle while the artillery and Luftwaffe did what they could to neutralize their opposition.

Throughout the day, high winds and heavy bursts of rain precluded the sort of air support that the three divisions needed, but from 0630 hours Stukas and medium bombers carried out attacks despite the low cloud base. However, such was the nature of the close-quarters fighting and terrible visibility that morning that the dive bombers found it extremely difficult to silence the enemy. One observer, SS-Oberschütze Paul Meuller, later recalled:

The Luftwaffe was not on form during [the 11th]. Not only were the aircraft slow in arriving at the pinch points, but their attacks were lame. We saw a number of Stukas pull out of their dives without releasing their bombs. I saw one fail to pull out of his dive and crash into the ground. Another two were shot out of the sky by enemy anti-aircraft fire. It was a bad day for the air arm, but conditions were vile and did not suit the flyers or their machines.

Another SS trooper watched in horror as an LAH unit was mistakenly attacked by its own aircraft:

> We called in Stuka assistance, which was still possible to do at this time. But once again things went wrong! Some bombs hit [Sturmbannführer Joachim] Peiper's III Panzer Grenadier Battalion and elements of [Obersturmbannführer] Rudolf von Ribbentrop's 6 Panzer Company of 1.SS Panzer Regiment . . . which was held in reserve on this day. In spite of the fact that an air liaison officer from the Luftwaffe was stationed with his armoured radio vehicle next to the battalion's staff vehicle, our Stukas again hit our own positions.

While a bridge was being constructed over the anti-tank ditch, the LAH Reconnaissance Battalion blocked Soviet movement between the Psel and the main road. On the right, the 1st Panzer Grenadier Regiment successfully cleared the woods north of Storozhevoe. In this way, Wisch's division contained the attacks on its flanks, which neither Das Reich nor Totenkopf were in a position to fend off as they, too, were meeting fierce resistance. Kruger's division was denied Vinogradovka by the 2nd Guards Tank Corps, and Priess's men found it difficult to expand their small bridgehead against concerted counterattacks. During the night of 10–11 July, with no armoured support because the bridge was not strong enough to take the weight of tanks, Totenkopf's panzer grenadiers had no option but to fight the 31st

Tank Corps with magnetic mines and fire bombs, and thwart the 33rd Guards Rifle Corps' onslaught with hand-to-hand fighting. Artillery support helped, but it was not until a tank bridge was completed in late morning that the medium panzers could cross. Their weight and fire-power helped retrieve the desperate situation, but by the end of the day most of Hill 226.6 was still in Soviet hands.

LAH, meanwhile, battled on. With the anti-tank ditch bridged by noon, armour and panzer grenadiers pushed forward with the aim of taking Hill 252.2 and then bounding on the final two miles to seize Prokhorovka. The high ground was taken after a bloody but relatively brief confrontation, which was followed by an attack on the Oktiabrskii State Farm. The resistance offered by the airborne forces was powerful. Backed by heavy artillery along with the dug-in KV-1s and T-34s of the 29th Tank Corps, the defences initially repelled the onslaught. Describing the approach of LAH's panzer grenadiers, a paratrooper later wrote that the front 'shuddered from exploding bombs, shells, and mines'. He continues:

> When only several hundred metres remained to the edge of the state farm, infantry poured out of the armoured transporters. Submachine gunners opened fire on the run, and concealing themselves behind the tanks, they began to assault. The distorted faces of the Fascists bore witness to the fact that their warlike ardour was roused by a fairly large dose of schnapps.
>
> 'Fire!' ordered the battery commander. A squall of 3rd Battalion fire met the Fascists. The long burst of ... heavy machine guns struck the infantry in the flanks and were echoed by the guardsmen's light machine guns and submachine guns. Divisional artillery and supporting artillery battalions [of the Reserve] laid down an immovable defensive fire in front of the state farm ... The infantry were separated from the tanks, and facing a hurricane of fire from the state farm, they withdrew to

the reverse slopes of Hill 215.4. The Fascists attacked the 3rd Battalion two more times before 1400 hours. However, these were only reconnaissances in force.

Although the Germans eventually prevailed and Oktiabrskii State Farm was taken at around 1700 hours, a move on Prokhorovka could not be undertaken for fear of producing an even more vulnerable salient. It was critical, therefore, that both Totenkopf and Das Reich moved up alongside LAH the following morning so that a corps effort could be made on the town. Hausser subsequently produced orders for 12 July that directed Totenkopf to seize Hill 226.6 and then advance along the north bank of the Psel to cut the Orel–Prokhorovka road, while Das Reich took Belenikhino and Vinogradovka before thrusting south of Prokhorovka. Once Hill 226.6 had been taken, LAH was to take Storozhevoe and Jamki and make a frontal assault on the town.

It was not just II SS Panzer Corps that was to attack on the morning of 12 July. Manstein was also expecting XLVIII Panzer Corps to cross the Psel River and begin its final approach on Oboyan. The aim, the field marshal said, was to 'maintain Fourth Panzer Army's momentum across the front. Oboyan and Prokhorovka are to be seized and the Soviet armoured reserve defeated.'

Meanwhile, Vatutin promulgated his own orders. At 0800 hours, the 5th Guards Tank Army was to:

Deliver a counterstroke in the direction of Komsomolets State Farm and Pokrovka and in co-operation with 5th Guards Army and 1st Tank Army destroy the enemy in the Kochetovka, Pokrovka and Greznoye regions and do not permit him to withdraw in a southern direction.

Rotmistrov made his final preparations for the counterattack during 11 July, but he did so apparently unaware of the advance that II SS Panzer

Corps was making. Despite undoubtedly hearing the sounds of battle, seeing the smoke-filled sky above the battlefield and being presented with reports about the situation at the front, the commander of the 5th Guards Tank Army seemed to be remarkably ill-informed about unfolding events. Indeed, that evening he and Marshal Vasilevsky – who had been directed by Stalin to assist in the coordination of the Soviet counterattacks in the southern salient – sped off to inspect the jumping-off positions of the 18th and 29th Tank Corps. Rotmistrov later wrote of the episode in his memoirs:

> Our route passed through Prokhorovka to Belenikhino, and the quick-moving [Jeep], bobbing up and down over the potholes, skirted round vehicles with ammunition and fuel, which were heading to the front. Transports with wounded slowly went past us. Here and there destroyed trucks and smashed transports stood by the roadside. The road passed through wide fields of yellowing wheat. Beyond them began a forest which adjoined the village of Storozhevoe. There, along the northern edge of the forest, were the jumping-off positions of the 29th Tank Corps. 'The 18th Tank Corps would attack to the right,' I explained to A.M. Vasilevsky. He intently peered into the distance and listened to the ever-growing rumble of battle. One could divine the front lines of our combined armies from the clouds of smoke and explosions of aerial bombs and shells. The agricultural installations of Komsomolets State Farm could be seen two kilometres distant on the right.
>
> Suddenly, Vasilevsky ordered the driver to stop. The vehicle turned off the road and abruptly halted amid the dust-covered roadside brush. We opened the doors and went several steps to the side. The rumble of tank engines could be clearly heard. Then the very same tanks came into sight. Quickly turning to me, and with a touch of annoyance in his voice, Alexsandr Mikhailovich

asked me, 'General! What's going on? Were you not forewarned that the enemy must not know about the arrival of our tanks? And they stroll about in the light of day under the Germans' eyes.' Instantly, I raised my binoculars. Indeed, tens of tanks in combat formation, firing from the march from their short-barrelled guns, were crossing the field and stirring up the ripened grain. 'However, Comrade General, they are not our tanks. They are German.' 'So the enemy has penetrated somewhere. He wants to pre-empt us and seize Prokhorovka.' 'We cannot permit that,' I said to A.M. Vasilevsky.

Ordering two tank brigades to plug the breach that Das Reich had made in his front, Rotmistrov was later shocked to learn of the true scope and strength of II SS Panzer Corps' attack. Hausser had taken the initiative and moved far closer to Prokhorovka than the 5th Guards Tank Army had expected, and even overrun some of its jumping-off points. Headquarters staff had to work quickly to identify new jumping-off points, alter missions, revise artillery and air plans and, finally, work up and promulgate new orders. The plan for a deliberate offensive had to be turned into a scheme for a meeting engagement. Commenting on what that situation must have been like for Rotmistrov's team, Wehrmacht staff officer Leo Spiegel has said:

Those men would have been up against a great time pressure. Although they had shown themselves to be capable enough in moving the Army so far so fast over the previous few days, to have one's plans turned over at the last moment is awful – but it is also quite common. The staff would have had procedures worked out and, no doubt, various sub-plans available to them for just such a situation – we always did. But one can never accurately predict what the enemy might do and so there is always a last minute scrambling around to make sure that everything is in place . . . What I can say without any fear of contradiction is that few men on the 5th Guards Tank Army staff would have got much sleep [on the night of 11–12 July] and they would have been anxious that the alterations to the plan that they had made were relevant and practical.

The time of the attack was brought forward to 0630 hours when the 18th, 29th and 2nd Guards Tank Corps were to deliver the hard blow along the axis of the Prokhorovka–Pokrovka road, aided by the 5th Guards Mechanized Corps to the south. The small reserve – the 53rd Guards Tank Regiment together with some tanks and the self-propelled guns of the 5th Guards Mechanized Corps – was to wait in the rear for deployment where and when needed during the course of the battle.

After days of slog and grind there was, all of a sudden, a far greater sense of urgency across the front than there had been since 4–5 July. Even though Rokossovsky received reports that Model was disengaging in the north as the Briansk Front prepared to attack the Second Panzer Army in the Orel salient, it was on the south that German and Soviet eyes were so inextricably fixed. Here the destiny of Zitadelle would finally be decided. Would the two German spearheads converging on Prokhorovka cripple the 5th Guards Tank Army and breathe new life into Zitadelle, or would the Soviets use the opportunity to kill off the German offensive and destroy the Wehrmacht's ability to launch offensive operations in the area? It was a question that consumed Manstein's headquarters and had a particular poignancy after Anglo-American forces began their invasion of Sicily on 10 July. With the soft underbelly of Europe under Allied attack, it was only a matter of time before German armour would need to be removed from the East to confront this new threat to the overstretched Reich. The Eastern Front's post-Zitadelle strength had taken on a new and more florid complexion. A pivotal moment in the Second World War had arrived.

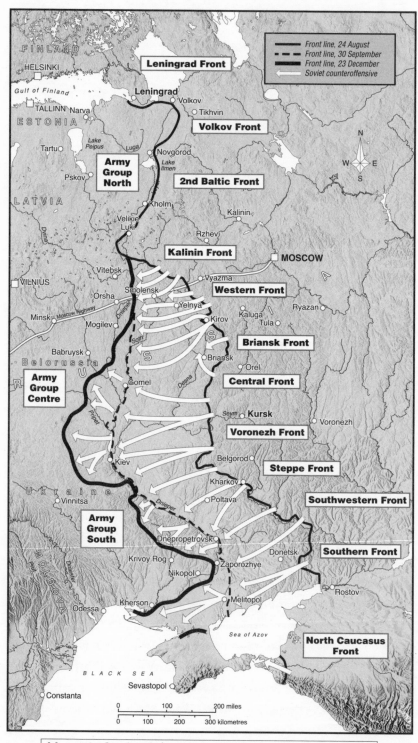

Map 10: Soviet Advances, August–December 1943

CHAPTER 9

Finale

(Zitadelle: 12 July and After)

While the rest of the 28th Guards Airborne Regiment were fighting on Hill 252.2 during the afternoon of 11 July, Pavel Krylov's platoon were detailed to help bring ammunition forward from a dump five miles east of Prokhorovka. As they waited for the five 9th Guards Airborne Division trucks on to which they would load the boxes, Krylov and his comrades smoked, chatted and joshed. Although they knew that they would be in the front line the next morning, their talk was banal and centred more on the machine gunner's dubious new haircut than their likely fate. They also used the time to devour their first hot meal in three days, supplied by a mobile field kitchen and slopped into their canteens by a soldier with a bad attitude. The 'stew' was made with unidentifiable ingredients that seemed to have little nutritional value, and Krylov wondered (out loud) how, on such rations, young Dimitri had got so fat. Their food finished, they continued to wait and amused themselves by trying to spot pretty girls among the stream of units that filed past the entrance to 'Ordnance

Depot 12 Prokhorovka' – tanks, towed artillery, anti-aircraft guns, infantry, jeeps, trucks. The whole gamut of the Red Army's fighting prowess seemed to be moving into position for the battle that even Krylov recognized as climactic.

The arrival of the trucks was greeted with sardonic cheering by the men, who then proceeded to bend their backs lifting the heavy cargo into the load space. They crammed the vehicles with as many boxes as they could, perched themselves precariously atop the freight and then wobbled out on to the Prokhorovka road. The journey forward in the gathering evening gloom was tortuously slow and it was not before 2300 hours that the convoy passed through a gun line and then into Prokhorovka itself. The small town was alive with vehicles. Krylov identified blurred shapes directing the traffic and trying to bring order to a situation that seemed desperately chaotic.

The trucks pulled up where the buildings gave way to open fields – just a mile, they were told, behind the front line. From here the platoon would have to walk, taking with them as many boxes as they could. The rest would be brought up through the lines during the night by others. Krylov grabbed the rope handle at one end of a box of anti-tank shells, Dimitri grasped the other, and the 30 men shuffled forward. The snake of soldiers followed a humourless guide who led them through masses of tanks, waiting in the unharvested wheat. The crews chatted in hushed tones or sprawled by their machines in a desperate attempt to snatch a few hours' valuable sleep.

After what seemed like an age, the men, their hands and arms aching from the dead weight of their burdens, approached their company lines. Silence was ordered and moments later the quartermaster appeared out of the darkness to take charge of the precious consignment. He was followed by the platoon commander, who had spent most of the evening in a briefing to outline the plan for the next morning. Krylov and his colleagues learned that they were to provide infantry support for the T-34s that they had just passed, and were acquainted with their tactical objective. The young officer then led his men to a cramped trench where, he advised, they got some sleep. What seemed like minutes later, Krylov was shaken awake by a ghost-like form: 'One hour before the attack,' it said. 'Eat something.' 'It was,' Krylov recalls, 'the worst early morning call that a man could ever receive.'

As dawn broke, both the Soviets and the Germans were undertaking their final preparations before their attacks across the southern salient. Low cloud ensured there was some residual heat from the previous day, visibility was good but the outlook was stormy. The combatants took up their field glasses and scrutinized the battlefield. SS-Rottenführer Johannes Bräuer, the driver of an armoured troops carrier in 11th (Armoured) Company, recalls: 'It wasn't until dawn on 12 July that one could properly see the surrounding area and the mass of vehicles and troops being drawn up around us. One could only guess that something big was in the offing.' Had he taken up a pair of field glasses, he would easily have discerned the major features of the battlefield. Looking three miles northwest, he would have been able to see Hill 226.6 standing on the north bank of the Psel along which Totenkopf was to advance. A similar distance to the south, Bräuer would have been able to pick out Das Reich's positions before Vinogradovka and the more undulating and complicated ground stretching northeast across which that division had to push. To his front right, the officer would have taken in the gently undulating ground before him – good tank country – and would have noted the front line incorporating Hill 252.2. This high ground stood as a sentinel adjacent to the embanked railway line and road, which ran parallel to the Psel and led into Prokhorovka just three and a half miles distant. It was between the Psel and the railway line that the Germans were about to launch their *schwerpunkt*, as were the Soviets.

Rotmistrov drove through Prokhorovka just before dawn and took up a position at 29th Tanks Corps' command post on orchard-covered high ground just to the south of the town. He swung his field glasses across his Army's positions, from the Psel through an arc taking in the land in front of Prokhorovka and down to Belenikhino over seven miles away. His formations had completed the move to their new jumping-off positions in the early hours of the morning and, having been told that all was well, he made ready to give the command to begin the attack.

In front of him were 294 fighting machines of II SS Panzer Corps and 616 of his own tanks. On that day, just over half of Rotmistrov's tanks were T-34s and most of the remainder were T-70s. Experienced commanders took on board as much ammunition as they could – particularly armour-piercing shells and high explosive – and all ensured that they were replete with fuel. Many took the risk of strapping extra fuel barrels on to their rear decks. As one T-34 commander explained to his crew: 'In a tank battle against the panzers, a stopped T-34 will shortly become a destroyed T-34. We cannot afford to run out of ammunition but, more importantly, we cannot afford to run out of fuel.'

The Soviet tanks were strongly supported by additional artillery and Katyusha regiments. Indeed, infantryman Mansur Abdulin noted: 'Neither before nor since had I seen so much artillery. The commanders of artillery units, with their guns of different calibres, had a hard time finding firing positions from which they could fire without disturbing their neighbours. There was not enough space for the gunners on the battlefield!'

The additional firepower was particularly focused in the centre of the battlefield behind 18th and 29th Tank Corps, which faced LAH. The tank crews were becoming increasingly impatient to get moving. 'We waited with dry mouths and wrenching stomachs,' says T-34 driver Yuri Ruslanova, 'and found it difficult to concentrate on anything.' Bräuer concurs, explaining that the final hours before combat were a blur: '[W]e enlisted men had no idea of what was soon to be happening to us. I had taken part in everything since the beginning of the eastern campaign ... but I had never experienced such a surprise attack and inferno. Everything happened in such a surprisingly short time that one didn't know what to do.'

At 0545, Wisch was informed at LAH headquarters that troops were reporting the dull throb of T-34 engines emanating from the enemy's lines along with clouds of blue-grey exhaust fumes. Rotmistrov was on the verge of unleashing his tanks, but Hausser struck first. At 0600 hours, a swarm of Bf-109s arrived over the battlefield heralding the arrival of Stukas and He-111s, which targeted Soviet positions. As they began to soften the enemy's defences, LAH's panzer regiment advanced from positions around Oktiabrskii State Farm and Hill 252.2. Warned to expect enemy tanks moving towards them, the commanders stood in their cupolas, keeping a watchful eye on the terrain before them as the artillery laid down a sharp barrage along the 9th Guards Airborne Division's front. Pavel Krylov found his world turned upside down:

> I do not know what our trench was hit by, but just as we were about to attack we noticed Stukas preparing to attack. I did not see an aircraft dive towards us but moments after a warning was yelled, the ground in front of us levitated. It was like a giant had grabbed the battlefield and shaken it. I was knocked to the ground, but was dragged to my feet and the platoon was told to look to its front and stand firm . . . Shells continued to drop all around us and then I saw, to my absolute horror, a dense line of enemy tanks approaching like a tidal wave about to break on top of us.

Krylov was far from the only soldier to be surprised at that moment. Back at 29th Tank Corps' headquarters, Rotmistrov watched in disbelief. His plan to seize the initiative was disintegrating before his eyes. However, as the German armour rolled forward, it ran straight into what the 5th Guards Tank Army commander described in his memoirs as 'a cyclone of fire unleashed by our artillery, and rocket launchers that swept the entire front of the German defences'. It was the preliminary bombardment timed for 0600 hours that was to precede the Soviet attack. The panzers, led by the Tigers, fanned out, the dust thrown up by their tracks mingling with the smoke of the exploding shells, which tore up the ground and set fire to the crops. As the last shells were sent spinning towards the enemy, Rotmistrov gave the code words 'Stal! Stal! Stal!' (Steel! Steel! Steel!). The tank commanders pulled down their hatches, the drivers engaged gear and the Soviet armour staggered forward and slowly gained speed.

Soviet tactics continued to emphasize the need to close with the enemy's armour as quickly as possible for fear of the Germans' powerful 88mm guns smashing them at long range. Rotmistrov was adamant that 'successful struggle with [Tigers and Ferdinands] is possible only in circumstances of close-in combat', and by exploiting 'the T-34's greater manoeuvrability and by flanking fire against the [weaker] side armour of the German machines'. Tigers were capable of disabling a T-34 at a range of over 4000 yards, but the Soviets seem to have massively overestimated the number that were available to Hausser. The reality was that II SS Panzer Corps had 15 – Totenkopf had 10, LAH had four and Das Reich just one. There were no Ferdinands or Panthers on the Prokhorovka battlefield.

Nevertheless, the 5th Guards Tank Army sought to charge the panzers in an early attack in order to catch the Germans unawares and allow the Soviet tank commanders to get their 76mm guns close enough to do damage before the enemy realized what was happening. But Hausser's pre-emption had delivered Rotmistrov's plans a fatal blow. Instead of a surprise attack, the T-34s found themselves racing forward, rapidly losing their shape and firing speculatively on the move against a vigilant enemy. There is little doubt that, in the circumstances, Rotmistrov's attacking tank corps would have been far better served by a slower, stealthier and better coordinated advance. As it was, the panzer commanders spotted a great cloud of dust rising between the ridges, and the appearance of Il-2 ground-attack aircraft confirmed the imminent arrival of a large enemy offensive. Panzer IV company commander Rudolf von Ribbentrop, son of the German Foreign Minister Joachim von Ribbentrop, describes the scene:

A purple wall of smoke rose into the air, produced by smoke shells. It meant: 'Tank warning!' The same signals were to be seen all along the crest of the slope. The threatening violet danger signals also appeared farther to the right at the railroad embankment.

Everything immediately became clear: beyond the hill, still out of sight of those in the valley, a major Soviet armoured attack was under way ... On reaching the crest of the slope we saw another low rise about 200 metres away on the other side of a small valley, on which our infantry positions were obviously located ... The small valley extended to our left, and as we drove down the forward slope we spotted the first T-34s, which were apparently attempting to outflank from the left.

The panzers went into a well-practised routine – they stopped, the commander identified a target, the gunner lined it up in his sights and a shell was sent scudding towards the victim. The whole clinical process took just a few seconds and was as efficient as it was effective. Ribbentrop continues:

We halted on the slope and opened fire, hitting several of the enemy. A number of Russian tanks were left burning. For a good gunner 800 metres was the ideal range.

As we waited to see if further enemy tanks were going to appear, I looked around, as was my habit. What I saw left me speechless. From beyond the shallow rise about 150–200 metres in front of me appeared fifteen, then thirty, then forty tanks. Finally there were too many to count. The T-34s were rolling forward toward us at high speed, carrying mounted infantry [standing on the engine compartment and clinging on to handles welded onto the hull] . . . Soon the first round was on its way and, with its impact, the T-34 began to burn. It was only fifty to seventy metres from us. At the same instant the tank next to me took a direct hit and went up in flames . . . His neighbour to the right was also hit and soon it was also in flames.

The avalanche of enemy tanks rolled straight towards us: Tank after tank! Wave after wave! It was a simply unimaginable assembly, and it was moving at very high speed.

On the receiving end of the German armour-piercing shells was Vasili Bryukhov, a T-34 commander in the 29th Tank Corps' 31st Tank Brigade.

The distance between the tanks was below 100 metres – it was impossible to manoeuvre a tank, one could just jerk it back and forth a bit. It wasn't a battle, it was a slaughterhouse of tanks. We crawled back and forth and fired. Everything was burning. An indescribable stench hung in the air over the battlefield. Everything was enveloped in smoke, dust and fire, so it looked as if it was twilight . . . Tanks were burning, trucks were burning.

Dr Olga Borisenko, attached to the 5th Guards Tank Army, saw the horrifying results of blazing armour and has testified: 'You wouldn't have thought that the metal could burn so fiercely. We had a dreadful time helping the wounded crews at the battlefield. Many of the men would come in covered in dirt. They'd tried to put out the flames by rolling on the ground. As a result their wounds got dirty and became infected.' Many, however, did not have a chance to escape their 'tracked coffins' as their armour was ripped open and, on occasion, their turrets were wrenched off. Ribbentrop has written:

We halted ten metres behind the stationary T-34 and turned. My gunner scored a direct hit on the Russian's turret. The T-34 exploded, and its turret flew about three metres through the air almost striking my tank's gun . . . Burning T-34s ran into and over one another. It was a total inferno of smoke and fire, and impacting shells and explosions. T-34s blazed, while the wounded tried to crawl away to the sides.

Bryukhov's tank eventually took a German round, but the result was not catastrophic:

My tank was hit. A round flew in from nowhere and hit the driving sprocket and the first road wheel. The tank stopped, turned to the side a bit. We immediately bailed out and sneaked into a shell crater. The situation didn't favour repair of the tank. That was Prokhorovka! . . . I got into another tank, but that was destroyed after a while. The round hit the engine, the tank caught fire, and we all bailed out. We hid in a shell crater and fired at German infantry and the crews of their knocked out tanks.

Probing forward on Ribbentrop's left, towards the 18th Tank Corps, was the panzer regiment's heavy company, with its four remaining Tigers. These were now being commanded by SS-Untersturmführer Michael Wittmann. The 170th and 181st Tank Brigades were attempting to smash through LAH between Oktiabrskii State Farm and the Psel. They were to continue to the village of Andreevka where they were to destroy Totenkopf's bridges over the river. However, Wittmann's Tigers were just waiting for the 100 Soviet tanks bobbing towards them to come into range, when they proceeded to pick them off with aplomb. Engines whined as the Tigers found new firing positions and their guns erupted once more. It is interesting to note that Rotmistrov's view was rather different and his account has the

Germans suffering badly at the hands of the advancing Soviet armour. Describing the contact, the general later wrote:

> The tanks were moving across the steppe in small packs, under cover of patches of woodland and hedges. The bursts of gunfire merged into one continuous mighty roar. The Soviet tanks thrust into the German advanced formation at full speed and penetrated the German tank screen. The T-34s were knocking out Tigers at extremely close range, since their powerful guns and massive armour no longer gave them an advantage in close combat. The tanks of both sides were in the closest possible contact. There was neither the time nor room to disengage from the enemy and re-form in battle order or operation information. The shells fired at close range pierced not only the side armour but also the frontal armour of the fighting vehicles. At such range, there was no protection in armour and the length of the gun barrels was no longer decisive. Frequently when a tank was hit, its ammunition and fuel blew up and the torn off turrets were flung through the air over dozens of yards. On the black, scorched earth the gutted tanks burnt like torches. It was difficult to establish which side was attacking and which was defending.

The battlefield descended into confusion. Hundreds of small confrontations took place across a broad front, and there was no respite for the tank crews, who fought for their lives on a field of battle more congested with armour than they had ever experienced before. T-34 driver Anatoly Volkov recalls:

> The noise, heat, smoke and dust of battle were extremely trying. Despite wearing protectors, my ears were extremely painful from the constant firing of the gun . . . The atmosphere was choking. I was gasping for breath with perspiration running in streams down

my face. It was a physically and mentally difficult business being in a tank battle. We expected to be killed at any second and so were surprised after a couple of hours of battle that we were still fighting – still breathing!

Chasing down the Soviet tanks were LAH assault guns. Their crews required little encouragement to dispatch enemy machines, as a German newspaper reporter, riding in a StuG III, has described:

We roll on again. Here we sight another T-34. Too short! Too far! Missed to the right. Clouds of smoke keep hiding him, yet he is barely 1,000 metres away; we knocked out the first enemy tanks at more than 2,000 metres! The next shot nearly hits the Bolshevist. 'Jammed,' yells the gunner. The very next second a terrible blow shakes us. Fragments flying about. Then another blow and a crash. 'Out!' screams the commander. 'Out, get out!' Like lightning we are up and tumbling into the cool grass, pressed flat, breathing in gasps.

It did not matter on which side of the increasingly ramshackle line in front of Prokhorovka the combatants fought, the danger was real and constant. The battle provided a vintage case-study of uncertainty (and occasionally chaos) upon which commanders, at all levels, tried to impress themselves. At the tactical level Ribbentrop explains:

On the smoke and dust-shrouded battlefield, looking into the sun, it would be impossible for our crews to distinguish us from a Russian tank. I repeatedly broadcast our code-name. 'All stations: This is Kunibert! We are in the middle of the Russian tanks! Don't fire at us!'

For the Soviet armour, though, in which all but the command tank had only a radio receiver, the battle was bewildering. In such circumstances, the panzer crews could out-think and out-fight their more numerous enemy. As George Nipe Jnr has observed:

> In warfare, numbers alone do not always mean superiority on any given battlefield. In spite of the mediocre armour and less than dominating main armament of the Panzer IIIs and IVs, the Germans remained tactically superior to the Russians due to flexible, aggressive command, better crew training, superior optics and a crucial advantage in communications capability . . . Russian tank units were run by officers who were trained to follow orders, not operate with personal initiative, because orders could not be easily transmitted to individual tanks or small units. As a result, time after time on the Eastern Front . . . Soviet armour losses were often catastrophic when confronted with the good quality German panzer units.

Yet despite the best efforts of the panzers to stop the Soviets from penetrating their line, some inevitably got through. Indeed, one observer later wrote:

> We found ourselves taking on seemingly inexhaustible masses of enemy armour – never have I received such an overwhelming impression of Russian strength and numbers as on that day . . . Soon many of the T-34s had broken past our screen and were streaming like rats all over the battlefield.

It was at this point that the anti-tank guns opened fire and tried to give the German line greater rigidity. The gun on which SS-Unterscharführer Mutterlose served was quickly in action, as he describes:

> We saw the turret of a very slow moving T-34 that was advancing out of a hollow. As it emerged completely, we saw Red Army

soldiers sitting on its rear deck. They were clearly outlined against the bright horizon. Not 20 metres away from it, a second T-34 appeared, and then yet a third and a fourth of those steel monsters. We stood behind our two 15cm field guns, ready to fire. Apparently, the Russians did not think that we could open fire on them. They continued to move on and appeared unperturbed. The soldiers who were riding on the tanks did not fire a round . . . I heard the bright, clear command voice of our battery officer, SS-Untersturmführer Protz: 'Fire!'

The first round thundered from our gun and then we heard the report of our neighbouring piece. But it looked like we had missed the tanks, for they moved on, unscathed. Neither seemed to have been hit. The Red Army soldiers remained mounted in the rear decks, where they ducked low.

At that point, it was all over for our two guns. Before the gunners could reload, the barrels of the leading T-34s turned toward us and, without even making a firing halt, they poured high-explosive rounds into our firing positions. It seemed like every foxhole was individually shelled. Shrapnel shrieked away through the air . . . With a leap we were out of our foxhole. We saw, horror struck, what had gone on around us. Death had reaped a rich harvest. Eight comrades lay there, all of them dead. Ghastly! Their bodies shredded! Two gunners were torn into unrecognizable fragments. All those still alive had been wounded.

The guns worked in close cooperation with panzer grenadiers, who reacted to the Soviet onslaught with great élan. Untersturmführer Gührs of the Reconnaissance Battalion, for example, reacted by confronting the steel with his own flesh and bone. He wrote:

They were around us, on top of us, and between us. We fought man-to-man, jumping out of our foxholes to lob our magnetic hollow charge grenades at the enemy tanks ... It was hell ... Our panzers helped us mightily. My company alone had destroyed fifteen tanks. The Soviet armoured phalanx had been halted. The battlefield was saturated with burning and disabled tanks. Some of the stricken continued to fire on the Tigers, until they too were hit again and destroyed.

Joachim Peiper's battalion was also in the thick of the action, and deployed four-man, tank-hunting teams. One grenadier stopped the tank – perhaps by throwing a Teller mine under its tracks – the second provided him with cover while the other two moved in from the sides and rear to destroy the vehicle with either explosive charges or a bag of hand grenades. Peiper's adjutant, Werner Wolff, took command of a leaderless company that morning, and they went on to claim 30 tank kills during the day. SS-Unterscharführer Erhard Knöfel later reported:

> We were singled out by a T-34 which rammed [our half-track]. We put our hollow charges to use, some of which failed in the tumult. SS-Untersturmführer Wolff knocked out a tank in the mêlée. He lay shoulder to shoulder with us but the day was long yet. Then we became involved with the Soviet mounted infantry ... self-propelled guns began 'reaping' with direct fire from the anti-tank ditch. The Soviet attack began to falter. All hell broke loose; jets of flame and tank turrets flew through the air. But we took losses too ... I was shot in the thigh while in the kneeling position tending to a wounded man. I removed my pistol belt and applied a dressing to the wound and then looked for cover. I found a hole nearby and was about to jump in, but what did I see? Two pairs of fear-filled eyes staring at me, the crew of a knocked-out enemy tank, unarmed like me.

Wolff's boss later reported to Hausser that Wolff had 'stood like a rock in the breakers in this fighting. With unfailing courage, he destroyed tanks himself, led his company against other tanks and also destroyed those tanks.' Such was the ferocity of the fighting that Peiper also found himself immersed in the sharp end of the battle, as the following account written by one of his men reveals:

> Smoke and fumes were so thick that they brought tears to the eyes. Hideous and malicious, that yellow cloud. Out of it, in grey, uncertain, blurred contours grew the mighty forms of the on-rolling Russian tanks that approached at high speed and seemed to stamp everything down into the ground.
>
> A clear call rang out from the right. Our commander stood there, crouching slightly forward, the stock of his rifle pressed against his shoulder and the barrel, on which the bulge of the grenade launcher was attached, followed the gigantically growing outline of the T-34 that was fast approaching, belching out clouds of exhaust fumes.
>
> At a distance of three metres, it rolled over the trench. At the same moment the commander's grenade struck it on the side. It rolled another 20 to 30 metres before it came to a halt, shivering and shaking.

The support that the ground forces received from the air that morning was limited. Although Rotmistrov later wrote:

> Soviet as well as German airmen tried to help their ground forces to win the battle. The bombers, close-support aircraft and fighters seemed to be permanently suspended in the sky over Prokhorovka. One aerial combat followed another. Soon the whole sky was shrouded by thick smoke of burning wrecks.

In reality, however, air operations were severely affected by the poor weather, and Soviet sorties were undermined by the decision to concentrate their air assets elsewhere that day. Eschewing a potentially unedifying battle over the German *schwerpunkt* around Prokhorovka, Vatutin, Vasilevsky and Rudenko decided to place the weight of the air power on the flanks. It was thought that by stopping XLVIII Panzer Corps on the left and (in particular) the forward momentum of III Panzer Corps coming up on the right, II SS Panzer Corps' thrust would peter out. Those Red Air Force aircraft that conducted sorties against Hausser's grouping, therefore, had a thorny task on their hands. Despite the Red Air Force's 893 sorties that day across the southern Kursk salient outnumbering the Luftwaffe's 654, reports from ground units suggest that the air was dominated by German aircraft, which harried, chased and shot down numerous enemy machines. Indeed, a report by the 31st Tank Brigade remarks: 'Our own air cover was fully absent until 13.00 hours . . . After 13.00 hours, our fighter cover began to appear, but only in groups of two to ten aircraft.' The 5th Guards Tank Army later noted: '[T]he enemy's aircraft literally hung above our combat formations throughout the entire battle while our own aircraft, and particularly the fighter aviation, was totally insufficient.'

Without the protection that the Red Army formations had begun to enjoy, tanks, artillery batteries, troop concentration areas and other key operational targets were pounded all day long. Among the pilots doing the pounding was the vastly experienced Captain Hans-Ulrich Rudel in his Ju-87G Stuka, armed with twin 37mm cannon. Describing his actions on 12 July, Rudel – who was to amass a tally of 519 Soviet tank kills by the end of the war – later said:

> With these gigantic offerings of enemy tanks, an attempt would be possible. The Soviet armour formations were provided with strong Flak defences, but I figured that if we flew at between 1,200 and 1,800 metres altitude, I would be able to nurse a

damaged aircraft to our own territory unless, of course, one fell like a stone. Loaded with bombs the aircraft of the first Staffel flew behind me in single cannon planes. This is how we tried it! In my first attack, four tanks exploded through the fire from my cannons. By the evening, the total had risen to twelve.

The one-sidedness of the air battle that day can be seen in one stark comparison: the Soviets lost 14 fighters over the Prokhorovka battlefield and the Germans just one. As Christer Bergström argues convincingly in his important work on the aerial confrontation over the Kursk salient: 'It is not too much to say that the Luftwaffe's decisive contribution to the famous battle of Prokhorovka has been underestimated in most published accounts.'

Yet despite the clear German dominance of the skies from the outset, the results of the opening armoured clash were not decisive. Although Rotmistrov had numerical advantage, by 0900 hours the men and machines of LAH had stood their ground and, using a mixture of firepower, obstinacy, guile and tactical prowess, resisted the initial onslaught. However, 15 minutes later, another wave of Soviet armour – the 5th Guards Tank Army's second echelon – surged forward between the Psel and the railway line. On LAH's right, groups of T-34s pushed forward with considerable artillery support. Once again they ran into ranks of German tanks at high speed and, at a range of just a couple of hundred yards, managed to dispatch four of them. The LAH history describes how the German machines fired at their enemy 'from a distance of 10 to 30 metres' and made 'every shell a direct hit because the Russians could not see through the dust and smoke'. The result was a three-hour battle in which 62 T-70s and T-34s were engaged in what 'could almost be termed hand-to-hand tank combat'.

On the left of the division, meanwhile, the relatively lightly armoured Reconnaissance Battalion failed to contain the 18th Tank Corps' persistent attack and began to lose its shape at around 1100 hours.

Observing the difficulties that the unit was facing from his command post on Hill 241.6, Wisch and his operations officer watched as four T-34s from 110th Tank Brigade managed to break loose from the Germans' clutches and push through towards the artillery positions, where they destroyed two 150mm heavy guns. They were eventually stopped either by the artillery firing over open sights or panzer grenadiers.

The divisional commander also observed a minor breakthrough near Hill 252.2 at around 1130 hours. A modest force from the 32nd Tank Brigade made a small breach before being repulsed. This vital high ground was probably the most fiercely contested part of the battlefield and the 9th Guards Airborne Division retook it at around 1300 hours. Pavel Krylov was in the thick of the action:

> The morning was a blur of action that did not stop. There were no breaks, no lulls, just constant fighting. We were initially pushed out of our positions by the Germans who attacked with panzers and their grenadiers. We were not expecting it, but luckily we had our wits about us as we were preparing for our own attack. Had the enemy attacked an hour earlier there would have been trouble ... We held off the initial attacks, but the prospect of our position being overwhelmed led to the order to withdraw [around 500 yards]. The ground over which we moved was full of dead and wounded, but back we went, with small groups covering us and under heavy fire. The Germans were in firm command of the hill from which they co-ordinated their attacks on our positions. We had to attack. We had to regain the hill and so [during the late morning] launched a number of assaults on it and eventually, with the help of tanks and artillery, were successful.

By early afternoon, therefore, the Battle of Prokhorovka in the central sector with LAH had come to reflect the wider Battle of Kursk. It had become a slogging match but with a difference – rather than the

Germans doing the attacking, it was the Soviets. Having moved forward to take Prokhorovka, on sighting Rotmistrov's armoured waves, LAH quickly realigned themselves for defence and absorbed the 5th Guards Tank Army's power with great success. But what of the other II SS Panzer Corps divisions? Although not fighting for territory as overtly critical as the battlefield between the Psel and the railway embankment, the confrontation on the flanks was important for the central sector. If Totenkopf and Das Reich could gain the upper hand, that would put pressure on the Soviet centre to withdraw towards Prokhorovka, while failure would leave any advance by LAH in an exposed salient.

Of the two flanking divisions, it was Priess's men of the 'Death's Head' Division who progressed most favourably. Tasked with seizing Hill 226.6 and then driving northeast, the formation was opposed by the 52nd Guards Rifle Division from the tired and depleted 6th Guards Army, and the 31st Tank Corps from the run down 1st Tank Army, along with the fresher 95th Guards Rifle Division from the 5th Guards Army. These formations had developed strong defences on and around Hill 226.6, but the Germans had managed to build a new 60 ton crossing that had allowed Totenkopf's 10 remaining Tigers to pass over to the north bank of the Psel by dawn and join the medium tanks and panzer grenadiers by mid-morning. A detachment of assault guns had been left behind on the south bank to protect the bridges, but the majority of the 121 operational panzer and assault guns had moved into the two and a half mile wide, one and a half mile deep bridgehead. Thus, despite the Soviet intention to snuff out the German lodgement, destroy the crossing points and push Totenkopf into the Psel, the mixed Red Army force found themselves unable to withstand Preiss's late-morning attack. Anatoli Abalakov of the 290th Guards Rifle Regiment says that 'the fighting was unrelenting and bloody'. Recounting his part in the battle, the young infantryman has said:

The enemy advanced with great fervour, desperate to take the high ground which we defended. Our orders were 'To The Last Man', never words that we wanted to hear as we knew that we were in for a terrible time . . . We managed to hold the assault for a while, but eventually we were forced back. Heavy artillery fire and dive-bombing by Stukas made the position untenable – but we had caused the Nazis casualties and did not collapse . . . That afternoon the Panzers moved forward, but our guns hit the bridgehead hard and caused many problems for the Germans trying to organise themselves.

Hill 226.6 – the key to that sector – was lost by 1330 hours, which allowed Totenkopf to push on as Abalakov describes. This would have been a problem had LAH managed to make a significant move towards Prokhorovka that morning, but as the division had been engaged in defence against the bulk of the 5th Guards Tank Army's armour, that had not been possible and so Totenkopf's increasingly weak offensive had limited operational significance. Priess's push, furthermore, was increasingly challenged by elements of the 5th Guards Army, which entered the battle straight from the march, and also the 24th Guards Tank and 10th Guards Mechanized Brigades, which had been sent to the area from the 5th Guards Tank Army's reserve. These formations were to head off Totenkopf's 3rd SS Panzer Regiment and then force them to withdraw. As Rotmistrov later wrote, without a hint of modesty: 'The decisive movement of these brigades . . . and the decisiveness of their meeting blow against the penetrating Hitlerite tanks stabilized the situation.' German armour was to reach the Karteschevka–Prokhorovka road, but their position was precarious and was likely to pose a threat only if Totenkopf could manage to broaden it, fill it with more units and withstand the inevitable Soviet counterattacks.

While their sister division was pushing its armour northeast on the left wing of Hausser's corps, it was all that elements of LAH and Das Reich could do to hold their positions south of the railway line. The Soviets attacked II SS Panzer Corps' flank from the embankment down to Belenikhino and closed quickly with the Germans behind a heavy artillery and Katyusha bombardment. Hubert Neuzert, an LAH gunner on a Marder III tank destroyer near the Storozhevoe collective farm, has produced a detailed account of his battle. With most of his division's armour north of the railway line, the pressure was on his unit and the anti-tank guns to stop the 25th Tank Brigade breaking through:

Racing at full speed and firing from all barrels, T-34 after T-34 rolled over the hill, right into the middle of our infantry positions. We opened fire with our five guns as soon as we saw the first tank, and it was only seconds before the first T-34 stood shrouded in black smoke. Sometimes we had to take care of Russian infantry riding on top of the tanks in hand-to-hand fighting.

Then suddenly, there were forty to fifty T-34s coming at us from the right. We had to turn and open fire on them. All of a sudden, three bold giants among them raced off across the basin towards the collective farm. They captured the road leading to it. I did not have a chance to fire. The gun on the right wing had a jammed mechanism, and we could not seem to get it fixed. So we had to shift positions through the farm buildings. I had barely taken aim when I had to fire at my first T-34. My shell went past it, and the shell case got stuck in the gun. I ducked between the houses once again, and was in front of one when I got the mechanism un-jammed. A T-34 appeared right in front of me when my assistant gunner yelled so loud ... 'Last shell in the barrel!' On top of everything else! I swivelled around to face the T-34 racing toward us. At a distance of about 150 metres the next tragedy struck. The rear support for the gun collapsed, and the barrel swung up to point to the sky. I used the force of swivelling the turret to bring the barrel of the 75mm gun down, managed to get the T-34's turret in my sights, and fired. A hit! The hatch opened and two men jumped out. One stayed put while the other hopped across the road between the houses.

To the south, meanwhile, Das Reich fought to repel the combined attentions of the 2nd Tank and 2nd Guards Tank Corps. The chief of the latter formation, Major-General A.S. Burdeiny, was particularly aggressive and pushed hard between Vinogradovka and Belenikhino. The commander of the defending Panzer Grenadier Regiment Der Führer, Sylvester Stadler, was extremely frustrated by this turn of events and observed: 'The Russian attacks on our flanks were pinning down half of our effectives and taking the steam out of our operation against the enemy at Prokhorovka.'

Kruger therefore placed what little hope he had of an advance in Panzer Grenadier Regiment Deutschland, operating on Stadler's left flank, but Heinz Harmel's offensive to help LAH take Storozhevoe was pre-empted by a furious assault by the 136th Guards Rifle Regiment and 26th Tank Brigade. Although the line held it was not until late morning that the assault on the well-prepared Storozhevoe could take place. Recognizing the tactical importance of the village, the Soviets had protected its approaches with a minefield, which was covered by mutually supportive positions employing fixed anti-tank guns as well as machine guns. The break-in battle was consequently gruesome. The mines were not properly cleared as the panzer grenadiers sought to move quickly through the obstacles and neutralize the strong points that were causing the regiment to stutter. Although Deutschland had penetrated the southern part of Storozhevoe by the early afternoon and completed a union with panzer grenadiers on the right of LAH, it was hardly the dramatic thrust that Kruger had hoped for. Had III Panzer Corps been lending support, however, the situation – and the wider battle for Prokhorovka – could have been very different.

The commander of III Panzer Corps had been exhorted to throw caution to the wind in order to bring the formation up to Hausser's side. However, since 5 July, any movement northwards had been extremely difficult. A breakthrough was eventually made by Breith's formation on the night of 11–12 July and, although the corps was days behind schedule, Manstein still hoped that it could make a decisive impact. In a remarkably audacious move, under the cover of darkness, a small armoured force from the 6th Panzer Division had seized a bridgehead over the Donets River. This column, consisting of tanks and panzer grenadiers in half-tracks but led by a captured T-34, fooled onlookers from the 107th and 81st Guards Rifle Divisions into thinking that they were a Soviet unit. A member of the *coup de main* force later explained the protocol for the advance:

> Radio silence. No fire to be opened. No talking. But smoking permitted. In fact, the men were encouraged to ride on top of the tanks, relaxed and smoking, as if this was a normal movement by a unit. 'But not a single word in German', the company commanders had impressed on their men.

The tension was palpable as the vehicles gathered at their assembly point, despite the officers' insistence that the men needed to look unperturbed. They remained understandably edgy when the time came to advance:

> The ghost column moved on . . . There was only the rumble of engines and the clank of the chains. Enemy columns passed shoulder to shoulder. The silhouette of the T-34 at the head of the German unit deceived the Russians.

They moved past manned and well-established emplacements

of anti-tank guns and multiple rockets. The moon shed a dim light. The Russians did not budge. Sleepily they were leaning on their positions along the road. They were used to such columns. All day long Soviet formations had been rumbling past them.

After six miles the T-34 broke down and blocked the road. It was a nervous time for all concerned – the infiltrators moved it off the road as the enemy looked on – but before long the column moved forward again and the first houses of Rzhavets were sighted through the gloom. It was at this point that more than 20 Soviet tanks rattled past them, and although showing no signs initially of having noticed that they were sharing the road with German vehicles, six T-34s swept back to take a closer look, surrounding the lead panzer – a command tank furnished with an imitation gun barrel made of wood. Its officer, Major Dr Franz Bäke, took the initiative and, with his orderly, attacked with sticky bombs.

Demolition charge attached to the first enemy tank. A few Soviet infantrymen were sitting on top of it and turned their heads in alarm. One of them raised his rifle, but Bäke snatched it from his hands. He leapt in the ditch for cover. He found himself chest-deep in water. There were two dull explosions. [The orderly] Lieutenant Zumpel, for his part, had attached his demolition charge to the other tank ... But this time there was only one bang. The other charge did not go off.

One of the T-34s menacingly traversed its cannon. Bäke jumped up on one of his own tanks, which was coming up, ducked behind the turret and yelled: 'Open fire!' The German gun-aimer was quicker than his Russian opponent. One shot and the Soviet tank was knocked out. But now all hell was let loose. The ghost journey was over.

The German armour took its opportunity and raced into the village. The main bridge over the Donets was destroyed before the grenadiers could secure it, but mixed armed teams managed to get to the north bank by a footbridge and established a bridgehead there before the Soviets realized what was happening.

By the morning of the 12th, the salient leading into Rzhavets had been expanded and the bridgehead deepened, despite the close attention of the Red Air Force. The leading elements of III Panzer Corps were just 12 miles south of Prokhorovka, and by 1700 hours, Breith's division had begun to cross the hastily repaired main bridge. Early the following morning, the 7th and 6th Panzer Divisions prepared to support the 19th Panzer Division – led by 20 Tigers – as it made a headlong dash to Prokhorovka. Having managed to contain II SS Panzer Corps, Vatutin and Rotmistrov were suddenly faced by the spectre of the imminent arrival of a further 100 German tanks and assault guns to support Hausser's attack. Clearly, III Panzer Corps had to be stopped and part of the reserve – centred on 21 KV-1s – was sent to join the defences north of the Donets. That defence, organized by a 69th Army engorged by 10 additional anti-tank regiments, was all that stood between Breith, Hoth and Manstein achieving an improbable union between the two panzer corps.

The emergence of the threat south of Prokhorovka had not monopolized Vatutin's concerns over recent days. On Hoth's left flank, XLVIII Panzer Corps also remained a danger and the Soviet commander wanted the formation's emasculation before it reached Oboyan. This objective became an important part of the Soviet counterattack plan as Grossdeutschland was preparing to position itself to cross the Psel. The initial strike was to be focused on Knobelsdorff's left flank, which would dislocate the corps' offensive operations, before targeting those divisions around the Oboyan road. On the morning of 12 July, therefore, the 5th Guards Tank Corps pinned down the 332nd Infantry Division while the 10th Tank Corps smashed into the 3rd Panzer

Division and tore holes in its defences. By the evening, Soviet armour was approaching Verkhopenye and had taken Berezovka, which unhinged the entire corps by cutting across its lines of communication. As Knobelsdorff's left flank caved in, the Soviet attacks spread to include Grossdeutschland and the 11th Panzer Division. Mansur Abdulin's 66th Guards Rifle Division, freshly arrived with the 5th Guards Army, attacked towards Sukho-Solotino that day and his account illustrates Vatutin's fervent desire to deny the Germans any more territory in the western sector:

> The roar of guns continued all day without pause. We infantrymen – surrounded by thick black smoke and covered in soot – looked like stokers, endlessly throwing coal into a furnace. Only the whites of our eyes and teeth were shining. We moved at a furious pace, among burning tanks, exploding shells, and fire from every conceivable sort of weapon. Every soldier, covered in sweat, was systematically doing his job, as if toiling in a giant workshop; forgetting about fear and pinning his hope on chance: 'Will I be killed or not?' There's nothing one can do to save oneself in this carnage, and the hands did what was necessary automatically.

It was here, rather than over the battlefield farther east, that the Red Air Force focused its operations on 12 July. From first light, fighters, bombers and ground-attack aircraft went about their business of degrading the enemy's defences, attacking his logistics and hampering his movement. Surgeon Albert Thimm, making his only visit to the front line that day to attend a conference, was struck by the strength of Soviet air power:

> I had served in Poland, France and in the East since 1941 and I had never seen enemy aircraft in such numbers. I spent the day

approximately five kilometres behind 11th Panzer Division's forward positions and our three vehicle convoy was attacked several times by fighters. We were trying to use the road to Oboyan for ease, but it was clogged with vehicles which the Soviet airmen took great delight in destroying. We were forced to move cross-country, but our movement sent up dust which was seen by pilots who attacked us. With so little cover, we were lucky not to be killed . . . I made my way back to the [hospital] during the night 12–13 July, covered in mud and a bundle of nerves. How those boys at the front took that sort of treatment day after day, I do not know.

Abdulin also witnessed much air activity as the Luftwaffe tried to retain local superiority to help support their beleaguered ground forces:

All day long planes fired at each other in the sky. There was a hail of splinters and bullets. That was familiar enough: but watch out, you might get killed by a falling aircraft! Pilots parachuted here and there. One had to be careful not to confuse our men with the Germans. We could often see how the parachuting pilots continued their fight by firing pistols at each other. We wanted to help them, but how?

The staving in of Knobelsdorff's flank and the disruption to his primary attacking formations south of Oboyan destroyed XLVIII Panzer Corps' offensive prospects. As the Grossdeutschland history explains:

As a result of these heavy defensive battles, the division's plans for a further advance to the north [on the 13th] were initially overtaken . . . The danger now lay on the left, west flank, especially since the 3rd Panzer Division was apparently too weak to win through there. The villages of Gertzovka and Berezovka were back in enemy hands and the danger that the Soviet forces were advancing into the rear of the German attack divisions was increasing.

Vatutin was determined to take advantage of the opportunity to end the threat to Oboyan, and over the next two days his formations proceeded to dominate the hapless XLVIII Panzer Corps. German plans to continue their offensive north were indefinitely shelved while they dealt with the developing crisis, which required active defence. Commenting on the health of Grossdeutschland, Mellenthin later wrote:

> [The division] was dangerously weak after heavy fighting lasting ten days, while Russian striking power had not appreciably diminished. In fact, it seemed to have increased . . . The terrific Russian counterattacks, with masses of men and material ruthlessly thrown in, were . . . an unpleasant surprise. German casualties had not been light, while our tank losses were staggering.

The same observations could have been made about XLVIII Panzer Corps. Although eventually avoiding a rout, the corps was forced to accept that its next movement was far more likely to be a withdrawal than an advance.

While attempts to neutralize the threat to Oboyan were getting under way, the battle for Prokhorovka continued to rage. By late afternoon on 12 July, Manstein was fully aware of the scope of the Soviet counterattacks and could do little more than look to Hausser to take Prokhorovka and provide some optimism. It was at this time that the LAH panzers, severely rattled by the earlier Soviet onslaught, moved from a defensive stance and began to attack once more. However, with the weather deteriorating from showers to low cloud and heavy rain, there was little chance of Luftwaffe support and the Soviets were resilient. Although both the 18th and 29th Tank Corps had suffered heavy losses, Wisch's armour could not make an impression on the Soviet line, which even launched some local counterattacks. Indeed, one crunching assault consisting of 120 tanks moved off behind a curtain of artillery and Katyusha fire and forced the LAH armour not only to stop, but to make some withdrawals as the enemy swarmed among them. In such circumstances, despite its best efforts, the formation could not establish any forward momentum and as the light faded, its attack on Prokhorovka withered.

By this time, Totenkopf had managed to enlarge its bridgehead and take the village of Polyzhaev, and its Tigers had pushed on to reach the Karteschevka–Prokhorovka road. The arrival of the 24th Guards Tank and 10th Guards Mechanized Brigades from Rotmistrov's reserve, however, suggested that further forward movement would be problematic. Although the German commanders did not know it at the time, Priess's position five and a half miles northwest of Prokhorovka was to prove Manstein's most northerly penetration in the southern Kursk salient. By the end of the 12th, Totenkopf had lost half of its armoured strength and was faced by fresh 5th Guards Tank Army formations that had been tasked with its destruction on the following day.

Das Reich, meanwhile, had been forced to take up a wholly defensive posture on the corps' right flank. The commanders of the 2nd Guards Tank and 2nd Tank Corps were aware that III Panzer Corps was beginning to make progress towards Prokhorovka and did everything in their power to fix Kruger's formation in place and degrade it. Throughout the afternoon of the 12th, the Soviets launched a series of counterattacks to test Das Reich's resolve and wear down its fighting ability. South of Vinogradovka, for example, 40 T-34s launched a typical Soviet attempt to drive a wedge between the division's two panzer grenadier regiments.

As they engaged, another assault was being mounted near Belenikhino where 26 T-34s captured at Kharkov, painted in German camouflage and bearing prominent German crosses, gave battle to 50 Soviet T-34s. Witnessing the unusual event, Sylvester Stadler later testified:

In a short period of time all 50 tanks, one after the other, were set ablaze by shells from the captured tanks with German crews. The Soviet tanks each had a barrel of fuel attached to its back. These could be set on fire by a well-aimed shot, and shortly after the whole tank exploded. Of the Soviet tanks, only the command tank at the point was equipped with a radio. For this reason, that tank was knocked out first. The other crews were perplexed; obviously they did not recognize the T-34s on the hill as their enemy.

Although these Soviet drives were repulsed, the feat was not achieved without casualties, the destruction of armoured fighting vehicles and depletion of ammunition stocks. In common with other parts of the Prokhorovka battlefield, the wider Soviet counterattack and, indeed, the entire Battle of Kursk, the Soviets were cleverly utilizing their greater resources to negate the Germans' superior tactical ability, and grind them to a halt.

By the end of 12 July, Manstein's offensive ambitions had been dealt a serious blow. As heavy rain turned the battlefields and rear areas into a quagmire, the German field marshal was left ruminating on a day when his left flank crumbled and II SS Panzer Corps had been fought to a standstill. Vatutin, however, could not afford to relax. The Soviets had suffered heavy losses in the successful attempt to defend Prokhorovka, and he still had to achieve his aim of forcing Hoth back and regaining lost territory. Stalin was particularly concerned at reports, subsequently proved erroneous, of the 5th Guards Tank Army losing around 650 tanks on that day for the total loss of a mere 17 German armoured fighting vehicles. 'What have you done to your magnificent tank army?' the Supreme Commander asked Rotmistrov with barely hidden menace that evening. Zhukov was immediately despatched from the Briansk Front, where he was overseeing the attack into the Orel salient against the Second Panzer Army, to take charge of 'co-ordinating the Steppe and Voronezh Fronts'. From this it was clear that the Supreme Commander believed Vatutin and Rotmistrov either required assistance in developing their future operations, or had lost control. Vasilevsky was banished from the battlefield and sent to oversee operations on the Southwestern Front.

Thus, as thunder rumbled, lightning flashed and rain hammered down on the sapped combatants, Hausser and Rotmistrov ordered their formations to rearm, refuel, reorganize and ready themselves. II SS Panzer Corps was to continue its attack. The 5th Guards Tank Army had suffered such prohibitive losses that it had little option but to defend. Rotmistrov consequently ordered his formation to work hard on the development of defence west of Prokhorovka, including the laying of minefields, digging new trenches and establishing strong points that were integrated into new defensive lines using the surviving armour and infantry from the 18th and 29th Tank Corps. The battle, however, continued in a diluted from throughout the night as both sides sought to improve their tactical positions, undertake reconnais-sance, recover damaged armour, and make their enemy's preparations as difficult as possible. Reflecting on his experiences and the challenges of the night that followed, Pavel Krylov has said:

> I was exhausted at the end of a very difficult day ... The enemy continued to probe after dark, but it was nothing too serious and we could get some food and ready ourselves for the next morning. Our officer told us about the wider situation – although the details were extremely vague – and we were complimented on

our day's work. The Germans, we were told, had been held along the line and we should expect to attack soon – but not yet . . . It was always nice to be told that you were part of a success, but I knew that we had taken heavy casualties and the enemy was unlikely to back down without another major effort. The battle was not over yet.

Krylov was correct. Even if Zitadelle was dead, there was still fighting to be done. Manstein remained hopeful that the arrival of III Panzer Corps would change his fortunes, while Vatutin recognized that the Germans would retain their hope for as long as II SS Panzer Corps remained on the offensive. Vatutin's key aims, therefore, were to hold Hausser and block Breith; Manstein demanded that II SS Panzer Corps capture Prokhorovka. The German aim was clear, but unachievable. The weather had taken its toll on the ability of both sides to resupply, but Hausser's troops were most disadvantaged by the poor ground conditions as they resumed their attacks on the morning of the 13th. With Rotmistrov's defences well set, the panzers and supporting panzer grenadiers found the going extremely difficult and made few inroads into the Soviet line. Despite his losses on the previous day, Rotmistrov drew strength from the old military dictum that 'defence is stronger than attack' in frontal assaults, and used his growing access to artillery to smash Hausser's embryonic attacks. LAH attacked with its 50 panzers and 20 assault guns in a two-pronged advance, one along the south bank of the Psel, and the other towards Oktiabrskii. Once again taking up his position at the 29th Tank Corps' command post, Rotmistrov looked on as LAH pushed forward, and later wrote:

More than fifty enemy tanks firing from the march or from short halts, followed by ranks of motorized infantry, advanced on our positions. Allowing the Germans to approach to a distance of 500 to 600 metres, our anti-tank artillery and tanks opened direct

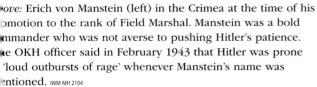

Above: Erich von Manstein (left) in the Crimea at the time of his promotion to the rank of Field Marshal. Manstein was a bold commander who was not averse to pushing Hitler's patience. The OKH officer said in February 1943 that Hitler was prone to 'loud outbursts of rage' whenever Manstein's name was mentioned. IWM MH 2104

Above: General Konstantin Rokossovsky was tortured by the NKVD and spent time in a Siberian Gulag before a rapid rise which saw him commanding the Central Front during the summer of 1943. IWM TR 2913

Above left: General Walter Model, commander of Kluge Ninth Army, who called for: 'More tanks! More officers! More artillery! Better training for the attack troops,' before the launch of Zitadelle. IMAGNO/GETTY IMAGES

Above right: A German office scrutinises a map with a colleague during preparation for Operation Zitadelle in Ju 1943. BUNDESARCHIV, BILD 101I-022-2916-13A, FOTOGRAF: WOLFF / ALTVATER

Left: Loading ammunition int one of Fourth Panzer Army's Tigers on the first day of Zitadelle. BUNDESARCHIV, BILD 101I-022-2948-24, FOTOGRAF: WOLFF

p right: One of the most ￼nic images of the Second ￼rld War: Junker Ju-87 ￼kas support the ground ￼ack on 5 July. These aircraft ￼ved at 370 miles per hour at ￼ angle of between 60 and ￼ degrees, and released a ￼0lb fuselage bomb and ￼o wing-mounted 110lb ￼mbs at around 1,500 feet.

TANK MUSEUM, BOVINGTON

ght: A German soldier in ￼tion with a Flammenwerfer ￼amethrower) 41, weighing ￼lbs with a range of around ￼ feet in eight shots. It used ￼ ignition system which ￼ssed hydrogen over a ￼ated element and produced ￼flame of around 1,300 ￼grees Fahrenheit.

TANK MUSEUM, BOVINGTON

elow: Panzer IIIs and IVs ￼dvance across terrain typical ￼ the southern Kursk salient ￼ring the first days of ￼peration Zitadelle.

DESARCHIV, BILD 101III-MERZ-014-12A, FOTOGRAF: MERZ

Left: The experienced 29-year-old SS-Untersturmführer Michael Wittmann commanded a platoon of five Tiger tanks. By the end of the first day alone, he and his crew had destroyed eight Soviet tanks and seven anti-tank guns.

THE TANK MUSEUM, BOVINGTON

Below: A German tank, incapacitated having suffered broken track in a minefield, left burning after being hit by a Soviet artillery shell during the night of 5–6 July.

THE TANK MUSEUM, BOVINGTON

Left: German infantry marching towards Pokrovka alongside a convoy of cars and motorcycles with sidecars. On warm days such as this, troops carrying heavy equipment suffered badly, with many becoming dehydrated.

BUNDESARCHIV, BILD 101I-219-0553A-30, FOTOGRAF: KOCH

b right: A 15cm Nebelwerfer
being loaded. This towed
apon fired six rockets to
maximum range of 7,600
rds. Due to the smoke trails
t the rockets left, however,
vas easy for the Soviets to
ate their firing positions
d bombard them. BUNDESARCHIV,
011-022-2943-20, FOTOGRAF: HARSCHNECK

ght: A column of Soviet
soners are led away from
battlefield. Although
red the fury of the
ghtmarish clash that was
king place in the north and
th of the Kursk salient,
ir ordeal was only just
ginning. BUNDESARCHIV, BILD 101I-022-2925-05,
RAF: WOLFF / ALTVATER

ttom right: A Panzer III tank
w of SS-Panzergrenadier
vision Das Reich take a
eak shortly after a rain
rm has washed over the
ttlefield. BUNDESARCHIV, BILD 101III-
AECKEL-208-25, FOTOGRAF: ZSCHÄCKEL

Left: The tank commander of a Tiger I attached to SS-Panzergrenadier Division Das Reich surveys the battlefield. A vehicle can be clearly seen traversing the ridge on the horizon, beginning to drop down into a shallow valley. BUNDESARCHIV BILD 101III-ZSCHAECKEL-206-34, FOTOGRAF: ZSCHÄCKEL

Below: German infantry ente a village during clearing operations on 8 July. A German war correspondent wrote that the outer defence: of each settlement consisted of 'wide mine belts, wire entanglements, flame-throwe barriers and tank ditches'.

BUNDESARCHIV, BILD 101I-022-2924-31, FOTOGRAF: KIPPER

Bottom left: A Tiger I scores a direct hit on an advancing T-34 somewhere on the Southern Front during 10 July.

BUNDESARCHIV, BILD 101III-GROENERT-019-23A, FOTOGRAF: GRÖNERT

Bottom right: German convoys were increasingly targeted by the Soviet Air Force. This convoy was destroyed by an aerial attack on 10 July; little of its cargo of food and other essential supplies could be salvaged.

BUNDESARCHIV, BILD 101I-219-0553A-23, FOTOGRAF: KOCH

ght: The fighting outside
krovka was particularly
ense due to its position on
e route to the vital southern
ojective of Oboyan. The
ysical and mental toll that
e battle took on the German
antry is captured in this
otograph taken on 8 July.
ESARCHIV, BILD 101I-219-0553A-10, FOTOGRAF: KOCH

ove left: Vehicles of II SS Panzer Corps
orientate themselves towards Prokhorovka on
July in order to confront the growing threat to
eir right flank. BUNDESARCHIV, BILD 101I-022-2924-14, FOTOGRAF: KIPPER

elow: A German Flakvierling 38 defending an
moured column from Soviet fighter bombers.
e four 20cm anti-aircraft guns were mounted
a single carriage which could be towed
hind a variety of vehicles.
DESARCHIV, BILD 101I-022-2926-38, FOTOGRAF: WOLFF / ALTVATER

Above right: The mangled wreckage of
another German convoy is by-passed by a
vehicle towing a field gun. 'The amount of
battlefield debris was demoralising,' recalls
one German officer. 'We frequently came
across smoking wrecks caused by air strikes
and artillery bombardments. Even in the rear
areas we feared for our lives.'

BUNDESARCHIV, BILD 101I-022-2924-15, FOTOGRAF: KIPPER

Right: SS-Standartenführer
Heinz Harmel, commander of
Das Reich's Panzer Grenadier
Regiment Deutschland. He was
a hard and uncompromising
soldier who launched a series
of furious attacks during the
Battle of Prokhorovka. BUNDESARCHIV,

BILD 101III-GROENERT-011-021A, FOTOGRAF: GRÖNERT

Above left: The Tiger I became another iconic weapon of the Second World War. It had a superb 88mm gun capable of penetrating a T-34's armour from a range of up to 1,800 yards. The Tiger also boasted armour that could defeat a Soviet 76mm gun at all but the closest range. BUNDESARCHIV, BILD 101I-022-2935-10A, FOTOGRAF: WOLFF / ALTVATER

Above right: An incapacitated T-34 is inspected by a German soldier. Major-General F.W. Mellenthin, Chief of Staff of XLVIII Panzer Corps, admired the all round capabilities of th[e] tank, and wrote: 'We had nothing comparable.' BUNDESARCHIV, BILD 101I-219-0553A-36, FOTOGRAF: KOCH

Above: The effectiveness of the Tiger I's armour can be seen in this photograph taken after the battle of Prokhorovka. The Soviet shell hit but failed to penetrate the hull and the tank – and its crew – lived to fight another day. BUNDESARCHIV, BILD 101I-022-2935-25A, FOTOGRAF: WOLFF / ALTVATER

Above: The cost of war. A German soldier is laid to rest hundreds of miles away from home on the Kursk battlefield. His grave is bordered by smoke-blackened bricks taken from a nearby farm. BUNDESARCHIV, BILD 101I-022-2948-19, FOTOGRAF: WOLFF

fire on them. Several enemy machines froze in place with broken tracks or began to rush about the fields engulfed in flames. Those which still moved forward exploded on mines. However, the Fascist motorized infantry still came forward . . . The fire of our Katyushas instilled terror in the Fascists. Suffering great losses, the enemy was forced to fall back, abandoning the burning tanks and the bodies of his dead soldiers and officers.

In his diary, SS-Sturmmann Warmbrunn recounts an incident that day when he was with Michael Wittmann, attacking positions held by the 32nd Tank Brigade near Oktiabrskii:

We were caught by a salvo from a Stalin Organ: it was as if the Red Army troops had been informed of our presence. We dropped to the ground and were showered by the remains of a wall. Wittmann said drily, 'We should be praying now.' Then I let out, 'To whom?' I don't think anyone ever laughed so hard at such a ticklish situation as Wittmann did then.

Not that far away and returning to front-line action after receiving a shrapnel wound on the first day of the offensive, LAH's SS-Oberschütze Rudi Bauermann recalls:

There seemed to have been little change in the state of play since 5th July. The enemy were well dug in and our attempts to engage him were foiled by minefields and well positioned anti-tank guns . . . We panzer grenadiers tried to infiltrate the line, but came under heavy machine gun fire which pinned us down. A tank must have seen what was happening and came over to lend some fire support. Half of the platoon moved in behind it as there was so little ground cover, but were soon flooding back to our position when the tank rolled over a mine and shed a track. It immediately came under artillery fire which eventually damaged its main armament and rendered it useless . . . The crew bailed out and joined us in a shell crater. 'That's the fourth time that I've hit a mine since the start of [Zitadelle],' the commander said to me, 'but I'd still rather be in a tank than out here with you lot!'

The two LAH attacks lasted little more than an hour before they impaled themselves on the Soviets' defences and could advance no further.

It was as well that LAH did not manage to batter its way through to Prokhorovka on the afternoon of 13 July for Totenkopf would have been in no position to help with resistance on their left flank. Limited to just 54 operational panzers and 20 assault guns, Priess's formation was still protecting its bridges on the south bank of the Psel. Not well placed to defend its current positions, it had little hope of breaking through Rotmistrov's reserve. Although the front at Prokhorovka at this time was remarkably reminiscent of a fist with a raised thumb, just like the emperor's signal for a beaten gladiator to be shown mercy in ancient Rome, an inverted thumb would have more accurately reflected Hausser's situation. In the face of concerted counterattacks by the 33rd Guards Rifle Corps, 10th Guards Mechanized Brigade and 24th Guards Tank Brigade, the division's overextended panzer regiment buckled. By noon, Priess informed Hausser that he needed to withdraw his armour back to Hill 226.6 if it was not to be encircled and destroyed piecemeal.

The ordered and professionally handled operation was successfully concluded by nightfall. The Soviets had tried to disrupt the movement by applying pressure across Totenkopf's front, but the division remained well organized and countered all enemy attempts to drive into the base of their lodgement. Lieutenant Vladimir Alexeev of the 170th Tank Brigade was attacking the village of Andreevka when his T-34 was hit by an armour-piercing shell. Helping the wounded driver out of his seat with his gunner, Alexeev noticed that 'parts of the leg were joined only by the sinews of the trousers . . . He got out as far as his waist and then lost consciousness.' The loader, meanwhile, could not be retrieved and had to be left in the blazing tank.

T-34 losses that day were high. Both German and Soviet accounts remark how many hulks were left on the battlefield after Rotmistrov's failure to break into Totenkopf's salient, but his counterattacks had removed the division's threat to the north of Prokhorovka. There is little doubt that Soviet casualties and tank losses were far higher than those suffered by Priess that day north of the Psel, but by throwing their resources at the taut division, the 5th Guards Tank Army had forced Hausser's left flank to pull back from a hard-won and tactically important position.

The one remaining danger for Vatutin, therefore, was the potential for III Panzer Corps to link up with Das Reich and reignite Hausser's offensive. Thus, as soon as Totenkopf began to pull back towards its bridgehead that afternoon, Rotmistrov detached one tank regiment of the 10th Mechanized Brigade from the battle north of the Psel and sent it to strengthen the defences on the southern approaches to Prokhorovka. On the 13th, the majority of Das Reich's units success-fully held their positions, but the division's panzer regiment endeav-oured to advance southeast from between Ivanovka and Vinogradovka to facilitate an early union with Breith's corps, which started the day barely six miles from Belenikhino. It managed a mile before being brought to a halt, and left Breith's divisions to cover the remaining distance. By the morning of the 13th – and under continuing Red Air Force raids – the 19th Panzer Division was ready to break out of III Panzer Corps' bridgehead north of the Donets. Yet although German commanders had anticipated that the Soviets would not be able to cope with such a dense concentration of firepower, the corps' narrow front served only to limit its ability to manoeuvre while presenting easy targets for the Soviet airforce and the artillery. By the end of the day, rather than having completed the union with Das Reich as expected, III Panzer Corps had been able to achieve little more than a slight broadening of its attacking front in the face of Trufanov's stoical resistance.

The ninth day of Zitadelle was a massive disappointment to Manstein and to the German High Command. With Model's command already withdrawing formations from the northern Kursk salient to tackle the rapidly developing threat to the Orel salient, and Oboyan and Prokhorovka still in Soviet hands in the south, it was decision time for the offensive. What is more, by 12 July the Allies had landed 160,000 troops and 600 tanks on Sicilian soil, which was not only likely to lead to the fall of the island, but to become the jumping-off point for an invasion of the Italian mainland. The stability of Mussolini's regime was looking extremely fragile, and there was a distinct possibility that Italy would fall out of the war. This situation demanded that German formations be moved into the country as soon as possible to meet the expected Allied offensive. OKW believed that, in such circumstances, Hitler would direct that Zitadelle be rapidly concluded so that men and equipment – II SS Panzer Corps prime among them – could be transferred to the Mediterranean. Those at headquarters were not surprised, therefore, when on 13 July Kluge and Manstein were summoned to the Wolfsschanze in East Prussia for a meeting with Hitler. On their arrival, the two soldiers found that Hitler's usually excellent manners had deserted him and after a cursory greeting the highly strung Führer launched into a diatribe against the situation in Italy. Bringing his rant around to issues that affected Kluge and Manstein, Hitler said:

> The loss of Sicily is practically certain because of the miserable Italian leadership. Perhaps Eisenhower will land tomorrow night on the Italian mainland or in the Balkans. I have to prevent that. As I have nothing more to withdraw anywhere after re-locating the 1st Panzer Division from France to the Peloponnese, these

reinforcements must be removed from the Kursk Front. Therefore, I am forced to discontinue Zitadelle!

Kluge was relieved at what he heard and replied that the decision would allow him to disengage the Ninth Army from the salient to deal with more pressing threats to the north. Manstein, however, felt the halting of the offensive would be precipitate for his force in the south. Although he had realized for some time that Zitadelle's grand intention of destroying the salient and everything in it was no longer possible, he had been driven on by the aim of rendering the Soviet armoured forces unable to present a viable threat in southern Russia. He later wrote of his reaction to Hitler's pronouncement:

Speaking for my own Army Group, I pointed out that the battle was now at its culminating point, and that to break it off at this moment would be tantamount to throwing a victory away. On no account should we let go of the enemy until the mobile reserve he had committed were completely beaten.

Manstein sincerely believed that the Germans were on the verge of an important military success – of breaking the 1st Tank Army and 5th Guards Tank Army permanently – and that withdrawing at this point would be to offer the Soviets an opportunity to strike back. In the words of Mellenthin: 'We were now in the position of a man who had seized a wolf by the ears and dare not let him go.' With III Panzer Corps about to arrive on the battlefield of Prokhorovka and Nehring's XXIV Panzer Corps *en route*, Manstein argued that his forces were in a strong position to complete the job, which would reduce pressure on the southern front.

It was a strong case and Hitler took a moment to think, before saying that he was willing to make a compromise: Zitadelle would be closed down in the north, but the southern offensive would continue with II SS Panzer Corps 'until it had achieved its aim of smashing the enemy's armoured reserve'. The Fourth Panzer Army was to hand over nearly one third of VIII Air Corps, however, as ground-attack formations were desperately needed to help counter Soviet operations against the Second Panzer Army in the Orel salient. Manstein was content that this was not an insurmountable problem and pinned his hopes on the early arrival of XXIV Panzer Corps to give his weary offensive a boost. It was only after Manstein returned to his headquarters on the 14th that he learned that Hitler had ordered Walter Nehring's corps back south to the First Panzer Army in preparation to meet a likely Soviet offensive between Kursk and the Sea of Azov. Manstein was understandably furious – the decision, taken without any consultation with Army Group South, undermined everything that the field marshal had argued at the Wolfsschanze. Nevertheless, he had long since realized that a general's lot was to appeal for the resources that he needed and to fight with less, and so he got on with the task in hand: the destruction of the Soviet armour south of the Psel.

His focus for Operation Roland was for II SS Panzer Corps to defeat the Soviets south and southwest of Prokhorovka. Totenkopf and LAH were to fix the Soviet defenders in position while Das Reich and III Panzer Corps were to reach out towards each other in an attempt to make that long anticipated but elusive union. If all went as Manstein's staff expected, the attack would lead to the encirclement of the enemy between the Lipovyi–Donets and the Northern Donets, which would then be cleared by the 167th and 168th Infantry Divisions. Prokhorovka, it was believed, would not be able to withstand the combined energy of the newly united panzer corps and fall after a brief struggle.

Roland began at 0400 hours on 14 July, when Das Reich attempted to push southeast, led by its two panzer grenadier regiments. After a hurricane bombardment on the Soviet lines to disorientate and neutralize the defending forces, men of the 1st and 2nd Battalions of

Der Führer advanced towards the defences held by the 4th and 25th Guards Tank Brigades. The division's history states:

> Solidly they accepted casualties from the extensive minefields across which they marched to gain the high ground south-west of Pravorot. The first houses in Belenikhino, a village at the foot of the high ground, were taken by midday, when the fighting was from house to house and hand-to-hand. Grenadiers used hollow charge grenades, while overhead Stukas dive-bombed the Russians, destroying their resistance inside and outside the village and destroying 12 of the Russian tanks that intervened in the battle. With Belenikhino at last in German hands, the grenadier battalions regrouped under the protection of the panzer regiment, then led the division's attacks for what remained of the day and continued throughout.

Das Reich's efforts on the 14th were considerable and were rewarded with some impressive territorial gains – including Belenikhino and Ivanovka – which left it just short of Pravorot (four miles south of Prokhorovka) at dusk. The fighting had been heavy and the 2nd Guards Tank Corps had lost more armour, which, considering Manstein's aim, was critical to the success of what Hausser's corps was being asked to achieve. The Germans would use their guile, professionalism and tactical nous to inflict significant losses on their less capable enemy. Yet still the Soviets held the line and remained willing to take the casualties in the expectation that the Germans would run out of time to achieve a strategic (or even operational) victory before they would be forced to withdraw as the result of the wider developing Soviet offensive action. This was Zhukov's view when he arrived at the front on 13 July. Indeed, he continued with the attritional strategy and plans being followed in the southern salient and noted in his memoirs: 'After examining the situation and the actions of our own and enemy troops I fully agreed with Vasilevsky's measures and decisions.'

The Germans were being tempted to 'burn themselves out', and the Soviet commanders south of Prokhorovka did all in their power to ensure that their adversary was given the means with which to do it. If they resisted stubbornly, Manstein's energy would inevitably be sapped and with every passing day his offensive would take a step nearer to being halted. The defence against III Panzer Corps, therefore, remained as resolute as ever. When at 0700 hours on 14 July Breith's divisions finally broke out of the bridgehead after a massive build-up of forces across a very narrow front, Trufanov's force did not collapse. 'We fought with everything available,' recalls gunner Stanislav Usov, who served with the 32nd Anti-Tank Artillery Brigade.

> We were just one of scores of batteries that had been moved into position to block the German advance. I did not know where we were, but it was impressed upon us that we must stop the panzers at all costs. We were forced to withdraw several times that day, but we did what we could to slow the attack ... Two comrades were killed during this time. Because of the close quarter nature of our work we were often vulnerable to the tanks. Miss a panzer and he will blast the position or crush you. We missed, and saw the turret traverse towards us. The next thing I remember was lying on my back around [20 yards] from the gun. The tank had moved on and I went back to find a horrible mess. My comrades had been pulverised by the blast. There were just scraps of bloody uniform and a gory mess where they had stood just seconds before.

To Trufanov, there was no mystery about what Breith was trying to do, and so he withdrew his forces away from the punch in order to avoid their encirclement. This meant, however, that the panzer divisions did make headway and the 7th Panzer Division finally made contact with Das Reich, but not until the afternoon of 15 July. However, III Panzer Corps was not well positioned to drive Hausser's formation forward as Manstein had hoped and planned. Fatigued by 10 days of intense fighting, targeted mercilessly by the Red Air Force and immediately confronted by the 48th Rifle Corps, 2nd Guards Tank Corps, 5th Guards Mechanized Corps and 35th Guards Rifle Corps, Breith struggled to hold his ground. Although both Totenkopf and LAH fought off concerted Soviet attempts to dislodge them during the day, and a link-up between the two panzer corps had been successfully accomplished, Operation Roland had failed. The intended encirclement had not been achieved, nor had the destruction of critical Soviet formations, so the prospects for further exploitation were immediately squashed.

The German line was coming under increasing pressure from mounting Soviet counterattacks across the southern salient, and with broader offensive action being reported as actual or likely both north and south of the salient, Manstein knew that his offensive must soon come to an end. The Soviets did not show any signs of collapse. Vatutin's command remained cohesive and well motivated. Pavel Krylov's unit was kept up to date with general developments, which, he said, 'served to enthuse and encourage us'. Many of those formations that had been in action since the first days of the battle were weary and stretched, but the Soviets did also have fresher divisions, brigades and corps that had been carefully husbanded and fed into battle only where and when needed. The Germans, by contrast, had no reserve to call upon and Manstein's weary men could not fight on indefinitely. Rudi Bauermann, for example, recalls fighting while in a stupor:

Although I had been at the front for just a few days, I could hardly keep my eyes open. We were fighting 24 hours a day – hard, physical fighting – and were exhausted. Perhaps my healing wound had weakened me, but I found the pace too great. In battle the constant rushes of adrenaline, challenges to body and mind, finally take their toll. I watched as shattered soldiers made all sorts of basic errors because they could no longer keep their mind on the job. It did not help that we became short of basic fighting commodities: ammunition, water and medical supplies. We were told that they were held up in the rear. It was demoralizing, particularly when we knew that we were faced by an army of plenty in strong positions.

The declining fighting power of both II SS and III Panzer Corps over subsequent days allowed the Germans to do little more operationally than hold the Soviets. As their own attacks began to peter out, Army Group South was catapulted into the planning misery of making preparations for a withdrawal from the salient while in contact with the enemy. The headquarters staff pleaded with OKW for extra resources for its formations in the salient, but were told that their situation was mere detail in a deteriorating strategic picture that anticipated a general Soviet offensive against the Wehrmacht in central-southern Russia. Although it took until 23 July for Hitler finally to order that the offensive in the southern salient be halted, it had become increasingly apparent to Manstein that the stalemated front offered little to his formations but protracted misery. In the immediate wake of the battle, the field marshal contended that his extended offensive had managed to damage the Soviet armour around Prokhorovka to the extent that 'the enemy no longer posed a threat in this sector in the medium term'. He later confessed that during this period he had severely misjudged Soviet resources and fighting capabilities. It was an admission that also held true for the entire German approach to the destruction of the Kursk salient.

Conclusion

The Battle of Kursk was destined to be Hitler's last offensive in the East and propelled Stalin towards victory. Operation Zitadelle stripped the Wehrmacht of its last vestiges of invincibility, diluted its fighting spirit and robbed it of hope. Once the Red Army's attacks began to smash into their enemy's overstretched formations in the wake of the clash, there was nothing that Hitler or his generals could do to stop them. Vasilevsky later wrote: 'As a result of the Kursk battle, the Soviet Armed Forces had dealt the enemy a buffeting from which Nazi Germany was never to recover . . . The big defeat at the Kursk Bulge was the beginning of a fatal crisis for the German Army.'

The Soviets' concerted retaliation began on 12 July with a counter-attack against the Orel salient, which quickly succeeded in lacerating the Wehrmacht's line and made deep penetrations. Orel fell on 5 August and two weeks later the bulge had been removed to a depth of 50 miles. A second Soviet attack had begun two days earlier, targeting the southern German salient centred on the critical communications hub of Kharkov. After stoical resistance by its defenders, that city fell on the 23rd and a few weeks later the Germans were in retreat along the entire southern front. Writing in his voluminous history of the Second World War, Winston Churchill opined: 'These three immense battles of Kursk, Orel and Kharkov, all within the space of two months, marked the ruin of Germany on the Eastern Front. Everywhere they had been outfought and overwhelmed.'

The outcome of Operation Zitadelle had not been forged merely in the heat of two weeks of fighting during July 1943, but over a protracted period during which Germany and the Soviet Union prepared for war. The direct cause of defeat, however, can be found in Hitler's confused strategic thinking before the invasion of the Soviet Union, which led him to set his armed forces a plethora of competing aims, including ideological and economic goals as well as military objectives. The result was that although the Wehrmacht was poised on the outskirts of Leningrad and Moscow by December 1941, it was incapable of converting operational success into strategic victory. This sorry situation was exacerbated by the lack of preparation that OKW had undertaken for a campaign in the East lasting more than a couple of months. Confident that Operation Barbarossa would be brought to a satisfactory conclusion within a matter of weeks, with the Red Army defeated well before the capital was reached, the subsequent failure totally unhinged Hitler's strategy. Rather than spending 1942 consolidating his new territorial acquisitions in the East, Hitler was instead compelled to compete in the sort of attritional slogging match that he had neither the resources nor the military wherewithal to win.

In blitzkrieg, OKW believed that it had a magic bullet that would fell all before it, but its weaknesses were already apparent, and it was particularly ill-suited to the vastness of the Soviet Union. Its frailties were subsequently exploited by the Soviets as Hitler was forced to extend his front as he reached down into the Caucasus for oil during 1942. His failure to capture that vital resource, together with the defeat at

Stalingrad that came hard on its heels, amounted to a massive physical and psychological blow from which Germany never recovered. All the signs were pointing towards a bleak future for Hitler's Eastern aspirations, but he was not looking (he could not bring himself to) for in the absence of any viable alternative, he had committed his nation to a fight to the death.

The Soviet Union's initial strategic aim during the summer of 1941 was simple if not easily achievable – survival. That accomplished, it was followed in 1942 by an equally simple and increasingly achievable aim – the annihilation of the Wehrmacht. Although poorly placed to survive the opening German onslaught after Stalin's purges, the subjugation of the peasantry and the brutal incorporation of new territories into the Soviet Union, the Red Army held out. Tenacious defence, the Wehrmacht's difficulty sustaining their initial momentum over vast distances and the invaders' cruelty towards the Soviet population were but a few of the factors associated with the Germans' undoing. Others were Stalin's careful harnessing of the Soviet Union's massive manpower, access to raw materials and the country's production potential, which became the foundation for the Soviets' eventual triumph. That endeavour formed the spine of an attritional strategy that, together with the gradual improvement in the fighting ability of the armed forces, proved to be a winning formula.

By the second summer of the Russo-German war, the Wehrmacht was being systematically worn down while the Soviet military machine was beginning its transformation into a highly capable offensive instrument. Although never trying to match the professionalism and tactical excellence of the Wehrmacht, the Soviets set themselves the realistic aim of stitching together a series of operational successes in an attempt to gain strategic victory. Over time, pre-purge doctrine was dusted down and gradually applied by the voluminous Soviet forces. Assisted by basic but decent weaponry, robust troops and a population desperate to win the 'Great Patriotic War', the Red Army's latent offensive ability was displayed in the wake of the Battle of Stalingrad against a decaying opposition.

Although Hitler believed that he was seizing the initiative with Zitadelle, the operation played directly into Soviet hands. Inspired by the Germans after a series of defeats that they desperately wished to avenge, the Soviets used the offensive to develop a massive trap. Eschewing his natural instinct to attack, Stalin agreed to the building of a web of defences to destroy Hitler's great scheme. The decision came about not only as the result of a deep understanding about how to meet and defeat blitzkrieg, but was also due to a developing maturity within the Soviet High Command. Patience and faith in the Front commanders within the Kursk salient were amply repaid. Utilizing their excellent intelligence, and assisted by Hitler's decision to postpone the launch of the operation to bolster his attack with Tigers and Panthers, the Red Army produced a superlative cobweb of defences. To overcome them and their enemy's numerical superiority, the Wehrmacht lent heavily on blitzkrieg, their professionalism and superior weaponry. Guderian and Manstein were not impressed, and even Hitler's belief in what the operation could achieve waned as the weeks passed. Eventually, Zitadelle's grand aim of providing a platform from which the Wehrmacht could relaunch its offensive action was dropped for the far more modest goal of shortening the front and damaging Soviet armour enough to create an opportunity for Germany to deal with the Allied threat in the Mediterranean. As German historian Karl-Heinz Frieser has argued, the Germans recognized that 'it was no longer possible to achieve a decisive victory on the eastern front, certainly not in a single battle'.

When Zitadelle began on 5 July, the strike immediately failed to achieve the surprise and dislocation of the enemy that senior commanders had hoped it would. For the operation to succeed, the planners had dictated, Kursk needed to be ensnared within four days. Anything slower than this, they argued, would allow the Soviets enough time to plug any gaps that had been made in their lines, and move their reserves into position. However, the attackers immediately ran into an obstacle-strewn battlefield constructed around copious lines of elastic defence, and neither Model's Ninth Army nor Manstein's Army Group South were capable of maintaining the momentum necessary to cling on to the offensive's exacting timetable. Although XLVIII Panzer Corps and, in particular, II SS Panzer Corps caused some concern in the southern salient, III Panzer Corps was occupied for long enough to render the Fourth Panzer Army's right flank cruelly exposed. The Ninth Army, meanwhile, was left floundering before the Olkhovatka heights, partly because Model had too little armour, but also because he diluted the armour he had into uninspiring penny-packets. In the end, the Soviet defences were simply too strong for the attackers to break down in the time available, and the Soviet performance was impressive enough for Mellenthin to write: 'The Russian High Command conducted the Battle of Kursk with great skill, yielding ground adroitly and taking the sting out of our offensive with an intricate system of minefields and antitank defences.' The Red Army simply soaked up the impact of the German offensive with their shield and deftly moved their reserve forward to act as the counterattacking sword.

Having worn the Germans down and organized themselves for a general counterattack, the Soviets struck on 12 July. In the north, where the Ninth Army's offensive had already died, Model was forced to react to an attack on the Orel salient to his rear, while in the south fresh tanks and infantry set about the Fourth Panzer Army. Even though II SS Panzer Corps could claim to have won a tactical victory in the monumental armoured clash at Prokhorovka, having destroyed 334 of Rotmistrov's armoured fighting vehicles to 16 July (for the loss of 54 of their own), Hausser's men did not do enough to change the course of the operation. Manstein endeavoured to salvage something from Zitadelle's wreckage over the next few days, but his subsequent attempt to dislocate the Soviet armour was merely a last gasp attack before withdrawal. With pressure mounting in the Mediterranean and threats rapidly developing to the north and south of the Kursk salient, Hitler finally called time on the operation.

Although the Germans had not relinquished their tactical supremacy throughout the battle, Zitadelle ultimately failed to achieve even the most unpretentious German aim, that of drawing the Soviets' offensive teeth in the region. As Manstein later lamented: 'And so the last German offensive in the east ended in fiasco, even though the enemy opposite the two attacking armies of the Southern Army Group had suffered four times their losses in prisoners, dead and wounded.' The field marshal was correct. The Soviets did suffer more casualties than the Germans during Operation Zitadelle. Rokossovsky and Vatutin lost 177,847 casualties, around 1,600 armoured fighting vehicles and 460 aircraft; Model and Manstein suffered 56,827 casualties and lost 252 tanks and 159 aircraft. But the losses on the Kursk battlefield were not as important as the ability to replace those losses. The Soviets were well placed to write off nearly 19,000 tanks in the second half of 1943, since waves of replacements were ready to take their place, but German prospects were scuppered by relatively slight decreases in their resources. As Frieser argues: 'It was not by tank duels that the Battle of Kursk – or even the Second World War – was won, but by the production battle in the factories ... The German Reich had lost the production battle long before the first shot was fired at Kursk in July 1943.'

The losses of manpower and armoured fighting vehicles at Kursk placed the Wehrmacht in a position whereby it could not resist the Soviet counterattacks during July and August, which, in turn, rendered it incapable of stopping the general offensive in the south during the autumn. The Germans had structured their armed forces around a doctrine of attack and suddenly found themselves on the defensive, and infantry divisions were naked before massed Soviet armoured attacks. The only possible solution to this was for the army to spread its armour more widely across its formations, but at the cost of under-mining any future attempt at delivering an operational level armoured offensive. Recognizing the impact that the Battle of Kursk had on the Germans' ability to defend themselves, Guderian later admitted: 'We had suffered a decisive defeat.'

Operations in the Kursk salient in July 1943 should not just be seen in terms of German failure, therefore, but also as a notable Soviet success. In the words of Antony Beevor: 'The Red Army had proved once again the dramatic improvement in the professionalism of its commanders, the morale of its soldiers and the effective application of force.' The Soviets used Zitadelle as the perfect opportunity to grind the Wehrmacht further down before applying their developing offen-sive skills in pursuit of strategic victory. 'The defeat of the main grouping of German troops in the Kursk area,' Zhukov wrote in his memoirs, 'paved the way for the subsequent wide-scale offensive oper-ations by the Soviet forces to expel the Germans from our soil completely ... and ultimately to crush Nazi Germany.' The Battle of Kursk was, as a consequence, not only a turning point in the campaign in the East, but in the wider Second World War. As Churchill noted, for Russia, 'Stalingrad was the end of the beginning; but the Battle of Kursk was the beginning of the end.'

Epilogue

It is a year after my visit to the Kursk battlefield with the Petriks and I have arranged to meet Anton in a café just outside Köln, where he is now working in one of the city's hospitals. Determined to use every last minute of my precious research time in Germany, I am using the café as the venue for a final interview with Raimund Rüffer, an extremely friendly former infantryman who joined the German army in 1939 as a private, attended officer school in 1942 and ended up at Kursk as a junior officer.

The session goes well, so well that I totally lose track of time and am still chatting to Raimund when I notice Anton being pointed in my direction by a waiter. I stand up in surprise and for the duration of our handshake fail to see that Mykhailo is standing just behind his son and is taking off his coat. My blood runs cold as I immediately become aware of the delicate situation that I have inadvertently sponsored – the meeting of two old foes. I apologize for my tardy time-keeping and reach out to greet Mykhailo as Anton tells me that his father is

staying with him for a month or two while his flat is being redeco-
rated. A good excuse, he explains, for Mykhailo to catch up with his
great-grandchildren and enjoy a change of scene.

I introduce Raimund, explaining that he also fought at Kursk – but
for the Wehrmacht. Mykhailo sits down without looking in the
German's direction. Sensing a difficulty, Raimund immediately makes
an excuse to leave, but Anton steps in and engages him in polite
conversation while Mykhailo sits in silence. I make my way over to the
bar, order some coffee and take the opportunity to nip out to my car
to collect some photographs that I had taken of the Kursk battlefield
the previous year. I hope that they might help to break the ice between
the two octogenarians – or at least thaw it a little.

I don't know what was said in the brief time that I was away, but on
my return to the table I find the three of them laughing uproariously.
Anton translates for his father, whose face cracks into a smile before
he gives a throaty chuckle. The coffee arrives and I pass around the
photographs, explaining where they were taken and their significance.
Raimund asks about the battlefield. He has not had the opportunity to
visit it since the war. Anton translates to ensure that his father is not
left out of the conversation. Suddenly, Mykhailo reaches into his jacket
pocket, produces a map and spreads it out on the table. It is the one
that I had given him of the Kursk salient with Soviet and German
dispositions marked in red and blue ink. He jabs his index finger at
Cherkasskoe and says simply: 'I was here.' Raimund points to the
northern salient before Maloarkhangelsk to identify his position. A
breakthrough. From that moment on it is impossible to break into the
exchange as, using Anton as an intermediary, the two old soldiers
compare their lives and experiences.

They have a great deal in common. They were born in the same year
to farming families, disliked school, despised their first officers and
were both injured during training. As infantrymen, their wars also had
much in common. It suddenly becomes apparent that the two men

suffered similar wounds on the first day of the battle. They compare scars, tell their stories and praise the medical teams who tended to them. But for Anton's patient translation, a casual observer might mistake the men for former colleagues in the same army. 'Blankets? No, our unit wasn't issued with blankets until December. Where were you in July 1942?' 'The rain was awful. My bunker flooded. What did you sleep on?' 'My boots dried solid and I used animal fat to keep them supple and waterproof. What did you use?' The conversation steers clear of politics, war aims and strategy and focuses on life at the sharp end – the shared privations and common experience of the infantry no matter what side they fought on. '*Frontschwein*,' Raimund calls the infantry, the troops who had more in common with the enemy's infantry than they did with their own army in the rear area. Mykhailo nods in agreement and breaks into another cackling laugh.

The two men had connected, but looking at his watch, Raimund realizes he has to leave us for another appointment. The two old soldiers stand up on creaking knees and shake hands, and then, impulsively, embrace each other. Their eyes sparkle. It was time to move on.

Notes

Introduction

p. xvi   'our history, our heritage . . .' student at RMAS, November 2009. Over the course of 2008–09 I questioned students, colleagues, friends, neighbours, relations (and even some strangers) about their perceptions of the Second World War. I base my comments on these unscientific, but revealing, findings

p. xvii   'people living in the countries of the old . . .' at the time of writing, May 2010, the British press and BBC are running stories and programmes about the invasion of France and, in particular, the 70th anniversary of the evacuation from Dunkirk. In August 2009 the 70th anniversary of the invasion of Poland passed almost unnoticed

p. xviii   'one of the most decisive . . .' John Hughes-Wilson in Karl-Heinz Frieser et al *Kursk – Sixty Years On* in *The RUSI Journal* Vol. 148 No. 5 October 2003, p. 78

Chapter 1: The Origins of Annihilation I

p. 1 'The day dawned stormy and was to become shocking ...' details taken from Franz Kurowski *Panzer Aces – German Tank Commanders of WWII* Stackpole Books, Mechanicsburg, PA 2004; Franz Kurowski *Operation 'Zitadelle' – July 1943: The Decisive Battle of World War II* J.J. Fedorowicz, Winnipeg 2003; and George M. Nipe *Decision in the Ukraine – Summer 1943 – II SS and III Panzerkorps* J.J. Fedorowicz, Winnipeg 1996. Details have also been supplied by various interviewees whose details can be found in the notes to Chapter 9

p. 3 'Then came stirring news ...' Richard Krebs writing as Jan Valtin in *Out of the Night* Kessinger, Whitefish, Montana 2005, p. 9

p. 4 'Most of us just want peace ...' letter from Hilda Brandt to Jessica Rowland dated 15 January 1919. Author's collection

p. 5 'Today in the Hall of Mirrors ...' *Deutsche Zeitung* 28 June 1919. Author's collection

p. 5 'This is not peace ...' quoted in Stephen J. Lee *Aspects of European History 1789–1980* Routledge 1988, p. 186

p. 5 'in profiteering, careless of whether ...' Nationalist pamphlet dated 20 July 1919, published in Munich. Author's collection

p. 6 'Everything went black before my eyes ...' Adolf Hitler *Mein Kampf* Hutchinson 1974, pp. 185–7

p. 7 '[W]e became nationalists ...' quoted in Frank McDonough *Hitler and Nazi Germany* Cambridge University Press, Cambridge 1999, p. 20

p. 7 'a man whose honourable façade ...' Traudl Junge (edited by Melissa Müller) *Until the Final Hour – Hitler's Last Secretary* Phoenix 2002, p. 2

p. 7 'The Government of the November Criminals ...' quoted in Lee *op. cit.*, p. 208

p. 8 'Marxism itself systematically plans ...' Hitler *op. cit.*, p. 370

p. 8 'The Jewish doctrine of Marxism ...' Hitler *op. cit.*, p. 55

p. 8   '[T]here are only two possibilities . . .' quoted in J.W. Hinden *The Weimar Republic* Longman, Harlow 1990, p. 93

p. 9   'quite in keeping with nature . . .' quoted in Richard Overy *The Dictators: Hitler's Germany and Stalin's Russia* Penguin Books 2005, p. 442

p. 9   'conquer his inhibitions . . .' quoted in Overy *The Dictators op. cit.*, p. 16

p. 9   'Here was an unassuming man . . .' copy of a letter from Paul Weber to Henry Hartmann dated 20 June 1928. Author's collection. The original is owned by Paul Weber's son, Theo

p. 10   'We are the result of the distress . . .' quoted in Alan Bullock *Hitler – A Study in Tyranny* Penguin 1952, p. 151

p. 11   'We want the Bill . . .' quoted in Bullock *op. cit.*, p. 270

p. 11   'You are under arrest, you pig . . .' quoted in Overy *The Dictators op. cit.*, p. 50

p. 12   'lawful for the necessary defence of the state . . .' quoted in Overy *The Dictators op. cit.*, p. 51

p. 12   'The people are impotent . . .' quoted in Patrick Wright *Tank* Faber and Faber 2000, p. 221

p. 12   'I swear by God this holy oath . . .' quoted in Robert Wolfson *Years of Change: European History 1890–1945* Edward Arnold 1978, p. 307

p. 12   'We officers were particularly disturbed . . .' interview with Alarick Lindner, 10 April 2005

p. 13   'It is not enough for people to be . . .' quoted in McDonough *op. cit.*, p. 53

p. 14   'As the time for the Führer's arrival . . .' quoted in Overy *The Dictators op. cit.*, p. 111

p. 14   'All afternoon Nazi raiding parties . . .' quoted in McDonough *op. cit.*, p. 54

p. 15   '[W]hen an opponent says . . .' quoted in Michael Burleigh *The Third Reich – A New History* Macmillan 2000, p. 235

p. 16 'educated physically, mentally and morally . . .' quoted in Lee *op. cit.*, p. 217

p. 16 'The Hitler Youth ended my sons' childhood . . .' letter from Karla Kortig to Nancy Price dated 12 August 1945. Author's collection

p. 17 'We are overpopulated and cannot feed . . .' quoted in McDonough *op. cit.*, p. 41

p. 18 'Germany's rightful status . . .' transcript of a speech by Adolf Hitler to a rally in Berlin, August 1936. Author's collection

p. 18 'The struggle against Versailles . . .' quoted in McDonough *op. cit.*, p. 82

p. 20 'The smaller the army . . .' quoted in Wright *op. cit.*, p. 218

p. 21 'Little more than twenty years . . .' Major-General Heinz Guderian *Achtung – Panzer! – The Development of Armoured Forces, Their Tactics and Operational Potential* Arms and Armour Press 1992, p. 212

p. 22 'had pieced together a firm conviction . . .' quoted in Overy *The Dictators op. cit.*, p. 4

p. 22 'insignificant and timid . . .' quoted in Overy *The Dictators op. cit.*, p. 129

p. 22 'War is the father of all things . . .' quoted in Overy *The Dictators op. cit.*, p. 442

p. 23 'last territorial demand in Europe . . .' quoted in B.J. Elliot *Hitler and Germany* Longman 1966, p. 92

p. 23 'to liquidate the remainder of Czechoslovakia . . .' quoted in McDonough *op. cit.*, p. 79

p. 23 'confidently placed the fate . . .' quoted in Bullock *op. cit.*, p. 485

p. 23 'Children, this is the greatest day . . .' quoted in Bullock *op. cit.*, p. 485

p. 24 'In a few weeks I shall stretch . . .' quoted in McDonough *op. cit.*, p. 84

p. 24 'With minor exceptions German . . .' quoted in McDonough *op. cit.*, p. 84

p. 25 'I have put on the uniform . . .' quoted in J. Noakes, J. and G. Pridham (eds) *Nazism 1919–1945: Volume 3: Foreign Policy, War and Racial Extermination – A Documentary Reader* University of Exeter, Exeter 1988, p. 755

p. 25 'I was shocked at what had become . . .' quoted in Elliot *op. cit.*, p. 97

p. 26 'We are ruthless . . .' quoted in Lee *op. cit.*, p. 218

p. 26 'Hitler sat motionless . . .' quoted in Noakes and Pridham *op. cit.*, p. 757

p. 27 'not exactly according to . . .' quoted in Noakes and Pridham *op. cit.*, p. 725

p. 29 'OKH would be grateful . . .' quoted in Alan Clark *Barbarossa – The Russian-German Conflict 1941–45* Macmillan 1985, p. 4

p. 30 'Russia is at present not dangerous . . .' quoted in Noakes and Pridham *op. cit.*, p. 764

p. 31 'The disgrace is now extinguished . . .' quoted in Ian Kershaw *Hitler: 1936–1945 Nemesis* Penguin 2001, p. 299

p. 32 'The Supreme Command intervened . . .' Heinz Guderian *Panzer Leader* Futura 1974, p. 117

p. 32 'the greatest commander . . .' quoted in William Carr *Hitler: A Study in Personality and Politics* Edward Arnold 1989, p. 90

Chapter 2: The Origins of Annihilation II

p. 35 'In May 1937, Marshal Mikhail Tukhachevsky . . .' details taken from Simon Sebag Montefiore's *Stalin – The Court of the Red Tsar* Phoenix 2004; John Erickson's *The Soviet High Command: A Military–Political History, 1918–41* Frank Cass 2001; Catherine Merridale's *Ivan's War – The Red Army 1939–45* Faber and Faber 2005 and Donald Rayfield's *Stalin and his Hangmen* Penguin 2005

p. 37 'Russia is a squalid place ...' letter from Lieutenant-Colonel Edward Leigh to his brother, James Leigh, dated 12 February 1914. The Leigh Family Archive, Sittingbourne, Kent

p. 37 'workers, led by the more educated ...' quoted in Wolfson *op. cit.*, p. 325

p. 37 'The authorities seem to be losing ...' letter from Lieutenant-Colonel Edward Leigh to his brother, James Leigh, dated 16 February 1917. The Leigh Family Archive, Sittingbourne, Kent

p. 39 'We need the real, nation-wide ...' quoted in Lee *op. cit.*, p. 86

p. 39 'How can you make a revolution ...' quoted in Overy *The Dictators op. cit.*, p. 180

p. 39 'Some 250,000 people ...' figure from Overy *The Dictators op. cit.*, p. 180

p. 39 'It was as if the regime would not be satisfied ...' Anonymous *Memoir of an Itinerant Russian*, privately published in the United States of America 1924

p. 39 'All the forces of the old world ...' transcript of a speech by Leon Trotsky in Moscow, 25 October 1923. Author's collection

p. 40 'The death of Lenin has been announced ...' Daniel Vogel diary entry dated 22 January 1924

p. 40 'Not everyone beaten by parents ...' Robert Service *Stalin: A Biography* Pan Books 2005, p. 19

p. 41 'thick-set, of medium height ...' quoted in Overy *The Dictators op. cit.*, p. 7

p. 41 'always manage to use power ...' quoted in Overy *The Dictators op. cit.*, p. 1

p. 42 'waiting room of an English ...' quoted in Mark Healy *Zitadelle – The German Offensive against the Kursk Salient 4–17 July 1943* The History Press, Stroud 2008, p. 52

p. 42 'It was an experience ...' an undated event detailed in a journal written by Pavlo Kulik in 1938. The volume was discovered among Kulik's effects by his son, Viktor, after his father's death in 1990

p. 43 'electrification and literacy . . .' quoted in Lee *op. cit.*, p. 16

p. 43 'they strove and succeeded . . .' quoted on SovLit.com accessed on 16 June 2009

p. 44 'Oil Production Figures Soar . . .' *Pravda* 15 September 1935. Author's collection

p. 45 'an oasis in the middle . . .' quoted in Richard Overy *Russia's War* Penguin Books 1999, p. 6

p. 45 'In a conflict of first-class opponents . . .' quoted in Chris Bellamy *Absolute War – Soviet Russia in the Second World War: A Modern History* Pan Books 2008, pp. 32–3

p. 46 'a new imperialist war . . .' quoted in Martin McCauley *Stalin and Stalinism* Pearson, Harlow 2008, p. 39

p. 46 'Again, as in 1914 . . .' quoted in Overy *The Dictators op. cit.*, p. 441

p. 46 'It was not mere accident . . .' Overy *The Dictators op. cit.*, pp. 443–4

p. 47 'The history of old Russia . . .' quoted in Geoffrey Roberts *Stalin's Wars – From the World War to Cold War, 1939–1953* Yale University Press, New Haven 2006, p. 20

p. 48 'We were told what . . .' Mikhail Batkin interview, 12 December 2009

p. 48 'They need to be taught . . .' quoted in Service *op. cit.*, p. 55

p. 48 'Seven million died . . .' figures from Bellamy *op. cit.*, p. 8

p. 48 'Nothing can be allowed . . .' quoted in Service *op. cit.*, p. 55

p. 49 'Commissar Ordzhonikidze . . .' *Time* Monday, 16 December 1935. Author's collection

p. 50 'In the Gorky automotive . . .' *Time* Monday, 16 December 1935. Author's collection

p. 51 '4.3 million tons . . .' figures from Overy *Russia's War op. cit.*, p. 17

p. 51   '60 per cent of Soviet industry . . .' figures from Bellamy *op. cit.*, p. 87

p. 51   'sworn enemies of Soviet power . . .' quoted in McCauley *op. cit.*, p. 43

p. 51   'In the Soviet leader . . .' quoted in McDonough *op. cit.*, p. 81

p. 51   'develop a first-class military . . .' transcript of a speech given by Stalin in August 1938, provided by Viktor Kulik

p. 52   'In 1913 real defence . . .' figures from McCauley *op. cit.*, p. 45 and Overy *Russia's War op. cit.*, p. 19

p. 52   'At the beginning of 1928 . . .' figures from Overy *Russia's War op. cit.*, p. 19

p. 53   '40,000 aircraft and 50,000 tanks' quoted in Overy *Russia's War op. cit.*, p. 11

p. 53   'The nature of modern weapons' quoted in Sheffield and Trew (eds) *100 Years of Conflict* Sutton, Stroud 2000, p. 119

p. 53   'The fears of the Bolshevik . . .' Rodric Braithwaite *Moscow 1941: A City and its People at War* Profile Books 2006, p. 48

p. 54   'The wrecking and diversionary-spying . . .' quoted in Roberts *op. cit.*, p. 18

p. 54   'Of the five marshals . . .' figures from Bellamy *op. cit.*, p. 46

p. 54   'One Russian source suggests . . .' Evan Mawdsley *Thunder in the East: The Nazi–Soviet War 1941–1945* Hodder Arnold 2005, pp. 20–21

p. 56   'disintegrate and subdue . . .' quoted in Gerhard Weinberg *The Foreign Policy of Hitler's Diplomatic Revolution in Europe 1933–36* University of Chicago Press, Chicago 1970, p. 340

p. 56   'the conquest of Russia . . .' and 'German aggression is typical . . .' quoted in the Soviet Studies Unit, RMAS Pamphlet No. 21 1992

p. 57   'era of brute force . . .' quoted in Bellamy *op. cit.*, p. 47

p. 57   'conniving in aggression . . .' quoted in Roberts *op. cit.*, p. 34

p. 58   'without clear and unambiguous . . .' quoted in Bellamy *op. cit.*, p. 50

p. 58   'The sinister news broke . . .' quoted in Roberts *op. cit.*, p. 16

p. 58   'The Soviet Union is very serious . . .' quoted in Bellamy *op. cit.*, p. 54

p. 58   'Europe is mine! . . .' quoted in Overy *Russia's War op. cit.*, p. 49

p. 58   'I know what Hitler's . . .' quoted in Overy *Russia's War op. cit.*, p. 50

p. 59   'A war is on between . . .' quoted in Roberts *op. cit.*, p. 36

p. 60   'convincing performance . . .' quoted in Ross Peterson unpublished lecture *A Work in Progress – The Red Army, 1939–41* University of Leeds 1994, p. 16

p. 60   'poorly motivated . . .' quoted in Bellamy *op. cit.*, p. 63

p. 60   'Attacking on a broad . . .' quoted in Bellamy *op. cit.*, p. 74

p. 61   'It was a winter . . .' interview with Georgy Uritski, 12 August 2009

p. 61   'Looking back . . .' interview with Georgy Uritski, 12 August 2009

p. 62   'We must ensure . . .' quoted in Peterson *op. cit.*, p. 21

p. 63   'Between January 1940 . . .' figures from Roberts *op. cit.*, p. 42

Chapter 3: Invasion

p. 67   'The news that the Germans were . . .' details taken from Overy *Russia's War op. cit.*, pp. 73–5; Merridale *op. cit.*, p. 77; Braithwaite *op. cit.*, p. 70; G. Zhukov *The Memoirs of Marshal Zhukov* Jonathan Cape 1971, pp. 235–6

p. 68   'One day the Russians . . .' quoted in David Irving *Hitler's War 1942–1945* Macmillan 1977, p. 143

p. 69   'For us there remained . . .' quoted in Mawdsley *op. cit.*, p. 7

p. 69   'Everything that I undertake . . .' quoted in McDonough *op. cit.*, p. 90

p. 69   'to smash the state . . .' quoted in Overy *Russia's War op. cit.*, p. 62

p. 69   '[t]he mass of the Russian Army . . .' quoted on www.germanhistorydocs.ghi-dc.org/pdf/eng/English57_new.pdf accessed 27 October 2009

p. 70 'of no great importance . . .' quoted in David M. Glantz *Before Stalingrad – Barbarossa and Hitler's Invasion of Russia 1941* Tempus, Stroud 2003, p. 13

p. 70 'a mystical conviction . . .' quoted in McDonough *op. cit.*, p. 86

p. 71 'a population of 190 million . . .' quoted in Bellamy *op. cit.*, p. 8

p. 72 'Yet even this drastic move . . .' figures from H.P. Willmott *The Great Crusade: A New Complete History of the Second World War* Pimlico 1992, p. 135

p. 72 'Some 625,000 hungry . . .' figures from Mawdsley *op. cit.*, p. 26 and Charles D. Winchester *Hitler's War on Russia* Osprey, Oxford 2007, p. 63

p. 72 'Hitler refused to let . . .' quoted in McDonough *op. cit.*, p. 40

p. 72 'Europe will hold its breath . . .' quoted in Overy *Russia's War op. cit.*, p. 64

p. 72 'I could scarcely believe . . .' Guderian *Panzer Leader op. cit.*, p. 142

p. 73 'Renewed study of the . . .' Guderian *Panzer Leader op. cit.*, p. 143

p. 73 'You only have to kick . . .' quoted in Roberts *op. cit.*, p. 85

p. 73 'The Soviet force that . . .' figures from Bellamy *op. cit.*, p. 175 and Mawdsley *op. cit.*, p. 19 and p. 30

p. 73 'I consider it necessary . . .' quoted in Roberts *op. cit.*, p. 76

p. 74 'Two or three years . . .' Zhukov *Memoirs op. cit.*, p. 227

p. 74 'Zhukov argued that 16,600 . . .' figures from Zhukov *Memoirs op. cit.*, p. 197

p. 76 'We have a non-aggression . . .' quoted in Braithwaite *op. cit.*, p. 58

p. 76 'The majority of the intelligence . . .' quoted in Braithwaite *op. cit.*, p. 55

p. 76 'We doubt the veracity . . .' quoted in Overy *Russia's War op. cit.*, p. 70

p. 76 'Soviet passivity in the face . . .' quoted in Mawdsley *op. cit.*, p. 8

p. 77 'so as to update their military training . . .' Zhukov *Memoirs op. cit.*, p. 196. I recognize that Zhukov wrote his memoirs after

Stalin's death and at the time of Nikita Khrushchev's anti-Stalin campaign and have endeavoured to verify Zhukov's claims (particularly where they reflect badly on Stalin) with other sources

p. 77   'It can't be true . . .' quoted in Merridale *op. cit.*, p. 73

p. 78   'A surprise attack by the Germans . . .' quoted in Glantz *Before Stalingrad op. cit.*, p. 287

p. 78   'Other elements of the Luftwaffe . . .' figures from Glantz *Before Stalingrad op. cit.*, p. 30

p. 79   'the beauties of the landscape . . .' quoted in Erhard Raus *Panzer Operations* Da Capo, Cambridge, MA 2003, p. 16

p. 79   'The first victim of the ambush . . .' quoted in Raus *op. cit.*, p. 17

p. 79   'Everything is going well . . .' Ivan Krylov *Soviet Staff Officer* The Falcon Press 1951, p. 115

p. 79   'We are being fired on . . .' quoted in Clark *op. cit.*, p. 44

p. 80   'At this moment a march . . .' quoted in Clark *op. cit.*, p. 44

p. 80   'Before three months have passed . . .' quoted in Winchester *op. cit.*, p. 41

p. 80   'attack the enemy and destroy . . .' quoted in Glantz *Before Stalingrad op. cit.*, p. 288

p. 80   'without regard for borders' quoted in Glantz *Before Stalingrad op. cit.*, pp. 288–9

p. 81   'commanding generals and their . . .' Zhukov *Memoirs op. cit.*, p. 247

p. 81   'One of the tanks drove . . .' Raus *op. cit.*, p. 23

p. 81   'Despite the continued German . . .' figure from Raus *op. cit.*, p. 34

p. 82   'The Russian mass . . .' quoted in Overy *Russia's War op. cit.*, p. 76

p. 82   'We did not foresee . . .' Zhukov *Memoirs op. cit.*, p. 51

p. 82   'No one has been . . .' quoted in Roberts *op. cit.*, p. 92

p. 83   '80 per cent of the . . .' Nigel Nicolson (ed) *The Harold Nicolson Diaries 1907–1963* Weidenfeld and Nicolson 2004, p. 187

p. 83   'Everyone was confident . . .' Gottlob Herbert Bidermann *In Deadly Combat – A German Soldier's Memoir of the Eastern Front* University Press of Kansas, Lawrence, Kansas 2000, p. 12

p. 83   'The dusty road was lined . . .' Bidermann *op. cit.*, p. 13

p. 84   'The sight of the line of retreat . . .' quoted in Jonathan Bastable *Voices from Stalingrad* David and Charles, Cincinnati, OH 2007, p. 18

p. 84   '[T]hree Junkers appeared . . .' Vasily Grossman *A Writer at War – Vasily Grossman with the Red Army 1941–1945* Pimlico 2006, p. 14

p. 85   '[H]owling bombs, fire . . .' Grossman *op. cit.*, pp. 8–9

p. 85   'The whole city was . . .' Zhukov *Memoirs op. cit.*, p. 255

p. 85   'Put your heads together . . .' Zhukov *Memoirs op. cit.*, p. 255

p. 85   'building up a defence . . .' Zhukov *Memoirs op. cit.*, p. 256

p. 85   'the first great victory of the campaign . . .' Guderian *Panzer Leader op. cit.*, p. 158

p. 86   'In less than three weeks . . .' quoted in Glantz *Before Stalingrad op. cit.*, p. 35

p. 86   'lack of resolve . . .' quoted in Merridale *op. cit.*, p. 77

p. 86   'the beating heart . . .' quoted in Peterson *op. cit.*, p. 6

p. 86   'On his arrival from Moscow . . .' and 'Leningrad must not fall . . .' figures and quote in Peterson *op. cit.*, p. 15

p. 87   'Sometimes bottlenecks were formed . . .' quoted in Merridale *op. cit.*, p. 88

p. 88   'an endless open space . . .' Bidermann *op. cit.*, pp. 15–16

p. 88   'For days great numbers . . .' Bidermann *op. cit.*, p. 15

p. 88   'The Soviets had been dealt . . .' figures quoted in Glantz *Before Stalingrad op. cit.*, p. 46

p. 88   'The objective to shatter the bulk . . .' quoted in Glantz *Before Stalingrad op. cit.*, p. 68

p. 89   'displaying confidence and calmness . . .' Yakov Chadaev, a senior administrator in the Council of People's Commissars, quoted in Roberts *op. cit.*, p. 90

p. 89   'Lenin founded our state . . .' quoted in Overy *Russia's War op. cit.*, p. 78

p. 89   'Stalin was in a very . . .' quoted in Roberts *op. cit.*, p. 90

p. 90   'Can I lead the country . . .' quoted in Overy *Russia's War op. cit.*, p. 70

p. 90   'some 1,523 factories . . .' figures from Glantz *Before Stalingrad op. cit.*, p. 65

p. 90   'The heroic feat of evacuation . . .' Zhukov *Memoirs op. cit.*, p. 266

p. 90   'He was concerned at the high desertion rates . . .' figures from Merridale *op. cit.*, p. 92

p. 91   'The result was another . . .' figures from Winchester *op. cit.*, pp. 60–61

p. 91   'We're living in dugouts . . .' quoted in Merridale *op. cit.*, p. 119

p. 92   'Some in trucks . . .' quoted in Merridale *op. cit.*, p. 87

p. 92   'We were all expecting war . . .' quoted in Merridale *op. cit.*, p. 77

p. 92   'bring into the limelight . . .' quoted on http://eng.9may.ru/eng_inform_war/m9005510 accessed 14 January 2010

p. 93   'fighting in the Minsk direction . . .' see Alexander Werth *Russia at War 1941–1945* Barrie and Rockliff 1964, pp. 179–80

p. 93   'At 6.30 a.m. practically every person . . .' quoted in Bastable *op. cit.*, p. 15

p. 93   'unprovoked aggressor . . .' quoted in Overy *Russia's War op. cit.*, pp. 79–80

p. 93   'Comrades! Our arrogant foe . . .' quoted in Braithwaite *op. cit.*, p. 96

p. 94   'the tone of [the speech] . . .' Krylov *op. cit.*, p. 119

p. 94   'frightened and bewildered people . . .' quoted in Merridale *op. cit.*, p. 84

p. 94   'As an observer . . .' quoted in Bastable *op. cit.*, p. 17

p. 94   'I lived through German rule . . .' quoted in Merridale *op. cit.*, p. 78

p. 95 'Posters on the wall ...' Werth *op. cit.*, p. 177

p. 95 'Women did take the place of men ...' figures from http://www.iwm.org.uk/upload/package/41/women/Women WarThemes.pdf accessed 14 January 2010

p. 95 'I remember that they ...' quoted in Braithwaite *op. cit.*, p. 122

p. 96 'There must be diversionist groups ...' quoted in Merridale *op. cit.*, p. 125

p. 96 'We feared the partisans ...' telephone interview with Dr Karl Hertzog, 18 August 2009

p. 97 'The individual soldiers ...' Bidermann *op. cit.*, p. 11

p. 97 'If only you had come ...' Guderian *Panzer Leader op. cit.*, p. 250

p. 98 'the 'Commissar Order' ...' http://www.holocaustresearch project.org/holoprelude/aboutthess.html accessed 14 January 2010

p. 98 'expected to 'cooperate' in Hitler's stated ambition ...' quoted in Winchester *op. cit.*, p. 55

p. 98 'The first day ...' Werth *op. cit.*, p. 374

p. 98 'It was a difficult time ...' interview with Alana Molodin, 1 November 2009

p. 98 'Once a soldier had ...' interview with (sergeant) A.G., 12 August 2008

p. 99 '[T]he enemy locked ...' quoted in Merridale *op. cit.*, p. 111

p. 99 'It is no longer ...' quoted in Merridale *op. cit.*, p. 122

p. 99 'A significant indication ...' Guderian *Panzer Leader op. cit.*, p. 194

p. 100 'This is a very grim war ...' Werth *op. cit.*, p. 194

p. 100 'If someone is brave ...' Grossman *op. cit.*, pp. 41–2

p. 101 'if we do not intend ...' quoted in Glantz *Before Stalingrad op. cit.*, p. 74

p. 101 'knees were shaking ...' Helmuth Pabst, *The Outermost Frontier – A German Soldier in the Russian Campaign* William Kimber 1957, p. 16

p. 101   'shrapnel from the anti-aircraft . . .' Werth *op. cit.*, p. 182

p. 102   '[T]he enemy offered . . .' Raus *op. cit.*, p. 51

p. 103   'fight to the last round . . .' Peterson *op. cit.*, p. 25

p. 103   'Voroshilov demanded, therefore . . .' quoted in Glantz *Before Stalingrad op. cit.*, p. 94

p. 103   'As Leeb considered . . .' Peterson *op. cit.*, p. 25

p. 103   'atrocious roads, intolerable heat . . .' Peterson *op. cit.*, p. 26

p. 104   '[O]ur forward machine-gun . . .' Bidermann *op. cit.*, pp. 22–4

p. 104   'The objective of future operations . . .' quoted in Glantz *Before Stalingrad op. cit.*, pp. 274–5

p. 105   'The occupation and destruction . . .' quoted in Braithwaite *op. cit.*, p. 181

p. 105   'This meant that my Panzer . . .' Guderian *Panzer Leader op. cit.*, p. 183

p. 106   'the appearance of a large . . .' quoted in Glantz *Before Stalingrad op. cit.*, p. 76

p. 106   'They captured 107,000 . . .' figures from Glantz *Before Stalingrad op. cit.*, p. 117

p. 106   'The South-Western Front . . .' Zhukov *Memoirs op. cit.*, p. 288

p. 107   'throwing all of his shock . . .' quoted in Glantz *Before Stalingrad op. cit.*, p. 121

p. 107   'a withdrawal towards Kiev . . .' Krylov *op. cit.*, p. 126

p. 107   'I have powerful defences . . .' Krylov *op. cit.*, p. 128

p. 107   'The Council of War . . .' Krylov *op. cit.*, p. 130

p. 108   'Guderian and his whole group . . .' quoted in Roberts *op. cit.*, p. 101

p. 108   'The trap was beginning . . .' figures taken from Glantz *Before Stalingrad op. cit.*, p. 91

p. 108   'Delay could result . . .' quoted in Roberts *op. cit.*, p. 101

p. 108   'There was a roar . . .' Grossman *op. cit.*, p. 17

p. 109   '440,000 men, 2,642 guns . . .' figures taken from Glantz *Before Stalingrad op. cit.*, p. 129

p. 110 'I fear that Leningrad . . .' quoted in Roberts *op. cit.*, p. 105

p. 110 'Leningrad: Our objective . . .' quoted in Glantz *Before Stalingrad op. cit.*, p. 101

p. 111 'I recall the day very well . . .' interview with Malana Ragulin, 18 September 2009

p. 111 'The Führer has decided . . .' quoted in Glantz *Before Stalingrad op. cit.*, p. 110

p. 112 'every village and every town . . .' Werth *op. cit.*, p. 190

p. 112 'first independent operation . . .' quoted in Roberts *op. cit.*, p. 99

p. 113 'More generally, the battle . . .' figures taken from Roberts *op. cit.*, p. 99

p. 113 'The battle of Smolensk . . .' Zhukov *Memoirs op. cit.*, p. 275

p. 113 'The whole situation . . .' 11 August entry quoted in Braithwaite *op. cit.*, p. 180

p. 114 'It all depended . . .' Guderian *Panzer Leader op. cit.*, p. 226

Chapter 4: Heading South

p. 117 'Alexander Werth was driven . . .' details taken from Werth *op. cit.*, pp. 561–2, and an interview with Soviet Stalingrad survivor Fedor Tiomkin on 15 June 2009

p. 119 '[t]he name Moscow will disappear forever . . .' quoted in Overy *Russia's War op. cit.*, p. 94

p. 119 'After very severe battles . . .' quoted in Merridale *op. cit.*, p. 122

p. 120 'Today begins the last . . .' quoted in Glantz *Before Stalingrad op. cit.*, p. 140

p. 121 'There are aircraft . . .' Grossman *op. cit.*, pp. 45–6

p. 121 'I thought I'd seen . . .' Grossman *op. cit.*, p. 48

p. 121 'the greatest battle . . .' quoted in Overy *Russia's War op. cit.*, p. 94

p. 122 'CAMPAIGN IN EAST . . .' quoted in Overy *Russia's War op. cit.*, p. 95

p. 122 'After the enormous . . .' interview with Captain Pavlik Boklov, 12 August 2009

p. 123 'The main danger . . .' Zhukov *Memoirs op. cit.*, p. 323

p. 123 '[T]housands upon thousands . . .' Zhukov *Memoirs op. cit.*, p. 344

p. 124 'The road bears . . .' Pabst *op. cit.*, p. 36

p. 124 '[the] roads rapidly . . .' Guderian *Panzer Leader op. cit.*, p. 234

p. 124 '[C]art and dirt roads . . .' Raus *op. cit.*, pp. 87–8

p. 125 'a contrast to the high . . .' Guderian *Panzer Leader op. cit.*, p. 235

p. 125 'Soviet resistance would . . .' quoted in Overy *Russia's War op. cit.*, p. 115

p. 125 'It is miserable . . .' Guderian *Panzer Leader op. cit.*, p. 246

p. 126 'stand firm and fight . . .' Werth *op. cit.*, pp. 233–4

p. 126 'Let us not . . .' Werth *op. cit.*, p. 235

p. 126 'During the night . . .' quoted in Overy *Russia's War op. cit.*, p. 97

p. 127 'If [the Germans] want . . .' quoted in Overy *Russia's War op. cit.*, p. 114

p. 127 'Let us fight to liberate . . .' quoted in Braithwaite *op. cit.*, p. 281

p. 127 'Are you sure we'll . . .' Zhukov *Memoirs op. cit.*, pp. 339–40

p. 128 'What [Stalin] was thinking . . .' quoted in Braithwaite *op. cit.*, pp. 290–91

p. 128 'The snow is falling thickly . . .' Pabst *op. cit.*, p. 39

p. 129 'From a quarter to six . . .' quoted in Bastable *op. cit.*, p. 22

p. 129 'I could never get . . .' telephone interview with Dr Karl Hertzog, 18 August 2009

p. 129 'Germans, frozen to death . . .' Grossman *op. cit.*, p. 86

p. 130 'Seven of our lads . . .' quoted in Merridale *op. cit.*, p. 120

p. 130 'Your breath catches . . .' Werth *op. cit.*, p. 551

p. 133 'Our attack on Moscow . . .' Guderian *Panzer Leader op. cit.*, p. 259

p. 133 'The enemy facing . . .' quoted in Braithwaite *op. cit.*, p. 303

p. 133 'At the end of October . . .' figures from Glantz *Before Stalingrad op. cit.*, p. 176

p. 134 'The enemy is exhausted . . .' quoted in Glantz *Before Stalingrad op. cit.*, p. 177

p. 134 '[we need] to assimilate . . .' quoted in Overy *Russia's War op. cit.*, p. 122

p. 134 'I ordered the engineer . . .' Raus *op. cit.*, p. 93

p. 135 'I had heard about . . .' quoted in Bastable *op. cit.*, p. 38

p. 135 'even for the last bicyclist . . .' quoted in Glantz *Before Stalingrad op. cit.*, p. 181

p. 136 'Only he who saw . . .' Guderian *Panzer Leader op. cit.*, pp. 254–5

p. 136 'Bock's force had lost . . .' figures from Willmott *op. cit.*, p. 157

p. 136 'regardless of rank . . .' Bidermann *op. cit.*, p. 82

p. 136 'The war was now really . . .' Guderian *Panzer Leader op. cit.*, p. 260

p. 137 'At this time . . .' Guderian *Panzer Leader op. cit.*, pp. 270–71

p. 138 '[Hitler has] prepared badly . . .' quoted in Braithwaite *op. cit.*, p. 324

p. 139 'It was a ham-fisted . . .' figures from Overy *Russia's War op. cit.*, p. 122

p. 139 'We had overrated . . .' Zhukov *Memoirs op. cit.*, p. 358

p. 139 'In severe, often unbelievably . . .' Zhukov *Memoirs op. cit.*, p. 361

p. 139 'As soon as the weather . . .' http://users.telenet.be/stalingrad/germanpart/dir41.html accessed on 17 February 2010

p. 140 'The whole Red Army . . .' Braithwaite *op. cit.*, p. 340

p. 141 'The artillery, rockets, flak . . .' Bidermann *op. cit.*, p. 128

p. 141 'The Soviet attempt . . .' figures from Willmott *op. cit.*, p. 215

p. 141 'Looking into the causes . . .' Zhukov *Memoirs op. cit.*, p. 369

p. 142 'lives were a military currency . . .' telephone interview with Dr Karl Hertzog, 18 August 2009

p. 142 'On the whole . . .' Pabst *op. cit.*, p. 27

p. 143 'It's a strange life . . .' Pabst *op. cit.*, p. 37

p. 143 'We are part of this war . . .' Pabst *op. cit.*, p. 84

p. 143 'An old woman . . .' Grossman *op. cit.*, p. 24

p. 144 'We were marching . . .' interview with Fedor Tiomkin, 15 June 2009

p. 144 'A member of my gun . . .' Bidermann *op. cit.*, p. 131

p. 145 'Time spent behind . . .' interview with Alarick Lindner, 10 April 1995

p. 145 'The soldiers returned . . .' Bidermann *op. cit.*, p. 143

p. 147 'head of state, executive . . .' Willmott *op. cit.*, p. 217

p. 147 'A new pragmatism . . .' Merridale *op. cit.*, p. 129

p. 148 'We must avoid closing . . .' http://users.telenet.be/stalingrad/germanpart/dir41.html accessed on 17 February 2010

p. 150 'Not a step backward! . . .' quoted in Overy *Russia's War op. cit.*, p. 158

p. 150 'occupy the entire eastern . . .' http://users.telenet.be/stalingrad/germanpart/dir45.html accessed on 19 February 2010

p. 150 'The capture of Stalingrad . . .' quoted in Bastable *op. cit.*, p. 27

p. 151 'Those were hard and dreadful . . .' Grossman *op. cit.*, pp. 130–31

p. 151 'Stalingrad is in ashes . . .' Grossman *op. cit.*, p. 125

p. 151 'The ground under . . .' quoted in Bastable *op. cit.*, p. 43

p. 152 'world opinion and the morale . . .' quoted in Bastable *op. cit.*, p. 45

p. 152 'I knew that the Battle . . .' Zhukov *Memoirs op. cit.*, p. 377

p. 153 'The time for conducting . . .' quoted in Bastable *op. cit.*, p. 104

p. 153 'It was not uncommon . . .' interview with Fedor Tiomkin, 15 June 2009

p. 154 'When I first got the rifle . . .' Grossman *op. cit.*, pp. 157–8

p. 154 'Stalingrad's rules of survival . . .' interview with Fedor Tiomkin, 15 June 2009

p. 155 '[T]he units of our corps . . .' quoted in Zhukov *Memoirs op. cit.*, p. 385

p. 155 'Approaching this place . . .' Grossman *op. cit.*, p. 151

p. 155 'We were relying . . .' from a copy of Elbert Hahn's journal, entry dated 22 August 1944. Author's collection. Hahn served on Field Marshal List's staff with responsibility for procuring local beasts of burden

p. 156 'loyalty to Germany' letter from Elbert Hahn to the author dated 18 September 2008

p. 156 'First, to continue wearing . . .' Zhukov *Memoirs op. cit.*, p. 382

p. 157 '1.1 million men, 13,500 guns . . .' figures from Zhukov *Memoirs op. cit.*, p. 397

p. 157 'The 19th of November . . .' http://209.85.229.132/ search?q=cache:VhF1gh8JXAQJ:ww2db.com/battlespec.php %3Fbattleid%3D3+German+Sixth+Army+Joachim+ Wieder&cd=1&hl=en&ct=clnk&gl=uk accessed 22 February 2010

p. 158 'We did not have the slightest idea . . .' quoted in Zhukov *Memoirs op. cit.*, p. 397

p. 158 'We have never imagined . . .' quoted in Winchester *op. cit.*, p. 91

p. 158 'dig in and await relief . . .' quoted in Winchester *op. cit.*, p. 100

p. 158 'Fuel will soon be exhausted . . .' quoted in Winchester *op. cit.*, p. 100

p. 159 'The Sixth Army believes . . .' quoted in Winchester *op. cit.*, p. 103

p. 159 '266 Ju-52s and 222 other aircraft . . .' figures from Winchester *op. cit.*, p. 101

p. 159 'A task of historic magnitude . . .' Raus *op. cit.*, p. 152

p. 160 'We're hoping to be out . . .' quoted in Bastable *op. cit.*, p. 209

p. 160 '[U]p to the end of December . . .' quoted in Winchester *op. cit.*, p. 113

p. 161 'Even those accustomed . . .' quoted in Bastable *op. cit.*, p. 219

p. 161 'I have no intention . . .' quoted in Antony Beevor, *Stalingrad, The Fateful Siege: 1942–1943* Viking Penguin, New York 1998, pp. 381–3

p. 161 'The Battle of Stalingrad . . .' figures from Winchester *op. cit.*, p. 91

p. 162 'Up till then one believed . . .' quoted in Overy *Russia's War op. cit.*, p. 185

p. 162 'I had not questioned . . .' interview with Marianne Koch, 20 August 2009

p. 163 'Only Joseph Stalin fully . . .' *Time* magazine's online archive http://www.time.com/time/subscriber/personoftheyear/ archive/stories/1942.html accessed 19 January 2010

Chapter 5: Uneasy Calm

p. 165 'Recently arrived SS-Untersturmführer . . .' Roger Hoch interivew, 6 March 2010

p. 167 '[O]ur troops received . . .' Zhukov *Memoirs op. cit.*, p. 90

p. 167 'There is always a sense . . .' interview with Fyodor Onton, 12 September 2009

p. 168 'Marshal Winter gave way . . .' quoted in Major-General F.W. von Mellenthin, *Panzer Battles* Ballantine Books, New York 1956, p. 258

p. 168 'Among his closest associates . . .' quoted in Healy *Zitadelle op. cit.*, p. 27

p. 168 'Hitler forbade retreats . . .' Healy *Zitadelle op. cit.*, p. 39

p. 169 'The early months of 1943 . . .' Mawdsley *op. cit.*, p. 262

p. 170 'With the German army . . .' figures from Willmott *op. cit.*, p. 253

p. 171 'In Russia the moral comfort . . .' Mellenthin *op. cit.*, p. 251

p. 171 'The war will be won . . .' figures from Winchester *op. cit.*, p. 116

p. 171 'At the time of the spring . . .' quoted in Winchester *op. cit.*, p. 154

p. 171 'The result was that in 1942 . . .' figures from Overy *Russia's War op. cit.*, p. 155

p. 172 'Now we shall win . . .' quoted in Overy *Russia's War op. cit.*, p. 195

p. 172 '[Wehrwolf] in winter . . .' Irving *op. cit.*, p. 489

p. 172 'In the intervening fourteen . . .' quoted in Kershaw *Nemesis op. cit.*, p. 577

p. 173 'he tried to induce sleep . . .' Irving *op. cit.*, p. 489

p. 173 'with the air of a victorious war-lord . . .' quoted in Kershaw *Nemesis op. cit.*, p. 578

p. 173 'Hitler refused to accept . . .' Overy *The Dictators op. cit.*, p. 532

p. 175 'The gap in organization . . .' Overy *Russia's War op. cit.*, p. 198

p. 176 'the strengthening of our armoured forces . . .' quoted in Roger Hoch *Mein Leben* dated 10 July 1964. In the early 1960s Hoch conducted research into the German armoured forces for an account of his life that he wrote and printed for his family archive

p. 176 'We could clearly bury . . .' quoted in Healy *Zitadelle op. cit.*, p. 41

p. 177 'The Soviets seemed intent . . .' figures from Healy *Operation Zitadelle op. cit.*, p. 43

p. 177 '[I]t is necessary for us . . .' quoted in Kurowski *Operation 'Zitadelle' op. cit.*, p. 4

p. 178 'The objective of the attack . . .' quoted in Kurowski *Operation 'Zitadelle' op. cit.*, p. 5

p. 178 'the Russian defences . . .' Mellenthin *op. cit.*, p. 261

p. 178 'Everything now depends . . .' quoted in Kurowski *Operation 'Zitadelle' op. cit.*, p. 8

p. 179 'Our offensive is of . . .' *Excerpts from Hitler's Speeches, Lectures and Addresses* June 1960. Author's archive

p. 179 '[A]s early as March . . .' David M. Glantz and Harold S. Orenstein (eds) *The Battle for Kursk 1943: The Soviet General Staff Study* Frank Cass 1999, p. 28

p. 180 'We can expect the enemy . . .' Georgi K. Zhukov *Marshal Zhukov's Greatest Battles* Cooper Square Press, New York 2002, p. 209

p. 180 'I consider it would be unsound . . .' quoted in Mawdsley *op. cit.*, pp. 264–5

p. 180 'The Supreme Commander listened . . .' quoted in Healy *Zitadelle op. cit.*, p. 53

p. 180 'meet the enemy attack . . .' Glantz and Orenstein *op. cit.*, p. 28

p. 181 'Appropriate orders were . . .' Zhukov *Greatest Battles op. cit.*, pp. 215–16

p. 181 '[O]ur intelligence was able . . .' quoted in Mawdsley *op. cit.*, p. 265

p. 182 'The Red Army would gain . . .' Mawdsley *op. cit.*, p. 264

p. 183 'heavy tank casualties . . .' Mellenthin *op. cit.*, p. 262

p. 184 'More tanks! More officers! . . .' quoted in W. Haupt *Army Group Center – The Wehrmacht in Russia 1941–1945* Schiffer Military History, Atglen, PA 1997, p. 148

p. 184 'produced air photographs . . .' Mellenthin *op. cit.*, p. 262

p. 185 'For two months . . .' Mellenthin *op. cit.*, p. 263

p. 185 'The attacking forces . . .' figures from N. Zetterling and A. Frankson *Kursk 1943: A Statistical Analysis* Cass 2000, p. 18

p. 185 'From the strategic aspect . . .' Mellenthin *op. cit.*, p. 262

p. 185 'Model's main effort was to be made . . .' figures from Zetterling and Frankson *op. cit.*, pp. 29–31

p. 186 'It was a risky plan . . .' Healy *Zitadelle op. cit.*, p. 101

p. 187 'My God, the man's an idiot . . .' quoted in Healy *Zitadelle op. cit.*, p. 27

p. 188 'our success will demand . . .' quoted in Lloyd Clark *Elite Fighting Units on the Eastern Front 1941–43*, an unpublished paper to the War Studies Society, King's College, University of London, November 1994, p. 3

p. 189 'If any one tank deserves . . .' Healy *Zitadelle op. cit.*, p. 62

p. 190 '[T]he power of their guns . . .' quoted in Lloyd Clark *op. cit.*, p. 6

p. 190 'It should also be noted . . .' figures from Healy *Zitadelle op. cit.*, pp. 375–6

p. 190 'I worked with the Heinkel . . .' interview with Ludwig Schein, 15 April 2009

p. 191 'Our job was made . . .' interview with Ludwig Schein, 15 April 2009

p. 191 'It was stated that . . .' Healy *Zitadelle op. cit.*, p. 105

p. 193 'In total, the Front . . .' figures from Zetterling and Frankson *op. cit.*, p. 20

p. 193 'Lieutenant-General I.M. Chistyakov's . . .' figures from Zetterling and Frankson *op. cit.*, pp. 33–5

p. 194 'This made the total Soviet . . .' figures from Zetterling and Frankson *op. cit.*, p. 20

p. 194 'The General Staff took steps . . .' Zhukov *Greatest Battles op. cit.*, pp. 216–17

p. 196 'I much preferred the . . .' interview with Dimitri Trzemin, 20 December 2008

p. 196 'The KV-1's limitations . . .' figures from Zetterling and Frankson *op. cit.*, p. 69

p. 196 'studying the situation . . .' Zhukov *Greatest Battles op. cit.*, p. 223

p. 197 'We had to remain aware . . .' Raus *op. cit.*, p. 200

p. 198 'In Army Group Centre's . . .' figures from Healy *Zitadelle op. cit.*, p. 75

p. 198 'Irregular activity meant . . .' telephone interview with Dr Karl Hertzog, 3 September 2009

p. 198 'The Ninth Army, for example . . .' figures quoted in Healy *Zitadelle op. cit.*, p. 93

p. 198 'In anticipation of heavy . . .' figure quoted in Merridale *op. cit.*, p. 177

p. 198 'The build-up of Soviet resources . . .' Dokumenty sovetskogo komandovaniia v period Velikoi Otechestvennoi voiny (aprel–mai 1943), Central Archive of the Russian Ministry of Defence, Podolsk

p. 198 'I recorded a conversation . . .' Werth *op. cit.*, p. 120

p. 199 'For nights on end . . .' Mellenthin *op. cit.*, p. 266

p. 199 'In mid-June we spent . . .' interview with Max Sulzer, 18 August 2008. Sulzer was knocked down by a speeding vehicle while assisting with some signals cable on 1 July and suffered a broken leg and two broken ribs

p. 199 'day and night . . .' quoted in Robert Kershaw *Tank Men* Hodder and Stoughton 2008, p. 247

p. 200 'We divided our sector . . .' interview with Fyodor Onton, 12 September 2009

p. 200 '503,663 anti-tank mines . . .' figures from Zetterling and Frankson *op. cit.*, p. 22

p. 201 'At last, we had some heavy . . .' Mansur Abdulin *Red Road from Stalingrad: Recollections of a Soviet Infantryman* Pen and Sword, Barnsley 2004, p. 89

p. 201 'The basic plan . . .' Nikolai Litvin *800 Days on the Eastern Front: A Russian Soldier Remembers World War II* University Press of Kansas, Lawrence, Kansas 2007, p. 10

p. 202 'Staffs, units, and formations . . .' Glantz and Orenstein *op. cit.*, p. 50

p. 203 'During 1943, Lend-Lease . . .' figures from Overy *Russia's War op. cit.*, p. 194

p. 203 'Before Kursk we went . . .' interview with Dimitri Trzemin, 20 December 2008

p. 203 'Survive and Succeed' pamphlet dated 16 March 1943, provided by Dimitri Trzemin. Author's collection

p. 203 'use speed to your advantage . . .' 'Survive and Succeed' pamphlet dated 16 March 1943, pp. 3–7

p. 204 'Whenever there was a lull . . .' Litvin *op. cit.*, p. 12

p. 204 'It is very hot . . .' Abdulin *op. cit.*, pp. 88–9

p. 205 'considering Russian dispositions . . .' Raus *op. cit.*, p. 197

p. 205 'XI Corps staff made . . .' Raus *op. cit.*, p. 196

p. 206 'We were used to the war . . .' interview with Tanya Vershvovski, 12 October 2009. Vershvovski, a 15-year-old orphan, was evacuated from the farm on the second day of the battle. The truck in which she was travelling was attacked by a

German aircraft, but she reached the rear area and ended up working on a farm near Gomel with her sister

p. 207 'The hardship in the countryside . . .' Merridale *op. cit.*, p. 180

p. 207 'The armies that would fight . . .' Merridale *op. cit.*, p. 183

p. 208 'Probably none of us . . .' quoted in Kershaw *Tank Men op. cit.*, p. 254

p. 208 'Typical concerns among front-line troops . . .' the author asked each of the interviewees for this book questions about their fears. In common with the same question asked of troops fighting in other theatres during the war, death, mutilation and fear of failure appeared most regularly in answers

p. 208 'the average T-34 survived . . .' figures from Merridale *op. cit.*, p. 187

p. 208 'Others from outside . . .' quoted in Kershaw *Tank Men op. cit.*, p. 250

p. 209 'It took place during . . .' quoted in Kershaw *Tank Men op. cit.*, p. 247

p. 209 '21 June 1943 is a date . . .' interview with V.M., 20 May 2009

p. 210 'In the intense air battle . . .' figures from Healy *Zitadelle op. cit.*, p. 73

p. 210 'It was a truly worrying . . .' interview with Bernard Roth, 20 October 2009

p. 212 'Today another two . . .' quoted in Merridale *op. cit.*, p. 188

p. 212 'On the night of 2 July . . .' quoted in Healy *Zitadelle op. cit.*, p. 191

p. 213 'Bad weather meant . . .' interview with Ludwig Schein, 15 April 2009

p. 213 'Stuck under my cape . . .' interview with Bernard Roth, 20 October 2009

p. 213 'We had a tarpaulin . . .' interview with Dimitri Trzemin, 20 December 2008

p. 214 'had the entire platoon . . .' Patrick Agate *Michael Wittmann and the Waffen SS Tiger Commanders of the Leibstandarte in WWII Volume One* Stackpole Books, Mechanicsburg, PA 1996, p. 93

p. 214 'Soldiers! Today you . . .' quoted in Haupt *Army Group Center op. cit.*, p. 152

p. 214 'While German officers . . .' Robin Cross *Citadel: The Battle of Kursk* Michael O'Mara Books 1993, p. 155

p. 215 'Don't rush me . . .' quoted in Kershaw *Tank Men* p. 255

p. 215 'I am in a flamethrowing team . . .' quoted in Cross *op. cit.*, p. 157

p. 216 'a symphony from hell . . .' quoted in Merridale *op. cit.*, p. 188

p. 216 'The shells came plunging . . .' interview with Bernard Roth, 20 October 2009

p. 216 '[W]e had expected . . .' quoted in Healy *Zitadelle op. cit.*, p. 196

p. 217 'I said to myself . . .' quoted in Kershaw *Tank Men op. cit.*, p. 259

Chapter 6: Breaking In

p. 219 'Ivan bullets zipped . . .' interview with Raimund Rüffer, 12 August 2009. Rüffer was attended to by a medic and sent immediately to field hospital where he underwent an operation. After several weeks' recuperation, he arrived back in Germany on 1 September

p. 221 'At last we were . . .' telephone interview with Johan Müller, 16 March 2009

p. 222 'I had just gathered . . .' quoted in Christer Bergström *Kursk: The Air Battle* Ian Allen, Hersham 2007, p. 27

p. 222 'Over the radio, crews . . .' figures from Healy *Zitadelle op. cit.*, p. 20

p. 222 'In their great excitement . . .' quoted in Bergström *op. cit.*, pp. 28–9

p. 223 'We ran into a heavy AAA . . .' quoted in Bergström *op. cit.*, p. 31

p. 223 'As we approached . . .' letter from T. Simutenkov dated 13 September 2008. Simutenkov had landed approximately six miles behind the front line and was picked up by the Red Army infantry. After a glass of vodka at an unknown unit headquarters, he was guided back down the line and, eventually, two days later, rejoined his squadron

p. 224 'The Germans gained air . . .' figures from Bergström *op. cit.*, pp. 77–8

p. 224 'Our aviation fought . . .' quoted in Bergström *op. cit.*, p. 32

p. 225 'We arrived for the battle . . .' interview with Gerd Küster, 21 September 2009

p. 226 'The guards rifle division . . .' quoted in Healy *Zitadelle op. cit.*, p. 205

p. 226 'Everything is shrouded . . .' David M. Glantz and Jonathan M. House *The Battle of Kursk* The University Press of Kansas, Lawrence, Kansas 1999, p. 96

p. 227 'The job needed a steady . . .' Paul Carell *Scorched Earth – Hitler's War on Russia: The Story of the German Defeat in the East* George G. Harrap 1964, p. 37

p. 227 'The task was time-consuming . . .' telephone interview with Henri Schnabel, 2 November 2009

p. 228 'We understood that this . . .' interview with Gunar Francks, 4 June 2009

p. 228 'The entire corps sector . . .' quoted in Bergström *op. cit.*, p. 31

p. 229 'It was enough to make . . .' Helmuth Spaeter *The History of the Panzer Corps Grossdeutschland Vol. II* J.J. Fedorowicz, Winnipeg 1995, p. 116

p. 229 'Soviet air forces repeatedly . . .' quoted in Bergström *op. cit.*, p. 32

p. 230 'Now was the moment . . .' interview with Mykhailo Petrik, 1 June 2008

p. 231 'counted twice as much . . .' Kershaw *Tank Men op. cit.*, p. 264

p. 231 'Providing quick and effective ground . . .' quoted in Bergström *op. cit.*, p. 29

p. 232 'We had the enemy pinned down . . .' interview with Mykhailo Petrik, 1 June 2008

p. 233 'Be careful, comrades! . . .' quoted in Kurowski *Panzer Aces op. cit.*, p. 303

p. 234 'I was not afraid of going . . .' interview with Michail Khodorovsky, 3 June 2008

p. 234 'It was 4:15 am . . .' quoted in Healy *Zitadelle op. cit.*, p. 207

p. 235 'I could not stand . . .' Roger Hoch interview, 6 March 2010

p. 236 'The worst was the anti-tank . . .' quoted in Kershaw *Tank Men op. cit.*, p. 264

p. 236 'You should always act . . .' Abdulin *op. cit.*, p. 89

p. 236 '[W]e worked our way . . .' quoted in Cross *op. cit.*, p. 174

p. 237 'I left my heavier kit . . .' letter from Stefan Witte dated 16 July 2008

p. 237 'The Tigers rumbled on . . .' quoted in Carell *op. cit.*, p. 60

p. 238 'This is the hour of the tank . . .' quoted in Healy *Zitadelle op. cit.*, pp. 213–14

p. 239 'move, pause and fire . . .' quoted in Kershaw *Tank Men op. cit.*, p. 267

p. 239 'I had an encounter . . .' quoted in Kershaw *Tank Men op. cit.*, p. 267

p. 240 'Follow me . . .' quoted in Kershaw *Tank Men op. cit.*, p. 261

p. 240 'I directed the driver . . .' quoted in Kershaw *Tank Men op. cit.*, p. 262

p. 241 'The T-34's turret . . .' quoted in Kurowski *Panzer Aces op. cit.*, p. 304

p. 241 'The day's work had cost . . .' quoted in Glantz and House *op. cit.*, p. 100

p. 242 'We sped westwards to . . .' letter from Nicolai Andreev dated 18 August 2009. Andreev became a casualty later that day when he was knocked unconscious by a German shell while the tank was rearming. After suffering days of headaches and eventually losing his sight temporarily, he was taken to a field hospital and diagnosed with a fractured skull

p. 243 '[S]uddenly, a 'red sunrise' . . .' quoted in Healy *Zitadelle op. cit.*, p. 217

p. 244 'The Russian artillery opens . . .' quoted in Cross *op. cit.*, p. 178

p. 244 'The Tigers were extremely . . .' interview with Rolf Schmidt, 16 August 2008

p. 245 'My foot presses forward . . .' quoted in Cross *op. cit.*, pp. 178–9

p. 246 '[T]he advancing infantry . . .' Raus *op. cit.*, p. 202

p. 246 'The first Soviet line . . .' figure from Raus *op. cit.*, p. 204

p. 248 'We were not convinced . . .' letter from (Major) Jan Möschen dated 16 May 2008

p. 248 'On the Western Front . . .' interview with Max Torst, 22 October 2009

p. 250 'We made several sorties . . .' interview with Koba Lomidze, 11 December 2009

p. 250 'I had not seen . . .' interview with Max Torst, 22 October 2009

p. 251 'We put an emphasis . . .' interview with (Lieutnant) Thomas Lohr, 24 October 2009

p. 251 'During the resultant three-hour . . .' figures from a letter from Thomas Lohr dated 12 November 2009

p. 252 'The sky blackened from smoke . . .' quoted in Glantz and House *op. cit.*, p. 88

p. 253 'It was a frightening moment . . .' interview with Fyodor Onton, 12 September 2009

p. 253 'The tanks continued to advance . . .' Litvin *op. cit.*, pp. 12–13

p. 254 'Everything had been done . . .' quoted in Carell *op. cit.*, p. 41

p. 254 '[i]ncapable of close-range . . .' quoted in Cross *op. cit.*, p. 165

p. 256 'Far ahead of the . . .' quoted in Healy *Zitadelle op. cit.*, p. 229

p. 257 'Higher headquarters had been hoping . . .' Raus *op. cit.*, p. 204

p. 258 'Have we gained control . . .' quoted in Bergström *op. cit.*, p. 40

p. 258 'cautiously optimistic . . .' quoted in a letter from (Major) Jan Möschen dated 16 May 2008

Chapter 7: Breaking Through

p. 261 'Nurse Olga Iofe dressed . . .' interview with Olga Iofe, 1 June 2008

p. 264 'We knew that the Germans . . .' interview with Sasha Reznikova, 16 April 2008

p. 264 '[The enemy] did not suspect . . .' M.E. Katukov *Na ostrie glavnogo udara* Voenizdat, Moscow 1976, p. 54

p. 266 'Although it was noon . . .' Katukov *op. cit.*, p. 54

p. 267 'We could still capture Teterevino . . .' quoted in R. Lehmann *The Leibstandarte Volume III* J.J. Fedorowicz, Winnipeg 1990, pp. 216–17

p. 268 'obscure battles along the flanks . . .' Glantz and House *op. cit.*, p. 111

p. 268 'a considerable defensive victory . . .' Raus *op. cit.*, p. 206

p. 268 '6 July: Today we took . . .' diary entry by Leo Koettel, dated 6 July 1943. Author's collection. Despite his duties, Koettel, who had kept a diary since the age of eight, managed to provide an entry for every day of the battle

p. 269 '[we] came to a halt under . . .' quoted in Healy *Zitadelle op. cit.*, p. 240

p. 269 'Never before had a major . . .' quoted in Healy *Zitadelle op. cit.*, p. 241

p. 270 'It was a hard slog . . .' letter from Peter Maschmann to his father dated 10 July 1943. Author's collection

p. 270 'momentum be maintained . . .' XLVIII Panzer Korps Operational Order 5 July 1943 NAM T-313 Roll 369 Anlagen 13 zum KTB Lagenkarten PzAOK4 Ia 25.3.43–30.7.43 PaAOK4, 34888/17 National Archives, Washington D.C.

p. 270 'The entire area has . . .' quoted in Glantz and House *op. cit.*, p. 107

p. 271 'It was not a job . . .' interview with Peter Maschmann, 15 August 2008

p. 271 '[A] heavy tank battle developed . . .' Spaeter *op. cit.*, pp. 121–2

p. 272 'II SS Panzer Corps reported . . .' figure from Healy *Zitadelle op. cit.*, p. 238

p. 273 'to exhaust the enemy at prepared . . .' quoted in Glantz and House *op. cit.*, p. 114

p. 274 'Rudel alone replaces . . .' http://www.pilotenbunker.de/ Stuka/rudel accessed 26 April 2010

p. 274 'The aircraft had a devastating . . .' Hans-Ulrich Rudel *Stuka Pilot: The War Memoirs of Hans-Ulrich Rudel* Barbarossa Books 2006, p. 50

p. 274 'We tried to hit the tanks . . .' Rudel *op. cit.*, p. 124

p. 275 'During repeated attacks . . .' Spaeter *op. cit.*, p. 22

p. 275 'The fleeing masses were caught . . .' Mellenthin *op. cit.*, p. 265

p. 276 'The ground gradually lit up . . .' Artyom Zeldovich unpublished memoir dated 1962 (unpaginated). Kursk chapter provided by Zeldovich's grandson, Stephan Osetrov

p. 277 'We had to keep pace . . .' interview with Karl Stumpp, 18 August 2009

p. 277 'The backbone of the German . . .' quoted in Healy *Zitadelle op. cit.*, p. 262

p. 278 'A couple of days later . . .' figures from Healy *Zitadelle op. cit.*, p. 262

p. 278 'The next two or three days . . .' quoted in Mark Healy *Kursk 1943: The Tide Turns in the East* Osprey 1992, p. 64

p. 278 'On no account must . . .' quoted in Healy *The Tide Turns in the East op. cit.*, p. 64

p. 279 'tie down enemy forces . . .' Zhukov *Greatest Battles op. cit.*, p. 76

p. 279 'Night fell but no rest . . .' Spaeter *op. cit.*, p. 30

p. 279 'This was the fourth night . . .' telephone interview with Henri Schnabel, 2 November 2009

p. 279 'I hardly recall the first days . . .' interview with Feliks Karelin, 18 May 2007

p. 280 'It was extremely hot . . .' quoted in Agate *op. cit.*, p. 64

p. 281 'SS Senior Corporal Pötter . . .' see Kurowski *Panzer Aces op. cit.*, p. 308

p. 281 'My own tiredness was offset . . .' interview with Leutnant Walter Graff, 16 August 2008

p. 283 'We are under extreme pressure . . .' diary entry of Georg Grosch dated 7 July 1943

p. 284 'I have to say that the Germans . . .' interview with Sasha Reznikova, 16 April 2008

p. 285 'The 3rd Company of Kunin's . . .' quoted in Carell *op. cit.*, p. 69

p. 285 'We saw in the distance . . .' quoted in Healy *Zitadelle op. cit.*, p. 272

p. 286 '[A] pack of T-34s and one . . .' quoted in Carell *op. cit.*, pp. 70–71

p. 287 'Ferocious, unparalleled tank battles . . .' quoted in Healy *The Tide Turns in the East op. cit.*, pp. 68–9

p. 287 'The Russian ground-attack aircraft . . .' quoted in Kurowski *Zitadelle op. cit.*, pp. 268–9

p. 287 'The rounds crack, whistle . . .' quoted in Kurowski *Zitadelle op. cit.*, pp. 269

p. 288 'The prospects for a breakthrough . . .' notes of a conversation between Manstein and Hoth taken by Major Jan Möschen, dated 16 May 2008

p. 288 'considerable Soviet armoured . . .' RS 2–2/13 II SS-Panzerkorps Anhang zum KTB Nr. 5: Vorbereitungen zum Unternehmen 'Zitadelle' 10 Apr–31 Mai 1943, Das Bundesarchiv, Freiburg

p. 289 'I decided to change . . .' quoted in Bergström *op. cit.*, p. 42

p. 290 'the decisive battle-winning . . .' Healy *Zitadelle op. cit.*, p. 249

p. 290 'The impact of their attack . . .' quoted in Bergström *op. cit.*, p. 44

p. 291 'Every second that passed . . .' interview with Herbert Forman, 2 August 2008

p. 291 'I took up a position . . .' interview with Marc Doerr, 3 August 2008

p. 291 'There was a lethal cocktail . . .' interview with Vladimir Severinov, 16 June 2009

p. 292 'The tanks came out . . .' interview with Herbert Forman, 2 August 2008

p. 294 'At around 6:00 a.m . . .' Litvin *op. cit.*, pp. 17–18

p. 295 'I saw my own unavoidable . . .' Litvin *op. cit.*, p. 20

p. 296 'All day the roar of battle . . .' Zhukov *Greatest Battles op. cit.*, p. 237

p. 297 'here was the key to . . .' Carell *op. cit.*, p. 45

p. 298 'By 7–8 July the Soviets were . . .' quoted in Bergström *op. cit.*, p. 53

p. 298 'Lieutenant Hänsch rallied . . .' Carell *op. cit.*, p. 46

p. 299 'We could see the tanks assembling . . .' letter from Valentin Lebedev dated 3 May 2008

p. 301 'Stories about 45mm cannons . . .' Grossman *op. cit.*, pp. 230–31

p. 302 'Artillery, mortars, Stalin organs . . .' quoted in Healy *Zitadelle op. cit.*, p. 282

p. 303 'At the head of my men . . .' quoted in Kurowski *Operation 'Zitadelle' op. cit.*, p. 60

p. 303 'The Russians laid down a curtain . . .' quoted in Carell *op. cit.*, p. 47

p. 304 'At a little over 700 yards . . .' quoted in Healy *Zitadelle op. cit.*, p. 285

p. 304 'particularly distinguished themselves . . .' Zhukov *Greatest Battles op. cit.*, p. 237

p. 305 'after fierce battles along . . .' quoted in Glantz and House *op. cit.*, p. 120

p. 305 'continue to maintain offensive . . .' letter from (Major) Jan Möschen dated 8 August 2008

p. 305 'it is now essential to inflict . . .' excerpt from *OKW War Diary* 11 July 1943

p. 306 'Here, on the sector of the Central Front . . .' quoted in Healy *Zitadelle op. cit.*, p. 286

Chapter 8: Anticipation

p. 309 'The partisans struck . . .' interview with Samuel Erwin, 3 February 2010

p. 310 'They were a constant menace . . .' interview with Felix Dresener, 19 February 2010

p. 311 'On 7 July, for example . . .' figures quoted in Healy *Zitadelle op. cit.*, p. 267

p. 311 'On the following day . . .' figures quoted in Glantz and House *op. cit.*, p. 137

p. 312 'If it was not bad enough . . .' interview with Igor Panesenko, 16 May 2009

p. 313 'It reminded me of a football . . .' interview with Igor Panesenko, 16 May 2009. Panesenko was marched to Tomarovka with around 200 other prisoners. He escaped on 11 July when a Soviet air raid on the town led to his captors fleeing. Taking the opportunity to break out of the flimsy barn in which they had been incarcerated, Panesenko ran and hid in the fields. He evaded capture for long enough to link up with friendly forces in mid-August

p. 313 'Our tanks soon ran into . . .' Spaeter *op. cit.*, p. 125

p. 314 'in hindsight the diversion . . .' quoted in Healy *Zitadelle op. cit.*, p. 290

p. 314 'commissar and Red Army . . .' Spaeter *op. cit.*, p. 127

p. 315 'We needed more aircraft . . .' interview with Ludwig Schein, 15 April 2009

p. 315 'Over the period 7–8 . . .' figures from Bergström *op. cit.*, p. 68

p. 316 '[W]e found the same scene . . .' quoted in Bergström *op. cit.*, p. 68

p. 317 'Suddenly I saw [Feldwebel] Lohberg's . . .' quoted in Bergström *op. cit.*, p. 68

p. 317 '[Our aviation] did not . . .' quoted in Glantz and Orenstein *op. cit.*, p. 137

p. 318 'LAH, for example, reported . . .' figures from RS 2–2/13 II. SS-Panzerkorps Anhang zum KTB Nr. 5: Vorbereitungen zum Unternehmen 'Zitadelle' 10 Apr–31 Mai 1943, Das Bundesarchiv, Freiburg

p. 318 'The whole area was flattened . . .' interview with Arnold Brenner, 17 April 2009

p. 319 'a very severe battle . . .' quoted in Kershaw *Tank Men op. cit.*, p. 256

p. 319 'Rotmistrov's 593 tanks . . .' figures from Glantz and House *op. cit.*, p. 327

p. 319 'Even now, writing several decades . . .' P.A. Rotmistrov *Stal'naia gvardiia* Voenizdat, Moscow 1984, p. 296

p. 319 'The move to Prokhorovka . . .' quoted in Kershaw *Tank Men op. cit.*, p. 257

p. 319 'What a great advantage it was . . .' interview with Semen Berezhko, 3 February 2010

p. 320 'the 80,000 men . . .' figures from Glantz and House *op. cit.*, p. 324

p. 320 'A panoply of former military . . .' Glantz and House *op. cit.*, p. 147

p. 320 'encircle and defeat the main . . .' quoted in Healy *Zitadelle op. cit.*, p. 304

p. 320 'anticipate an engagement with . . .' quoted in Healy *Zitadelle op. cit.*, p. 95

p. 320 'Having failed to penetrate . . .' quoted in Healy *Zitadelle op. cit.*, p. 299

p. 321 'Moreover, the Fourth Panzer Army . . .' figures from Zetterling and Frankson *op. cit.*, p. 103

p. 321 'Under cloud covered skies . . .' quoted in Kurowski *Operation 'Zitadelle' op. cit.*, p. 148

p. 321 'At last I have a moment . . .' journal entry by Ralph Faber dated

10 July 1943, provided by his daughter, Sophie Barker. Author's collection

p. 322 'We attacked a column south ...' interview with Boris Vassilieva, 16 July 2009

p. 322 'When we approached the target ...' quoted in Bergström *op. cit.*, p. 74

p. 323 'squadron after squadron of Stukas ...' quoted in Mellenthin *op. cit.*, p. 273

p. 323 'Many of our soldiers and commanders ...' quoted in Glantz and House *op. cit.*, p. 156

p. 324 'I suddenly saw fiery arrows ...' quoted in Spaeter *op. cit.*, p. 128

p. 324 'The highest point on the approaches ...' Carell *op. cit.*, p. 72

p. 325 'After days of fighting ...' Heinrich Huber telephone interview, 10 July 2008

p. 325 'The scene along the banks ...' interview with Anatoli Abalakov, 12 June 2008

p. 326 'There was lively enemy ...' quoted in Kurowski *Operation 'Zitadelle' op. cit.*, pp. 149–50

p. 328 'Each day we expected ...' interview with Rolf Schmidt, 16 August 2008

p. 328 'I was sent to see the operations ...' interview with Major Leo Spiegel, 18 May 2009

p. 329 'Should the attack be continued ...' quoted in Healy *Zitadelle op. cit.*, p. 310

p. 330 'Breakthrough ...' Rolf Schmidt diary entry dated 11 July 1943

p. 331 'Enemy infantry are retreating ...' RH 21–4/122 Panzergruppen, Panzerarmeen Operation 'Zitadelle' 15 Mai–9 Juli 1943, Das Bundesarchiv, Freiburg

p. 331 'All day we fought for scraps ...' interview with Arnold Brenner, 17 April 2009

p. 332 'Having fought on the road to Prokhorovka ...' interview with Lev Drachevsky, 1 May 2009

p. 333 'From nowhere came . . .' notes on Zitadelle written by Alexander Simm dated August 1952. Author's collection

p. 333 'The Luftwaffe was not . . .' interview with Paul Meuller, 2 February 2010

p. 334 'We called in Stuka assistance . . .' quoted in Bergström *op. cit.*, p. 75

p. 335 'When only several hundred . . .' quoted in Glantz and House *op. cit.*, pp. 173–4

p. 336 'maintain Fourth Panzer Army's . . .' RH 21–4/122 Panzergruppen, Panzerarmeen Operation 'Zitadelle' 15 Mai–9 Juli 1943, Das Bundesarchiv, Freiburg

p. 336 'Deliver a counterstroke . . .' quoted in Healy *Zitadelle op. cit.*, p. 322

p. 337 'Our route passed through Prokhorovka . . .' Rotmistrov *op. cit.*, pp. 181–2

p. 338 'Those men would have been . . .' interview with Major Leo Spiegel, 18 May 2009

Chapter 9: Finale

p. 341 'While the rest of the 28th Guards . . .' interview with Pavel Krylov and Dimitri Lachinov, 12 February 2010

p. 343 'It wasn't until dawn on 12 July . . .' quoted in Agate *op. cit.*, p. 125

p. 344 'In front of him were 294 . . .' figures from Zetterling and Frankson *op. cit.*, p. 107. For detail on the vexed subject of the number of tanks involved in the Battle of Prokhorovka and the number eventually destroyed, see Chapter 7 of Zetterling and Frankson's most illuminating and helpful volume

p. 344 'In a tank battle against the panzers . . .' letter from Y. Sirmnov dated 16 August 2009

p. 344 'Neither before nor since . . .' Abdulin *op. cit.*, p. 91

p. 344 'We waited with dry mouths . . .' telephone interview with Yuri Ruslanova, 6 February 2010

p. 344 '[W]e enlisted men . . .' quoted in Agate *op. cit.*, p. 125

p. 345 'I do not know what our trench . . .' interview with Pavel Krylov and Dimitri Lachinov, 12 February 2010

p. 345 'a cyclone of fire unleashed by our artillery . . .' quoted in Healy *Zitadelle op. cit.*, p. 331

p. 346 'successful struggle with [Tigers and Ferdinands] . . .' quoted in Healy *Zitadelle op. cit.*, p. 328

p. 347 'A purple wall of smoke rose . . .' quoted in Kurowski *Panzer Aces op. cit.*, pp. 178–9

p. 348 'The distance between the tanks . . .' Artem Drabkin and Oleg Sheremet *T-34 in Action – Soviet Tank Troops in WWII* Stackpole Books, Mechanicsburg, PA 2006, p. 131

p. 348 'You wouldn't have thought . . .' quoted in Kershaw *Tank Men op. cit.*, p. 273

p. 349 'We halted ten metres behind . . .' quoted in Kurowski *Panzer Aces op. cit.*, p. 181

p. 349 'My tank was hit . . .' Drabkin and Sheremet *op. cit.*, p. 131

p. 350 'The tanks were moving across . . .' quoted in Carell *op. cit.*, pp. 81–2

p. 350 'The noise, heat, smoke . . .' interview with Anatoly Volkov, 8 August 2009

p. 351 'We roll on again . . .' quoted in Healy *Zitadelle op. cit.*, p. 337

p. 351 'On the smoke and dust-shrouded . . .' quoted in Kurowski *Panzer Aces op. cit.*, p. 180

p. 352 'In warfare, numbers alone do . . .' Nipe *op. cit.*, pp. 39–40

p. 352 'We found ourselves taking . . .' quoted in Cross *op. cit.*, p. 215

p. 352 'We saw the turret of a very slow . . .' quoted in Kurowski *Operation 'Zitadelle' op. cit.*, pp. 164–5

p. 353 'They were around us . . .' quoted in Lehmann *op. cit.*, p. 234

p. 354 'We were singled out by a T-34 . . .' quoted in Agate *op. cit.*, p. 66

p. 355 'stood like a rock in the breakers . . .' quoted in Kurowski *Operation 'Zitadelle' op. cit.*, p. 160

p. 355 'Smoke and fumes were so thick . . .' quoted in Kurowski *Operation 'Zitadelle' op. cit.*, p. 161

p. 355 'Soviet as well as German . . .' quoted in Bergström *op. cit.*, p. 80

p. 356 'Despite the Red Air Force's . . .' figures from Bergström *op. cit.*, p. 78

p. 356 'Our own air cover was fully . . .' quoted in Bergström *op. cit.*, p. 81

p. 356 '[T]he enemy's aircraft. . .' quoted in Bergström *op. cit.*, p. 80

p. 356 'With these gigantic offerings . . .' quoted in Bergström *op. cit.*, p. 79

p. 357 'It is not too much to say that . . .' quoted in Bergström *op. cit.*, p. 81

p. 357 'from a distance of 10 to 30 . . .' Lehmann *op. cit.*, p. 236

p. 358 'The morning was a blur . . .' interview with Pavel Krylov and Dimitri Lachinov, 12 February 2010

p. 360 'The enemy advanced with great . . .' interview with Anatoli Abalakov, 12 June 2008

p. 360 'The decisive movement of these brigades . . .' Rotmistrov *op. cit.*, pp. 189–90

p. 361 'Racing at full speed and firing . . .' Lehmann *op. cit.*, pp. 234–5

p. 362 'The Russian attacks on our flanks . . .' quoted in Healy *Zitadelle op. cit.*, p. 341

p. 363 'Radio silence. No fire . . .' quoted in Carell *op. cit.*, p. 84

p. 364 'Demolition charge attached . . .' quoted in Carell *op. cit.*, pp. 84–6

p. 366 'The roar of guns continued . . .' Abdulin *op. cit.*, p. 91

p. 366 'I had served in Poland, France . . .' telephone interview with Albert Thimm, 6 December 2009

p. 367 'All day long planes fired . . .' Abdulin *op. cit.*, p. 92

p. 367 'As a result of these heavy . . .' Spaeter *op. cit.*, pp. 129–30

p. 368 '[The division] was dangerously weak . . .' Mellenthin *op. cit.*, p. 276

p. 370 'In a short period of time all . . .' quoted in Healy *Zitadelle op. cit.*, p. 342

p. 371 'What have you done . . .' quoted in Healy *Zitadelle op. cit.*, p. 348

p. 371 'coordinating the Steppe . . .' quoted in Healy *Zitadelle op. cit.*, p. 348

p. 371 'I was exhausted at the end . . .' interview with Pavel Krylov and Dimitri Lachinov, 12 February 2010

p. 372 'More than fifty enemy tanks . . .' Rotmistrov *op. cit.*, p. 194

p. 373 'We were caught by a salvo . . .' quoted in Agate *op. cit.*, p. 128

p. 373 'There seemed to have been . . .' interview with Rudi Bauermann, 2 March 2009

p. 375 'parts of the leg were joined . . .' quoted in Kershaw *Tank Men op. cit.*, p. 274

p. 376 'What is more, by 12 July . . .' figures from Irving *op. cit.*, p. 535

p. 376 'The loss of Sicily is practically . . .' quoted in Healy *Zitadelle op. cit.*, p. 353

p. 377 'Speaking for my own Army Group . . .' quoted in Nipe *op. cit.*, p. 56

p. 377 'We were now in the position . . .' Mellenthin *op. cit.*, p. 277

p. 378 'until it had achieved its aim . . .' quoted in Glantz and House *op. cit.*, p. 254

p. 379 'Solidly they accepted casualties . . .' James Lucas *Das Reich: The Military Role of 2d SS Division* Arms and Armour 1991, p. 112

p. 379 'After examining the situation . . .' Zhukov *Memoirs op. cit.*, p. 461

p. 380 'We were just one of scores . . .' interview with Stanislav Usov, 3 March 2009

p. 381 'Although I had been at the front . . .' interview with Rudi Bauermann, 2 March 2009

p. 382 'the enemy no longer posed . . .' quoted in Healy *Zitadelle op. cit.*, p. 355

Conclusion

p. 383 'As a result of the Kursk battle . . .' quoted in Glantz and House *op. cit.*, p. 279

p. 384 'These three immense battles . . .' Winston Churchill *The Second World War Volume VI Triumph and Tragedy* Penguin 1985, p. 230

p. 386 'it was no longer possible . . .' Karl-Heinz Frieser et al *op. cit.*, p. 79

p. 387 'The Russian High Command . . .' Mellenthin *op. cit.*, p. 278

p. 387 'Even though II SS Panzer Corps . . .' figures from Zetterling and Frankson *op. cit.*, pp. 108–9

p. 388 'And so the last German offensive . . .' quoted in Glantz and House *op. cit.*, p. 256

p. 388 'Rokossovsky and Vatutin lost . . .' figures from Zetterling and Frankson *op. cit.*, Chapter 8

p. 388 'It was not by tank duels . . .' Karl-Heinz Frieser et al *op. cit.*, p. 80

p. 389 'We had suffered a decisive defeat . . .' Guderian *Panzer Leader op. cit.*, pp. 251–2

p. 389 'The Red Army had proved . . .' quoted in Karl-Heinz Frieser et al *op. cit.*, p. 80

p. 389 'The defeat of the main grouping . . .' quoted in Glantz and House *op. cit.*, p. 278

p. 389 'Stalingrad was the end . . .' quoted in Karl-Heinz Frieser et al *op. cit.*, p. 82

Bibliography

Primary sources
United Kingdom
National Archives, Kew, London
CAB 66/34/11 Weekly Resume (No. 180) of the Naval, Military and Air Situation from 0700 February 4th to 0700 February 11th 1943

CAB 66/34/21 Weekly Resume (No. 181) of the Naval, Military and Air Situation from 0700 February 11th to 0700 February 18th 1943

CAB 66/37/24 Weekly Resume (No. 195) of the Naval, Military and Air Situation from 0700 20th May to 0700 27th May 1943

CAB 66/37/37 Weekly Resume (No. 197) of the Naval, Military and Air Situation from 0700 3rd June to 0700 10th June 1943

CAB 66/39/13 Weekly Resume (No. 202) of the Naval, Military and Air Situation from 0700 8th July to 0700 15th July 1943

CAB 66/39/30 Weekly Resume (No. 203) of the Naval, Military and Air Situation from 0700 15th July to 0700 22nd July 1943

HW 1/1606 Central Russian front: German preparations for Zitadelle operation, Apr 13, PM query to CIGS; CIGS reply, Apr 15

Air Ministry (ACAS[I]) The Rise and Fall of the German Air Force (1933 to 1945) Air Ministry Pamphlet No. 248

Germany

Das Bundesarchiv, Freiburg

RH 20–99 Armeegruppen, Armeen und Armeeabteilungen Armee (AOK 9)

RS 2–2/13 II SS-Panzerkorps Anhang zum KTB Nr. 5: Vorbereitungen zum Unternehmen 'Zitadelle' 10 Apr–31 Mai 1943

RL 11/157 Truppenführungsstäbe der Flakartillerie Teilnahme im Orelbogen von Januar bis Juli 1943 (Einsatz Sowjetunion-Mitte). Studie von General Buffa

RH 21–4/121 Panzergruppen, Panzerarmeen Operation 'Zitadelle' 2 Apr–19 Juni 1943

RH 21–4/122 Panzergruppen, Panzerarmeen Operation 'Zitadelle' 15 Mai–9 Juli 1943

RH 24–48/113 XXXXVIII Armeekorps (mot.)/Panzerkorps Vorbereitungen zum Unternehmen 'Zitadelle' Mai–Juni 1943

Soviet Union

Central Archive of the Russian Ministry of Defence, Podolsk

Dokumenty sovetskogo komandovaniia v period Velikoi Otechestvennoi voiny (aprel–mai 1943)

B. Gurkin – Dokumenty i materialy: '*Podgotovka k kurski bitve*' Voenno-istoricheskii zhurnal No. 6

O. Gurov and V. Kovalev '*Pobeda na kurskoi duge*' Voenno-istoricheskii zhurnal No. 7

United States

National Archives, Washington D.C.

NAM T-312 Roll 56 Kriegstagbuch No. 2, AOK 8, Ia Tagliche Lagekarten vom 1.7.43–31.12.43 AOK 8, 44701/14

NAM T-312 Roll 320 Anlage zu KTB Nr. 8, AOK 9 Ian, 26 Mar–18 Aug 1943 AOK 9, 35939/7

NAM T-312 Roll 1253 Feindlagenkarten vom 1.7.1943 bis 30.9.1943, AOK2, Ic/AO KTB AOK2, 37418/128 Part 1

NAM T-313 Roll 171 Chefkarten, 23 Anlagen, Anlagenband 36 zum KTB PzAOK2 Ia 1 Jun–13 Aug 1943 PzAOK2, 37075/49

NAM T-313 Roll 369 Anlagen 13 zum KTB Lagenkarten PzAOK4 la 25.3.43–30.7.43 PaAOK4, 34888/17

Other archives

Letter from Lieutenant-Colonel Edward Leigh to his brother, James Leigh, dated 12 February 1914. The Leigh Family Archive, Sittingbourne, Kent

Letter from Lieutenant-Colonel Edward Leigh to his brother, James Leigh, dated 16 February 1917. The Leigh Family Archive, Sittingbourne, Kent

Newspapers, diaries, correspondences, unpublished sources and author's archive

Letter from Nicolai Andreev to the author, dated 18 August 2009

Letter from Hilda Brandt to Jessica Rowland, dated 15 January 1919

Letter from Elbert Hahn to the author, dated 18 September 2008

Letter from Karla Kortig to Nancy Price, dated 12 August 1945

Letter from Valentin Lebedev to the author, dated 3 May 2008

Letter from Thomas Lohr to the author, dated 12 November 2009

Letter from Peter Maschmann to his father, dated 10 July 1943

Letter from Jan Möschen to the author, dated 16 May 2008

Letter from T. Simutenkov to the author, dated 13 September 2008

Letter from Y. Sirmnov to the author, dated 16 August 2009

Letter from Paul Weber to Henry Hartmann, dated 20 June 1928

Letter from Stefan Witte to the author, dated 16 July 2008

Deutsche Zeitung 28 June 1919

Pravda 15 September 1935

Time 16 December 1935

Nationalist pamphlet dated 20 July 1919, Munich

Transcript of a speech by Adolf Hitler to a rally in Berlin, August 1936

Transcript of a speech by Leon Trotsky in Moscow, 25 October 1923

Transcript of a speech by Stalin in August 1938 (location unknown)

Excerpts from Hitler's Speeches, Lectures and Addresses, June 1960

Communist Party pamphlet *Survive and Succeed*, 16 March 1943

Diary of Daniel Vogel

Diary of Leo Koettel

Diary of George Grosch

Diary of Rolf Schmidt

Journal of Ralph Faber

Journal of Elbert Hahn

Journal of Pavlo Kulik

Soviet Studies Unit, RMAS Pamphlet No. 21 1992

Ross Peterson unpublished lecture *A Work in Progress – The Red Army, 1939–41*, University of Leeds 1994

Lloyd Clark *Elite Fighting Units on the Eastern Front 1941–43*, an unpublished paper for the War Studies Society, King's College, University of London, November 1994

Roger Hoch *Mein Leben*, 10 July 1964

Artyom Zeldovich memoir 1962

Excerpt from *OKW War Diary*, 11 July 1943

Notes on Zitadelle written by Alexander Simm, dated August 1952

Interviews

Anatoli Abalakov

Mikhail Batkin

Rudi Bauermann

Semen Berezhko

Pavlik Boklov

Arnold Brenner

Marc Doerr

Lev Drachevsky

Felix Dresener

Samuel Erwin

Herbert Forman

Gunar Francks

A.G.

Walter Graff

Dr Karl Hertzog

Roger Hoch

Heinrich Huber

Olga Iofe

Feliks Karelin

Michail Khodorovsky

Marianne Koch

Pavel Krylov

Gerd Küster

Dimitri Lachinov

Alarick Lindner

Thomas Lohr

Koba Lomidze

V.M.

Peter Maschmann

Paul Meuller

Alana Molodin

Johan Müller

Fyodor Onton

Igor Panesenko

Mykhailo Petrik

Malana Ragulin

Sasha Reznikova

Bernard Roth

Raimund Rüffer

Yuri Ruslanova

Ludwig Schein

Rolf Schmidt

Henri Schnabel

Vladimir Severinov

Leo Spiegel

Karl Stumpp

Max Sulzer

Albert Thimm

Fedor Tiomkin

Max Torst

Dimitri Trzemin

Georgy Uritski

Stanislav Usov

Boris Vassilieva

Tanya Vershvovski

Anatoly Volkov

Internet

www.whitehouse.gov

www.mtholyoke.edu/acad/intrel/ww40.htm

www.germanhistorydocs.ghi-dc.org

www.eng.9may.ru

www.iwm.org.uk

www.holocaustresearchproject.org

www.users.telenet.be/stalingrad/germanpart/dir41.html

www.209.85.229.132/search?q=cache:VhF1gh8JXAQJ:ww2db.com/
  battlespec.php%3Fbattleid%3D3+German+Sixth+Army+
  Joachim+Wieder&cd=1&h1=en&ct=clnk&gl=uk

www.time.com

www.pilotenbunker.de/Stuka/rudel

www.SovLit.com

Published sources

Articles

Frieser, Karl-Heinz et al *Kursk – Sixty Years On* in *The RUSI Journal* Vol.
  148 No. 5 October 2003

Glantz, David M. *Soviet Operational Intelligence in the Kursk Operation,
  July 1943* in *Intelligence and National Security* Vol. 5 No. 1 January
  1990

Glantz, David M. *Prelude to Kursk: Soviet Strategic Operations, February–
  March 1943* in *The Journal of Slavic Military Studies* Vol. 8 No. 1 March
  1995

Glantz, David M. *The Failures of Historiography: Forgotten Battles of the
  German–Soviet War (1941–45)* in *The Journal of Slavic Military Studies*
  Vol. 8 No. 4 December 1995

Glantz, David M. *Soviet Military Strategy During the Second Period of War
  (November 1942–December 1943): A Reappraisal* in *The Journal of
  Military History* Vol. 60 No. 1 January 1996

Simms, Captain Benjamin R. *Analysis of the Battle of Kursk* in *Armor* Vol.
  CXII No. 2 March–April 2003

Books

All books are published in London unless otherwise stated:

Abdulin, Mansur *Red Road from Stalingrad: Recollections of a Soviet
  Infantryman* Pen and Sword, Barnsley 2004

Agate, Patrick *Michael Wittmann and the Waffen SS Tiger Commanders of the*

Leibstandarte in WWII Volume One Stackpole Books, Mechanicsburg, PA 1996

Anonymous *Memoir of an Itinerant Russian*, privately published in the United States of America 1924

Armstrong, Richard N. *Red Army Tank Commanders: The Armored Guards* Schiffer Military History, Atglen, PA 1994

Bailer, Seweryn (ed) *Stalin and his Generals: Soviet Military Memoirs of World War II* Souvenir Press 1970

Barnet, Corelli (ed) *Hitler's Generals* Weidenfeld and Nicolson 1989

Bartov, O. *Eastern Front 1941–45* St Martin's Press 1996

Bastable, Jonathan *Voices from Stalingrad: Unique First-Hand Accounts From World War II's Cruellest Battle* David and Charles, Cincinnati, OH 2007

Beevor, Antony *Stalingrad, The Fateful Siege: 1942–1943* Viking Penguin, New York 1998

Bellamy, Chris *Absolute War – Soviet Russia in the Second World War: A Modern History* Pan Books 2008

Bergström, Christer *Kursk: The Air Battle* Ian Allen, Hersham 2007

Bidermann, Gottlob Herbert *In Deadly Combat – A German Soldier's Memoir of the Eastern Front* University Press of Kansas, Lawrence, Kansas 2000

Braithwaite, Rodric *Moscow 1941: A City and its People at War* Profile Books 2006

Bullock, Alan *Hitler – A Study in Tyranny* Penguin 1952

Burleigh, Michael *The Third Reich – A New History* Macmillan 2000

Caplan, Jane (ed) *The Short Oxford History of Germany – Nazi Germany* Oxford University Press, Oxford 2008

Carell, Paul *Scorched Earth – Hitler's War on Russia: The Story of the German Defeat in the East* George G. Harrap 1964

Carr, William *Hitler: A Study in Personality and Politics* Edward Arnold 1989

Carr, William *Arms, Autarky and Aggression: A Study in German Foreign Policy, 1933–1939* Edward Arnold 1989

Churchill, Winston *The Second World War Volume VI Triumph and Tragedy* Penguin 1985

Clark, Alan *Barbarossa – The Russian-German Conflict 1941–45* Macmillan 1985

Cross, Robin *Citadel: The Battle of Kursk* Michael O'Mara Books 1993

Dallin, A. *German Rule in Russia 1941–45* Macmillan 1981

Drabkin, Artem and Sheremet, Oleg *T-34 in Action – Soviet Tank Troops in WWII* Stackpole Books, Mechanicsburg, PA 2006

Dunn, Walter S. *Kursk – Hitler's Gamble, 1943* Stackpole Books, Mechanicsburg, PA 1997

Elliot, B.J. *Hitler and Germany* Longman 1966

Erickson, John *The Road to Berlin* Weidenfeld and Nicolson 1983

Erickson, John *The Soviet High Command: A Military–Political History, 1918–41* Frank Cass 2001

Fey, Will *Armor Battles of the Waffen-SS 1943–45* Stackpole Books, Mechanicsburg, PA 1990

Frieser, Karl-Heinz et al *Das Deutsche Reich und der Zweite Weltkreig. Die Ostfront 1943/44* Deutsche Verlags-Anstalt, Munich 2007

Fugate, Bryan I. *Operation Barbarossa – Strategy and Tactics on the Eastern Front 1941* Spa Books, Stevenage 1984

Glantz, David M. *Before Stalingrad – Barbarossa and Hitler's Invasion of Russia 1941* Tempus, Stroud 2003

Glantz, David M. *Colossus Reborn* The University Press of Kansas, Lawrence, Kansas 2005

Glantz, David M. *From the Don to the Dnepr – Soviet Offensive Operations December 1942–August 1943* Frank Cass 1991

Glantz, David M. *The Military Strategy of the Soviet Union* Frank Cass 1992

Glantz, David M. *Soviet Military Intelligence in War* Frank Cass 1990

Glantz, David M. *Stumbling Colossus* The University Press of Kansas, Lawrence, Kansas 1998

Glantz, David M. *When Titans Clashed: How the Red Army Stopped Hitler* The University Press of Kansas, Lawrence, Kansas 1995

Glantz, David M. and House, Jonathan M. *The Battle of Kursk* The University Press of Kansas, Lawrence, Kansas 1999

Glantz, David M. and Orenstein, Harold S. (eds) *The Battle for Kursk 1943: The Soviet General Staff Study* Frank Cass 1999

Grossman, Vasily *A Writer at War – Vasily Grossman with the Red Army 1941–1945* Pimlico 2006

Guderian, Heinz *Panzer Leader* Futura 1974

Guderian, Major-General Heinz *Achtung – Panzer! – The Development of Armoured Forces, Their Tactics and Operational Potential* Arms and Armour Press 1992

Haupt, W. *Army Group Center – The Wehrmacht in Russia 1941–1945* Schiffer Military History, Atglen, PA 1997

Haupt, W. *Army Group South – The Wehrmacht in Russia 1941–1945* Schiffer Military History, Atglen, PA 1998

Healy, Mark *Kursk 1943: The Tide Turns in the East* Osprey 1992

Healy, Mark *Zitadelle – The German Offensive against the Kursk Salient 4–17 July 1943* The History Press, Stroud 2008

Heiber, Helmut and Glantz, David M. (eds) *Hitler and his Generals – Military Conferences 1942–1945* Enigma Books, New York 2003

Heinl, Robert Debs Jnr *Dictionary of Military and Naval Quotations* US Naval Institute Press, Annapolis, MD 1978

Henig, Ruth *Versailles and After: 1919–1933* Routledge 1995

Hinden, J.W. *The Weimar Republic* Longman, Harlow 1990

Hitler, Adolf *Mein Kampf* Hutchinson 1974

Irving, David *Hitler's War 1942–1945* Macmillan 1977

Jukes, Geoffrey *Kursk: The Clash of Armour* Purnell 1968

Jung, Hans-Joachim *The History of the Panzerregiment Grossdeutschland* J.J. Fedorowicz Publishing Inc, Winnipeg 2000

Junge, Traudl with Melissa Müller *Until the Final Hour – Hitler's Last Secretary* Phoenix 2002

Katukov, M.E. *Na ostrie glavnogo udara* Voenizdat, Moscow 1976

Kershaw, Ian *Hitler: 1936–1945 Nemesis* Penguin 2001

Kershaw, I. and Lewin, M. *Stalinism and Nazism: Dictatorships in Comparison* Cambridge University Press, Cambridge 1997

Kershaw, Robert *Tank Men* Hodder and Stoughton 2008

Kershaw, Robert *War Without Garlands – Operation Barbarossa 1941–1942* Ian Allen, Hersham 2000

Krylov, Ivan *Soviet Staff Officer* The Falcon Press 1951

Kurowski, Franz *Infantry Aces – The German Soldier in Combat in WWII* Stackpole Books, Mechanicsburg, PA 1994

Kurowski, Franz *Operation 'Zitadelle' – July 1943: The Decisive Battle of World War II* J.J. Fedorowicz, Winnipeg 2003

Kurowski, Franz *Panzer Aces – German Tank Commanders of WWII* Stackpole Books, Mechanicsburg, PA 2004

Kurowski, Franz *Panzer Aces II – Battle Stories of German Tank Commanders of WWII* Stackpole Books, Mechanicsburg, PA 2004

Lee, Stephen J. *Aspects of European History 1789–1980* Routledge 1988

Lehmann, R. *The Leibstandarte Volume III* J.J. Fedorowicz, Winnipeg 1990

Litvin, Nikolai *800 Days on the Eastern Front: A Russian Soldier Remembers World War II* University Press of Kansas, Lawrence, Kansas 2007

Lucas, James *Das Reich: The Military Role of 2d SS Division* Arms and Armour 1991

Lucas, James *The German Army Handbook 1939–1945* Sutton Publishing Ltd, Stroud 1998

Lucas, James *War on the Eastern Front: The German Soldier in Russia 1941–1945* Greenhill Books 1998

Ludendorff, Erich von *My War Memoirs, 1914–1918* Naval and Military Press, Uckfield 2005

McCauley, Martin *Stalin and Stalinism* Pearson, Harlow 2008

McDonough, Frank *Hitler and Nazi Germany* Cambridge University Press, Cambridge 1999

Manstein, Erich von *Lost Victories* Greenhill Books 1987

Mawdsley, Evan *Thunder in the East: The Nazi–Soviet War 1941–1945* Hodder Arnold 2005

Mellenthin, Major-General F.W. von *Panzer Battles* Ballantine Books, New York 1956

Merridale, Catherine *Ivan's War – The Red Army 1939–45* Faber and Faber 2005

Müller, Rolf-Dieter and Ueberschär, Gerd R. *Hitler's War in the East 1941–1945 – A Critical Assessment* Berghahn Books, Providence 1997

Newton, Steven H. *Kursk – The German View: Firsthand Accounts of the German Commanders who Planned and Executed the Largest Tank Battle in History* De Capo, Cambridge, MA 2002

Nicolson, Nigel (ed) *The Harold Nicolson Diaries 1907–1963* Weidenfeld and Nicolson 2004

Nipe, G.M. *Decision in the Ukraine – Summer 1943 – II SS and III Panzerkorps* J.J. Fedorowicz, Winnipeg 1996

Noakes, J. and Pridham, J. and G. (eds) *Nazism 1919–1945: Volume 3: Foreign Policy, War and Racial Extermination – A Documentary Reader* University of Exeter, Exeter 1988

Overy, Richard *The Dictators: Hitler's Germany and Stalin's Russia* Penguin Books 2005

Overy, Richard *Russia's War* Penguin Books 1999

Overy, Richard *War and the Economy in the Third Reich* Oxford University Press, Oxford 1994

Overy, Richard *Why the Allies Won* W.W. Norton and Company, New York 1996

Pabst, Helmuth *The Outermost Frontier – A German Soldier in the Russian Campaign* William Kimber 1957

Parotkin, Major-General Ivan (Editor-in-Chief) *The Battle of Kursk* Progress, Moscow 1974

Raus, Erhard *Panzer Operations* Frontline Books, Cambridge, MA 2003

Rauss, Erhard Generaloberst et al *Fighting in Hell – The German Ordeal on the Eastern Front* Greenhill Books 1995

Rayfield, Donald *Stalin and his Hangmen* Penguin 2005

Reese, Roger R. *Stalin's Reluctant Soldiers – A Social History of the Red Army, 1925–1941* University Press of Kansas, Lawrence, Kansas 1996

Restayn, J. and Moller, N. *Operation Citadel Vol. I: The South* J.J. Fedorowicz, Winnipeg 2002

Restayn, J. and Moller, N. *Operation Citadel Vol. II: The North* J.J. Fedorowicz, Winnipeg 2006

Roberts, Geoffrey *Stalin's Wars – From the World War to Cold War, 1939–1953* Yale University Press, New Haven 2006

Rokossovsky, K.A. *A Soldier's Duty* Progress, Moscow 1985

Rotmistrov, P.A. *Stal'naia gvardiia* Voenizdat, Moscow 1984

Rudel, Hans-Ulrich *Stuka Pilot: The War Memoirs of Hans-Ulrich Rudel* Barbarossa Books 2006

Schneider, Wolfgang *Tigers in Combat Vol I* J.J. Fedorowicz, Winnipeg 1994

Schneider, Wolfgang *Tigers in Combat Vol II* J.J. Fedorowicz, Winnipeg 1998

Schukman, H. *Stalin's General* Weidenfeld and Nicolson 1993

Sebag Montefiore, Simon *Stalin – The Court of the Red Tsar* Phoenix 2004

Service, Robert *Stalin: A Biography* Pan Books 2005

Sheffield, Gary and Trew, Simon (eds) *100 Years of Conflict* Sutton, Stroud 2000

Shtemenko, S.M. *The Soviet General Staff at War* Progress, Moscow 1985

Sokolov, Marshal Sergy (Foreword) *Main Front – Soviet Leaders Look Back on World War II* Brassey 1987

Spaeter, Helmuth *The History of Panzer Corps Grossdeutschland Vol. II.* J.J. Fedorowicz, Winnipeg 1995

Spezzano, R. *Kursk 1943 Vols 1–6* RZM Southbury, CT 2002

Stein, George H. *The Waffen SS: Hitler's Elite Guard at War 1939–1945* Cornell University, New Haven 1966

Trang, Charles *Totenkopf* Heimdal, Bayeux 2006

Valtin, Jan *Out of the Night* Kessinger, Whitefish, Montana 2005

Weeks, Albert I. *Stalin's Other War: Soviet Grand Strategy, 1939–1941* Rowman and Littlefield, Lanham, MD 2002

Weinberg, Gerhard *The Foreign Policy of Hitler's Diplomatic Revolution in Europe 1933–36* University of Chicago Press, Chicago 1970

Weinberg, Gerhard L. *Germany, Hitler and World War II* Cambridge University Press, Cambridge 1995

Werth, Alexander *Russia at War 1941–1945* Barrie and Rockliff 1964

Wieder, Joachim and von Einsiedel, Heinrich Graf *Stalingrad: Memories and Reassessments* Cassell 2002

Williamson, Gordon *Loyalty is my Honour – Personal Accounts from the Waffen-SS* BCA 1995

Willmott, H.P. *The Great Crusade: A New Complete History of the Second World War* Pimlico 1992

Winchester, Charles D. *Hitler's War on Russia* Osprey, Oxford 2007

Wolfson, Robert *Years of Change: European History 1890–1945* Edward Arnold 1978

Wright, Patrick *Tank* Faber and Faber 2000

Zetterling, N. and Frankson, A. *Kursk 1943: A Statistical Analysis* Cass 2000

Zhukov, Georgi K. *Marshal Zhukov's Greatest Battles* Cooper Square Press, New York 2002

Zhukov, G. *The Memoirs of Marshal Zhukov* Jonathan Cape 1971

Zhukov, G. *Reminiscences and Reflections 2 vols* Progress, Moscow 1985

Order of Battle

Germany
Army Group Centre – **Field Marshal Günther von Kluge**
Ninth Army – **Colonel-General Walter Model**
XX Corps (von Roman)
45th Infantry Division
72nd Infantry Division
137th Infantry Division
251st Infantry Division

XLVI Panzer Corps (Zorn)
7th Infantry Division
31st Infantry Division
102nd Infantry Division
258th Infantry Division

XLI Panzer Corps (Harpe)
18th Panzer Division

86th Infantry Division
292nd Infantry Division

XLVII Panzer Corps (Lemelsen)
2nd Panzer Division
9th Panzer Division
20th Panzer Division
6th Infantry Division

XXIII Corps (Freissner)
216th Infantry Division
383rd Infantry Division
78th Assault Division

***Army Group South* – Field Marshal Erich von Manstein**
***Fourth Panzer Army* – Colonel-General Hermann Hoth**
LII Corps (Ott)
57th Infantry Division
255th Infantry Division
332nd Infantry Division

XLVIII Panzer Corps (von Knobelsdorff)
3rd Panzer Division
11th Panzer Division
Panzergrenadier Division Grossdeutschland
167th Infantry Division

II SS Panzer Corps (Hausser)
SS Panzergrenadier Division Leibstandarte Adolf Hitler (LAH)
SS Panzergrenadier Division Das Reich
SS Panzergrenadier Division Totenkopf

Army Detachment Kempf – General Werner Kempf
III Panzer Corps (Breith)
6th Panzer Division
7th Panzer Division
19th Panzer Division
168th Infantry Division

Corps Raus (Raus)
106th Infantry Division
320th Infantry Division

XLII Corps (Mattenklott)
39th Infantry Division
161st Infantry Division
282nd Infantry Division

Reserve
XXIV Panzer Corps (Nehring)
SS Panzergrenadier Division Wiking
17th Panzer Division

Luftwaffe
Luftflotte 4
VIII Air Corps

Luftflotte 6
1st Air Division

Soviet Union
Central Front – General Konstantin Rokossovsky
13th Army – Puchov

17th Guards Rifle Corps
6th Guards Rifle Division
70th Guards Rifle Division
75th Guards Rifle Division

18th Guards Rifle Corps
2nd Airborne Guards Rifle Division
3rd Airborne Guards Rifle Division
4th Airborne Guards Rifle Division

15th Rifle Corps
8th Rifle Division
74th Rifle Division
148th Rifle Division

29th Rifle Corps
15th Rifle Division
81st Rifle Division
307th Rifle Division

48th Army – **Romanenko**
42nd Rifle Corps
16th Rifle Division
202nd Rifle Division
399th Rifle Division
73rd Rifle Division
137th Rifle Division
143rd Rifle Division
170th Rifle Division

60th Army – **Chernyakhovsky**
24th Rifle Corps

42nd Rifle Division
112th Rifle Division

30th Rifle Corps
121st Rifle Division
141st Rifle Division
322nd Rifle Division
Independent 55th Rifle Division

65th Army – **Batov**
18th Rifle Corps
69th Rifle Division
149th Rifle Division
246th Rifle Division

27th Rifle Corps
60th Rifle Division
193rd Rifle Division
37th Guards Rifle Division
181st Rifle Division
194th Rifle Division
354th Rifle Division

70th Army – **Galanin**
28th Rifle Corps
132nd Rifle Division
211th Rifle Division
280th Rifle Division
102nd Rifle Division
106th Rifle Division
140th Rifle Division
162nd Rifle Division

2nd Tank Army – **Rodin**
3rd Tank Corps
16th Tank Corps

16th Air Army – **Rudenko**
3rd Bombing Air Corps
6th Mixed Air Corps
6th Fighter Air Corps

Independent Formation
Independent 9th Tank Corps
Independent 19th Tank Corps

Voronezh Front – **General Nikolai Vatutin**
6th Guards Army – **Chistyakov**
22nd Guards Rifle Corps
67th Guards Rifle Division
71st Guards Rifle Division
90th Guards Rifle Division

23rd Guards Rifle Corps
51st Guards Rifle Division
52nd Guards Rifle Division
375th Rifle Division
Independent 89th Guards Rifle Division

7th Guards Army – **Shumilov**
24th Guards Rifle Corps
15th Guards Rifle Division
36th Guards Rifle Division
72nd Guards Rifle Division

25th Guards Rifle Corps
73rd Guards Rifle Division
78th Guards Rifle Division
81st Guards Rifle Division
Independent 213th Rifle Division

38th Army – Chibisov
50th Rifle Corps
167th Rifle Division
232nd Rifle Division
340th Rifle Division

51st Rifle Corps
180th Rifle Division
240th Rifle Division
Independent 204th Rifle Division

40th Army – Moskalenko
47th Rifle Corps
161st Rifle Division
206th Rifle Division
237th Rifle Division

52nd Rifle Corps
100th Rifle Division
219th Rifle Division
309th Rifle Division
Independent 184th Rifle Division

69th Army – Kruchenkin
48th Rifle Corps
107th Rifle Division

183rd Rifle Division
307th Rifle Division

49th Rifle Corps
111th Rifle Division
270th Rifle Division

1st Tank Army – Katukov
6th Tank Corps
31st Tank Corps
3rd Mechanized Corps

2nd Air Army – Krasovskii
1st Bombing Air Corps
1st Assault Air Corps
4th Fighter Air Corps
5th Fighter Air Corps

Front Assets
35th Guards Rifle Corps
92nd Guards Rifle Division
93rd Guards Rifle Division
94th Guards Rifle Division
Independent 2nd Guards Tank Corps
Independent 3rd Guards Tank Corps

Steppe Front – Colonel-General Ivan Konev
5th Guards Army – Zhadov
32nd Guards Rifle Corps
13th Guards Rifle Division
66th Guards Rifle Division
6th Airborne Guards Rifle Division

33rd Guards Rifle Corps
95th Guards Rifle Division
97th Guards Rifle Division
9th Airborne Guards Rifle Division
Independent 42nd Guards Rifle Division
Independent 10th Tank Corps

5th Guards Tank Army – **Rotmistrov**
5th Guards Mechanized Corps
29th Tank Corps

5th Air Army – **Gorunov**
7th Mixed Air Corps
8th Mixed Air Corps
3rd Fighter Air Corps
7th Fighter Air Corps

Rank Equivalents

Waffen-SS	Wehrmacht	British Army	American Army
Reichsführer-SS	None	None	None
None	General Feldmarschall	Field Marshal	General
SS-Oberstgruppen-Führer	Generaloberst	General	General
SS-Obergruppenführer	General der Infanterie, der Artillerie etc	Lieutenant-General	Lieutenant-General
SS-Gruppenführer	Generalleutnant	Major-General	Major-General
SS-Brigadeführer	Generalmajor	Brigadier	Brigadier-General
SS-Oberführer	None	None	None
SS-Standartenführer	Oberst	Colonel	Colonel
SS-Obersturmbannführer	Oberstleutnant	Lieutenant-Colonel	Lieutenant-Colonel
SS-Sturmbannführer	Major	Major	Major
SS-Hauptsturmführer	Hauptmann	Captain	Captain
SS-Obersturmführer	Oberleutnant	Lieutenant	First Lieutenant
SS-Untersturmführer	Leutnant	Second Lieutenant	Second Lieutenant
SS-Sturmscharführer	Stabsfeldwebel	Regimental Sergeant Major	Sergeant Major

Waffen-SS	Wehrmacht	British Army	American Army
SS-Standarten-Oberjunker	Oberfähnrich	None	None
SS-Hauptscharführer	Oberfeldwebel	Regimental Sergeant Major	Master Sergeant
SS-Oberscharführer	Feldwebel	Company Sergeant Major	Sergeant First Class
SS-Standartenjunker	Fähnrich	None	None
SS-Scharführer	Unterfeldwebel	Staff Sergeant	Staff Sergeant
SS-Unterscharführer	Unteroffizier	Sergeant	Sergeant
SS-Rottenführer	Obergefreiter	Corporal	Corporal
SS-Sturmmann	Gefreiter	Lance Corporal	None
SS-Oberschütze	Oberschütze	None	Private First Class
SS-Schütze	Schütze	Private	Private

Index

Note: Individual units are listed under 'army units'. Page numbers in **bold** denote major sections. A page number in *italic* denotes an entry in the Order of Battle section.

Abalakov, Anatoli 325–6, 359–60
Abdulin, Infmn Mansur 201, 204–5, 236, 344, 366, 367
Achtung – Panzer! (Guderian) 21
air force, German 28, 159, *450*
  Battle of Prokhorovka 345, 355–7, 367
  losses (aircraft) 210, 224, 257, 272, 357, 388
  Luftflotte 4 190, 222, 272, 273, 297, *450*
  Luftflotte 6 190, *450*
  Operation Barbarossa 71, 78–9, 84–5, 101–2
  Operation Zitadelle 273–4
    preliminaries 190–92, 210
    5th July 221–4, 228–9, 231–2, 235, 250
    6th–8th July 266–7, 273, 283–4, 297–8
    9th–11th July 315–17, 322–3, 333–4
  Stalingrad bombardment 151–2
air force, Soviet
  2nd Air Army 193, 196, 272, *455*
  5th Air Army 194, *456*
  16th Air Army 193, 249–50, *453*
  17th Air Army 193
  Battle of Prokhorovka 355–7, 366–7
  defence of Kursk salient
    preliminaries 175, 193, 194, 196, 210
    5th July 221–4, 228–30, 249–50, 257–8
    6th–8th July 287–8, 289–90, 297–8, 299–300

    9th–11th July 315–17, 322
  German invasion (Operation Barbarossa) 73, 79, 86, 88, 108–9
  losses (aircraft) 79, 86, 88, 109, 210, 224, 257, 357, 388
  weaknesses 74, 232
Alanbrooke, Sir Alan Francis Brooke, 1st Viscount 42
Alexeev, Lt Vladimir 239, 240, 319, 374–5
Alexeyev, Infmn Mikhail 135
Alexsandrovka 255
Andreev, Nicolai 242
Anti-Comintern Pact 56
anti-Semitism 8, 15
anti-tank guns 201, 204
Antonov, Gen Aleksei 174
army, German
  atrocities 97–100
  losses (mechanical) 109–10, 124–5, 198, 251, 259, 272, 305, 311, 388
  rearmament and development 19–22
  tactical superiority 352
  tanks *see* tanks, German
army, Soviet
  losses (mechanical) 81–2, 86, 87, 88, 108, 109, 121, 251, 284, 388
  morale and discipline 90–92
  motivation 97, 99–101

numerical advantage 170–71, 194–5
rearmament and development 51–3,
  61–2, 147–8, 174–5
recruitment 94–6
tanks *see* tanks, Soviet
weaknesses 51–2, 73–5, 80–81, 119–20,
  195
army units, German *448–50*
2nd Panzer Division 290, 297, *449*
2nd Panzer Grenadier Regiment 332
II SS Panzer Corps 188, 224, 233, 264–5,
  273, 282, 284, 320–21, 378, *449*
III Panzer Corps 188, 242, 282, 362–3, 365,
  375–6, 378, 380–81, *450*
3rd Panzer Division 213, 224, 233, 269–70,
  449
4th Panzer Division 302–3
6th Infantry Division 249, 297, 300, *449*
6th Motorized Infantry Brigade 79
6th Panzer Division 242, 243, 268, 269, 282,
  327, *450*
  Battle of Prokhorovka 363–5
  Operation Barbarossa 79, 81–2, 102
  Operation Typhoon 124–5, 131
7th Panzer Corps 297
7th Panzer Division 244–5, 268, *450*
9th Panzer Division 290, 293, 297, 300, *449*
XI Corps (Corps Raus) 188, 245–6, 268, *450*
11th Panzer Division 214, 224, 232, 269–71,
  313–14, *449*
17th Panzer Division 121, *450*
18th Panzer Division 297, *448*
19th Panzer Division 243–4, 268, *450*
20th Panzer Division 249, 251, 290, 297,
  298, 302, *449*
XXIII Corps 186, 249, *449*
XXIV Panzer Corps 188, 378, *450*
XLI Panzer Corps 186, 249, 252, 256,
  296–7, *448–9*
XLII Corps 188, *450*
XLVI Panzer Corps 186, 249, *448*
XLVII Panzer Corps 186, 249, 252, 256,
  290, 296–7, *449*
XLVIII Panzer Corps 224, 273, 275, 282,
  284, 314, 324, *449*
  Battle of Prokhorovka 367–8
  Zitadelle preliminaries 187, 213
78th Infantry Division 294
86th Infantry Division 252–3, 294, 297, *449*
292nd Infantry Division 252–3, 293, 297,
  449
503rd Heavy Tank Battalion 242–3, 282,
  327
505th Heavy Tank Battalion 186, 250–51,
  290, 297
Army Detachment Kempf 188, 242, 268,
  282, *450*

Army Group Centre *448–9*
  Operation Barbarossa 71, 84–6, 101–2,
    104, 106, 112–13
  Operation Typhoon 119, 123–4, 132,
    136
  Operation Zitadelle 185
Army Group Don 158, 159
Army Group North 70–71, 86, 102–3,
  109–12
Army Group South 132, *449*
  Army Group A 150, 155, 156
  Army Group B 150–51
  Operation Barbarossa 71, 87–8, 103,
    108
  Operation Blau 149, 150–51
  Operation Zitadelle 185, 187, 382
Eighteenth Panzer Army 102
Eleventh Army 132
First Panzer Army 87, 103, 109, 132
Fourth Panzer Army 86, 102, *449*
  Operation Typhoon 119, 120, 131
  Operation Zitadelle 187, 190, 259, 311,
    320–21, 378
Grenadier Regiment 230
Ninth Army 185–6, 198, 247–56, 259, 296–7,
  305–6, *448–9*
Panzer Grenadier Regiment Deutschland
  362
Panzergrenadier Division Grossdeutschland
  224–30, 232, 269–71, 275–7, 284–8,
  313–15, 331, *449*
  Battle of Prokhorovka 365–6, 367–8
  Zitadelle preliminaries 187, 213–14
Second Army 185
Second Panzer Army
  Operation Barbarossa 84, 104, 106,
    107–8, 109
  Operation Typhoon 119, 120–21, 124,
    131, 135–6
Seventeenth Army 132
Sixth Army 106, 132, 151, 152, 158–9,
  160–61
SS Einsatzgruppen 97
SS Panzer Corps 169
SS Panzergrenadier Division Das Reich
  233–4, 238–40, 265, 282, 317–18,
  325–7, 336, 369, 375, 378–9, *449*
SS Panzergrenadier Division Leibstandarte
  Adolf Hitler (LAH) 233–5, 240–41,
  265–6, 282, 317–18, 325–7, 335–6, *449*
  after 12th July 372–4, 378
  Battle of Prokhorovka 357, 358–9,
    361–2, 368–9
SS Panzergrenadier Division Totenkopf
  233–4, 241–2, 282, 317–18, 325–6, 336,
  449
  after 12th July 374, 378

Battle of Prokhorovka 359–60, 369
Third Panzer Army 84, 104, 110, 119, 120,
    131, 135
army units, Romanian
    Fourth Romanian Army 158
    Third Romanian Army 157
army units, Soviet *450–56*
    1st Guards Cavalry Corps 131
    1st Guards Tank Army 240
    1st Tank Army 193, 247, *455*
    2nd Guards Tank Corps 247, 283, 362, 369
    2nd Tank Army 192, 257, *453*
    2nd Tank Corps 326–7, 362, 369
    3rd Anti-Tank Brigade 304
    3rd Mechanized Corps 284, 288, *455*
    4th Army 192
    4th Guards Army 194
    5th Guards Army 194, 311, 320, 360, *455–6*
    5th Guards Tank Army 194, 272, 320, 336,
        346, 357, *456*
    5th Guards Tank Corps 247, 365
    5th Tank Army 311
    6th Guards Army 193–4, 198, 215, 224,
        247, *453*
    7th Guards Army 193, 194, 215, 247, 268,
        282, *453–4*
    9th Guards Airborne Division 358
    10th Guards Mechanized Brigade 360
    10th Tank Corps 283, 365–6
    13th Army 192, 193, 293, 299, *450–51*
    15th Guards Rifle Division 247, *453*
    16th Tank Corps 289, *453*
    17th Guards Rifle Corps 257, 299, *450–51*
    17th Guards Rifle Division 289
    18th Rifle Corps 257, *452*
    18th Tank Corps 357
    19th Tank Corps 292
    24th Guards Tank Brigade 360
    25th Tank Brigade 361–2
    26th Tank Brigade 362
    27th Army 194
    29th Anti-Tank Brigade 288
    29th Rifle Corps 252, *451*
    31st Tank Corps 283, 288, *455*
    32nd Tank Brigade 358
    38th Army 193, *454*
    40th Army 193, *454*
    47th Army 194
    51st Guards Rifle Division 247, *453*
    53rd Army 194
    62nd Army 151, 152
    64th Army 151, 152
    65th Army 192, *452*
    66th Guards Rifle Division 366, *455*
    69th Army 193, *454–5*
    70th Army 192, *452*
    90th Guards Rifle Division 247, *453*

93rd Guards Rifle Division 247, *455*
110th Tank Brigade 358
136th Guards Rifle Regiment 362
170th Tank Brigade 349
181st Tank Brigade 349
307th Rifle Division 293, 300, *451*, *455*
309th Rifle Division 288, *454*
316th Rifle Division 131
Briansk Front 107–8, 121
Central Front 106, 192–3, *450–53*
Kalinin Front 135
Leningrad Front 110, 138
Northern Front 74, 86, 102
Northwestern Front 74–5, 86
Reserve Front 106, 122, 133
Southern Front 75, 87–8
Southwestern Front 75, 87–8, 108, 138
Steppe Front 194, *455–6*
Volkhov Front 138
Voronezh Front 193–4, 263, *453–5*
Western Front 75, 84, 85, 122, 135
atrocities 97–100
Austria 22

Bäke, Maj Dr Franz 364
Barbarossa, Operation **67–114**
    air operations 71, 78–9, 84–5
    casualties, German 109, 113, 125, 133
    casualties, Soviet 86, 88, 108, 109, 113
    causes of German defeat (summary) 384–5
    causes of Soviet victory (summary) 385–6
    German advance 80–89, 101–14
    Hitler's commitment to invasion 29–30, 68–9
    Kiev 106–9
    Klein-Kargarlyk 103–4
    launched 67–8, 77–80
    Leningrad 86–7, 102–3, 109–12
    Minsk 85–6
    Operation Typhoon *see* Moscow
    planning, German 69–73, 104–6, 113–14,
        384–5
    planning, Soviet 73–5
    Smolensk 101, 104, 112–13
Batkin, Mikhail 48
battles *see* campaigns, battles and engagements
Bauer, Ludwig 199
Bauermann, Oberschütze Rudi 373–4, 381–2
Beer Hall Putsch 7–8
Beevor, Antony xvii, 389
Belenikhino 370, 379
Belgorod 168, 169
Belov, Nikolai 212
Below, Nicholas von 168–9
Berezhko, Semen 319–20
Berezovka 366
Bergström, Christer 357
Beria, Levrentiy 91

Beyer, Wilhelm 161
Bidermann, Infmn Gottlob 83, 88, 97, 103–4,
    136, 140–41, 144–6
Blau, Operation 148–57
    German planning 150–51
    Soviet Operation Uranus 156–8
    Stalingrad 150–55
blitzkrieg 21, 26
Blokhin, Capt Vasili 36
Blomberg, Col-Gen Werner von 12
Bock, Gen Fedor von 71, 112–13, 129, 132,
    135, 137
Boklov, Pavlik 122
Bolshie Maiachki 282
Borchers, SS-Obergrenadier Günther 215
Borisenko, Dr Olga 348
Braithwaite, Rodric 53
Brandt, Hilda 4
Brauchitsch, Gen Walther von 28, 29, 133, 137
Bräuer, SS-Rottenführer Johannes 343, 344–5
Breith, Gen Hermann 188, 268, 330, *450*
Brenner, Arnold 318, 331
Briansk 121
bridge construction (defences) 200
bridgeheads 242–5, 363–5
Bryukhov, Vasili 348, 349
Budenny, Mar Semyon 35, 36, 107
Burdeiny, Maj-Gen A.S. 362
Busse, Gen 329
Butovo xxiii–xxvi, 213, 232
Butyrki 255
Bykovka 240

Cairncross, John 182, 210
Caldwell, Erskine 93, 94
campaigns, battles and engagements
    for major subjects *see* Barbarossa; Moscow;
        Prokhorovka; Stalingrad; Zitadelle
    German offensives (after declaration of
        war) 30–32
    German territorial expansion (prior to
        declaration of war) 22–6, 59
    Kharkov 132, 138, 140, 141–2
    Operation Blau 148–57
    Operation Mars 159
    Operation Winter Storm 158–60
    Rostov 132
    Sevastopol 140–41
    Soviet invasion of Finland 60–61
    Soviet spring offensive (1942) 137–9
Carell, Paul (Paul Schmidt) 26–7, 226–7, 254,
    286, 298
casualties
    Finnish 61
    German xv, 26, 139, 142, 159
        Operation Barbarossa 109, 113, 125, 133
        Operation Typhoon 136

Operation Zitadelle 241, 246, 259, 267,
    272, 298, 305, 318, 325, 388
    Stalingrad 161
    Soviet xv, 60, 61, 139, 141, 142, 159
        defence of Kursk salient (Operation
            Zitadelle) 388
        field hospitals 261–2
        German invasion (Operation
            Barbarossa) 86, 88, 108, 109, 113
        Stalingrad 161
Chamberlain, Neville 23, 30
Chekhov, Anatoly 154
Cherkasskoe 232–3
Chistyakov, Lt-Gen I.M. 193, 232, 233, 237, *453*
Chuikov, Lt-Gen Vasily 153, 155, 160
Churchill, Winston 30, 32–3, 58, 82, 181–2,
    384, 389
civilian populations 97–8, 206–7
code-breaking 181–2
collectivization 48
Communist Party 11, 38, 43–4, 53–4
comradeship 208
Cowles, Virginia 14
Crimea 132, 140–41
Czechoslovakia 23, 57

Denmark 30
deserters 90–91
Dessloch, Gen Otto 190, 272
Deutsche Zeitung (newspaper) 5
Dexler, Frederik 310
Dictators, The (Overy) 46
Dietrich, Otto 121–2
Doerr, Oberst Hans 153
Doerr, Marc 291
Drachevsky, Lev 332
Dresener, Felix 310–11
Dunkirk 31, 32

Eastern Front, historical awareness of in West
    xv–xviii
Ehrenburg, Ilya 162
Enigma cipher machines 181–2
Enshin, Maj-Gen M.A. 293
Eremenko, Lt-Gen A.I. 121
Erwin, Johannes 309–10

Faber, Ralph 321–2
Fedyuninsky, Col I.I. 87
Ferdinand tank 183, 189–90, 254–5
    see also tanks, German
field hospitals 261–2
Finland 39, 60–61
Five Year Plans (Soviet Union) 46–51
flame-throwers 236
Foch, FM Ferdinand 5
Forman, Herbert 292

Four Year Plan (Germany) 17
France 19, 27, 30–31, 57–8
Francks, Hauptmann Gunar 228
Frantz, Maj Peter 286, 323–4
Frederick I Barbarossa 70
Frieser, Karl-Heinz 386, 388
Friessner, Gen Johannes 186, 249, *449*
Frunze, Mikhail 45, 52

Gapeyonok, Nikolay 223
Germany
    see also Hitler, Adolf
    after World War One 3–5
    economy 17–18, 171
Gertsovka 214, 233
Getman, Maj-Gen A.L. 311, 323
Glantz, David xvii, 268, 320
Goebbels, Joseph 13, 14, 27, 31, 76, 80, 168
Golikov, Lt-Gen Filip 76
Gomel 85
Göring, Hermann 17, 18, 27, 28, 159, 171
Gostishchevo 283–4
Graff, Lt Walter 281
Gräser, Gnr Helmut 2
Great Britain 19, 26–7, 32–3, 57–8, 82–3
Greim, Col-Gen Robert Ritter von 190
Gremuchii 241
Greznoye 275
Grossman, Vasily 84–5, 93, 100, 108–9, 121,
    122, 129–30, 143, 151, 301
Grossmann, Horst 249
Guderian, Col-Gen Heinz xxi, 21, 32, 136–7,
    172–3, 254
    Operation Barbarossa 72–3, 85, 97, 99–100,
        101, 105–6, 114
    Operation Typhoon 124, 125, 129, 131, 133
    Operation Zitadelle 176, 183–4, 189–90, 389
Gührs, Ustuf 353–4

Haarhaus, Lt 287–8
Hahn, Elbert 155–6
Halder, Col-Gen Franz 28, 70, 88, 110, 113, 156
Harmel, Heinz 362
Harpe, Gen Josef 186, 249, 305, *448*
Hausser, SS-Obergruppenführer Paul 169, 188–9,
    233, 242, 265, 289, 327, 333, *449*
Healy, Mark 314
Henry, Harald 129
Henry, Infmn Herbert 83–4
Hertzog, Karl 96, 98, 129, 142, 198
Hill 226.6 359–60
Hill 252.2 358
Hindenburg, FM Paul von 3, 10, 11
Hitler, Adolf
    see also Germany
    Anti-Comintern Pact 56
    assassination attempt on 173

and British and French declaration of war
    26–7
character 9–10
control of armed forces 27–9, 31–2, 146–7,
    156, 173–4
daily routine 146
declares war on United States 136–7
determination to destroy Soviet Union 29–30,
    68–9
economic policy 17–18
foreign policy 18–19, 21–3
health 150, 172–3
ideology 5–6, 8–9
and invasion of Britain 32–3
military rearmament and development 19–22
Nazification of Germany 11–17
non-aggression pact with Soviet Union 24,
    58–9
Operation Barbarossa 69–73, 80, 88, 104–6,
    111, 113–14, 384–5
Operation Blau 148–9, 150–51, 152, 156,
    158
Operation Typhoon 105, 119, 120, 121, 125,
    133
Operation Zitadelle 258, 376–8, 382
    preliminaries 168–9, 176–9, 183–5, 212,
        214
    other offensives (after declaration of
        war) 30–32
rise to power 6–12
sacks commanders 137, 156
and Soviet resources 139–40
territorial expansion (prior to declaration of
    war) 22–6, 59
trade agreement with Soviet Union 63–4
Hitler Youth 16
Hoch, SS-Ustuf Roger 165–6, 235
Hoepner, Col-Gen Erich 86
Hoernlein, Lt-Gen Walter 228, 229, 275, 276–7
Hoth, Col-Gen Hermann xxii, 187, 188, 268,
    271–2, 288–9, 320, 330, *449*
House, Jonathan 268
Huber, Hans 236
Huber, SS-Sturmmann Heinrich 325
Hughes-Wilson, John xviii
Hünersdorff, Maj-Gen Walter von 243

intelligence gathering 181–2, 196–7, 210–12
Iofe, Olga 261–2
Irving, David 172
Italy 31, 56, 376
Ivanovka 379

Japan 56
Jews, anti-Semitism 8, 15
Jodl, Alfred 158

Kageneck, Clemens Graf 242–4, 269
Karelin, Infmn Feliks 279–80
Kassnitz, Col 228
Katukov, Lt-Gen M.E. 237, 264, 266, 285, *455*
Katyusha rockets 134–5
Keitel, FM Wilhelm xxi, 27, 32
Kempf, Gen Werner xxii, 188, 289, 329–30, *450*
Kessel, Mortimer von 249, 256
Keyneres, Miklós 222–3
Keynes, John Maynard 5
Kharkov 132, 138, 140, 141–2, 168, 169, 384
Khodorovsky, Michail 233–4
Khrushchev, Nikita 278
Kiev 106–9
Kirponos, Col-Gen M.P. 75, 87, 108, 109
Klein-Kargarlyk 103–4
Kleist, Col-Gen Ewald von 87, 106, 150
Kless, Gen Friedrich 298
Kluge, FM Günther von xxi, 137, 198, 305, 376–7, *448*
Knobelsdorff, Gen Otto von 187, 229–30, 270, 289, *449*
Knöfel, SS-Unterscharführer Erhard 354
Koch, Marianne 162
Kochetovka 318
Koettel, Leo 268–9
Komsomolets State Farm 327
Konev, Col-Gen Ivan xxi, 135, 194, 273, *455*
Korovino 233
Kortig, Karla 16
Kozhedub, Lt Ivan 316, 322
Krause, Fw Günther 300
Krebs, Richard 3
Kriachkov, Feodor 50
Kriachkov, Ivan 50
Krivoshein, Gen 284
Kruchenkin, Lt-Gen V. 330, *454*
Kruger, SS-Gf Walter 238
Krüger, SS-Ustuf 264
Krylov, Capt Ivan 79, 94
Krylov, Pavel 341–3, 345, 358, 371–2, 381
Kuechler, Col-Gen Georg von 137
Kulik, Pavlo 42
Kursk
    Battle of *see* Zitadelle, Operation
    German occupation 168
Küster, Gerd 225
Kuznetsov, Col-Gen F.I. 74, 86
KV-1 tank 81, 196
    see also tanks, Soviet

Lang, Maj Frederich 191
Lau, SS-Panzerschütze Walter 214
League of German Maidens 16
Lebedev, Valentin 299
Leeb, Gen Ritter von 70–71, 103, 111, 112, 137
Lehwess-Litzmann, Obstlt Walter 222

Leigh, Lt-Col Edward 37–8
Lemelsen, Gen Joachim 186, 249, 305, *449*
Lend-Lease scheme 171–2
Lenin, Vladimir 38–40, 41, 43, 44–5
Leningrad 86–7, 102–3, 109–12, 138
Levitan, Yuri 93
Lindner, Alarick 12–13, 145
Liskow, Spr Alfred 78
List, FM Wilhelm 155, 156
Litvin, Nikolai 201, 204, 253–4, 294–6
Litvinov, Maxim 56, 172
Lochmann, Franz 269
Lohberg, Fw 317
Lomidze, Koba 249–50
Lotoshino 98
Lozovsky, Solomon 92
Luchki 267
Ludendorff, Gen Erich 3
Luftwaffe *see* air force, German

Maisky, Ivan 57
Maloarkhangelsk 249
Manstein, FM Erich von xxi, 141, 158, *449*
    Operation Zitadelle 288–9, 320, 329, 330, 336, 388
    after 12th July 372, 376–8, 382
    preliminaries 168–9, 176–7, 178, 187, 188
Mars, Operation 159
Maschmann, Peter 270–71
Maslovo Pristani 246
Mattenklott, Gen Franz 188, *450*
Mawdsley, Evan 169–70, 182
Maykop 155
Mein Kampf (Hitler) 8–9
Mellenthin, Gen Friedrich von 171, 178, 184–5, 199, 275, 368, 377, 387
Merridale, Catherine 147, 207
Meuller, Oberschütze Paul 333–4
Meyer, Hauptmann Bruno 283–4
Mickl, Maj-Gen 232
Mikhailovka bridge 242–3
mines 205, 226–8, 253, 270–71
Minsk 85–6
Miroshnikov, Lt 100–101
Model, Col-Gen Walter xxi, 184, 185–6, 247–8, 256, 296–7, 305–6, *448*
Molodin, Alana 98
Molotov cocktails 255
Molotov, Vyacheslav 47, 58, 68, 89
morale and discipline 90–92
Morell, Dr Theo 173
Moscow
    air bombardment 101–2
    German planning 105, 119
    Operation Typhoon 119–32
        Briansk 121
        failure of 133

Mozhaisk 123
  Soviet counteroffensive 133–6
  Soviet defences 120, 123, 126
  Soviet pre-emptive attacks 128
  Vyazma 120, 121
  weather conditions 125, 128–31
  Soviet defences 85
Mozhaisk 123
Müller, Johan 221
Mussolini, Benito 31, 376
Mutterlose, SS-Unterscharführer 352–3

Napoleon I, Emperor 120
Nationalsozialistische Deutsche Arbeiterpartei
  see Nazi Party
Nazi Party 5–11
  see also Hitler, Adolf
Nazification of Germany 11–17
Nehring, Gen Walter 188, 450
Neuzert, Hubert 361–2
Nicholas II, Tsar 38, 39
Nicolson, Harold 83
Niemann, Gerhard 244, 245
Nipe, George Jnr 352
Norway 30
Novorossisk naval base 155
Novosselovka 313–14
NSDAP see Nazi Party

Oberkommando der Luftwaffe (OKL) 28
Oberkommando der Marine (OKM) 28
Oberkommando der Wehrmacht (OKW) 27, 384
Oberkommando des Heeres (OKH) 27, 28
Oboyan front 314–18, 324
OKH (Oberkommando des Heeres) 27, 28
OKL (Oberkommando der Luftwaffe) 28
OKM (Oberkommando der Marine) 28
Oktiabrskii State Farm 335–6
OKW (Oberkommando der Wehrmacht) 27, 384
Olesha, Yuri 43–4
Olkhovatka heights 296–300, 302–5
Onton, Fyodor 200, 253, 255
order of battle 448–56
Orel 383, 384
Out of the Night (Krebs) 3
Overy, Richard 46, 173–4, 175

Pabst, Helmuth 101, 124, 128, 142–3
pacts and agreements 19, 56, 57
  Anti-Comintern Pact 56
  German–Soviet non-aggression 24, 58–9
  German–Soviet trade 58, 63–4
  Treaty of Versailles 4–5, 18
Panesenko, Igor 312–13
Panfilov, Maj-Gen Ivan 131
Panther tank 183–4, 189, 190, 224–5
  see also tanks, German

partisans 96, 197–8, 309–11
Paulus, FM Friedrich 72, 118, 158–9, 161
Pavlov, Gen D.G. 75, 77–8, 85, 86
Peiper, Joachim 354, 355
Petrik, Anton xxiv–xxv, 390–92
Petrik, Mykhailo xxiv–xxvi, 230, 232–3, 390–92
Petrov, Konstantin Giorgevich 49–50
planning, German
  Operation Barbarossa 69–73, 104–6, 113–14,
    384–5
  Operation Blau 150–51
  Operation Typhoon 105, 119
  Operation Zitadelle 176–9, 183–8, 305–6
planning, Soviet
  Battle of Prokhorovka 336–9
  defence of Kursk salient 179–83, 306
  German invasion (Operation Barbarossa) 73–5
  Operation Uranus 156–7
Plotnikov, S. 50
Poel, Lt-Gen N.K. 214–15
Poland 19, 23–6, 39, 59–60
Polyzhaev 369
Ponyri 294–6, 300–301
Ponyri Station 293–4
Popiel, Lt-Gen N.K. 285
Popov, Lt-Gen M.M. 74, 110
Pötter, Snr Cpl 281
Pravda (newspaper) 44
Priess, SS-Gf H. 241
prisoners 83, 97–9, 106
Prokhorovka, Battle of 1–2, **341–71**
  air operations 345, 355–7, 366–7
  Belenikhino 370
  Berezovka 366
  Hill 226.6 359–60
  Hill 252.2 358
  losses (mechanical), German 357
  losses (mechanical), Soviet 357
  Polyzhaev 369
  Rzhavets bridgehead 363–5
  Soviet preparations 336–9, 341–3
  Storozhevoe 362
  Storozhevoe collective farm 361–2
propaganda 13, 15, 92–4, 95
Psel, River 325–6
Pukhov, Lt-Gen N.P. 193
purges
  Hitler's 11–12, 137
  'Red Terror' 38–9
  Stalin's 35–6, 53–5, 91

radio communication 203
Rado, Sándor 182
Ragulin, Malana 111
rank equivalents 457–8
Raus, Gen Erhard 79, 81, 102, 124, 134,
  159–60, 188, 197, 205, 246, 257, 450

Razuvayev, Nikolai 151–2
recreation 208–9
recruitment 94–6
Red air Force *see* air force, Soviet
Red Army *see* army, Soviet
'Red Terror' 38–9
Reichenau, Gen Walther von 137
Reinke, Hauptmann 309
reservists 96
Reznikova, Rflmn Sasha 264, 285
Rhineland 22
Ribbentrop, Joachim von 24, 26
Ribbentrop, Rudolf von 347–9, 351
Richthofen, Gen Wolfram 159
Rodin, Lt-Gen A.G. 192, 257, *453*
Roes, Wilhelm 216–17, 236
Röhm, Ernst 11–12
Rokossovsky, Gen Konstantin xxi, 54–5, 128,
    192, 256–7, 258, 263, 289, 296, *450*
Roland, Operation 378–81
Rommel, Erwin 32
Rössler, Rudolf 182
Rossmann, Ofw Edmund 316–17
Rostov 132, 149, 168
Roth, Lt Bernard 210–11, 213, 216
Rotmistrov, Lt-Gen Pavel 272, 319, 336–8, *456*
    after 12th July 372–3, 375
    Battle of Prokhorovka 343–4, 346, 349–50,
       355, 360, 371
Rudel, Capt Hans-Ulrich 273–4, 356–7
Rudenko, Lt-Gen Sergey 193, 258, 289, 290, *453*
Rüffer, Lt Raimund 219–21, 390–92
Rundstedt, FM Gerd von 71, 103, 132, 137
Rusanova, Lidiya 134
Ruslanova, Yuri 344
Russian Revolution 36–9
    see also Soviet Union
Russo-German war, historical awareness of in
    West xv–xviii
Rzhavets bridgehead 363–5
Rzhev 138

SA (*Stormabteilungen*) 7, 11–12
Sacharov, Aleksandr 208
Sagun, Ivan 239–40
Samodurovka 302
Samoilov, David 92
Saucken, Gen van 302–3
Schein, Ludwig 190–91, 192, 213, 315
Schellenburg, Walter 25–6
Schmerov, Ivan 50
Schmidt, Obersturmbannführer Paul (Paul
    Carell) 26–7, 226–7, 254, 286, 298
Schmidt, Rolf 244–5, 328, 330
Schmükle, Gerd 209
Schnabel, Henri 227–8, 279
Schörner, Mar Ferdinand 274

Schütz, Obersturmführer 265
Schutzstaffel (SS) 11
Scorched Earth (Carell) 227
Seeckt, Gen Hans von 20
Seidemann, Maj-Gen Hans 231
Service, Robert 40
Sevastopol 140–41
Severinov, Vladimir 291–2
Shaposhnikov, Mar Boris 53, 106, 107, 134
Shcherbakov, Col-Gen Alexander 126
Shumilov, Lt-Gen M.S. 194, 268, 282, *453*
Simm, Ustuf Alexander 333
Simonov, Konstantin 95–6
Simutenkov, Snr Lt T. 223–4
Smolensk 101, 104, 112–13
snipers 153–4
Sorge, Richard 76
Soviet Union
    see also Russian Revolution; Stalin, Joseph
    collectivization 48
    construction of defences 62–3
    economy 44, 51, 171–2
    Five Year Plans 46–51
    propagation of Communist ideology 43–4
Spanish Civil War 22
Speer, Albert 22
Spiegel, Maj Leo 328–9, 338–9
SS (Schutzstaffel) 11
Stadler, Sylvester 362, 370
Stakhanov, Aleksy 49–50
Stalin, Joseph
    see also Soviet Union
    character 41–2
    counteroffensive (early 1943) 168
    defence of Kursk salient 180–81, 183,
       209–10, 257–8, 272–3, 306, 370–71
    defence of Moscow 123, 127–8, 133
    and Five Year Plans 46–7, 48–9, 51
    foreign policy and German threat 45–6,
       55–8, 67–8, 75–8
    German invasion (Operation Barbarossa)
       80, 85, 89–91, 93–4, 106–8, 110
    German summer offensive (Operation Blau)
       149–50, 151
    and invasion of Finland 60–61
    and invasion of Poland 59–60
    and Lend-Lease scheme 172
    non-aggression pact with Germany 24, 58–9
    openness to advice 174
    purges of Communist Party and military
       35–6, 53–5, 91
    rise to power 40–41, 90
    Soviet defences 62–3
    spring/summer offensives (1942) 137–9, 140
    Time magazine's 'Person of the Year 1942' 163
    trade agreement with Germany 63–4
Stalin, Yakov 91

Stalingrad 117–19, 150–62
  casualties 161
  Operation Blau 150–55
  Operation Uranus 156–8
  Operation Winter Storm 158–60
Stavropol 155
Steiger, Martin 234
Stormabteilungen (SA) 7, 11–12
Storozhevoe 362
Storozhevoe collective farm 361–2
Strasser, Gregor 7
Stumpp, Karl 277
Sudetenland 23, 57
Sukho-Solotino 318
Sulzer, Infmn Max 199
Svechin, Aleksandr 52
Syrtsevo 275–6, 284–5

T-34 tank 195
  see also tanks, Soviet
T-70 tank 195
  see also tanks, Soviet
tank crews, comradeship 208
'tank panic' 253–4
tank-hunting teams 236, 354
tanks, German
  Ferdinand 183, 189–90, 254–5
  losses 109, 241, 251, 259, 272, 277–8, 305,
    311, 327, 388
  Panther 183–4, 189, 190, 224–5
  production 148, 171
  repairs 277
  Tiger 183, 189–90, 239–40, 277–8, 346
tanks, Soviet
  KV-1 81, 196
  losses 81–2, 86, 87, 88, 108, 109, 121, 251,
    284
  production 148, 171
  T-34 195
  T-70 195
Temkin, Gabriel 92
Teploe 302–4
Teterevino 274–5
Thimm, Albert 366–7
Tiger tank 183, 189–90, 239–40, 277–8, 346
  see also tanks, German
Time magazine 49–50, 163
Timoshenko, Mar Semyon 61, 67, 77, 78, 85, 86,
  109, 138, 140
Tiomkin, Infmn Fedor 144, 153–4
tiredness, troops' 279–81
Tiulenev, Maj-Gen I. 75
Torst, Maj Max 248, 250
training 202–5
Treaty of Versailles 4–5, 18
Tresckow, Maj-Gen Henning von 173
Triandafillov, Vladimir 52

Trotsky, Leon 39, 41
Trufanov, Maj-Gen 380
Trzemin, Dimitri 203, 213
Tukhachevsky, Mar Mikhail 35–6, 52–3
Tupikov, Maj-Gen V.I. 108
Typhoon, Operation *see* Moscow

United States 136–7
Uranus, Operation 156–8
Uritski, Infmn Georgy 60–61
Usov, Stanislav 380

Vasilevsky, Gen Aleksandr 73–4, 174, 181, 212,
  337–8, 371, 383
Vassilieva, Boris 322
Vatutin, Gen Nikolai xxi, *453*
  defence of Kursk salient 193, 263, 268,
    272–3, 278, 288, 320–21, 336, 372
  and German invasion (Operation
    Barbarossa) 78, 85, 86–7
Verkhopenye 285–8, 312–13
Versailles, Treaty of 4–5, 18
Vershvovski, Tanya 206
Vogel, Daniel 40
Volkov, Anatoly 350–51
volunteers 94–6
Voronezh 149
Voroshilov, Mar Kliment 53, 57–8, 60, 61, 62, 90,
  103
Vyazma 120, 121, 138

Warlimont, Gen Alfred 173
Warmbrunn, SS-Sturmmann 373
Weber, Paul 9–10
'Wehrwolf' complex 146
Weimar Republic 4–5
Wendorff, Helmut 214
Werth, Alexander 94, 95, 98, 100, 112, 117–19,
  126, 130–31, 198
Wiedemann, Fritz 72
Wieder, Joachim 154–5, 157–8
Wietersahm, Hauptmann von 314
Wilhelm II, Kaiser 3
Willmott, H.P. 147
Winter Storm, Operation 158–60
Wisch, SS-Gf Theodor 240, 325
Witte, SS-Mann Stefan 237
Wittmann, SS-Ustuf Michael 1–2, 240–41, 266,
  281, 349, 373
Wolff, SS-Ustuf Werner 354–5
women 95, 123
World War One 3–6

Yeremenko, Gen Andrei 107–8
Yezhov, Nikolai 36

Zahn, Sgt Ebbert 165

Zeitzler, Col-Gen Kurt xxi, 156, 177, 184,
258
Zeldovich, Artyom 276
Zheleznov, Nikolai 239
Zhukov, Mar Georgi xxi, 54–5, 90
    defence of Kursk salient 179–81, 194–5,
        196, 215–16, 296, 306, 371, 379–80, 389
    defence of Moscow 122–3, 127–8, 133–4
    German invasion (Operation Barbarossa)
        67, 74, 77, 78, 81, 82, 85, 87, 106–7,
        110, 111, 112, 113
    spring/summer offensives (1942) 138, 139,
        141
    Stalingrad 152, 156–7, 160, 161, 167
Zitadelle, Operation **165–389**
    preliminaries **165–217**
        air operations 210
        bridge construction 200
        combat training, German 205
        combat training, Soviet 202–5
        German preliminary offensive 213–14
        intelligence gathering, German 210–11
        intelligence gathering, Soviet 181–2,
            196–7, 210, 211–12
        local civilian population 206–7
        Manstein's counteroffensive 169
        partisan attacks 197–8
        planning, German 176–9, 183–8
        planning, Soviet 179–83
        provisioning 198–9
        Soviet bombardment 215–16
        Soviet defences 200–202
        Soviet offensives 167–8
        start date 177–8, 212
    5th July **219–59**
        air operations 221–4, 228–30, 231–2,
            235, 249–50, 257–8
        Alexsandrovka 255
        bridgeheads 242–5
        Butovo 232
        Butyrki 255
        Bykovka 240
        Cherkasskoe 232–3
        German casualties 241, 246, 259
        Gertsovka 233
        Gremuchii 241
        Korovino 233
        losses (mechanical), German 224, 251,
            257, 259
        losses (mechanical), Soviet 224, 251, 257
        Maloarkhangelsk 249
        Maslovo Pristani 246
        preliminary bombardment 221
        Soviet defences 226–8, 237, 246–7, 249,
            251–7

6th–8th July **261–306**
        6th July 263–73, 289–96
        7th July 273–81, 296–301
        8th July 282–9, 296–7, 302–4
        air operations 266–7, 283–4, 287–8,
            289–90, 297–8, 299–300
        Bolshie Maiachki 282
        German casualties 267, 272, 298, 305
        Gostishchevo 283–4
        Greznoye 275
        losses (mechanical), German 272, 305,
            311
        losses (mechanical), Soviet 284
        Luchki 267
        Olkhovatka heights 296–300, 302–5
        Ponyri 294–6, 300–301
        Ponyri Station 293–4
        Samodurovka 302
        Soviet counteroffensives 266, 268, 283–4,
            286–90, 292–3
        Soviet defences 263–4, 265–6, 268–9,
            270–71, 272–3, 282, 288, 296–9,
            301
        Syrtsevo 275–6, 284–5
        Teploe 302–4
        Teterevino 274–5
        Verkhopenye 285–8
    9th–11th July **309–39**
        9th July 312–20
        10th July 320–29
        11th July 329–39
        advance on Prokhorovka 318–21,
            324–39
        air operations 315–17, 322–3, 333–4
        German casualties 318, 325
        German losses (mechanical) 327
        Kochetovka 318
        Novosselovka 313–14
        Oboyan front 314–18, 324
        Oktiabrskii State Farm 335–6
        planning, German 305–6
        planning , Soviet 306
        Sukho-Solotino 318
        Verkhopenye 312–13
    12th July *see* Prokhorovka, Battle of
    after 12th July **371–82**
        13th July 371–8
        14th July 378–80
        Belenikhino 379
        Ivanovka 379
        Operation Roland 378–81
        Soviet counteroffensives 383–4
    factors leading to outcome (summary)
        386–9
Zorn, Gen Hans 186, 249, *448*